Essay Writing

for Canadian Students
with Readings

Seventh Edition

Topic Sentences
w/ Write Away

Essay Writing
for Canadian Students
with Readings

Seventh Edition

Roger
DAVIS
Red Deer College

Laura K.
DAVIS
Red Deer College

Kay L.
STEWART

Chris J.
BULLOCK
Professor Emeritus,
University of Alberta

PEARSON

Toronto

Vice-President, Editorial Director: Gary Bennett
Editor-in-Chief: Michelle Sartor
Acquisitions Editor: David S. Le Gallais
Sponsoring Editor: Kathleen McGill
Marketing Manager: Jennifer Sutton
Supervising Developmental Editor: Suzanne Schaan
Project Manager: Lesley Deugo
Manufacturing Manager: Susan Johnson
Production Editor: Avivah Wargon
Copy Editor: Carolyn Zapf
Proofreaders: Cheryl Cohen, Tilman Lewis
Compositor: MPS Limited, a Macmillan Company
Permissions Research: The Editing Company
Art Director: Julia Hall
Cover and Interior Designer: Anthony Leung
Cover Image: Bambu Productions, Gettyimages

10 9 8 7 6 5   [EB]

Library and Archives Canada Cataloguing in Publication

Essay writing for Canadian students with readings / Roger Davis ... [et al.]. — 7th ed.

Previous eds. written by Kay L. Stewart.
Includes bibliographical references and index.
ISBN 978-0-13-255759-7

1. Exposition (Rhetoric). 2. English language—Rhetoric.
I. Davis, Roger Nathan, 1971–

LB2369.E88 2013   808'.042   C2011-905451-5

ISBN 978-0-13-255759-7

To those we have taught,
and those who have taught us.

Brief Contents

Contents

Part 2 Readings 201

Published Writings 203

Sample Essays 348

Preface to the Seventh Edition

To the Student

If you are trying to figure out how to cope with essay assignments in your college or university courses, you are the student we had in mind when we wrote this book.

We present a systematic approach to writing essays. Because we believe that writing is a skill you can learn, rather than a talent you are born with, we are convinced this method will work for most writers. Feel free to adapt it to suit your needs.

To the Instructor

If you are new to *Essay Writing for Canadian Students*, you will notice that we present the writing process as a systematic set of procedures for planning, drafting, and revising deductively organized academic essays. Like most teachers, we have found that many weaknesses in student writing stem from confused thinking about the assignment, the subject of the essay, or both. For this reason, we stress the analytic skills that help students to explore the subjects they write about more completely. We recognize that one disadvantage of this approach is that it may seem to limit creativity. The deductively organized analysis is, after all, only one kind of academic essay. Nevertheless, we believe there is value in an approach that encourages critical thinking.

Part 1 Rhetoric

The Rhetoric section takes students through the process of writing and revising a wide range of essays and writing assignments: summaries and essays in various disciplines (Chapters 2, 3, 4, and 5); essays analyzing literature, comparing, evaluating, and persuading (Chapters 6, 7, 8, and 9); and research papers (Chapters 10 and 11). Part 1 emphasizes the importance of reading and thinking analytically.

In this section of the book, we have

- Revised the overview of essay writing and included a new sample essay on the film *The Matrix.*

- Expanded the discussion of methods of analysis (also called rhetorical modes) and revised the discussion of disciplinary and analytic categories.

- Revised and reconfigured the discussion on analysis essays (formerly called content analysis essays) to take into account the notion that all writing involves engagement with a text or texts, broadly understood.

- Revised and reconfigured the discussion on writing essays about literature (formerly called textual analysis essays) to take into account that essays in English consider both content and form—what a text says and how it creates meaning.

- Moved the discussion of reading analytically and writing summaries to early in the book, since any act of writing involves active reading and analysis.

- Updated Special Categories for Writing Essays about Literature (called textual analysis essays in the sixth edition's Appendix 3) and moved the discussion into Chapters 3 and 6. The relocation of the material gives the reader more direct and immediate access to the material.

- Through the revisions noted above, reduced the number of chapters from 14 to 11, streamlining the text to provide better focus and avoid repetition.

Part 2 Readings

We have selected essays published in a wide range of sources both to illustrate the types of writing we discuss in the Rhetoric section and to provide timely subjects for students to write about.

- About one quarter of the Readings are new to this edition.
- The Published Writings centre on four broad subject areas: language/literature, health/medicine/addiction, social justice/environmentalism/globalization, and multiculturalism/personal identity/sports, with

interesting links between these categories. Students therefore have a wealth of material to analyze, compare, and evaluate.

- The new Sample Analysis Essay and the new Sample Essay on Literature show the results of the processes of gathering material, drafting, and revising covered in Chapters 3, 4, 5, and 6.

Part 3 Handbook for Final Editing

The Handbook gives students the tools they need to recognize and correct problems in sentence structure, grammar, punctuation, and format. New to this edition is an answer key to the exercises in the Handbook.

Throughout, we've added, deleted, and changed material to make explanations clearer, exercises more useful, and examples more interesting.

How to Use This Book

Because it serves as a combined rhetoric, reader, and handbook, *Essay Writing for Canadian Students* has been used successfully in a wide variety of courses, from introductory literature to advanced writing. The scope and structure of the book allow you to tailor your course to suit your own teaching style and the needs of your students. Some instructors prefer to begin by systematically reviewing handbook material on sentence structure, grammar, and punctuation. Others plunge their students into writing essays, assigning handbook material as needed. Still others may ask students to read and respond informally to some of the published writings before assigning the first formal essay.

Your selection of rhetoric chapters will likely depend on the kind of course you are teaching. All students can benefit from Chapters 1, 2, and 3, which provide an overview of the writing process and strategies for tackling essay assignments.

Writing courses

If you are teaching a writing course, you will likely use Chapter 2 on reading analytically and writing summaries, and Chapter 3 on analysis essays. The latter, which examines various methods of analysis such as cause/effect analysis, process analysis, and systems analysis, lays the groundwork for students to respond to and write about texts from a wide variety of academic disciplines. Chapters 4 and 5 give detailed instructions for drafting and revising essays, with clear examples of good and weak thesis statements, topic sentences, introductions, conclusions, and middle paragraphs. You might follow up with Chapter 7, Writing Comparison Essays; the sample topic for this chapter is a comparison of two essays from the Readings. You could then introduce the more complex skills required for evaluating arguments and writing critiques found in Chapter 8. Chapter 9 calls on students to put these skills to work by constructing their own arguments about controversial issues or by writing reviews. Students could expand their persuasive essays into research papers by following the procedures set out in Chapters 10 and 11.

Literature and media courses

If you are teaching a course in literature, film studies, or other media, you might emphasize the chapter devoted to writing essays on literature (Chapter 6). The sample topic for this chapter is a poem by William Carlos Williams. Chapter 1, Essay Writing: An Overview, also includes a sample essay on the film *The Matrix,* as well as a discussion of that essay. You may want students to write two or three essays analyzing a single subject before you ask them to tackle a comparison essay (Chapter 7) or an evaluative essay/review (Chapter 8). Classic pieces by E. M. Forster, George Orwell, W. S. Merwin, Jonathan Swift, and Virginia Woolf provide opportunities for comparison with contemporary writers in both subject and style.

However you structure your course, we hope you and your students find *Essay Writing for Canadian Students* stimulating and productive.

MyCanadianCompLab

The moment you know

Educators know it. Students know it. It's that inspired moment when something that was difficult to understand suddenly makes perfect sense. Our MyLab products have been designed and refined with a single purpose in mind—to help educators create that moment of understanding with their students.

MyCanadianCompLab delivers **proven results** in helping individual students succeed. It provides **engaging experiences** that personalize, stimulate, and measure learning for each student. And, it comes from a **trusted partner** with educational expertise and an eye on the future.

MyCanadianCompLab can be used by itself or linked to any learning management system. To learn more about how MyCanadianCompLab combines proven learning applications with powerful assessment, visit www.mycanadiancomplab.ca. MyCanadianCompLab—the moment you know.

Supplement for Students

Visit **MyCanadianCompLab** (www.mycanadiancomplab.ca) to access diverse resources for composition in one easy-to-use place:

- Sections on writing, research, and grammar cover all the key topics in the text, providing additional instruction, examples, and practice. Exercises offer the opportunity to practise the skills learned in class, and include both self-grading quizzes and writing activities. Writing samples provide examples of different types of writing and different documentation styles; some are annotated to highlight key aspects or to stimulate reflection and discussion. Videos illustrate aspects of the writing process through scenarios, or provide grammar and editing tutorials through onscreen revision.

- An online composing space includes tools such as writing tips and editing FAQs, so you can get the help you need when you need it, without ever leaving the writing environment. Within this space, you'll find access to EBSCO's ContentSelect, a database of articles from academic journals that can be used for research and reference.

- The portfolio feature allows you to create an e-portfolio of your work that you can easily share with your instructor and peers.

Use the access code packaged with new copies of this textbook to log on to MyCanadianCompLab, or purchase separate access through your campus bookstore or directly through the website.

Supplements for Instructors

The **Instructor's Manual** is available for downloading from a password-protected section of Pearson Canada's online catalogue (www.pearsoncanada.ca/highered). Navigate to your book's catalogue page to access the supplement. See your local sales representative for details and access.

Technology Specialists. Pearson's Technology Specialists work with faculty and campus course designers to ensure that Pearson technology products, assessment tools, and online course materials are tailored to meet your specific needs. This highly qualified team is dedicated to helping schools take full advantage of a wide range of educational resources by assisting in the integration of a variety of instructional materials and media formats. Your local Pearson sales representative can provide you with more details on this service program.

Acknowledgments

First and foremost, we, Roger Davis and Laura Davis, would like to thank Marian Allen for introducing us to this project, and for inviting us to participate in its authorship. Over the years she has created this book and contributed to it, and we express our gratitude for her guidance and mentorship. We would also like to thank Kay Stewart and Chris Bullock for the great work they have done on the previous editions of this textbook. Their insights have been invaluable, and it has been wonderful to continue work on such an excellent and successful textbook. Marian and Kay spent many summers developing the materials that led to the first edition of *Essay Writing* (1980), at that time the only university-level writing textbook by Canadian authors for Canadian students. Without Marian, Kay, and Chris's enthusiasm, hard work, and practical wisdom about students' needs, this project would never have come to fruition, nor have lasted through so many editions.

We would like to thank Laura's research assistant, Meagan Roberts, a BA English student in the University of Calgary's Collaborative Degree Program at Red Deer College. Meagan helped edit the Rhetoric section of this edition. We would like to thank Roger's former student, Deanna Wierenga—who made consistently excellent contributions to his classroom environment—for her willingness to write a student draft of the Sample Research Essay for consideration. We would also like to thank Chris Bullock's former students whose work we've used in exercises in this edition. More generally, we are grateful to all our students at Grant MacEwan University, Red Deer College, and the University of Alberta. They have helped us to see what did and didn't work in teaching writing and have generously allowed us to use their writing.

We would also like to thank the reviewers who made valuable suggestions for improvements in this edition: Nancy E. Batty, Red Deer College; Blair Hemstock, Keyano College; George W. Lyon, Mount Royal University; Kate O'Neill, University of Calgary/Red Deer College; Susan Pajewski, Mount Royal University; and Rachel F. Prusko, Grant

MacEwan University. We would also like to thank our colleagues who provided us with feedback and suggestions for improvements, particularly Peter Slade at Red Deer College. Many thanks as well to the staff at Pearson Education Canada for their help and timely nudges along the way: Kathleen McGill, our efficient and kindly Sponsoring Editor; Rema Celio and Suzanne Schaan, our excellent Developmental Editors; Avivah Wargon, our Production Editor, whose intelligence, experience, and cheerful notes smoothed a sometimes bumpy path; Lesley Deugo, Project Manager, for all the important behind-the-scenes work. Kay, Chris, and Marian would like to thank the following editors for their hard work on previous editions: Pearson staff Patty Riediger, Patti Altridge, and Avivah Wargon, as well as freelance editors Cheryl Cohen, Lesley Mann, and Lisa Berland.

Finally, we, Roger and Laura, would like to thank our family for their years of support, particularly our parents, siblings, and especially our three children, Rachael, Kai, and Clara, who always add fun and laughter to a hard day's work.

Rhetoric

(Part 1)

Writing Essays: An Overview

(1)

Essay Writing: Purposes

Essay Writing: Product

Essay Writing: Process

In this book we focus on essay writing for two reasons. First, the thinking skills you practise in the process of writing essays are central to the work you do in college or university. Second, the procedures you learn for writing and revising essays will help you with many other kinds of writing assignments.

Essay Writing: Purposes

Writing to Learn

How can writing essays help you to develop thinking skills? One way is by encouraging you to explore your ideas. This purpose is reflected in the French word from which the term *essay* comes: *essai,* meaning "attempt." The term was first used by the French author Michel de Montaigne, who published a book of short prose pieces entitled *Essais* in 1580. This title suggests the personal, exploratory nature of Montaigne's attempts to understand the world around him by writing on everyday subjects such as the art of conversation or liars. You may study informal essays of this type in composition and literature courses, and create them as well.

Since Montaigne's day, the term *essay* has come to include formal writing on a wide range of subjects, from the nature of love in Shakespeare's *King Lear* to theories about the origins of the universe. Writing academic essays of this kind will help you to develop systematic analytic thinking. It is this more formal type of essay writing that you will most often be asked to do in your university and college courses, and that we will focus on in this text.

Thinking about a **subject*** and writing about a subject are different processes. Thinking is largely internal and abstract, while writing requires you to make your thoughts external and concrete. If you were taking a painting course, you would recognize that no matter how good the instructor's lessons might be or how much you thought about painting, you would learn to paint only by painting. The same holds true for writing. Through writing essays, whether formal or informal, you develop greater awareness of the language you and others use to make meaning. What may be less obvious is that you learn the theories, concepts, and procedures of academic disciplines more thoroughly by actively employing them in writing essays.

---

* Terms in bold are defined in the Glossary of Rhetorical Terms (492–95).

Writing to Communicate

Some of the writing you do—such as class notes, responses to reading, drafts that go nowhere—may have no reader other than yourself. Other types of writing, like texting, have very specific, immediate purposes and may be deleted without much further thought. Writing essays, however, is a means of sharing your understanding of a particular issue with others and generally involves a more sustained engagement with the issue you are writing about.

Most academic essays require an argument or opinion that will persuade the reader. Contrary to the popular belief that everyone has a right to an opinion of his or her own, not all opinions have equal merit: some opinions can be harmful (such as racism) or even incorrect (that the Earth is flat). Moving beyond mere factual information, an essay will draw conclusions about a particular topic and support a position or course of action related to that topic. The merit of an argument or opinion relies on the reasons and evidence you give to support that position as well as its ability to persuade the reader.

In an academic essay, this combination of an opinion and the reason(s) supporting it is called a **thesis**. A thesis is like a hypothesis in a scientific experiment: it is the statement or assertion that is to be proved. Proof in an academic essay consists of the logical, orderly development of your thesis through explaining your reasons and giving **evidence** (such as factual information, examples, and quotations from authorities) to support those reasons. By explaining your thesis carefully and giving evidence to support it, you are likely to persuade readers to take your opinion seriously, whether or not they agree with it.

Essay Writing: Product

If both informal essays and formal academic essays present writers' opinions on particular subjects, then the writer must consider the audience for whom a piece is being written and the presentation of the material.

Audience

Most informal essays are written for a popular audience, and the subject material is usually fairly general in nature. Magazine articles and newspaper stories often contain much factual material and are geared toward information or entertainment as a starting point for discussion. These types of essays do not represent sustained analyses of topics.

Formal essays on an academic subject, in contrast, are written for specialized audiences already familiar with the subject. Readers of these essays want to know the writer's thesis from the beginning and to have the evidence supporting the thesis laid out in a logical, orderly fashion. They also appreciate essays that are well written according to the conventions of the discipline. Most of the essays you write in college and university courses will be of this second type. You will be writing for instructors and classmates who know something about the subject and want to hear your opinion on it. For such academic audiences, then, you do not need to include broad generalizations or unnecessary summary in the essay, particularly in the introduction. Try to be as specific as possible.

Structure

Many students have learned the five-paragraph essay **structure** that includes an introduction, three body paragraphs, and a conclusion. The five-paragraph essay is an acceptable, if simple, approach to the essay. However, the five-paragraph essay can become a crutch if a writer uses it as a template for every essay. This model's main drawback is that it tends to make writers think in terms of three subpoints, which is not always the best approach to thinking about any given topic. The structure begins to dictate content when it is generally preferable to let content dictate the structure, a point Fred Stenson implicitly makes in his essay "In Search of a Modest Proposal" (Readings).

Whether you write five, seven, nine, or any other number of paragraphs in your essay, it is important that you have an **introduction**, **middle paragraphs**, and a **conclusion**. Here is a brief description of these elements:

INTRODUCTION
The introduction presents the thesis of the essay. It may also establish the **context** for the discussion (for example, by defining necessary terms or giving historical background). The introduction should not include broad generalizations that will not be supported in your essay, nor should it contain references to examples or ideas that will not be analyzed.

MIDDLE PARAGRAPHS
Middle paragraphs present subpoints of your essay, which support your thesis statement. **Topic sentences** explain each subpoint and how it relates to your thesis. However, you may have two paragraphs that support a single subpoint—with a different example explained in each paragraph. One paragraph may fully explain a subpoint of your thesis, or you may need more than one paragraph to explain a subpoint. We will show you how to create an

"umbrella" topic sentence—a topic sentence for two middle paragraphs—in Chapter 5.

CONCLUSION
The conclusion ties together the points developed in the middle paragraphs and mentions the wider implications of the discussion, if any.

Sample Essay: Analysis of a Film

So that you can see what this kind of essay might look like in practice, here is an example. The assignment asked students to choose their favourite film, to identify a key **theme** or topic, and to make an argument about their understanding of the material. The main structural elements of the essay have been labelled.

Writing Sample

FREE WILL AND FATALISM IN *THE MATRIX*

Introduction

Released in 1999, the movie *The Matrix* has found a central place in popular culture, certainly more so than its two sequels. Aside from its compelling action scenes, part of the film's popularity derives from its questioning of the principle of personal freedom, a principle that is usually an unchallenged assumption in North America. The film's fundamental premise is that reality is an illusion and that most humans live their lives inside a computer-generated world called "the matrix," manipulated by the machines of the future. The film asks the audience to consider the extent to which they are in control of their decisions and how much technology and other social conditions influence or determine their lives. The two characters Neo and Cypher represent opposite positions in the debate between free will and fatalism, yet the film's treatment of both characters suggests that neither free will nor fatalism are absolute positions but are related terms in the decision-making process.

Thesis
statement

Topic sentence

Through his involvement with technology, the film's main character Neo (Keanu Reeves) has the opportunity to choose between knowledge and ignorance, and ultimately to escape from his prison. An office worker by day and computer hacker by night, Neo is searching for more meaning in his life, perceiving that something is wrong with his apparent reality. It is through the hacker network that Neo meets Trinity (Carrie-Anne Moss) who leads him to Morpheus (Laurence Fishburne). Morpheus offers Neo the chance to learn about the matrix, but he must make a choice between the blue pill (to remain ignorant inside the matrix) or the red pill (to learn the truth and escape the matrix). In choosing the red pill, Neo takes control of his future, which begins his quest through the film to overcome the constraints of the matrix and to become humanity's liberator.

Middle
paragraph 1

To some extent, Neo is god-like in his power at the end of the film, and he has attained this power through choosing to question his surroundings.

Transition
Topic sentence

    In contrast to Neo, Cypher represents the opposite reaction to the realization that something is wrong with reality. Cypher has already escaped the matrix and works with Morpheus to liberate other humans from their prison. However, Cypher has grown tired of his struggle against the harsh conditions of life in the real or non–computer-generated world. Ironically, when one of the matrix's agents asks Cypher, a technical operator out-

Middle
paragraph 2

side of the matrix, to betray Morpheus, Cypher willingly agrees on condition that he be reinserted back into the matrix. Cypher asks to be rich and important in his new life inside the matrix and suggests the life of an actor; he wishes to remember nothing of the outside world. Essentially, Cypher consciously adopts a life inside the illusion provided by technology, a move equivalent to committing suicide in his real life so he can become an actor in a fictional world.

Topic sentence

    Two extremes of the debate are therefore clear. On the one hand, Neo follows his own intuition to discover the limits of technology in order to overcome them and to live in the real world. On the other hand, Cypher, who already knows the limits of technology,

Middle
paragraph 3

cooperates with technology in order to live, once again, inside the illusion of the matrix. Neo appears to embody self-determination and the triumph of free will. Cypher appears to embody resignation and fatalism.

Transition
Topic sentence

    However, the film complicates this simple contrast. While Cypher appears to side with an ignorant life inside the matrix, he makes a free choice to betray his friends. Although we may understand his reasons, we ultimately disagree with his decision. In the case of Neo, Morpheus and his crew believe that Neo is "the one." That is, there is a myth inside the matrix that a special person will emerge from within the matrix to liber-

Middle
paragraph 4

ate humanity. In other words, Neo is predestined to fulfill his role of "the one," which implies that he is not acting totally out of free will. In this way, the film reminds its viewers that our choices and situations are not as simple as they might first appear. Free will and fatalism are not discrete and separate; rather, they are intimately intertwined with one another.

Conclusion

    Overall, the film suggests that the very idea of free will is a concept that is, perhaps, part of our social conditioning. The contradiction the film explores is that the ability to choose—free will—may be an illusion leaving no meaningful choice. While Cypher apparently gives up in the face of real-world challenges, Neo offers hope that choice is possible, despite the influence of the matrix. Thus, the matrix represents not only technology but also larger social conditions such as politics, interpersonal relationships, and spiritual beliefs. As the internet and other technologies like social media become more pervasive in our lives, *The Matrix* reminds us to question whether these technologies allow us greater personal freedom to make our own choices and to realize our individuality or whether they limit our creativity by replacing meaningful face-to-face communication with computer-mediated friendships. The question becomes less about the possibility of free will than about the ability to understand why and how we make our choices within the circumstances in which we make them.

Discussion of the Sample Essay

"Free Will and Fatalism in *The Matrix*" illustrates the effective use of structural elements common to college and university essays. The introduction provides basic information about the film and introduces the topics of free will and fatalism. It concludes with the thesis statement, which posits that the film complicates a simple division between free will and fatalism as evidenced in the characters of Neo and Cypher. The thesis is debatable, because one could argue that free will and fatalism are distinct and separate concepts.

The thesis statement also serves as a guide to the structure of the essay as a whole. It sets out a simple proposition—that free will and fatalism are opposite terms—and establishes that this distinction does not capture the complexity of the film. The essay will demonstrate how each character represents either free will or fatalism, and it will then show how each character demonstrates the opposite position in his actions.

The middle paragraphs develop the characters in terms of the concepts under discussion by referring to specific details from the film. The first two middle paragraphs deal with separate characters to develop them individually, while the following two paragraphs deal with the characters together in comparison with each other. Also notice that this structure does not follow a simple five-paragraph essay structure that deals with three subpoints. But that does not mean that the essay has a flawed structure. Notice how the point made in each paragraph builds upon the previous one: the second paragraph contrasts Cypher to Neo, who was discussed in the first paragraph; the third paragraph develops the two contrasting characters in relation to the relevant concepts; and the fourth paragraph, developing from the third, explains the intertwining of the concepts of free will and fatalism. Each paragraph in the essay furthers the overall argument.

In the middle paragraphs of the essay, each of these points is clearly made in a topic sentence. Each topic sentence identifies the aspect of the film to be discussed and connects that aspect to the thesis by stating how it contributes to the topics of free will and fatalism. The topic sentences and some other sentences also provide transitions between one paragraph and the next.

The framework you create by establishing this kind of relationship between the thesis, topic sentences, and transitional devices will give your reader valuable assistance in following your line of thinking.

The conclusion sums up the argument of the essay and points to the wider implications of the argument. Rather than making broad generalizations, the conclusion takes a minor theme of the essay (technology) to ask further questions about how the technology in the film (*The Matrix*) might be related to our real lives (the internet, Facebook, and other social media) in terms of the major themes of the essay, namely free will and fatalism.

Essay Writing: Process

Most people don't write an essay—or anything intended to be read by others, for that matter—by sitting down with paper and pen (or computer) and rising an hour later with a finished product. The final draft is the last stage of a highly complex process of thinking and writing, rethinking and rewriting. If you want to produce an interesting, thoughtful essay like the one on *The Matrix,* you have to be prepared to give time and serious attention to your subject. Without that willingness, you will not learn how to write from this book or from any other. But if you make the effort, you can learn to write essays that have something to say and say it well.

To help you learn the skills you need, we will begin by discussing reading analytically and writing summaries, important prequels to writing an essay (see Chapter 2). Throughout the rest of the book, we will focus on the major stages of writing academic essays:

Stage 1:   Clarifying Essay Topics
Determining what your assignment requires and exploring ideas to define a topic

Stage 2:   Gathering Material
Using methods of analysis to stimulate your thinking and to organize ideas, information, and specific details about your topic

Stage 3:   Formulating a Thesis Statement
Forming a main idea and selecting points to support it from the material you have gathered

Stage 4:   Drafting
Selecting and organizing material in a first draft

Stage 5:   Revising the Thesis Statement and Essay Structure
Checking for possible problems in your thesis statement and essay structure, and making necessary changes

Stage 6:   Revising Individual Paragraphs
Checking for possible problems in your introduction, middle paragraphs, and conclusion, and making necessary changes

Stage 7:   Final Editing
Improving your sentence structure and word usage, and correcting errors in grammar, punctuation, mechanics, and format

We are not claiming that the methods and the stages we propose are the only way to write or to write effectively; we don't even claim that they reflect exactly what writers—including ourselves—do when we write. For many of us, writing is far messier and more intuitive than our model would suggest. You may find that the order in which we present writing activities suits your method of composition perfectly; on the other hand, you may find yourself writing a draft to clarify your understanding of a topic or mentally revising the structure before a word hits the page. Try out our suggestions, adjust them to your needs, and fit them into a writing process that works for you.

Exercise

Answer each of the following questions in a sentence or two.

1. We suggest that writing essays can help you think through your ideas and communicate them to other people. Which of these purposes is most relevant to you as a writer? Why?

2. What is your usual approach to writing an essay? How effective do you find this approach? Which stage(s) of the process do you find easiest? Hardest?

Reading Analytically and Writing Summaries

(2)

Most of the material you need for writing essays in college and university will come from written sources. The reading you do will likely be much more difficult than your reading for high school. You may find the concepts new and the vocabulary unfamiliar. Or you may grasp the details but miss the overall point. Reading analytically is often the first step for most university and college level writing, so it is important that you learn how to read analytically before you begin to write about any text or texts. For this reason, we address the topic of reading analytically here, before discussing the major stages of essay writing. Along similar lines, writing a summary of a text is often a first step for developing an educated opinion (thesis) and writing an essay about it. As the main focus of essay writing is the development of a thesis statement, this chapter will also discuss the topic of writing summaries.

STAGE 1   Honing Your Reading Skills

The guidelines that follow will help you to **analyze**, and therefore to understand, what you read. We will explain how to analyze texts in a variety of disciplines, such as history, psychology, and political science (see Chapters 3–5). We will also aid you in explaining the relation between content and form (**literary analysis**) when you are writing about literature and film (see Chapter 6, Writing Essays on Literature). This ability to understand and analyze what you read is crucial when you are asked to explain, **compare**, or **evaluate** ideas and events you have read about (see Chapter 7, Writing Comparison Essays, and Chapter 8, Evaluating Arguments and Writing Critiques). It is an indispensable skill when you are writing **research papers** (see Chapter 10, Gathering Material for Research Essays). The readings in Part 2 provide many opportunities for you to practise the skills we outline in this chapter.

STAGE 2   Gathering Material: Analyzing Nonfiction Writing

STEP 1   Figuring Out the Basic Ideas

What is the writer's *subject*?

Check the title For most nonfiction, you will be able to identify the subject in the title or first few paragraphs. The titles of scholarly books and articles, for example, customarily state their subject: "The Effects of Television Violence on Preschoolers"; "Masculine Roles in Pat Barker's War Trilogy"; *Ukrainian Settlements in Ontario, 1870–1900*.

Not all titles, however, will identify the writer's subject so precisely. Writing intended for a general audience may have a title designed to create interest or convey the writer's attitude rather than state a subject, as in Fred Stenson's "In Search of a Modest Proposal" (Readings). Other titles may be ironic or otherwise misleading, as in W. S. Merwin's "Unchopping a Tree" (Readings).

Check the introductory paragraph(s) Because titles can be misleading, it's always a good idea to check the first few paragraphs to confirm or correct your sense of the writer's subject. If, for example, you relied on the title of E. M. Forster's "My Wood" (Readings), you might say that Forster's subject is a piece of property he owns. From reading the introduction, however, you would find that Forster states his subject in three ways: "What is the effect of property on the character? . . . If you own things, what's their effect on you? What's the effect on me of my wood?" This introduction makes it clear that Forster is using his own experience to illustrate a broader ethical question. You might say, then, that his subject is the effects that owning things have on a person's character.

Check your sense of the whole Sometimes identifying the subject won't be easy. The writer may seem to discuss several subjects; the details may be so fascinating that you lose the big picture; or the subject may be more complex than it initially appears. Try to think about the work as a whole. How would you describe its particular focus, in ten words or less? Consider, for instance, "He Was a Boxer When I Was Small" (Readings). On one level, of course, the subject is obvious—Lenore Keeshig-Tobias is writing about her father. But lots of people write about their fathers. How would you describe her particular focus?

Reviewing your sense of the whole will help you to avoid distorting what you read by assuming the first subject the writer mentions is the actual subject, or by overemphasizing a minor point.

What is the writer's *main idea* about the subject?

Check for an explicitly stated thesis Reread the piece, focusing on the main point the author is making about the subject. You may find a one- or two-sentence thesis statement in the introduction (as in David Suzuki's "It Always Costs" [Readings]); in the conclusion (as in Forster's "My Wood" [Readings]); or at another appropriate point (as in George Orwell's "Shooting an Elephant" [Readings]).

To make sure you understand what you have read, restate the thesis in your own words. By the time you reach the end of "My Wood," for example, you may recognize that the phrases "enormously stout, endlessly avaricious, pseudo-creative, intensely selfish" summarize Forster's thesis about the effects of owning property. But can you explain what Forster means by those terms in your own words? If so, you can be confident that you understand his main idea.

Restating the thesis and main points in your own words not only ensures that you understand the material but also reduces the temptation to keep quoting sentence after sentence. Use brief quotations sparingly to give a sense of the writer's tone or to define a key term that you then explain. Make sure you include the page reference for all quotations. For further information about how to handle quotations, see Part 3, Handbook for Final Editing, H2 Quotations.

If you do not understand a key term, you may miss the overall point of the piece. In the Readings, we have defined many terms for you. When you encounter unfamiliar terms in your course materials, you can look them up in your textbook or in a specialized dictionary like M. H. Abrams's *A Glossary of Literary Terms.*

Make an implied thesis explicit In pieces that are ironic, humorous, or based on personal experience, the main idea is often strongly implied but not stated directly. In "Unchopping a Tree" (Readings), for example, the absurdity of the process Merwin describes clearly suggests an opposite meaning. But you will not find a sentence or two spelling out Merwin's point.

What do you do if there is not an explicitly stated thesis? You may have a strong enough sense of the whole to sum up its main idea from an initial reading. You will often get a more accurate sense, however, if you examine the work more closely. Jot down your initial ideas, then reconsider them after you have completed your analysis.

How does the writer develop this main idea? Understanding how the writer organizes material to illustrate the main points will help you to see the relation between main points and supporting details. When you are reading secondary sources for a research paper, keep in mind disciplinary categories (which we discuss in Chapters 3 and 6). *Disciplinary categories* are key terms specific to a discipline or field of study. In writing essays on literature, for example, literary critics may develop their interpretation through disciplinary categories such as *plot, characterization,* and *setting.* Or they may employ terms specific to a particular literary approach, such as *postcolonial theory* or *gender studies.* In such cases, you may need to find definitions for key terms in order to understand the main ideas. You will find more information on gathering material for research essays in Chapter 10. Pay particular attention to lists of points in the introduction, to typographical devices such as headings, to key terms in topic sentences, and to transitions. Focus on the ideas being presented, not the details. Write a sentence or two explaining the main idea of each section in your own words.

There are six main methods writers use to develop ideas in nonfiction.

1. Telling a story What are the main stages in the narrative? What point does the writer make (or what point can you make) about each stage?

In nonfiction, a narrative is a (true) story told to illustrate a point. It has a beginning and an end and several incidents in between, though the incidents may not be recounted in chronological order. The incidents are usually grouped into stages, marked by significant external or internal changes. Summarize the point made by each of the main stages: not "The first section tells about their first week kayaking up the Mackenzie," but "In their first week kayaking [stage], they had to learn to work as a team [point]."

- Key transitions
  Time words, such as *before, after, one morning, the next day*
  Example: Orwell, "Shooting an Elephant" (Readings)

Although we don't demonstrate how to write narrative essays in this text, we have included a few examples in the Readings to illustrate this form.

2. Analyzing causes and effects What are the main causes and/or effects? What point does the writer make (or what point can you make) about each cause and/or effect?

As we will discuss with greater detail in Chapter 3, cause/effect analysis is one of the most common ways to write about ideas and events. Watch for two types: *independent causes and effects,* and *cause and effect sequences.* Independent causes and effects are often enumerated ("one cause," "another effect," "the most important . . ."). You may find it harder to follow the development of a cause and effect sequence, where the first cause produces an effect that in turn causes a further development (as in Benjamin Franklin's caution about neglect: "For want of a nail the shoe was lost; for want of a shoe the horse was lost; for want of a horse the rider was lost").

Independent causes/effects

- Key transitions
  Number words, such as *first, second, third;* other words signalling addition, such as *also, further, most important*
  Example: Forster, "My Wood" (Readings)

Cause/effect sequence

- Key transitions
  Words indicating cause and effect, such as *therefore, consequently, as a result*
  Example: Bruce Alexander and Stefa Shaler, "Addiction in Free Markets" (Readings)

3. Analyzing a process What are the main stages in the process? What point does the writer make (or what point can you make) about each stage?

A process has a beginning and an end, and can be divided into stages marked by significant changes. Summarize the point made by each of the main stages: not "The next stage is denial," but "The writer explains the next stage, denial, as the mind's attempt to protect the body from feeling pain."

- Key transitions
  First, next, third, final step/stage
  Example: Alison Gopnik, "Kiddy Thinks" (Readings [analyzed below])

4. Analyzing a system What are the main parts? What point does the writer make (or what point can you make) about each part?

Anything composed of parts that work together to create a whole can be considered a system. Writers often divide their subject into parts and discuss each part in a clearly identified section of their work, such as a chapter in a book or a block of paragraphs in an essay. Identify each main part and summarize the point the writer makes about it: not "Penal institutions are one aspect of the criminal justice system," but "Penal institutions, according to the writer, are the weakest link in the criminal justice system."

- Key terms and transitions
  The parts to be discussed may be identified in the introduction. Watch for repetition of key terms and for terms such as these: *aspect, element, feature, part*
  Example: Virginia Satir, "Systems: Open or Closed?" (Readings)

5. Comparing and contrasting What are the main similarities and differences the writer discusses?

Comparisons are built upon analysis, and so the writer may use **methods of development** such as cause/effect, process, or systems analysis. The two basic **methods of organizing comparison** essays are the *block method* and the *point-by-point method* (see Chapter 7). Look for similar kinds of material about each subject. Make sure you note both similarities and differences.

- Key terms and transitions

Compare, contrast, similar, different, in contrast, on the other hand, similarly, likewise

Example: David Suzuki, "Food Connections" (Readings)

6. Evaluating strengths and weaknesses What are the main points in the writer's argument? Are these points identified (or can you identify them) as strengths/weaknesses, costs/benefits, advantages/disadvantages? According to what **standard of evaluation**? For a detailed discussion of this term, see Stage 1: Clarifying Evaluation Topics: Checking for the Logical Standard in Chapter 8.

Writing that is intended to persuade readers is often harder to follow than other kinds of writing. There are several reasons. The subject itself may be complex, and so the writer may need to define terms; the writer's opinion about the subject may include both points in favour and points against; or the writer may introduce other opinions with which he or she agrees or disagrees. These sections may distract you from the main line of argument. Try to identify the type of analysis underlying the argument, such as cause/effect, process, or systems analysis. Use the writer's thesis as a guide to the points to watch for. Summarize each one. Then note how other points relate to the main line of argument.

- Key transitions

Words that suggest the writer is indicating disagreement or qualification: *although, despite, nevertheless, while it is true that*

Example: Dan Gardner, "The Missing Piece to the Gang-Violence Debate" (Readings)

If the work you are reading does not seem to fit one of the six patterns above, don't despair. Some pieces, especially long ones, may combine different types of development. Some may simply not be well organized. Do your best to identify and summarize the main points.

What are the main types of evidence/detail the writer uses? For what purpose(s)? Each main point in a piece of nonfiction writing will be developed through evidence and details of the kinds listed below. The term *evidence* describes the specific information used to support an argument (think of the evidence offered in a murder trial). The term *details* refers specifically to particular actions in narratives and particular images in descriptions; more broadly, it refers to any material that explains or illustrates a general statement. Details may become evidence when used for a persuasive purpose (think of a Crown prosecutor reviewing the details of a murder case to decide which ones can be used as evidence of the defendant's guilt).

How much attention you pay to specific details will depend on your purpose in reading. If you are writing a research essay, you may find both the general ideas and the specific information useful to you. If you are studying for an exam, on the other hand, you may focus more on general principles, with a few selected facts or examples. If you are writing a summary of the piece as an assignment, you may be more interested in the kinds or quality of the evidence/details than in the specific information.

Note in a sentence or two which of these main types of evidence/detail the writer uses, and for what purpose.

- Examples

  Specific instances that illustrate a general point or principle. Taking a lost wallet to the police station could be used as an example of honesty.

- Facts and figures

  Specific information such as names of people, places, events; titles of publications; and names of characters

  Precise numbers, as in measurements, statistics, dates

  Research studies and other "hard" evidence

- Quotations and other references to authorities

  Quotations from people interviewed or texts consulted

  References to recognized authorities on the subject or to authoritative texts (such as the Bible, the Quran), without direct quotation

- Narrative/descriptive details

  In telling a story or describing something, a writer may use few details (as in Caesar's "I came, I saw, I conquered") or many (as in an account of kayaking from Alaska to Tierra del Fuego). The details may seem fresh and vivid or flat and clichéd. The writer may use details for purposes such as creating suspense and conveying emotion.

- Other: definitions, analogies, allusions

  To make their explanations clearer, their arguments more persuasive, or their experiences more vivid, writers may define terms, provide analogies (the behaviour of gas molecules is like the behaviour of people in an elevator), or make passing references—allusions—to well-known historical figures and events ("My hopes sank like the *Titanic*"). For more on analogies, see Identifying kinds of evidence in Chapter 8.

Analyzing a piece of nonfiction writing is often preparation for evaluating the ideas and information it presents. For suggestions about how to evaluate a writer's arguments and evidence, see Chapter 8, Evaluating Arguments and Writing Critiques.

STEP 2   Gaining a Broader Perspective

Once you've figured out the basic ideas in a piece of nonfiction, it's time to stand back and take another look at the work as a whole. As a result of considering the work's purpose and tone, you may modify your sense of the work's subject or thesis. Thinking about the work's context may lead you to a deeper understanding. After you've reread or thought about the whole piece, write a sentence or two answering the questions posed below.

Purpose   Is the writer's main purpose to inform, to persuade, or to share personal experience? In "Kiddy Thinks" (Readings), for example, Gopnik's purpose is to explain the stages in children's cognitive development. In "It Always Costs" (Readings), on the other hand, Suzuki's main purpose is to persuade readers to accept his views. Keeshig-Tobias's purpose in "He Was a Boxer When I Was Small" (Readings) is to share her memories of her father and her insights into his behaviour. Consider these possibilities carefully. You may discover that works seemingly designed to explain or to share personal experience are actually making a persuasive point.

In summarizing, choose words that show you understand the author's purpose. Use the author's name every few sentences to make clear you are stating another person's ideas, not your own.

PURPOSE	WORDS THAT CONVEY PURPOSE
To share experience	Tells the story, reflects upon, describes
To inform	Explains, discusses, examines, analyzes
To persuade	Argues, claims, makes the point, criticizes

Tone   Does the writer use humour, satire, or irony? If so, how does that affect your understanding of the piece?

Context: subject   What knowledge of the subject or the cultural/historical circumstances can you bring to your understanding of the work?

Take a few minutes to consider how the piece fits with other things you know about the subject. For instance, perhaps your knowledge of the "troubles" that plagued Northern Ireland for many years could enrich your understanding of Jonathan Swift's "A Modest Proposal" (Readings).

Context: writer What do you know about the writer? Does the writer mention the source of his or her knowledge about the subject? Does the writer identify herself/himself with a specific political, religious, or intellectual position? What does the work itself suggest about the writer's perspective?

Writers often give some indication of the experience or training that qualifies them to speak about their subject, as you can see in the Suzuki piece "It Always Costs" (Readings). They may also identify the political, religious, or intellectual framework that guides their thinking, as Polly Toynbee identifies herself with the political left in "Inequality Is the Real Enemy" (Readings). The writer's perspective may be implied rather than stated. For example, Forster's biblical allusions in "My Wood" (Readings) suggest a particular religious framework. Considering the above questions will help you to see the values that inform the piece of writing.

STEP 3   Writing a Summary

When you finish your analysis, use your notes to write a brief summary of the piece. The summary will help you remember what you've read. You may also incorporate the summary, or parts of it, in your essay. This summary should include the following:

1. Complete bibliographic information about the piece: author, title, and other details as appropriate for the type of publication (see Part 3, H3 Documentation).

2. The writer's thesis, in your own words, near the beginning of the summary.

3. An overview of the organization of the piece and the main points in each section. State these points in your own words, but include brief quotations to capture the tone of the piece. Put quotation marks around any three or more consecutive words from the piece. If the piece is longer than a page, give page numbers in parentheses after each quotation and paraphrase. Page numbers are handy in case you need to refer to specific material again. They are crucial when you are documenting research papers.

4. The main types of evidence and an explanation of their purpose.

5. Key terms and their definitions.

For an example, see the following sample topic.

Sample Topic: Analyzing the Content of Alison Gopnik's "Kiddy Thinks"

Gopnik's article "Kiddy Thinks" (published in the *Guardian Weekly*, February 3–9, 2000) is reprinted in the Readings. You will follow this example more easily if you read Gopnik's article first.

STEP 1   Figuring Out the Basic Ideas

What is the subject? The title suggests that the article is about children and thinking. The sentences in the boxed text on page 237 tell us that the author, Alison Gopnik, is a developmental psychologist. We would therefore expect this article to be about the stages at which the thinking abilities of babies change.

What is the main idea? Gopnik states her thesis quite clearly at the end of her introduction. Here she says that the traditional view that babies and young children think quite differently from adults is wrong. Babies are not passive little blank slates; instead they use the same strategies that scientists use to understand both people and their environment.

How does the writer develop this main idea? Gopnik develops her thesis through process analysis. Step by step, she sets out the stages at which babies and young children acquire specific thinking skills. As she explains each stage, Gopnik also shows how babies "observe, formulate theories, make predictions, and do experiments" (237). Like adult scientists, babies can also change their theories if they get enough contradictory evidence.

What are the main types of evidence/detail the writer uses? For what purpose(s)? For the most part, Gopnik relies on examples taken from her experiences as a parent and from her work as a developmental psychologist. Because these examples are specific and involve familiar situations (the baby reaching for the lamp cord), they provide evidence many readers would find convincing. Gopnik also establishes her own credentials as an expert in the cognitive development of children by mentioning near the beginning of the essay that she co-authored a book entitled *How Babies Think*.

STEP 2   Gaining a Broader Perspective

Purpose and tone Gopnik's main purpose is to provide readers with information on how children develop crucially important cognitive skills: the awareness that children are people with thoughts and feelings and that they live with other people who have both similar and different thoughts and feelings; the awareness that the predictions children make about reality may or may not be accurate. Gopnik's tone is friendly but serious; her point is not shaped by humour, satire, or irony.

Context Traditional assumptions about children's inability to think rationally are part of the academic context of this essay. Gopnik says that "in the past 30 years we have learned more about what young children know and how they learn than we did in the preceding 2,500 years. And this has revolutionised our view of children" (237). She ends her article by discussing the social context. Many parents (the most likely readers of this essay) feel anxious and guilty about their ability to spend time with their children. Should parents quit their jobs? Should they take courses and buy educational toys and equipment for their children? While Gopnik is reassuring, she makes the point that more flexible work schedules and government funding for high-quality daycare would make it easier for parents to give children the attention they deserve.

STEP 3   Writing a Summary

Now that you have gathered information for an analysis of a piece of nonfiction writing, you can clarify the connections among your points by writing a summary.

SAMPLE SUMMARY

"KIDDY THINKS"

Alison Gopnik's essay "Kiddy Thinks" (*Guardian Weekly*, February 3–9, 2000) sets out the stages at which babies and young children acquire crucial thinking skills. The major stages of this cognitive development are as follows: at birth babies know that adults are like them; at nine months babies can differentiate happiness, sadness, and anger, and they watch the adults around them for clues as to how they should respond; between fourteen months and eighteen months babies begin to understand that other people may think and feel differently than they do; two-year-olds spend much of their time testing that knowledge, but they aren't very good at hiding objects; three-year-olds understand the concept of hiding objects; four-year-olds understand that objects aren't always what they appear.

As Gopnik explains each stage, she presents examples from personal experience and from her experiments as a developmental psychologist as evidence to support her thesis that even young babies use sophisticated and rational thinking skills. Gopnik suggests that babies behave like adult scientists as they "observe, formulate theories, make predictions, and do experiments" (237). Like adult scientists, babies change their theories if they get enough contradictory evidence. Gopnik concludes her essay by urging readers to support flexible work schedules and government-funded, high-quality daycare so that parents can give these tiny scientists the attention they deserve.

Working on Your Own Assignment

Develop better reading strategies to help you understand nonfiction, such as articles in books, magazines, newspapers, and scholarly journals.

- Figure out the basic ideas by identifying the writer's subject, thesis, main points, and supporting evidence.

- Deepen your understanding of the material by considering the writer's purpose, tone, and context.

- Write a brief summary that will help you remember what you have read.

Exercises

A.   Write a summary of one of the following essays from Part 2, Readings. Use the sample topic above as a guide.

- David Suzuki, "It Always Costs"

- Polly Toynbee, "Inequality Is the Real Enemy"

B.   Write two or three sentences identifying the major strengths and weaknesses of the following summary. Then revise the summary. You will find E. M. Forster's "My Wood" in Part 2, Readings.

> "What is the effect of property on the character?" E. M. Forster asks in "My Wood," and then proceeds to give us the answer (225). "In the first place, it makes me feel heavy" he says (225), referring to the fact that owning things weighs people down both physically and morally. "In the second place, it makes me feel it ought to be larger" he continues (226). "A little more, and then a little more" he says (226), pointing to our greed for more and more possessions. Furthermore, "property makes its owner feel that he ought to do something to it" (226). He realizes, however, that his impulse to change things "spring[s] from a foolish desire to express myself and from an inability to enjoy what I have got" (226). The final effect of property is to make a person selfish. As Forster says, "I shall wall in and fence out until I really taste the sweets of property" (227). He sums it all up by saying that his property has made him "[e]normously stout, endlessly avaricious, pseudo-creative, intensely selfish" (227).

Writing Analysis
Essays: Clarifying
Essay Topics and
Gathering Material

(3)

We turn now to the writing of analysis essays. As we discussed in Chapter 2, it is important to have reading and comprehension skills in order to write about a text or a subject in any discipline. It is also important to be able to summarize what you have read. Now that you understand and have worked on those skills, you are ready to learn how to analyze a text and communicate your analysis to others. In other words, you are ready to write an analysis essay.

When you write analysis essays, you focus both on the content of your source material and on how it is presented: you pay attention to what is said and how it is said. You may examine behaviour, data, events, written works, and other sources of information and ideas. Every written text is created from particular materials available to its writer. In a history course, for example, you may be asked to survey various historical documents and writings in order to answer a question about a particular aspect of the First World War. In a literature course, you may be asked to analyze characters' national or gendered identities in order to determine the author's and characters' relationship to the world in which they live.

STAGE 1 Clarifying Essay Topics

STEP 1 Defining Unfamiliar Terms and Understanding Your Assignment

Make sure that you understand all the terms used in the assignment. Learning about a subject includes learning the vocabulary that specialists in the subject use. In psychology courses, you may learn the meaning of such terms as *conditioned response, narcissism,* and *depression.* In literature courses, you are likely to discuss the meaning of such terms as *myth, point of view,* and *tragedy.* As these examples suggest, the specialized vocabulary of each discipline is likely to include terms seldom used outside the field as well as terms used in a more restricted way than you would use them in everyday speech. You can often clarify the meaning of terms by consulting your course text(s) or specialized dictionaries. Many texts contain glossaries that briefly define concepts and other specialized terms.

Understanding what your assignment is asking of you is also important when you begin the process of writing an essay. Essays can take a variety of forms: they may be largely descriptive or they may be highly analytic. Knowing what an essay can do and what type of essay your topic requires will help you deliver a more effective assignment.

No matter what subject you are studying, you will write essays that present arguments—you will be using *rhetoric* (the title of Part 1), the art of persuasive speech or writing. The tradition of rhetoric dates back to ancient times: one of the first written accounts was Aristotle's *On Rhetoric.* Rhetoric is concerned with not only the argument but also the language that makes the argument. This tradition is related to current essay writing because it is the foundation of the thesis statement: an opinion (the argument) with evidence (the reasons, expressed in language, why the argument is worth believing).

When you are writing an essay that requires you to make an argument, you need to think about your subject in two related ways: analysis and critique. *Analysis* is a process where you break down something into its various distinct parts. Related to analysis, *critique* involves an evaluation of (that is, forming an opinion or making a judgment about) some or all of those distinct parts that you identify in the analysis. For example, you could dismantle your car into all its identifiable parts: tires, hubcaps, windows, handles, fans, belts, spark plugs, and so on. However, if something were wrong with your car, you would need the critical capacity to evaluate which part is faulty. You might be able to identify all the parts, yet you might or might not be able to determine what is wrong.

The beginning chapters of the rhetoric section primarily address analysis and what we call methods of analysis. The latter chapters of the rhetoric section address critique and evaluation. However, the main focus of essay writing is the development of a thesis statement, so you will find elements of both analysis and critique in these early chapters, because a thesis involves both these processes. Engaging in an analysis is not the same as holding an opinion; similarly, having an opinion does not necessarily presuppose a thorough analysis.

STEP 2   Exploring Your Subject

Most essay topics set limits on what you should cover: the concept of the state in Plato's *Republic;* the use of the vampire myth in *Dracula* and *Interview with the Vampire;* Canadian and US policies on endangered species. Occasionally, however, you may face a fairly indefinite topic, such as "Write a 1000-word essay on how technology affects your life," or you may be invited to come up with a topic of your own.

Whether your topic is narrowly defined or open-ended, you can use various techniques—such as freewriting, brainstorming, and tree diagramming—to explore your topic and to define its limits. Limiting your topic allows you to examine your subject thoroughly enough to speak as an expert to less well-informed readers. If you try to write a five-page essay on a broad subject, such as computers or every aspect of a novel, your treatment is likely to be superficial. Narrowing your focus enables you to examine your subject in greater depth. It also helps you organize your information gathering and your writing. If you are unsure of the scope or intent of your assignment, ask for clarification from your instructor.

Here are three quick ways of generating ideas about your topic:

Freewriting Each time you come up with an idea, does another part of your brain say, "That's no good," or "You'll look silly if you say that"? Freewriting is one way of circumventing this mental critic. If you tend to agonize over a blank page, then freewriting may set your mind in motion.

Freewriting consists of writing continuously for ten minutes or longer, without stopping to organize, correct, or evaluate what you are doing. If your first attempt at freewriting does not give you a clear sense of what you might want to focus on in your essay, try variations on the freewriting process. You might, for example, look over your first freewriting material for the idea that seems most promising and then use this idea as a springboard for a second spurt of freewriting. Or, if you are trying to find an aspect of a text that interests you, you might freewrite a fantasy dialogue with the author, asking questions and recording the replies. This dialogue may reveal possibilities that you would not have reached by more conventional means.

Brainstorming This is another way of circumventing your mental critic. Brainstorming consists of putting down, in point form, everything you can think of about your topic, however obvious or bizarre the ideas may seem. Begin by writing your subject in the middle of a page and then jot down ideas as they come to you. When you have finished, you will have a mixture of generalizations and details radiating from your central subject. You can then draw lines to connect related points. For example, if you wanted to explore the film *The Matrix*, as discussed in Chapter 1, you might come up with a brainstorming diagram such as the one in Figure 3.1.

Much of the material you generate while brainstorming will never make it into a final version of your essay, but it's always better to have too much material than too little. From the diagram, you might pursue the aesthetics of action and violence in the film as an essay topic, or you could choose to explore the problematic opposition of free will and fatalism, as shown in the sample essay in Chapter 1.

Tree diagramming Tree diagramming is a more systematic form of brainstorming. When you use this technique, you divide your broad subject into categories and subcategories in the form of an ever-expanding tree.

FIGURE 3.1
Sample Brainstorming Diagram

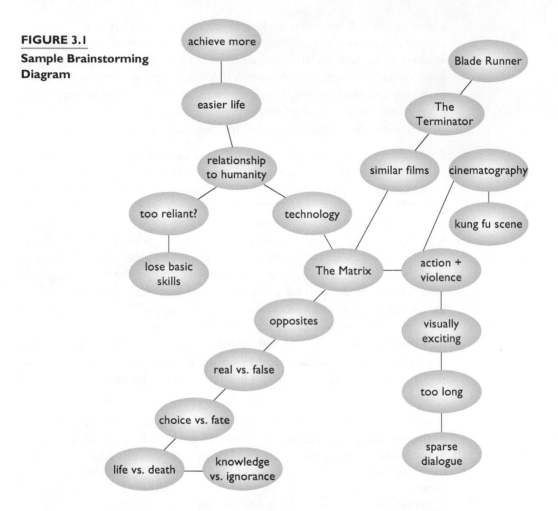

Because a tree diagram encourages you to develop equivalent categories, it is especially useful for narrowing comparison topics and developing arguments for and against something. For example, you might construct a tree diagram as a means of exploring arguments for and against Canada's role as a peacekeeper. Figure 3.2 represents the type of diagram you would generate by using this technique.

These discovery techniques are obviously useful for narrowing a broad subject such as technology. Even when the topic is limited, you can use these techniques to prime your thinking or to discover an angle that interests you.

FIGURE 3.2
Sample Tree Diagram

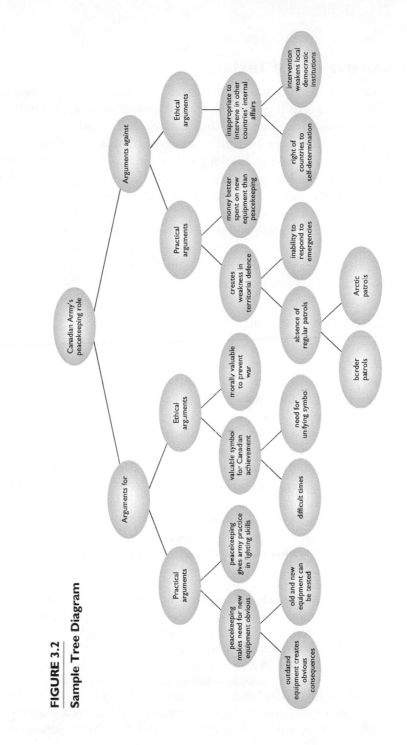

STAGE 2   Gathering Material

STEP 1   **Analyzing the Text**

Writers write essays on *texts*—a term that we use broadly to encompass disciplinary texts (history or anthropology textbooks, for example), but also interviews, advertisements, emails, signs, and visual or performance art. In an analysis essay, you gather material by thinking about the text you are considering and by breaking it down into parts in order to understand its meaning and its importance in culture and society. To gather material for an analysis essay, then, you must analyze the text and identify what is important and noteworthy about it.

If you are writing an essay on another essay—as is the case with the Sample Topic in this chapter—then you will also need to identify what method of analysis the author is using for his or her essay. Identifying the method used is a way to analyze the text.

STEP 2   **Choosing Methods of Analysis**

Writers have identified various methods of analysis (sometimes called rhetorical modes) that are useful in examining subjects. The following list of modes is not exhaustive, but it includes basic definitions of some major methods of analysis that you may be asked to use when you are writing essays for college or university courses.

In this section, we will touch briefly on the modes of *description, narration, division and classification*, and *comparison and contrast*, followed by a more detailed discussion of *definition,* **cause/effect analysis, process analysis,** and **systems analysis**. The latter four methods of analysis are common to most academic disciplines and to analytic thinking in general.

Because of its importance and prominence in many courses, we have included an entire chapter on how to write a comparison essay (see Chapter 7). In that chapter you will learn how to analyze the similarities and differences between works.

Description   Description mostly involves giving details about a person or thing. The most obvious type of description is spatial and physical. For example, if you were describing a person, you might give details such as hair colour, eye colour, height, weight, and clothes worn (physical details), and organize them in a logical structure by starting from head to toe, back to front, or side to side, depending on the subject of description (spatial details). Other possibilities for description might include temporal and abstract details. You could, for example, write about a building in a city where certain historical aspects are significant. Such descriptive writing might include abstract ideas like what the building means to the citizens of the city. Good descriptive writing will avoid a shopping list approach to detail in favour of an analysis of the importance of the included details.

Narration Narration is the act of telling in language; generally speaking, all writing has an element of narration. Most frequently, narration involves telling a story, as seen in all types of writing from newspaper articles to memoirs to fiction to how-to manuals. Narration usually relates the details of what happened and in what order, although many writers toy with narrative strategies by telling events out of order or through other experimentation. Narration is similar to description, but description primarily focuses on the person or thing itself while narration is more concerned with the sequence of details over time. In some cases, both happen simultaneously.

Division and classification Division and classification are basic human ways of thinking that allow us to separate units into groups and subgroups, often in some logical structure. For example, the classification of biological organisms into kingdom-phylum-class-order is a top-down ordering. The organization of books into alphabetical order is a left-to-right ordering. The palette of colours with red-yellow-blue in the centre and orange-green-purple (and other colours) surrounding it in various combinations is a centre-out ordering. To produce good division and classification writing, it is essential that the *basis of classification* be clearly defined. There can be different reasons for dividing groups of things into subgroups. For example, we may want to classify foods in terms of their colours, their protein values, their availability, or their cost.

Comparison and contrast Comparison and contrast writing analyzes the similarities and differences of two or more things. Like division and classification, good comparison and contrast writing will identify the **basis of comparison** and explain the reason(s) for the comparison. In academic writing, comparison and contrast writing will examine related opinions or theses on any given topic. For example, a biology class might ask you to write a paper on Lamarck's and Darwin's competing theories of evolution. An economics class might ask that you analyze the benefits and drawbacks of owning a car versus taking public transit. Similarly, an environmental studies class might ask the same question about transportation, but the basis of comparison could be quite different, one being economic in nature, the other environmental. Unless the objects are identical, comparison and contrast always involves both similarity and difference.

Definition Definition is very common in college and university writing. The most obvious source for definitions is the dictionary, but dictionaries sometimes make poor sources for academic definitions because they are written for brevity. As we discussed earlier, most disciplines develop a specialized vocabulary for their own purposes, and dictionary definitions fail to capture this depth or complexity. For example, claiming you are "depressed" would mean one thing to a friend and quite another thing to a clinical psychiatrist. Given that most academic writing is aimed at a specialized audience, it is preferable to use definitions that are more thorough, developed, or specific within that particular discipline. Avoid using simple definitions from sources such as a standard student dictionary or dictionary.com. If you feel compelled to use a dictionary, the most exhaustive dictionary of the English language is the *Oxford English Dictionary* (*OED*), which traces all words back to their first appearance in written English.

Later in this chapter we explain that disciplinary categories (for example, the category of *human needs* in psychology) must be understood within the context of the discipline or course of study. Definitions of terms can also be discipline specific. This specificity is why it is important to understand terms used in your assignment in relation to your course, not just in relation to a standard dictionary. It may be necessary to refer to terms as they are outlined in your textbook or in a specialized dictionary, such as a glossary of literary terms.

If you are using a definition method of analysis, you will need to employ an *extended definition*. Whereas a *formal definition* is a short, specific definition, as outlined in a dictionary, for example, an extended definition is more complex and multifaceted. It is a sustained and thorough definition of a concept or an idea, often as it applies to a particular discipline, context, or situation. If your essay topic asks you to explore a particular concept or term in sufficient detail, then you may want to use a definition method of analysis.

The following essay topics (based on works reprinted in the Readings) would be conducive to a definition method of analysis: "Explore the meaning of *addiction* as it is outlined by Gabor Maté in 'Embraced by the Needle' and Bruce K. Alexander and Stefa Shaler in 'Addiction in Free Markets'"; "With reference to David Suzuki's 'It Always Costs' and 'Food Connections,' and W. S. Merwin's 'Unchopping a Tree,' explain *environmentalism*." Such assignments ask you to explore the complexities of a term and how that term might be understood by different authors and in various contexts.

A definition method of analysis works best when the term you are defining is open to different interpretations. For instance, if asked to respond to the essay assignment "What success means to you," no two students will write the same answer. Similarly, environmentalism might be understood and explained differently by Suzuki and Merwin. If the term or concept you are examining is vague or multidimensional, then it is particularly important to engage in an analysis of the term and to explain clearly what it means within the context of your essay. A definition can expand or limit the scope of a term, depending on the purpose of the exercise.

When employing the definition method of analysis, you can divide the concept you are defining into different parts. What is it that can provide your readers with a sense of the whole? The parts that you recognize in your concept are your categories for analysis. For example, if you are writing an essay on environmentalism and drawing upon essays by Suzuki and Merwin (Readings), then you might recognize that conservation or preservation is important to both authors' understanding of environmentalism. Suzuki wishes to preserve aspects of traditional farming and marketing in "Food Connections," whereas Merwin wishes to preserve forests in "Unchopping a Tree." The idea of conservation, then, can be one of the categories through which you explain environmentalism.

Conversely, you may wish to place your term within the context of a larger concept—explain your term in relation to a larger whole. If you are writing an essay on the notion of environmentalism, you can relate it to the larger concept of *ecology*. While placing your concept in a larger category, it is important to explain exactly how it fits into that larger notion. Doing so will make clear the term's meaning and your understanding of it.

You may also want to analyze your term by comparing or contrasting it with other similar concepts. If you are defining *social worker*, for instance, you may compare and contrast the role of social worker with that of a psychologist or counsellor. If you are comparing your term to something similar, then make sure to point out the difference(s) in order to make the specific meaning of your term clear.

Another way of providing an extended definition of your term is to provide examples of it. An example of environmentalism might be choosing an organic food from a local market, rather than from a large grocery store, one of Suzuki's suggestions in "Food Connections" (Readings).

You may use one or more of these techniques in order to define your term. Above all, it is important to make clear to your readers how the works you are analyzing and how you—as the author of your essay—understand the term. Analyzing definitions is therefore an important method since you can use it to exemplify your understanding and to communicate specific meanings of concepts to your readers.

Cause/effect Cause/effect analysis explores the factors that have brought about a behaviour, event, or other phenomenon (its causes, in other words) or the changes that this phenomenon has itself brought about (its effects). Analysis of causes answers *why* questions: Why do some people become addicted and others not? Why do we disapprove of hockey violence and yet keep watching the game? Analysis of effects answers *what* questions: What are the effects of addiction on parenting, or on self-esteem? What are the consequences of accepting violence in sports?

In writing cause/effect analysis essays, your eventual goal is to arrive at a thesis—an opinion about causes, effects, or the relationship between causes and effects. However, you need to be modest about your claims. As ecologist David Suzuki points out in "It Always Costs" (Readings), we can't necessarily predict the effects of our actions. Nor can we always identify causes with certainty. The relationship between causes and effects is complex and often quite conjectural, even in the sciences. Certainly most phenomena do not have either a single cause or a single effect. For example, Gabor Maté in "Embraced by the Needle" (Readings) and Bruce Alexander and Stefa Shaler in "Addiction in Free Markets" (Readings) offer somewhat different causes of addiction. Both accounts have much validity, as C. Jones points out in her comparison essay "Perspectives on Addictions" (Readings: Sample Essays).

Because the goal of most academic disciplines is to probe beneath the surface of the phenomena they study, cause/effect analysis is often required in academic essay assignments. Assignments containing the word *why* usually ask you to analyze causes, as in "Write an essay discussing the reasons why addiction to prescription drugs is so common in North America." Assignments that require you to analyze effects usually indicate this focus by using words such as *effects, consequences,* or *results.* If you are unsure whether cause/effect analysis suits your subject, try turning the essay topic into a *why* or *what* question. If rewording the assignment in this way does not make cause/effect analysis obviously appropriate, you may want to consider other types of analysis.

In the early stages of planning your essay, of course, you may not know the answer to your question about causes or effects. You still may decide that this kind of analysis is the best way to explore your subject. For example, in "Na Na Na Na, Hey Hey Hey, Goodbye" (Readings), Tim Bowling's subject is his ambivalence toward hockey, which he can explain only by exploring the reasons why his attitude exists. Thus his subject provides a strong motivation for writing a cause/effect analysis essay.

Process analysis A process generally has a beginning and an end, with various stages in the middle. Like cause and effect, it is a progression of related events through time. Unlike cause and effect, however, a process analysis deals with larger stages that may differ from the isolated events of cause and effect. The process may consist of either a sequence of actions directed toward a definite end, such as the process of making a handicraft or a machine, or a series of identifiable changes over time, such as the process of aging. We divide the process into stages according to the points at which changes occur in the actions or states that make up the process.

Using this textbook as an example, the rhetoric section could be read as a process analysis. Disregarding the stages and steps this textbook discusses, a writer could simply produce an introduction, three body paragraphs, and a conclusion. The resulting five-paragraph essay might look like an essay, but it would lack the necessary stages of development, the comprehensive working through of the process that yields a good, persuasive essay. For example, missed developmental stages could mean the essay lacks the intellectual deliberation upon other viewpoints that may conflict with or contradict the essay's thesis. The essay, by definition, is a process of working through an idea and cannot be achieved through a formulaic approach to writing offered by some simple how-to essay writing guides.

When you are writing a process analysis essay, your goal is to develop a thesis about the relationship between the stages that make up your subject. Remembering this purpose will help you to avoid slipping into two kinds of writing that superficially resemble process essays but actually have very different goals: *how-to writing* and *narrative essays.*

- How-to writing consists of sets of instructions that tell you, for example, how to finger the easiest chords on your new guitar or how to minimize the use of pesticides in your garden. How-to writing may seem similar to process analysis essays about actions directed toward an end. You can avoid confusing these two kinds of writing if you remember that the aim of how-to writing is to enable the reader to *do* something, while the aim of a process analysis essay is to have the reader *believe* something, namely the author's thesis about the relationship between the action stages. A handbook on fingering guitar chords, for instance, would explain how to move from simple chords like A and E to more complex chords like F and B minor, whereas an essay analyzing the process of learning folk guitar might present the thesis that the process is unexpectedly complex because the early stages are interdependent.

- The second kind of writing that can be confused with process analysis, the narrative essay, uses nonfictional material to tell a story with a more or less explicit thesis. George Orwell's "Shooting an Elephant" (Readings) is a narrative essay in which the author describes the stages of his own awakening to the evils of imperialism. Not all narrative essays have an emphasis on stages; the ones that do, like Orwell's, may seem hard to distinguish from process essays that analyze identifiable changes over time. The key distinction is that narrative essays deal with *individual* stages; process essays analyze *general* stages of development. Thus in "Shooting," Orwell presents the stages through which one particular "young and ill educated" Englishman, a police officer, struggles to understand his true role in the East. Are these stages common to everybody who comes to a similar understanding of the significance of imperialism? It is not part of Orwell's aim to answer this question. A process analysis essay on the same subject might claim, for example, that many representatives of colonial powers go through the same process of psychological denial followed by recognition, then social accommodation followed by alienation.

Process analysis topics in academic disciplines may require you to analyze a series of directed actions, such as the procedure for casting bronze, the steps necessary to stage a Greek tragedy, or the steps required to improve the habitat for spotted owls. Analyzing a series of changes over time is a common assignment in disciplines like history (for example, analyzing the stages in the development of parliamentary democracy), psychology (analyzing the development of cognitive thinking), or anthropology (analyzing the development of Mayan religious iconography). Notice the key words in these assignments: *procedure, steps, stages, development.* Similar terms, such as *emergence, evolution, growth,* and *progress,* may also indicate process analysis.

Process analysis may also be one of several possible ways of responding to a general topic. For example, if you were given the topic "Write an essay exploring the significance of globalization," you might decide to analyze globalization in terms of its historical evolution. This is the analysis that underpins James Howard Kunstler's "Globalisation's Time Is Up" (Readings). The process approach supports his point that globalization is a transient phenomenon, rising and falling with the passage of time.

Two kinds of stages that you may develop in your process analysis essay are *chronological stages* and *action stages.*

Chronological stages Since process is an unfolding over time, periods of time form natural categories for process analysis. However, chronological stages should not be arbitrarily divided segments of time; each should correspond to a marked change in the ongoing process. For example, if you were writing a process analysis essay on the development of children's thinking, you might generate material by reflecting on what is going on in each segment of a child's early life in which a new stage of thinking begins, as Alison Gopnik does in "Kiddy Thinks" (Readings). Not all children reach the same development stages at the same age, so it is the change that matters to the process, not the exact timing. Many process essays, including those by Gopnik and Kunstler (Readings), are organized chronologically.

Action stages When you are analyzing a process that consists of a series of actions, action stages are useful categories for gathering material. Look for points at which the nature of the action changes. Each of these changes marks a new stage in the process. If initially you come up with only one or two action stages, think of the actions that necessarily precede and/or follow the actions you have identified.

The following assignment is an example of a process analysis essay topic.

- **Discuss** the gradual way in which the character of Neo in the film *The Matrix* comes to realize that his world is fictional.

The assignment asks you to examine Neo's process of change and discovery. You would divide the process of discovery into stages and analyze each stage. In developing the essay, you would focus each paragraph on a different stage in the process; the stage would become the topic of the paragraph and the main point would be about the significance of the stage. This method works well in theory and in expert hands, but process essays about texts often fall into the trap of just retelling the story. Be aware of this tendency if you choose the process analysis method of development.

Essentially, if your subject can be divided into stages, process analysis is one way of gathering material. Whether it is the best way depends on the kind of point you eventually want to make.

Systems analysis Whereas a *process* is the progression through general stages to some kind of end, a *system* is a combination of interrelated parts that constitutes a unified whole. To use the essay as an example, the writing of an essay is a process; the product of an essay is a system. The various parts of the essay—the thesis, the development of details, the wider implications, the audience, the context of the writing—all contribute to how the essay works. So, for example, if an essay lacked the development of details, the reader might understand the point of the argument (the thesis) but not how the writer arrived at the thesis (development of details). Or, if a writer failed to consider the essay's audience, the writer might risk alienating that audience by not considering their viewpoint. In other words, a writer who is "for" a particular position will write differently for an audience who shares similar views than for an audience who is "against" that position. In any case, when one part of a system fails to function properly or adequately, the entire system may be compromised. The system may fail, or it may find a new equilibrium. Good writing about systems will consider all parts of the system in order to make an argument.

In school you have no doubt studied planetary systems and the many systems that make up the human body. Out of school, your activities and even your mood may be influenced by the prevailing weather system. The news is filled with debates about the health care system. Yet you may not fully understand why each of these is called a system.

A system is a unified whole that is made up of many parts. This meaning can apply to a set of events, such as the French Revolution; a set of data, such as a bookkeeping system; a set of phenomena, such as an ecosystem; or a set of ideas, such as neo-liberal economic theory. It even applies to essays whose parts (thesis statement, topic sentences, and the like) contribute to a whole (the essay itself).

Whether it involves a set of phenomena or a set of ideas, a system will have *essential parts,* which are those elements needed to keep the system going, and a *goal* or *function,* which is what the system is in place to do. When writing systems analysis essays, you need to be particularly thorough in gathering material, because you cannot afford to leave out any essential part.

The purpose of systems analysis essays is to analyze the parts in order to understand the system as a whole and its goal or function. If you were analyzing the criminal justice system within a democracy, for example, you might conclude that the parts (lawmakers, courts, lawyers, juries, prisons, and so forth) are designed to achieve the goal of balancing the defendant's rights with the rights of society. In contrast, the criminal justice system in a dictatorship would have a different function, such as maintaining the authority of those in power.

Essay assignment topics may specifically ask for systems analysis. For example, an assignment could ask you to identify the key features of J. K. Galbraith's economic theories, the elements necessary for a salmon stream to be viable, the main aspects of verbal and non-verbal communication in families, the key beliefs of the '70s generation of feminists, or the defining components of systems of poetic metre. Notice the adjectives (*key, necessary, main, defining*) and nouns (*features, elements, aspects,* and *components*) in these topics. Words like these refer to essential parts of something, and thus indicate that you are being asked to view the subject as a system. Assignments may also ask you to focus on the function of one or more parts in relation to the whole, as in "Discuss the role played by planning committees in the organization of the 2010 Winter Olympic Games."

As a way of seeing the world, systems analysis has become increasingly common since the mid-twentieth century, when disciplines like ecology reinforced the interconnectedness of human society with the whole surrounding environment. For assignments that do not specify the method of analysis you are to use, systems analysis is a good choice if your subject can be divided up into essential parts and if you can make a valid and thoughtful point about the interconnectedness of these parts.

When you are writing a systems analysis essay, check first to see whether there is an appropriate set of disciplinary categories for the system you are analyzing. If you were analyzing the needs of wilderness forests as a system, for example, the ecological categories of carbon cycle, water cycle, nutrient cycle, and energy cycle would give you comprehensive categories for collecting material. As you move your attention away from the sciences toward culture and society, decisions about which parts are essential become a matter of informed, well-educated, or researched opinion. It is obvious that trees need water, but is an emphasis on equal pay an essential part of the ideology of 1970s feminism?

When you are writing about subjects that are governed mainly by informed opinion, it will be the details you gather that will make your claims about essential parts more or less convincing to your reader. If you are having trouble coming up with categories of essential parts, try brainstorming. Or, if the function of the whole seems more important than a detailed analysis of the parts, you may find that you can explain the significance of one system more forcefully by comparing it with a similar system. If you were writing an essay on traditional food markets as distribution systems, for example, you could gather more material by considering modern food markets in the same light. The resulting comparison might give you an essay similar to David Suzuki's "Food Connections" (Readings). For more on comparison essays, see Chapter 7.

Systems analysis is a method often used in writing essays on literature. In analyzing a literary text (a poem, a film, an essay) as a work of art, you are examining it as a system of interrelated parts. The artistic choices about such matters as verse form, structure, and **style**, in particular **diction**, help to shape literature's meaning—the whole work of literature as a system. Analyzing a literary text as a system gives you practice in examining a text closely. You could, however, also use cause/effect or process analysis to analyze literary texts. For instance, you could look at the historical, social, economic, or psychological causes that may have shaped a particular text, or at the text's aesthetic or social effects. This kind of cause/effect analysis is increasingly popular in literature courses, as we attempt to understand how and why literature "means" in our historical and contemporary world. You could also examine the process by which a text was composed, published, or performed. This kind of process analysis would be helpful, for example, if you were learning to publish or perform a creative text yourself. For more on writing essays on literature, see Chapter 6.

As is clear from the preceding discussion, many of these methods of analysis (rhetorical modes) are related to, or build upon, each other. For example, the method of division and classification shares traits with comparison and contrast. The cause/effect method is similar to process and systems analyses. An essay using a comparison and contrast analysis may need to define or describe the two things being compared. Any given essay may therefore use one method of analysis for the entire essay or, more usually, draw upon two or more methods of analysis.

If you were writing an essay on the causes and effects of addiction for Maté and Alexander and Shaler (Readings), you would be using the cause/effect method of analysis. It would also be important, however, to analyze what *addiction* means to the authors and to provide an explanation of those meanings in your essay. Thus you would also be using the definition method of analysis.

If you were to compare and contrast the reasons Tim Bowling likes or dislikes hockey in "Na Na Na Na, Hey Hey Hey, Goodbye" (Readings) with the reasons Kofi Annan thinks sports are important to politics in "Football Envy at the UN" (Readings), you would be using both comparison and cause/effect for your methods of analysis. Because you are comparing two works, you are using a comparison method of analysis; because you are examining the *reasons* for the author's beliefs, you are using a cause/effect method of analysis.

STEP 3   Choosing Disciplinary or Analytic Categories

When you gather material for writing analysis essays, you often do so within the framework of a particular academic discipline, such as education, Spanish, or psychology. Academic disciplines all define their own content (the area or areas of knowledge with which they are concerned) and develop specialized vocabularies for categorizing their material. We call these *disciplinary categories*. For example, in one school of psychology, the needs for safety, belonging, love, respect, self-esteem, and self-actualization are categorized together as human needs.

Sometimes ready-made disciplinary categories are not available to you. Suppose that in an essay for a literature course, you wish to examine how several Anglo-Canadian writers represent First Nations and Métis characters in their writing. You might look at how such characters are represented in the literature socially, economically, and physically (for example, physical appearance). These categories are not literary categories *per se*. Rather, they are your own categories around which you might wish to gather material for an essay: they are not disciplinary but *analytic categories*. By contrast, in an essay for a literature course, you may be asked to determine how the form of a poem conveys its meaning. In this case, you may choose the disciplinary categories of figurative language, diction, and **tone** to structure your essay. When you gather material for an essay, you will need to place that material into categories. Those categories may be either disciplinary or analytic. The categories you choose in the planning stage of your essay will be determined by the methods of analysis you intend to employ.

STEP 4   Choosing Methods of Proof

As stated earlier, engaging in an analysis is not the same thing as proving an argument. An argument involves critique because it involves an evaluation or a judgment. In his writing *On Rhetoric*, Aristotle identified three main methods of proof: *ethos*, *logos*, and *pathos*. A persuasive essay will use at least one of these three methods of proof to persuade the audience that the thesis is worth believing. While much contemporary writing about essays will focus on *logos*, it is worth considering the other methods of proof when writing your essays. The main purpose of evaluation is to determine the strengths and weaknesses of something, and the proofs will set the standards of evaluation.

Ethos   The Greek term *ethos* gives us our current word *ethics*. In terms of essay writing, *ethos* means two things. First, the person making the argument (the writer) should have an ethical character. That is, he or she should appear to have integrity and honesty, and is, therefore, believable rather than questionable. Second, the argument should be worthy of public consideration because it serves the public good. In this way, it is ethical in nature. In Aristotle's time, arguments were made in the interests of the public, a fact that is sometimes lost in today's classroom environments.

Logos   The Greek term *logos* gives us our current word *logic*. In terms of essay writing, *logos* also means two things. First, the argument should be logical and reasonable; that is, we can work through its internal logic and arrive at a sound conclusion. Second, *logos* has connotations of writing, language, and words, so the words we choose when discussing a topic are important. For example, if we were trying to persuade someone to eat spinach, saying "Eat your spinach because I say so" is quite different from saying, "Spinach is high in vitamins, calcium, and fibre, so eating it would be good for you." The purpose is the same (eat your spinach), but the expression is different (command versus explanation). The second example is more persuasive because it provides specific details to support the argument and uses more appropriate language and tone.

Pathos   The Greek term *pathos* refers to the emotions. While some might argue that emotion should not factor significantly into essays, emotion is nonetheless an effective tool to persuade a reader. While manipulating the reader's emotions would contradict the value of the writer's *ethos*, emotion can influence your reader when used appropriately. Like *logos*, you can invoke emotion by choosing the correct words to write an effective essay. For example, using a word like *murder* or *killing* has a different emotional effect than the more legal term *homicide*. However, keep your audience in mind because specialists in a field will expect a certain terminology and may dislike or resent blatant emotionally charged terminology.

Other methods for proving arguments can include practical and aesthetic considerations, which can be considered in terms of *ethos, logos,* and *pathos*. For example, an aesthetic evaluation considers taste (*pathos*) as well as character (*ethos*) when deciding if a particular person would enjoy a particular movie. A practical evaluation considers the most reasonable course of action (*logos*) given the people involved (*ethos*) with the least amount of disturbance (*pathos*).

STEP 5   Connecting the Parts to a Whole

Depending on which method(s) of analysis you have chosen, you have categorized your information according to a definition, sequences of causes and effects, stages in a process (chronological or action), aspects of a concept, or parts of a system. It is important to distinguish between the methods of analysis that you have chosen to organize your own essay and the methods of analysis that you recognize and understand in a work. If you are writing a process essay, the disciplinary or analytic categories you recognize may be identical to the categories you use to organize and write your essay. Thus if you are planning an essay on how to play folk guitar, you recognize action stages of strumming and fingerpicking, and you use those same stages or categories to organize your own essay.

However, the categories you choose to structure your own essay are often not the same as those you recognize in your study of the text(s). For example, in reading Laura Robinson's "Girl Unprotected" (Readings), you see that Robinson uses a cause/effect method in her essay: she argues that coach Frost's power over and abuse of his junior hockey players resulted in those players' abuse of girls. While Robinson uses a cause/effect method of analysis in her writing, you might use a systems analysis method in your own essay. In response to Robinson's essay, you might argue that the system of abuse in junior hockey can be broken down into various parts: violence in the game and problems in the roles and responsibility of management, players, and fans. These parts ultimately make up the whole: the system of abuse in Canadian hockey. It is important to realize that the way in which you connect the parts will help to determine your overall argument: your thesis statement. We will explore this stage in the essay writing process in Chapter 4.

Special Categories for Analyzing Texts

When you are gathering materials for your essay from behaviour, data, events, and/or written or visual works—all texts—you can ask particular questions in order to develop your analysis. Here are some questions you can ask yourself when analyzing your subject, and when you are choosing disciplinary or analytic categories and connecting the parts to the whole. While asking these questions, you are paying attention to *how* the work means, not just *what* it means. You may ask a few or many of these questions, depending on what kind of text you are analyzing.

A. Identifying Textual Features

Subject, genre/subgenre, context

1. What issue, idea, event, or person is this work about?

2. Does this work belong to a particular **genre and subgenre** (genre: novel, film, essay, poem; subgenre: fantasy novel, science fiction film, personal essay, lyrical poem)?

3. Can you identify the likely audience for this work (for example, academic, popular)? Is knowledge of the intended audience and/or the social, historical, or cultural situation in which the work was produced relevant to understanding the work?

Evidence and detail The material used to support evaluative or analytic points, or to give substance to explanation, narration, or description.

1. What material does the author use to support evaluative or analytic points? Examples? Facts? Statistics? References to, or quotations from,

authorities on the subject? Imaginary situations? Predictions? (See Chapter 8 for kinds of evaluative arguments and detail.)

2. Does the author give substance to narration by extended accounts of a small number of events or by brief accounts of many events? Is description panoramic (using selected details to summarize a wide range of experience), or dramatic (using lots of details to convey a particular experience)?

Structure The selection and arrangement of points, narrative incidents, and/or descriptive detail.

1. Does the work use the structure appropriate to a particular genre and subgenre (for example, inductive reasoning for a personal essay)?

2. Does the work use the structure appropriate to a particular mode of discourse?

   a. Is the main purpose of the work to present an analysis, summary, or evaluation? If so, what principle determines the order in which points are presented (for example, order of ascending interest, pro–con structure)?

   b. Is the main purpose of the work to present a narrative or a description? If so, what principle governs the order (for example, past to present, near to far)?

   c. If the work mixes analysis, summary, and/or evaluation with narration and/or description, what is the organizing principle?

   d. Does the work uses spatial or chronological principles of structure? (For example, are flashbacks used, or are events summarized?)

   e. Is the work divided into parts? Do these parts correspond to stages in the development of the action?

Diction

1. Is the level of usage in the work that of formal, educated speech; informal, everyday speech; the colloquial speech associated with a particular dialect or subculture; or a mixture of these levels? Are there shifts between levels of usage?

2. Is a specialized vocabulary (for example, the vocabulary of a biologist or a banker) important to this work?

3. Are there significant patterns of word choices (for example, euphemisms designed to hide unpleasant facts)?

Sentence structure

1. What are the characteristic features of the author's sentences? Long or short? Simple or complex? Is there a distinctive use of parallelism or other rhetorical devices?
2. Are there significant exceptions to, or changes in, the author's habitual sentence structure?

Tone

1. How would you describe the tone of the work?
2. Is there a narrator or speaker who is distinctly different from the author? How would you characterize the narrator's or speaker's attitude toward the subject and/or the reader? How would you characterize the author's attitude toward the reader?
3. How is the tone conveyed?
4. Are there shifts in tone? If so, where, and to what purpose?
5. How apparent, and how important to the work, is the personality of the author?

B. Connecting the Parts to the Whole

1. If the work belongs to a distinct genre and/or subgenre, in what ways does it conform to and depart from the conventions of the genre?
2. How does the title relate to the work as a whole?
3. What is the relationship between structure and evidence/detail? For example, is one part of the evaluation or analysis supplied with more evidence or detail than another?
4. What is your interpretation of the author's thesis or theme, based on your analysis of the work and your sense of how its elements are related?
5. Does the author state a thesis or theme directly?

Sample Topic: Nostalgia in Tim Bowling's "Na Na Na Na, Hey Hey Hey, Goodbye"

The aim of this section is to demonstrate ways of gathering material for a sample essay assignment. Essay assignments will ask you to analyze a text or texts. Whether those texts consist of documents, data gathered from interviews, newspaper clippings, or a work of literature, your task will be to scrutinize the text(s) closely and present an educated opinion, a thesis on your findings. The sample essay we discuss here analyzes Tim Bowling's essay "Na Na Na Na, Hey Hey Hey, Goodbye" in relation to the notion of *nostalgia*. Bowling's essay can be found in the Readings section of this textbook; the sample student essay on Bowling's work—the one we explain here—can be found in the Sample Essays section of the Readings. We recommend that you read both Bowling's essay and the sample student essay before you continue to read this section.

STAGE 1   Clarifying Essay Topics

STEP 1   Defining Unfamiliar Terms and Understanding Your Assignment

Let's suppose that your instructor has asked for a 1000 word essay on Tim Bowling's attitude toward hockey in "Na Na Na Na, Hey Hey Hey, Goodbye" (Readings). There do not seem to be any terms that you need to look up in order to clarify your understanding of the essay topic. *Attitude* seems clear enough. Just to be sure, though, you look up *attitude* in a dictionary and find that you need to pay attention to the tone that comes through in Bowling's work. At this point, you may also want to ask yourself relevant questions for identifying textual features, as discussed earlier in Special Categories for Analyzing Texts. You want to make sure, for example, that you are clear on the genre of the work. Thus you determine that the genre is an essay and that the subgenre is a personal essay. As you read through Bowling's essay, you pay attention to details, structure, diction, tone, and so on. You will also need to understand the subject (professional hockey) and the context (1993 semifinals of the Stanley Cup) of the work.

Can you identify the method of analysis that Bowling uses in his essay? What kind of parts does Bowling's essay break down into? What is the whole—the thesis—that Bowling is trying to convey? In short, what is Bowling's point? These are questions you will ask in order to understand Bowling's essay more thoroughly. You may not use the same method of analysis that Bowling does, and you should not break your own essay into the same parts that Bowling does. Nevertheless, you need to understand how Bowling's essay works in order to plan and write your own essay.

STEP 2   Exploring Your Subject

You may engage in freewriting, brainstorming, or tree diagramming to further explore the topic of your essay.

STAGE 2   Gathering Material

STEP 1   ## Analyzing the Text

There are different ways to gather material, depending upon what kind of essay you are writing. As you will see in Chapter 10, for example, you will gather material for a research essay by finding and reading scholarly articles and books on your topic. As you will see in Chapter 7, you will gather material for a comparison essay by thinking about and itemizing the similarities and differences between texts, events, or concepts. In an analysis essay, you gather material by analyzing the text at hand. Whether that text is a historical document, an advertisement, or a literary essay, you will break it down into parts in order to discover the whole—how it means and why it is important.

Discovering the text's method(s) of analysis Upon reading and re-reading Bowling's essay with an eye to what kind of method(s) of analysis he is using, you find that he uses the cause/effect method of analysis to write his essay. You discover this method because you read the text closely and find that Bowling asks questions about why he likes and dislikes professional hockey, and then attempts to answer his own questions. Associating hockey with Canadian icons such as Tim Horton and the Tragically Hip (cause) makes Bowling like hockey (effect). The violence that Bowling notices in the game, such as the Sheldon Kennedy and Todd Bertuzzi cases (cause), makes Bowling dislike hockey (effect). Thus you discover the parts (causes and effects) that make up the whole system of Bowling's essay.

Now that you have discovered that Bowling uses a cause/effect method of analysis, you need to find out what those parts—those causes and effects—add up to. What is the whole? What is Bowling's point? What is his thesis? As you answer these questions, you engage in an analysis of the text.

Because Bowling writes a personal essay, not a formal essay, his thesis statement is implicit rather than explicit. Unlike the formal essay you will write, he does not provide a concrete thesis statement near the beginning of his essay. Therefore, you will need to determine the answer to his questions by interrogating the text as a whole. Upon doing so, you find that Bowling does not really answer his own question. He neither solely likes nor dislikes hockey. He remains ambivalent about the game throughout the essay. You discover Bowling's attitude, in part, by how he ends his essay. He seems to have given up on it, deciding to dislike it, when he says, "I won't be watching" (215). But then he qualifies that stance by questioning whether or not he really will be able to stop watching (215). You decide that Bowling's thesis is that there are positive and negative aspects to the sport of hockey—he remains both drawn to it and aware of the problems within it. This kind of thesis, one that is not a simple either/or position, is common in academic work. Often the issues that writers discuss are complicated and cannot be simplified into a single or easy stance.

STEP 2   Choosing Methods of Analysis

Now that you have determined Bowling's method of analysis (cause/effect) and the thesis of his essay (that he is stuck in a love/hate relationship with professional hockey), you will need to work on choosing the method of analysis for your own essay. Be wary of choosing the same method of analysis that the author does. Similarly, do not choose the same thesis statement that the author does. Your goal is not to summarize the essay, but to engage in your own analysis of it.

With your new knowledge of Bowling's method of analysis and thesis statement, you reread Bowling's essay. This time, you think more about the essay topic—Bowling's attitude toward hockey—and try to read between the lines, looking to see how Bowling's attitude might come across in the essay. You notice that there are various notions that keep arising in Bowling's essay. For example, Bowling keeps referring to his childhood and to Canada and what it means to be Canadian. In order to understand how these notions arise in Bowling's text, you brainstorm and freewrite. Here is the chart that you write to gather your material and organize your thoughts.

Childhood	playing hockey with marbles in the kitchen as a kid (par. 2) boards were blank; you could hear the whistle being blown (par. 14)
Canada	2002 Winter Olympics, loonie under the ice, Canada's win (par. 11) Don Cherry (par. 12), Tim Hortons, Tragically Hip (par. 7) millions of Canadians "grew up on the lore of the game" (par. 7)
Violence	Sheldon Kennedy and Todd Bertuzzi (par. 10) says the game has "outdated machismo code" (par. 6) Al Purdy's comment that hockey is "ballet and murder" (par. 9)
Hockey as narrative/story	"primal pull of narrative" (par. 7) hockey as the "Great Canadian Novel" (par. 7)

After you have engaged in freewriting, brainstorming, note-taking, and making charts such as the one above, you will probably have a rough idea about the kinds of parts—analytic categories—into which your essay can be divided. Upon examining these categories you can decide on a method of analysis. In terms of the work you have done on Bowling's essay, you notice that the categories you have identified above are not causes and effects, nor are they stages in a process. They are also not aspects of a definition. Rather, they seem to be parts of a whole of some sort. You don't know what that whole is, because you have not yet determined it: you have not yet created your thesis statement or argument. However, you sense that upon further examination of these categories, you might be able to understand what kind of attitude Bowling has toward hockey. Note that the list of categories you have created through brainstorming, freewriting, note-taking, and charting will probably be much longer than what you end up using in your final essay. That's okay. It's better to have too much material to work with than too little. You can eliminate some of your categories once you have decided upon a thesis statement and started to draft your essay.

Upon examining the various possible methods of analysis, you decide that a systems analysis will work best. The various categories in your chart—childhood, Canada, and so on—will lead to a thesis statement and will be able to relate to an overall argument. You have determined your method of analysis and some possible parts or categories to use in your essay. Now you can work on formulating an argument and creating a tentative thesis statement, which we will discuss in the next chapter.

As you work on your assignment, know that it's okay to go back and forth between the analysis of the text itself—looking at its parts, thinking of their importance in relation to the whole—and the method(s) of analysis and categories that you will use in order to express those ideas. Learning to analyze a text, to break it down and really understand it in an intellectual way, can be one of the most difficult but rewarding things you will learn. You analysis of a text is intimately related to how you organize and write about it. For that reason, gathering material and writing about that material are really very closely linked in analysis essays. We remind you, as we did in Chapter 1, that although we outline how to work toward an analysis essay in stages and steps, the writing process doesn't always occur in such a linear way—it's fine to go back and forth between these stages and steps as you work on your assignment.

Working on Your Own Assignment

Clarifying the demands of your topic is a necessary first step toward writing a good essay.

- Identify terms that need to be defined and what your assignment is asking of you.
- Use freewriting, brainstorming, or tree diagramming to discover an aspect of your subject that interests you.

The purpose of writing analysis essays is to come to a better understanding of the nature and significance of your material by dividing it into relevant parts.

- Analyze the text by breaking it down into parts and thinking about what is most important.
- Decide whether you should define, or use cause/effect, process analysis, or systems analysis (or a combination of them).
- Decide on which disciplinary or analytic categories you will use.
- Decide on a method of proof: *logos*, *ethos*, or *pathos*, or a combination of them.
- Connect the parts to a whole.

Exercise

Respond to each of the following questions in a sentence or two.

1. What is the main purpose of writing an analysis essay?
2. What kinds of texts might you analyze in your preparation to write an analysis essay?
3. Why is it important to determine the method(s) of analysis and categories the text(s) use before you can determine the method(s) of analysis and categories to use for your own essay?
4. Why should you avoid using the same method of analysis as the author and repeating the author's thesis statement as your own?
5. What is the difference between a summary of a text and an analysis of a text?

Writing Analysis
Essays: Formulating
a Thesis Statement
and Drafting

(4)

Sample Topic: Nostalgia in Tim Bowling's "Na Na Na Na, Hey Hey Hey, Goodbye"

In Chapter 3 we discussed the early stages of writing analysis essays: clarifying essay topics and gathering material. In this chapter we will show you how to use your material to formulate a thesis statement and draft an essay. The principles discussed will apply to most of the writing you do for college and university courses.

STAGE 3   Formulating a Thesis Statement

At the heart of every essay is the writer's thesis, the main idea that gives shape and meaning to the piece of writing. Writers of informal essays (essays based on personal experience) may not state their theses directly, leaving readers to work out how details add up to a main idea. In formal academic writing, by contrast, readers expect to find a thesis statement, usually one or two sentences stating the writer's opinion about the subject and the main reasons or support for that opinion. We will demonstrate how to arrive at a tentative thesis statement that will serve as the starting point for drafting your essay.

STEP 1   Forming an Opinion

An opinion is a belief or judgment based on your interpretation of events, ideas, behaviours, or other phenomena. Consider a simple example. "The temperature is 30°C" is a statement of fact; the statement can be proved to be true or false. "It's too hot for a hike" is a statement of opinion; your hiking partner might disagree, but the opinion would nevertheless be true for you. Similarly, if you were writing an essay on the First World War, you would not try to prove that particular battles were fought on particular days. That information is a matter of fact, not opinion. But not everyone agrees about the main causes of the war. So your thesis might be that the main causes of the war were economic rather than political.

When you write about familiar subjects, you may have an opinion before you begin. When the subject is new to you, as in most academic writing, your opinion usually emerges as you perceive connections among the categories you have used for your analysis. Even if you are writing about a familiar subject, you may find that new materials, evidence, and perspectives cause you to alter your opinion on that subject.

From the material that you generated by analyzing Tim Bowling's "Na Na Na Na, Hey Hey Hey, Goodbye" (Readings) for instance, you could arrive at opinions like these:

- Tim Bowling likes hockey because it has been part of his life since he was a child [causal analysis]
- Tim Bowling works through his reasons, one by one, for liking and disliking hockey [systems analysis]

- Tim Bowling dislikes violence in hockey [definition if examining the meaning of violence; systems analysis if looking at violence as a system with various kinds of violence within it]
- Tim Bowling expresses nostalgia when reminiscing about hockey [definition if examining the meanings of nostalgia; systems analysis if looking at nostalgia as a system with parts]

Opinions by themselves are incomplete. Opinions become thesis statements only when they are shaped by the reasoning used to support them.

Check your opinion against your essay topic to make sure you are still on track. In the sample topic we have been working with, the instructor asked for an essay on "Tim Bowling's attitude toward hockey in 'Na Na Na Na, Hey Hey Hey, Goodbye.'" Do all the thesis opinions above relate to the essay topic? Let's examine each of them. The first thesis opinion, analyzing Bowling's reasons for liking or disliking the sport, comes too close to repeating Bowling's own method of analysis and thesis statement. The second thesis opinion, considering Tim Bowling's reasons as a process the author goes through, doesn't really show Bowling's attitude toward the sport. The third thesis opinion, Bowling's dislike for violence in the sport, does show Bowling's attitude toward hockey. This topic could be promising, although it might not demonstrate the entirety of Bowling's opinion, since he also seems to like the sport. The fourth thesis opinion, on Bowling's feeling of nostalgia toward hockey, adheres to the essay topic. Nostalgia—one's longing for a home or past—can be seen as a kind of attitude.

Sometimes you will find that one opinion stands out as the most relevant to the essay topic. If this is the case (as we have just seen), then use that one. If you have several possibilities for a thesis opinion and each represents a good gathering of material and is an appropriate response to the assignment, then you should choose the one that you are most interested in exploring. Or, you may want to consider the possibility of combining or synthesizing two or more possibilities into a single opinion. Be careful not to take on too much material.

STEP 2 Supporting Your Opinion

A good thesis statement requires not only an opinion but also one or more reasons to support it. Without reasons that emphasize your particular interpretation of your subject, a thesis opinion merely sounds like a vague generalization. If you want your reader to be interested in what you have to say and to take your opinion seriously, you have to give good reasons.

Reasons—your support for your thesis—need to be grounded in evidence. The evidence you use will depend upon the discipline within which you are working. In literature courses, your evidence will be found in your primary text or **primary source** (the work of literature you are analyzing) and, if the essay requires research, in **secondary sources** (works of critics who have written about the text). In history courses, your evidence may be found in historical documents (primary sources) and in writings about those documents (secondary sources). In psychology courses, your evidence may be found in data from interviews or psychological studies. All disciplines require evidential support for thesis opinions.

Your reasons will be a short form of the points you plan to develop in detail in the body of your essay. At this stage of the writing process, you may not have worked through your material completely enough to give precise reasons. You can often use your methods of analysis to guide you as you write your draft. If you added the analytic categories of your systems analysis (see Chapter 3) to the corresponding thesis opinion that we discussed earlier, you would come up with a tentative thesis statement like this:

Tentative thesis statement	Tim Bowling expresses nostalgia when reminiscing about hockey: he dislikes violence in hockey, but he longs for his childhood, his Canadian home, and hockey as story.

This tentative thesis statement now includes both an opinion and the main points—analytic categories—you will cover in your essay. It still sounds tentative, though, because it lacks the specific insights that will later distinguish your final copy from your draft. Writing a draft often helps you to clarify and deepen your thinking about your subject. In Chapter 5 you will see how to revise your thesis statement to incorporate new insights and to make it more forceful.

STAGE 4   Drafting

Write your draft well before your essay is due. It's tempting to wait until you feel inspired or until the night before the due date, but it's better to take a cue from professional writers. They cannot afford to wait for inspiration, nor do they expect to produce a perfect piece of writing the first time. Their method is almost always to write out a rough draft, let it sit for a while, and then submit it to a process of revision and fine-tuning. This is the method we recommend.

Some writers find an outline helpful at this stage, and in this chapter we explain how to develop a *draft outline* to guide the process of drafting. Others prefer to write a draft and then use a *revision outline* to organize their material. We will illustrate that method in Chapter 5.

Since you will eventually revise what you have written, let the writing flow, even if you find yourself departing from your outline or mental plan. You may discover new and better ideas as you write. You can revise your thesis statement, structure, and individual paragraphs when you finish drafting (see Chapter 5). Resist the temptation to polish sentences that you may discard when you revise.

STEP 1   Selecting Material and Making Points

In formulating your tentative thesis statement, you focus on the analytic categories that provide the best support for your thesis. You may discover, however, that these categories give you too much material. It is always better to explain a few points in depth than to skim over a great many. In a short essay (500–1000 words), you can usually develop two to five main points. Thus the first step in writing a draft is to consider which paragraph topics and material to include.

- Take another look at the material generated by analyzing Tim Bowling's "Na Na Na Na, Hey Hey Hey, Goodbye" in Chapter 3. You may not be able to include all of these ideas in a short essay. Upon examining the analytic categories you've generated— childhood, Canada, violence, and hockey as narrative/story— you find that violence is not as relevant to your thesis opinion on nostalgia as are the other categories. You might decide to focus, then, on the three categories that are most relevant to your thesis opinion. But don't discard your notes on violence, including your freewriting and brainstorming. You may be able to discuss some of your ideas on violence in the text in relation to one of the three analytic categories you've chosen. Now you can turn your material into points that relate to your thesis statement. From your selected categories you arrive at the following paragraph topics and points:

TOPIC	POINT
Childhood	Bowling desires a return to his childhood, which is characteristic of nostalgia
Canada	Bowling links hockey to his Canadian home, and nostalgia is a longing to go back home
Hockey and narrative/story	Bowling says that the narrative of hockey "pull[s]" (par. 7) him into it, just as nostalgia draws one into one's past and one's home

STEP 2 Organizing Your Material

When organizing your material, there are two issues to consider:

- Whether to organize your essay with a **deductive** or **inductive structure**
- How to present your points in an effective sequence

In each case, the audience for whom you are writing will influence your choice.

Choosing deductive or inductive structure When you argue deductively, you start with a premise and test it against examples to prove its validity. Try to think of counter-examples that would disprove or contradict the premise. Your thesis will likely say something about the validity of the premise (for example, its strength or its applicability in various contexts) and the reasons for testing the validity. This structure provides a framework that makes it easier for readers to grasp the significance of specific details. Most academic writing on literature and in the humanities follows this pattern (for an example, see Joyce MacDonald's "The Problem of Environmental Costs: Suzuki vs. Merwin" [Readings: Sample Essays]). You will find deductive structure appropriate for writing essays and research papers in academic courses where your readers are familiar with the subject and want to know your interpretation of it.

In contrast, when you reason inductively, you start from a specific case or cases and move toward the principles involved. To organize an essay inductively, you present events, points, or details first and withhold the thesis to be derived from them until later. Inductive structure is often used to create interest in narrative and descriptive essays (for an example, see George Orwell's "Shooting an Elephant" [Readings] and E. M. Forster's "My Wood" [Readings]). Inductive reasoning can also be useful in writing for hostile audiences who may disagree with an explicit thesis. However, in most formal academic writing, you should state your thesis early in the writing and then walk the reader through the points of development to show how you came to that thesis statement. An essay that is structured inductively can still state the thesis in the introduction, but the rest of the essay (the body paragraphs) will follow an inductive structure.

When organizing your essay, avoid organizing your points chronologically. This method of narration, or telling a story, is usually not a good method for developing an analysis essay. Avoid the temptation to describe the unfolding of a plot or to list historical events, throwing in some commentary on the details as you go. The problem with this method is that your comments stay isolated from one another. You will be much less likely to fall into this kind of summary plus commentary if you have gathered material systematically and worked out a thesis statement to guide the writing of your draft.

Sequencing your points effectively Depending on the method of analysis you are using, the best order for presenting your material may not be obvious. For example, if you are writing a process analysis essay, you might present your points in *chronological order*. But what if you are writing a definition essay or a systems analysis essay? For these types of essays, it might be more difficult to determine the best order to present your points. The most common arrangement for these types of essays is an *order of ascending interest*. You begin with your least important point and end with your most important point. That way, you more easily keep your readers' attention and leave the strongest impression.

- In organizing your essay on Tim Bowling's "Na Na Na Na, Hey Hey Hey, Goodbye," for example, you might decide to begin with Bowling's individual relationship to his childhood and move to the wider context, that of nation and narrative. By progressing in this manner, you will highlight the importance of hockey and nostalgia beyond Bowling's individual experience.

You will face the basic decisions about organizing material—choosing deductive or inductive structure and sequencing your points effectively—no matter what kind of essay you are writing. Some types of essays bring other considerations as well. You will find suggestions for organizing comparison essays in Chapter 7; for using pro–con structure to organize a persuasive essay in Chapter 9; and for organizing research papers in Chapters 10 and 11.

STEP 3 Making a Draft Outline

At this point, you may find it useful to make a draft outline to guide you as you write your draft. Put your tentative thesis statement at the top of the page. Remember to change the sequence of support, if necessary, in response to decisions you have made about organizing your draft. Then list your main points and subpoints in the sequence you have decided upon. You may also want to note the most important evidence that supports each point, such as specific examples.

STEP 4 Drafting Individual Paragraphs

Sketching the introduction You can sketch out the introduction by writing a sentence or two about the context of your topic and then stating your thesis (if you are giving your essay a deductive structure) or asking the question your essay will answer (if you are using an inductive structure). If you can't get started without a polished introduction, consult Revising Your Introduction in Chapter 5.

Drafting middle paragraphs Use each point in your draft outline as the basis for a topic sentence for one or more paragraphs. Paragraphs, like essays, can be organized either deductively or inductively, so your topic sentence may appear at the beginning or end of the paragraph. In academic essays, it is most common and often advisable to organize your paragraphs deductively. When you are writing analysis essays, try not to bury your topic sentence in the middle of a paragraph where your main point may be overlooked. Explain the point fully by such methods as defining terms, referring to authorities, and providing additional information. Support each point by giving examples, citing facts and figures, and using other specific details. We discussed how writers develop their material in Chapter 2.

Sketching the conclusion Rather than slapping a perfunctory summary on your draft, let your thinking carry you naturally into your conclusion. Often ideas come together as you write, and a better thesis emerges—if you let it. Your conclusion should never be an exact or nearly exact reproduction of your introduction.

When you have finished your draft, let it sit for a day or two. Then revise it, using the suggestions in Chapter 5 as a guide.

Working on Your Own Assignment

- Formulate a tentative thesis statement by figuring out what main idea connects your analytic categories.
- Decide what points to make and how to organize them.
- Make a draft outline to keep you on track as you write.
- Write a draft, paying most attention to developing your middle paragraphs.

Exercises

A. Respond to each of the following in a sentence or two.

1. Explain the difference between a fact and an opinion, using an example of your own.
2. What is a thesis statement?
3. What are the advantages of writing a draft?

4. Explain the difference between inductive structure and deductive structure. How would you decide which one to use?

5. Define the term *order of ascending interest* and give an example.

B. Work out a draft outline for an essay on a selection from the Readings section of this book. Put your thesis statement at the top of the page. List your main points in the order you plan to discuss them. Note the most important evidence you will use to support each point.

C. Write a draft of your essay, paying particular attention to developing each of your points. Keep your draft for later use.

Writing Analysis Essays: Revising

(5)

Sample Topic: Nostalgia in Tim Bowling's "Na Na Na Na, Hey Hey Hey, Goodbye"

Revision means literally "re-vision," seeing again. When you write a first draft, you are essentially writing it for yourself, to clarify your ideas and to try out your tentative plan for the essay. If you continue reading your work from this perspective, however, you may find it hard to see what changes are needed because you know what you mean to say. To "see again," you have to be able to adopt the perspective of your reader, to evaluate what you have written as it would appear to your intended audience.

Allow enough time before the due date to let your draft sit for a day or two after you have completed Stages 1 through 4. You will then be able to examine it more objectively when you revise.

The goal of revision is to improve your writing on three levels:

- The conceptual level: Does this essay reflect the best thinking you are capable of doing about the topic?

- The organizational level: Have you organized and presented your ideas effectively?

- The stylistic level: Is your writing clear, engaging, and free from errors?

This chapter will guide you through the process of evaluating and revising your work on the conceptual and organizational levels. You will find many suggestions for improving your style in Part 3, Handbook for Final Editing.

STAGE 5 Revising the Thesis Statement and Essay Structure

Before you begin rewriting, read through your draft to assess its overall strengths and weaknesses in content and organization. Then examine your thesis statement and essay structure, as outlined below, to see if you can improve the framework of ideas in your essay. One of the difficulties in writing analysis essays is maintaining a clear boundary between the essay you are writing and the text or texts you are writing about. We will look at different aspects of this problem and how to overcome them at each stage of revising.

STEP 1 Making a Revision Outline

You can keep track of the changes you need to make by using a revision outline—an outline of the draft you have actually written, together with suggestions for changes. Using two columns, you note in the left hand

one the points you make in your introduction, each of your middle paragraphs, and your conclusion. Record these points exactly as they stand
in the draft, not as you intended them to be. As you go through the
revision process, enter suggestions for changes in the right-hand column.
You will find an example of a revision outline for the sample topic, on
nostalgia in Tim Bowling's "Na Na Na Na, Hey Hey Hey, Goodbye,"
on page 66.

STEP 2   Revising Your Thesis Statement

Whether you write a draft as soon as you have gathered material or follow the suggestions for formulating a tentative thesis statement given in
Chapter 4, you will likely need to revise your thesis statement because writing the draft has helped you understand your subject better.

Check both the *content* of your thesis statement and its *presentation.* To
assess the effectiveness of your thesis statement, check that it

- gives an opinion with reasons or points to support it;
- suggests you have a good understanding of your subject;
- interests readers in your interpretation of your subject;
- is a response to the essay assignment, but does not simply
  repeat it;
- is supported by reference to aspects of the text or texts you are
  analyzing in your essay.

If you find any of the following problems with your thesis statement,
revise as indicated.

PROBLEMS WITH THESIS STATEMENTS	EXAMPLES/SOLUTIONS	
Merely restating the subject	AVOID	"I will discuss nostalgia in Tim Bowling's 'Na Na Na Na, Hey Hey Hey, Goodbye.'"
	USE	"Bowling's nostalgia for hockey as it was in the past is evident in his references to his own childhood, his linking of hockey to distinctly Canadian icons, and his understanding of hockey as narrative."

(*Continued*)

(Continued)

Merely stating facts	AVOID	"Tim Bowling knows a lot about hockey."
	USE	"Tim Bowling's knowledge of the history of hockey is demonstrated in his description of events surrounding the 1993 Stanley Cup semifinals and in his reference to many hockey icons and legends."
Failing to give reasons	AVOID	"There are many reasons why Tim Bowling likes hockey."
	USE	"While Tim Bowling's knowledge of hockey shows an admiration for the sport, his criticism of the violence in hockey reveals a more conflicted attitude toward it."
Failing to separate your opinion from other writers' opinions	AVOID	"Many writers have discussed violence in hockey."
	USE	"Although many writers have discussed violence in hockey, I argue that Tim Bowling provides a more nuanced take on the problem, since he also recognizes 'the grace and beauty of the game when played well' (213)."
Failing to signal essay structure	REVISE	. . . thesis statement or paragraph order so that points follow the order suggested by the thesis statement.
No longer fits content of essay	CHECK	. . . for better thesis statement in draft conclusion.
Too vague or mechanical	AVOID	"Tim Bowling shows his like and dislike for hockey."
	USE	"Tim Bowling demonstrates his love for the game of hockey, but he also recognizes that many real problems have become inseparable from the culture of hockey in Canada, including corporate ownership and violence."

The last problem, the tentative thesis statement that is too vague or mechanical, is the most common one. Writing your draft will often provide the insights you need to make your tentative thesis statement more precise and more interesting. Problems with thesis statements in analysis essays also arise from focusing on a critic's opinion at the expense of *your* supported opinion on these subjects.

- Take a look at the tentative thesis statement for the draft essay on nostalgia in Tim Bowling's "Na Na Na Na, Hey Hey Hey, Goodbye":

Tentative thesis statement Tim Bowling expresses nostalgia when reminiscing about hockey: he dislikes violence in hockey, but he longs for his childhood, his Canadian home, and hockey as story.

In the process of drafting an essay to support this thesis statement, you might well decide that you could be even more clear and specific about the points you make. You would therefore revise your thesis statement:

Writing Sample

Revised thesis statement Bowling's nostalgia for hockey as it was in the past is evident in his references to his own childhood, his linking of hockey to distinctly Canadian icons, and his understanding of hockey as narrative.

STEP 3 Revising Your Essay Structure

Each of your middle paragraphs should constitute or contribute to one specific point that supports your thesis. The **order of your middle paragraphs** should follow the order suggested by your revised thesis statement. Use the left-hand column of your revision outline to note any of the problems discussed below and revise as suggested in the right-hand column.

PROBLEMS WITH ESSAY STRUCTURE	SOLUTIONS
Failure to paragraph	Indicate on your revision outline where each new point begins and divide your material accordingly.

(Continued)

(Continued)

Paragraphs too long	Divide paragraphs longer than half a page and use an "umbrella" topic sentence (see below).
Paragraphs too short	Combine several short paragraphs under one topic sentence or explain your points more fully (see below).
Paragraphs don't support revised thesis statement	Delete irrelevant material.
Point(s) made in revised thesis statement lack support	Add new paragraph(s).
Paragraphs don't follow order suggested in revised thesis statement	Indicate appropriate order on draft outline.
Paragraph order not effective	Show new order on draft outline.

"Umbrella" topic sentences Sometimes you may have more material on one aspect of your subject than you can comfortably fit into a single paragraph. If a paragraph is more than three quarters of a page, you can often divide it and then use an "umbrella" topic sentence to tie related paragraphs together, as in the following example:

"Umbrella" topic sentence	Bowling's nostalgia is represented in his fondness for both his childhood and Canada as a nation.
Topic sentence for paragraph A	Bowling expresses a longing for his past that is characteristic of nostalgia.
Topic sentence for paragraph B	Bowling's nostalgia for the old-fashioned game of hockey is also evident in his linking of hockey to Canadian icons.

- The thinking that led you to revise the thesis statement for the sample assignment also indicates that you should examine the sequence of paragraph topics in your essay. You will now want the sequence indicated in your thesis statement. You may think of your thesis statement as moving from narrow to wide, from the individual and personal (childhood) to the national (Canada) and beyond the national (narrative in general). You can now fill in more detail in the right-hand column of your revision outline.

REVISION OUTLINE

PARAGRAPH TOPIC	POINT
Nostalgia and childhood	Bowling thinks about moments in his childhood that were linked with hockey and exemplifies those moments with fondness (for example, playing with marbles on the kitchen floor).
Nostalgia and Canada	Bowling connects his happy memories of hockey with Canadian icons such as the loonie—the Canadian one-dollar coin—and ex-Maple Leafs defenceman Tim Horton's doughnut chain.
Nostalgia and narrative	Bowling explains how following hockey games and newscasts about hockey is like reading a bestselling novel or work of fiction.

- For the essay that results from this revision outline, see C. Stonehouse, "Nostalgia in Tim Bowling's 'Na Na Na Na, Hey Hey Hey, Goodbye,'" in Part 2, Readings: Sample Essays.

STAGE 6   Revising Individual Paragraphs

Once you have revised your thesis statement and identified ways, if necessary, to improve your essay structure, you are ready to consider changes to individual paragraphs.

STEP 1   Revising Your Introduction

Your introduction gives your readers a chance to prepare, emotionally and intellectually, for the essay that is to follow. In the opening sentences, check that you have identified your subject and provided a context for your essay and the thesis statement to follow. For instance, you might give relevant background information about historical events or define a key concept. Also check that your introduction includes your thesis statement (for deductively organized essays) or the question your essay will answer (for inductively organized essays). Most academic essays in the humanities will be organized deductively.

If you have done research, you may be tempted to display your knowledge by presenting various critical perspectives. If you are working with a literary text, you might want to provide details of the author's life and other publications. This practice is sometimes appropriate. In a research essay there are good reasons to begin with a statement of the critical debate (see Chapter 11); in a shorter analysis essay, however, you need to introduce your thesis statement quickly rather than provide extraneous information.

In revising your draft introduction, check that

- you provide all the necessary details to identify the work(s) you are analyzing, such as the author and title of the work, or the historical/psychological/sociological/cultural context and framework you are addressing;
- these details and any criticism you present are relevant to the subject identified by the assignment and to your thesis statement;
- you avoid large generalizations about life or literature that are intended to be impressive rather than to illuminate the thesis statement;
- you include any other material your readers might need to understand the thesis statement or appreciate its significance;
- you make an effective transition from context material to thesis statement;
- you make any changes required as a result of changes to the essay structure.

Check your introduction for the following problems:

PROBLEMS WITH INTRODUCTION	EXAMPLES/SOLUTIONS	
Sweeping generalizations	NOT	"Throughout history people have been nostalgic about their pasts." See Chapter 8 for this and other problems with argumentation.
		(Continued)

(Continued)

Mechanical statements	**NOT**	"There are three ways that Bowling shows nostalgia."
	BUT	"Bowling's nostalgia for hockey as it was in the past is evident in his references to his own childhood, his linking of hockey to distinctly Canadian icons, and his understanding of hockey as narrative."
Too much detail		Keep your introduction to between four and six sentences.
		Save examples for your middle paragraphs. However, don't confuse saving examples with being vague and elusive. Even though you will provide concrete examples to demonstrate your points in your middle paragraphs, you still need to give your readers a very clear and concrete idea about your argument and your main points.
Misplaced thesis statement		Your thesis statement does not need to go in a specific place in your introductory paragraph, but you do need to include your thesis statement somewhere in the introductory paragraph. Think carefully about where to place it. You should lead up to it with context, or follow it with specific details or points about your overall argument.

- In revising your introduction, you would ask yourself what comments are necessary to set the stage for your revised thesis statement. You might decide to include a definition of nostalgia and provide a link to the essay assignment by referring to Bowling's ambivalent relationship to hockey in connection with his feeling of nostalgia. When providing definitions of concepts, consult reliable sources. If you are using a basic dictionary, for instance, you may also want to consult a specialized dictionary on your subject—especially if you are working with a literary term or a historical or sociological concept. By adding a fuller statement of context, you might come up with a revised introduction like the one below.

Writing Sample

Revised introduction   Tim Bowling's entertaining essay about NHL hockey, "Na Na Na Na, Hey Hey Hey, Goodbye," is an exploration of the author's own ambivalent attitude toward that sport in Canada. On the one hand, Bowling demonstrates his love and appreciation for the game. On the other hand, however, Bowling recognizes the many real problems that have become inseparable from the culture of hockey in Canada, including corporate ownership and violence. Bowling never really resolves his dilemma about hockey, remaining in a "love/hate" relationship with the game throughout the essay. Interestingly, though, while cataloguing his reasons for and against supporting the game, Bowling exemplifies a feeling of nostalgia. *The Oxford English Dictionary* explains that nostalgia derives from the Greek roots "nostos," meaning "home," and "algia," meaning "pain." M. H. Abrams's *A Glossary of Literary Terms* explains that "nostalgia" is a longing for a past that is pristine and idyllic—like the garden of Eden before the Fall of Adam and Eve. Thus, nostalgia is a painful separation from and longing for one's home, a home that is also construed as one's personal or ancestral past. Bowling's nostalgia for hockey as it was in the past is evident in his references to his own childhood, his linking of hockey to distinctly Canadian icons, and his understanding of hockey as narrative.

STEP 2   Revising Your Middle Paragraphs

Checking topic sentences

- Does each paragraph contain a topic sentence that announces the subject of that paragraph and makes a *point* about the subject?
- Does that point support some aspect of your thesis statement?

When you revise, make sure that each middle paragraph has a topic sentence. The topic sentence states the main idea that other sentences in the paragraph explain and support. In this way, it functions as a mini thesis statement, controlling the content of the paragraph and showing how the paragraph relates to the thesis.

Paragraphs, like essays, can be organized either deductively or inductively. If your essay is organized deductively, your reader will expect your paragraphs to be organized deductively also, with your topic sentence at or near the beginning (a transitional sentence may come first). If your essay is organized inductively, many of your paragraphs may be as well, with your topic sentence at or near the end of each paragraph.

Watch for these potential problems:

PROBLEMS WITH TOPIC SENTENCES	EXAMPLES/SOLUTIONS
No sentence stating subject and point	Add a sentence linking the main idea of the paragraph to the thesis statement.
Subject stated, no point made	"Bowling discusses his childhood." If you use a sentence like this one as a transition, make sure the next sentence states your point. Better yet, combine them: "Bowling's childhood memories of hockey are tinged with a fondness and a longing that are characteristic of nostalgia."
Point not linked to thesis	"Bowling links hockey to Canadian icons." Revise to relate to nostalgia. "Bowling's nostalgia for the old-fashioned game of hockey is not only evident in the description of his childhood but also in his linking of hockey to Canadian icons." (Note that this sentence also provides a transition from the previous paragraph, about childhood.)
Misplaced topic sentence	Don't bury topic sentences in the middle of the paragraph. Don't end a paragraph with the topic sentence for the next paragraph.

Checking paragraph development

- Is the point you make in your topic sentence sufficiently explained and supported by specific details?

Explanations serve as a bridge between main ideas and specific details. You may explain your point by defining terms, giving reasons, or moving to a subpoint. To be convincing, each point and subpoint should be supported by specific details, including facts and figures (such as names, dates, statistics); examples (such as representative instances, case studies, hypothetical examples); and quotations from or references to authorities. If you're writing an essay about literature, your evidence will include references to and quotations from the primary text, and may include references and quotations from secondary sources.

PROBLEMS WITH PARAGRAPH DEVELOPMENT	SOLUTIONS
Inadequate detail	Add examples, facts and figures, quotations, or references to texts or authorities, as appropriate.
Misleading detail	For help in identifying problems such as misleading statistics and misused authorities, see Chapter 8.
Irrelevant detail	Delete details that don't support your thesis statement.
Inadequate explanations	Add quotations, cited paraphrased material from primary or secondary texts, definitions, reasons, sub-points, and other material as necessary.

When writing an essay about literature, make sure not to slide back into telling "what happens" rather than using evidence to make a point. Sometimes we are carried away by a story, the development of a metaphor, or a compelling scene in a film or play. Use evidence such as quotations or paraphrases from the primary text to support your points.

Reread each middle paragraph carefully. Do you need to

- add examples or direct quotations?

  Direct quotation is often the best possible evidence. The point of your paragraph should be clearly supported. For guidelines on using quotations effectively, see Part 3, H2 Quotations.

- revise and shorten the details so that they become evidence for the point?

- explain how the evidence supports the point?

  Claiming that a quotation or detail supports a point is not sufficient, since other readers may understand the text differently. You need to explain the connection between your point and the quotation.

Note on your revision outline whether each paragraph follows this pattern.

REVISION OUTLINE

TOPIC SENTENCE	EVIDENCE	EXPLANATION OF EVIDENCE
Author's notion of hockey connected to his childhood memories of hockey	Memory of playing hockey with marbles on the kitchen floor	Mother as symbol of love, home, comfort

- To see how you would identify and correct problems with topic sentences and paragraph development, consider this paragraph from the draft essay on nostalgia in Tim Bowling's "Na Na Na Na, Hey Hey Hey, Goodbye":

Bowling discusses his childhood in the early 1960s. Bowling says, "I'd play with hockey cards on the linoleum floor of the kitchen, passing a marble back and forth and re-enacting great goals and saves as my mother clattered dishes in the sink nearby" (211). Bowling states, "When I was a boy, the boards, ice and score clock were free of advertising; goals and assists meant more than salaries; and players and teams had distinct characters" (215). This vision of hockey in Bowling's past is contrasted with a present day hockey game at which "you're . . . bombarded with supersonic noise and flashing lights and company logos" (215). Hockey has not yet fallen into the corruption of corporate takeover and violence.

- When you check this paragraph, you find there is no topic sentence. Your subject was intended to be how Bowling's childhood memories relate to hockey and how those memories are nostalgic, but the first sentence of the paragraph only mentions Bowling's childhood. While you provide quotations as evidence to support your point, you don't explain those quotations. You need to state your interpretation of the quotations and how they relate to the point of the paragraph and the thesis of the essay. You would note these problems on your revision outline and then use your notes as a guide to revising.

Writing Sample

Revised middle paragraph

Bowling's childhood memories of hockey are tinged with a fondness and a longing that are characteristic of nostalgia. For instance, speaking of his childhood in the early 1960s, Bowling says, "I'd play with hockey cards on the linoleum floor of the kitchen, passing a marble back and forth and re-enacting great goals and saves as my mother clattered dishes in the sink nearby" (211). Bowling's first hockey memory is in his kitchen, the domestic space of home, and Bowling is alongside his mother, a symbol, perhaps, of love, comfort, and belonging. Furthermore, Bowling states, "When I was a boy, the boards, ice and score clock were free of advertising; goals and assists meant more than salaries; and players and teams had distinct characters" (215). Here, hockey in Bowling's childhood is understood as pristine, untouched, and not yet corrupted by corporate culture. This vision of hockey in Bowling's past is contrasted with a present day hockey game at which "you're . . . bombarded with supersonic noise and flashing lights and company logos" (215). Bowling's recollection of playing hockey with marbles on his kitchen floor is nostalgic in that it exemplifies a longing for home, domesticity, and love; his recollection of the blank "boards, ice and score clock" (215) is nostalgic in its description as pure and idyllic: hockey has not yet fallen into the corruption of corporate takeover and violence.

STEP 3   Revising Your Conclusion

Many people find conclusions as hard to write as introductions. As a result, draft conclusions tend to be skimpy and mechanical. When you revise, make sure that your conclusion achieves its purpose: to leave your readers with a strong sense of the importance of what you have written.

A good conclusion for an academic essay generally summarizes and expands the thesis and main points, and sets them within a broader context. In drafting, however, you may have merely summarized your thesis and main points or, conversely, shifted into large generalizations about life or literature. Either of these choices will likely fail to satisfy your readers, who want to see what greater understanding of the text your discussion has made possible and also what the implications are for the larger issues that the assignment and text have raised.

In revising, then, ask these key questions about your draft conclusion:

1. Does your conclusion expand the original thesis statement by drawing upon the more specific ideas you have developed in the body of the essay?

2. Have you briefly discussed the broader implications of your essay? We all want to feel that what we have written is important. You can show readers that your analysis of a subject or text(s) has a broader significance by putting it within a larger context. That context might be such things as opinions expressed by scholarly critics or reviewers, similarities to and differences from other works by the same writer, placement in a larger historical time period, movement from a specific case to a more general category, or the relevance of issues raised in

the text to your readers. (In some cases, you may need to revise your introduction so that it refers to the context you will return to in your conclusion. This return to the initial context gives conclusions the sense of both extending and completing a circle.)

Finally, check to see if your draft conclusion reveals any of the following problems.

PROBLEMS WITH CONCLUSIONS	EXAMPLES	
Sweeping generalizations	**NOT**	"We all feel nostalgic about our childhood."
Mechanical repetition of thesis and points	**NOT**	"In conclusion, we have seen that Tim Bowling is nostalgic because he refers to his childhood, Canada, and narrative."

- Let's see what happens when you apply these principles to revising the conclusion of the draft essay on nostalgia in Tim Bowling's "Na Na Na Na, Hey Hey Hey, Goodbye."

Draft conclusion   In conclusion, we have seen that Tim Bowling is nostalgic because he refers to his childhood, Canada, and narrative. We can relate to the essay because, like Tim Bowling, we all feel nostalgic about our childhoods.

- This conclusion does not reflect the way the thesis statement has been developed in the essay. Furthermore, the statement of broader implications does not emerge out of the points made in the essay. It also is not true: some people have not had happy childhoods and may not long for them. You should revise to produce a conclusion that reflects what you have discovered in the process of your analysis and the implications of those discoveries. To expand a thesis and draw out its implications, you have to take the time to reflect on what your analysis has led you to discover about the subject and the text or texts you have analyzed.

Writing Sample

Revised conclusion At the end of his essay, Bowling asks, "Can I resist the lure of *nostalgia* and the pull of narrative?" (215, my emphasis). This statement is the only one in which Bowling mentions the word "nostalgia," but the notion of nostalgia is prevalent throughout his essay. From his recollection of childhood memories of hockey, which include domestic and motherly images, to his linking of hockey to Canadian national icons, to his connection of hockey to narrative, Bowling wishes to come back to a past in which hockey was free from corruption, a past which was also supposedly idyllic, innocent, and comforting. Perhaps Bowling's desire is typical of twenty-first century Canadians who remember or have heard about their ancestor pioneers. Bowling's "Na Na Na Na, Hey Hey Hey, Goodbye" is not just an exploration of the author's reasons for liking or disliking the game of hockey: it is an engagement with the fond memories of his past, an engagement that might apply, in one way or another, to many Canadians.

After you have revised your conclusion, make adjustments to your introduction, if necessary, to ensure that the two are in accord.

STAGE 7 Final Editing

The last step in writing an analysis essay is to give your essay a final edit. Final editing is discussed in Part 3, Handbook for Final Editing. The chart at the beginning of Part 3 will help you identify problems with sentence structure, grammar, punctuation, and format.

- The sample essay that results from revisions and final editing is C. Stonehouse, "Nostalgia in Tim Bowling's 'Na Na Na Na, Hey Hey Hey, Goodbye,'" in Part 2, Readings: Sample Essays.

Working on Your Own Assignment

- Turn your draft outline into a revision outline by recording what you have actually done in your draft and what needs to be changed.

- Revise your thesis statement as necessary to reflect new ideas, changes in the structure of your essay or your introduction, and greater attention to diction and sentence structure.

- If you are providing context in your introduction, check that the context provides information that directly leads toward your thesis statement.

- Check that your thesis statement is not a description of the text or texts, but rather your supported opinion on the assignment topic.
- Check that your draft is not a running summary of the text, but rather is organized around a series of topics in ascending interest.
- Check to make sure that your middle paragraphs expand upon ideas presented in your thesis statement and that they are arranged in an effective sequence.
- Check each middle paragraph for topic sentence, transitions, supporting details, quotations and paraphrased material, and explanations.
- Check that the detail in the middle paragraphs does not simply describe a section of the text or texts, but rather is used as evidence to support a point.
- Check that the connection between point and detail in the middle paragraphs is sufficiently explained, especially in the case of direct quotations.
- Keep your reader in mind as you revise your introduction and conclusion. Check that your conclusion restates and expands the thesis and suggests broader implications appropriate to the subject and texts you are analyzing.
- When you are satisfied with the content and organization of your essay, turn to Part 3, Handbook for Final Editing, for help in improving the style.

Exercise

E. M. Forster's "My Wood" (Readings) is an inductively organized essay, with a question at the beginning and a thesis statement at the end. Write a revision outline showing how you would change the inductive structure into a deductive structure. Consider whether changing the structure means changing the thesis statement. If yes, write the new thesis statement.

Writing Essays on Literature (6)

Sample Topic: Tone in William Carlos Williams's "This Is Just to Say"

In the previous three chapters we discussed how to write analysis essays, and we showed you how to clarify essay topics, gather material, formulate a thesis statement, write a draft, and revise your essay. Essays on literature are analytical, and so the stages and steps in the previous chapters are relevant to you when writing an essay on literature. Essays on literature require particular emphasis, however, because you will be paying more attention to textual features, figurative language, and how meaning is produced.

In literature courses, you may focus more on the relationship between content and form of expression than you do in other courses. In creating written texts, writers use the *material* of language. Ways of using language to achieve certain effects are *techniques*. Writers learn some techniques from studying other writers, but they may also develop new ways of using language. Thus, when you analyze written text as art, you focus on the relation between form and content. Similarly, when you analyze performances as art, as in plays, films, and television programs, you pay attention not only to the content or meaning but also to the particular ways in which the director uses the materials and techniques available. You will write essays based on information available to you from written and visual texts and documents. In literature courses, you will also write essays based on how that information is presented.

STAGE 1 Clarifying Essay Topics

Some assignments in literature classes ask you to analyze a literary text as a system, although they may not use this terminology. Such essay topics focus on the aesthetic elements of the text: how the work of literature functions as art. For example, your essay assignment might read, "Explain how the author uses figurative language in the text in order to convey a theme." You would then consider the work of literature as a system that employs metaphor, symbol, or image (categories) in order to convey a thematic message (thesis). Make sure not to confuse the literature's theme or thesis with the thesis of your own essay on the literature.

STAGE 2 Gathering Material

STEP 1 Using Disciplinary or Analytic Categories

In Chapter 3 we explained that disciplines (for example, Spanish, psychology, history, and English) develop their own vocabularies to describe concepts specific to their disciplines. When you draw upon these specialized vocabularies to analyze a text or texts and organize your essay, you use *disciplinary categories.* When you determine your own categories through your analysis of the text(s), you use *analytic categories.* Since this chapter focuses on writing essays on literature, we will explain some of the disciplinary categories available to you within the field of English. Whether you use disciplinary or analytic categories in the organization of your own essay, the disciplinary terms below will help you to understand how a literary text produces meaning. You may draw upon and use these terms, whether or not you use disciplinary categories to organize your essay.

There are three basic questions for a systems analysis of a literary text: What are the parts of the text? What is their function within the work? How do the parts relate to each other? You can analyze a wide range of works by gathering material about these parts: *subject, genre, context, methods of development, structure, style, tone,* and *point of view.* Here is a brief explanation of each of these terms.

Subject Subject is the general issue(s) or concern(s) of the text, as you perceive it (them).

Sometimes your assignment will identify a subject for you, such as manhood in a Hemingway short story or the meaning of love in Emily Brontë's *Wuthering Heights.* But often you will have to decide what you think the subject is. Your statement about a text's subject(s) will be most useful to you if it is both tentative and precise: "This film seems to be about the meaning of heroism in war." If you keep your statement of subject tentative, you will find it easier to modify or change if necessary. And if you make it precise, you will have a better starting point from which to ask: how does the text treat this subject? Avoid both plot summary ("this film is about a soldier who . . .") and vague generalization ("this film is about man against man" or "this film is about war").

Genre The word *genre,* which means "kind," has traditionally been used to refer to the categories into which literary works may be grouped because of similarities in form, subject, or technique. In contemporary theory, genre has been redefined as "a form of human expression loosely adhering to certain conventions that may change over time."* This definition broadens the traditional meaning to encompass a wide range of what can be considered texts: not only literary works but also other verbal and/or visual texts such as films, television programs, speeches, and paintings.

---

* Jerald Zaslove. "Bakhtin and the Image of Language: A Friendly Critique of Martin Jay's *Downcast Eyes.*" Paper presented at the conference of the Canadian Association of Art History, Vancouver, 1998. Lecture.

Works can be divided into major genres and minor genres (subgenres). The major genres you are likely to study are nonfiction, fiction, poetry, drama, and film. Each of these has many subgenres; for example, the genre of poetry includes the subgenres of the sonnet, the ballad, and the ode, among others. Some texts cross genre boundaries. "New journalism," for instance, is nonfiction writing that uses many techniques of fiction.

Each major and minor genre has its own conventions, rules that authors either adhere to or break for their own purposes. The conventions that govern fantasy, for instance, are quite different from those that govern realistic fiction. Identifying the genre and subgenre of a text makes you more conscious of the rules the author is working with and/or against. This knowledge will not only improve your analysis, but also help you avoid serious mistakes. Some students, for example, confuse short stories with autobiographical essays and assume that short stories are accurate accounts of the writers' own experiences. A handbook of literary or film terms will explain the conventions of many kinds of works.

Context   Context means the historical and/or cultural situation in which the text was produced, including the specific audience (if any) for which it was intended.

Texts generally reflect the outlook and concerns both of the author/director and of the era in which they are created. You may therefore find that you understand a text better if you know something about the author or director and about such factors as the historical events, social conditions, and cultural issues that enter into the work, and about the audience for which a work might have been intended. You may find this kind of information in an introduction or notes to the text itself, or you may need to look it up in the reference section of your library or online through your library catalogue or database. Be careful not to substitute information of this kind for a close analysis of the text. A poet may have had a drinking problem, for instance; that doesn't mean every poem he or she wrote is about alcoholism.

For certain kinds of essay assignments, it can be important to examine the literature you are analyzing within the historical, social, and political contexts from which it arose. For example, if you are writing an essay about the narrator's attitude toward death in a story by Edgar Allan Poe, it may be relevant to examine the story within nineteenth century America, the movement from religious beliefs to Darwinism, and/or the time period's interest in psychology, spirituality, and the gothic mode. While this kind of analysis might be too much to attempt in a short essay, you may wish to incorporate it into a research essay on literature, which we discuss in Chapters 10 and 11.

Methods of development Methods of development are the specific elements, such as points, events, and descriptions, by which the author/director unfolds or elaborates the central issue or concerns of the text.

A text consists of material that develops the overall point—the theme or thesis—of the work. You can analyze this material by examining the methods of development commonly used in specific genres or subgenres. In imaginative works that tell a story (whether in poetry, fiction, drama, or film), you would pay attention to details of events, setting, and characterization. In imaginative works that do not tell a story, you might find that the theme is developed through reflections, observations, or impressions. A love poem, for example, might be developed through a list of the beloved's virtues, or a nature poem through detailed observations of the landscape. For information on characteristic methods of development in various genres, consult handbooks of literary and rhetorical terms and handbooks that focus on specific literary forms.

Structure The term *structure* refers to the way that units of material are organized to convey a theme or thesis.

In thinking about structure, you need to be aware both of the general principles of structure within various genres and of the particular ordering of material within the text you are analyzing. Novels, drama, and film often organize events into a rising and falling action; short stories more often, though not always, focus on a single moment of revelation; essays often, though not always, arrange a series of points into an order of ascending interest. In addition to these broad structural principles, each work will have its particular way of organizing material.

Consider the following points when you analyze the structure of specific texts:

Generic principles of structure Among the conventions of various subgenres are conventions about structure. If you know that a poem is a sonnet, for instance, you can anticipate that its fourteen lines will be organized into one of two structures: an octave of eight lines setting out a problem and a sestet of six lines suggesting a solution; or three quatrains of four lines, each quatrain developing one idea, and a concluding couplet that sums up the previous lines or presents them in a new light. If you find variations on these forms, think about why the author violated the conventions. You can find information about the structural conventions of various genres in dictionaries of literary and rhetorical terms and in handbooks of specific literary forms.

Spatial and chronological principles of structure Space and time often function as principles in structuring material. Notice patterns of spatial structuring: contrasts between characters identified with different settings, such as city and country; events organized as a journey; changes in a character that occur as a result of moving from a familiar to an unfamiliar place.

Time is used as a structural principle in the following ways, among others: a chronological unfolding of events; movement between the present and the past; cycles of days, seasons, or years.

Typographical devices as indicators of structure Typographical devices often reinforce other kinds of structure. The most obvious are those that divide works into chapters or acts and scenes. Watch for the less obvious as well, such as the arrangement of lines on the page for some kinds of poetry.

Within the overall structure of the work, you may notice the way smaller blocks of material are organized. The overall structure of an essay, for example, might be chronological, but a paragraph of description within the essay might be organized according to a spatial arrangement of near to far. Making an outline of the text, or of its major divisions, will help you to identify its structural principles.

Style Style is the characteristic or distinctive mode of expression within a text.

In analyzing style, you examine a text at its most detailed level—the level of lines, sentences, scenes (in plays), or shots (in films). While many elements enter into the style of a work, three are most important for written texts: diction, figurative language and allusions, and the rhythm created by sentence structure and other methods.

Diction Diction refers to the kinds of words the author or characters use, in both language level (colloquial, informal, formal) and origin (for example, ethnic dialect, legal jargon). What is the effect of these choices? One essayist may use the informal language of everyday speech to seem like "one of us," for instance, while another writer may use the specialized vocabulary of economics to speak as a colleague to other experts.

Figurative language Figurative language includes *images* (figures of speech such as metaphor and simile, or visual, oral, tactile, and kinesthetic images) and *symbols* (objects or actions that stand for a more abstract idea or value, such as a pair of scales to symbolize justice).

Allusions Allusions are references to literary, historical, mythological, or religious events and figures, such as Adam and Eve. Repeated images, symbols, or allusions that form a pattern are particularly important. For instance, the images of Emily Dickinson's poem "Because I could not stop for Death" form a pattern in which life is seen as a journey with Death as a kindly companion.

Sentence structure Sentence structure determines the rhythms of prose and, with other devices, of poetry and drama. Is there a high proportion or distinctive use of basic sentences, long or short sentences, sentence fragments, parallelism, or inversion? How do line length and sound patterns contribute to the rhythms of poetry? How does the pacing of dialogue and action contribute to the effects of drama?

In analyzing the style of film and television productions, you focus on the way the camera is used, with less attention on the language. Shooting techniques, visual images and symbols, and editing techniques together create the style.

To analyze style, you may need the help of resources such as a handbook of poetics or dictionaries of slang, symbols, or film terms.

Tone Tone refers to the attitude of the author/narrator toward the self, the subject of the text, and the reader, as conveyed by the style. In plays and films, this quality is referred to as the *mood* or *atmosphere* of the work.

When you read silently, you likely hear the words inside your head as though they were being spoken by the author or character. The voice may seem like that of a modest gentleman or a frightened child, a witty woman of the world or a dreamy adolescent. It is this sense of a voice speaking that we mean by the attitude toward the self that a written work creates.

The tone (created through stylistic choices) establishes a particular relationship among the author or narrator, the subject of the text, and the audience. The author of an essay might, for example, adopt a playful attitude toward the subject of addiction to coffee and treat the reader as either playmate or disapproving parent. Or the essayist might deliver a serious lecture about the dangers of caffeine and treat the reader either as a peer with whom to share ideas or as a pupil to be instructed. In plays and films, the tone or mood may be established through music, lighting, costuming, and other devices.

Terms commonly used to describe tone or mood include *sentimental, businesslike, authoritative, comic, nostalgic, menacing, reflective, playful,* and *serious.* The piece is ironic when we understand its meaning to be different from, or the opposite of, what is expressed.

Point of view The perspective from which the text is presented is called point of view. On the next two pages you will read about the distinctions commonly made in analyzing point of view. Notice the difference in terminology for each genre: when referring to fiction, we say *narrator*, when referring to poetry, we say *speaker*, and when referring to nonfiction, we say *writer* or **persona**. Make sure to use the proper terminology for the genre of literature you discuss in your essay.

Fiction: Who is the narrator (storyteller)?

First-person narration

MAJOR PARTICIPANT:	The story is told in the first person by an "I" who has a major role in the events (Vanessa telling the story of her encounter with Piquette in Margaret Laurence's "The Loons" [Readings]).
MINOR PARTICIPANT:	The story is told in the first person by an "I" who recounts events but does not have a major role in them (the unnamed narrator of William Faulkner's short story "A Rose for Emily").

Omniscient narration The story is told in the third person by an anonymous narrator who has access to the thoughts and feelings of more than one character (as in D. H. Lawrence's short story "The Horse-Dealer's Daughter").

Limited omniscient narration The story is told in the third person by an anonymous narrator who has access to the thoughts and feelings of only one character (as in Nathaniel Hawthorne's short story "Young Goodman Brown").

Objective narration The story is told in the third person as though recorded by a camera, with no access to the thoughts or feelings of any character (as in Ernest Hemingway's short story "Hills Like White Elephants").

Poetry: Who is the speaker? Like fiction, poetry can be expressed in the first person or the third person. The most important distinction is between the first-person speaker who is a character completely separate from the poet (as in dramatic monologues such as Robert Browning's "My Last Duchess") and the first-person speaker who seems hard to distinguish from the person who wrote the poem (as in lyric poems such as Robert Frost's "Stopping by Woods on a Snowy Evening"). Although it's tempting to treat the second type as wholly autobiographical ("Frost was driving a wagon one night and . . ."), this "I" too is a literary creation, one that allows poets to transform purely individual insights and experiences into ones their readers can more easily share. That's why you ordinarily refer to the speaker of the poem rather than to the poet.

Nonfiction: Who is speaking—writer or persona? As you may have gathered by now, nonfiction writers generally speak for themselves, in either the first or third person, or they create a persona to speak for them. A persona is like a character an actor might play. The writer adopts a role, usually for purposes of humour or irony. In "A Modest Proposal" (Readings), for example, Jonathan Swift creates a persona quite different from himself to comment on conditions in Ireland.

STEP 2   Connecting Textual Features to Figure Out the Work's Theme/Thesis

In most texts, the features we have just described work together to convey an overall point about the subject. The term *thesis* is generally used to refer to the more explicit point made in essays, while *theme* refers to the more indirect points made by imaginative literature.

At first glance it may seem difficult to distinguish theme or thesis from subject. To some extent the difference is between the general and the specific. The subject is the general topic of discussion in the work; the theme or thesis is the specific point the work makes about the subject. You might describe the subject of Alice Munro's short story "Thanks for the Ride" as the dating rituals of adolescence and her theme as the necessity of recognizing the class barriers that obstruct some relationships.

A word of caution is in order here. To analyze texts effectively, you will need to formulate a clear statement of thesis or theme. But remember: it is impossible to capture everything that could be said about any complex and interesting work in a brief phrase, and the statement reflects only your current interpretation, which may change with time or reflection. There may also be discordancies, gaps, or contradictions in the text that you will need to take into account. As you write your essay, keep your mind open to other possible interpretations. Remember, too, that the thesis or theme of the text is not the same as the thesis of your essay; finding your own thesis belongs to the next stage of the writing process.

Sample Analysis of a Poem: William Carlos Williams's "This Is Just to Say"

We will demonstrate how to clarify essay topics and gather material for essays on literature by working through a sample topic, an analysis of William Carlos Williams's "This Is Just to Say." You will find it easier to follow the discussion if you first read the poem carefully.

PUBLISHED WRITING

THIS IS JUST TO SAY

I have eaten
the plums
that were in
the icebox

5   and which
you were probably
saving
for breakfast

Forgive me
10   they were delicious
so sweet
and so cold

"This Is Just to Say," by William Carlos Williams. From *The Collected Poems of William Carlos Williams*. Vol. 1: 1909–1939. Ed. A. Walton Litz and Christopher MacGowan. New York: New Directions, 1991.

STAGE 1   Clarifying Essay Topics

Let's suppose that you are working on the following essay assignment:

> Write a 500 word essay in which you analyze the tone or the attitude of the speaker in William Carlos Williams's "This Is Just to Say."

Clarifying terms Tone is the one word in the assignment that may leave you feeling uncertain. The assignment seems to identify tone with the speaker's attitude. To be sure, you check a dictionary of literary terms and learn that tone is the attitude a speaker/writer takes toward the subject, reader, and self.

Recognizing genre and scope Look at Special Categories for Analyzing Texts in Chapter 3 for questions to ask when analyzing a literary text such as a poem. Also, gather material by focusing on the disciplinary categories noted earlier. Though the assignment focuses on tone, you will need to gather material in the other categories as well. You can decide which categories are most relevant to the poem and the essay assignment.

STAGE 2   Gathering Material

STEP 1   Using Disciplinary or Analytic Categories

Begin by examining relevant disciplinary categories. Make observations and take notes, as we do below.

Subject   The immediate subject is the speaker telling someone (perhaps a friend or a lover) that he has eaten the "plums" in the "icebox." There may be a deeper subject, which hints at the relationship between the speaker and the person to whom he is speaking or for whom he is leaving the note. At this point, we don't know whether the speaker is a "he" or a "she." Later we decide to interpret the speaker as a "he."

Genre and context   "This Is Just to Say" is a free-verse poem. William Carlos Williams is an American poet of the Modern time period. You look up *modernism* in a specialized dictionary, M. H. Abrams's *A Glossary of Literary Terms*, and find that some key elements of modernism are a break from Western culture and tradition, and a questioning of the certainty of the self and established belief systems in religion, philosophy, and politics (167).

Poetic structure   You note that "This Is Just to Say" is clearly divided into three stanzas. In the first stanza, the speaker states his action of eating the plums; in the second stanza, he speculates on his friend's or lover's intentions for the plums; in the third stanza, he apologizes for his action and describes how the plums tasted. You also note that the lines of each stanza are short, consisting of only two or three words each. The short lines and frequent line breaks create a slow reading of the poem. The reader must deliberate on each word and the cluster of words in each line.

Diction   The diction in the poem is simple and easy to understand. Some of the words are sensuous, and describe the taste and feel of the plums. You observe that specific and sensuous descriptions are evident in words such as "delicious," "sweet," and "cold." You look up some of the words in the poem and find that they have more than one possible meaning. The word "just," for instance, in the title of the poem, can mean either *merely* or *fair*. Upon a first reading, the poem implies that the meaning is *merely*, but keep in mind the other meaning of "just." One of the themes of the poem seems to be fairness—the speaker feels that he has done something unfair by eating the plums. He apologizes for his action. Scrutinizing the words of the poem even further, you wonder to what "this," in the title of the poem, refers. Does the word "this" refer to the note that the speaker leaves, the poem itself, or the action of eating the plums? One or more of these interpretations may be relevant. Make note of all of them.

Tone   The tone of "This Is Just to Say" is perhaps the most intriguing aspect of the poem. The tone is casual rather than formal. You can imagine the speaker quickly writing a note to a friend or lover and posting it on the fridge. Upon close examination, however, the tone reveals a complexity in the relationship between the speaker and the person to whom he writes. The speaker feels a sense of guilt at his action of eating the plums, evident in the phrase "forgive me." And yet he still points out how delicious the plums were. You deduce that this poem is likely written from one lover to another.

Point of view   In "This Is Just to Say," the point of view seems to be that of a speaker who is leaving a fridge note to a friend or a lover. It is written in first person narration and appears to be quite simple. We only ever receive the speaker's perspective on the situation. The speaker only speculates—but doesn't know for sure—that his friend or lover was "probably saving" the plums "for breakfast." Although the speaker could be a man or a woman, there are no indications that the speaker is a woman. You should not assume that the speaker is a man simply because the author is, but in this case, it seems to be a man who is speaking in the poem.

STEP 2   Connecting Textual Features to Figure Out the Work's Theme/Thesis

The material you have gathered emphasizes the complex attitude of the speaker toward his act of eating the plums and toward his lover to whom he speaks. You have examined the analytic categories that you deem relevant: subject, genre, context, poetic structure, diction, tone, and point of view. Your analysis of these categories has led you to understand the speaker's attitude as more complex that it initially appears. The speaker doesn't simply write a note and leave it on the fridge. He states his action of eating the plums, describes the sensuousness of that act, and admits his guilty feelings about the act to his lover. Your analysis has led you, then, to a deeper understanding of the poem and the speaker's attitude toward his subject.

STAGE 3   Formulating a Thesis Statement

You now know that when you are asked to analyze a verbal and/or visual text, you are usually expected to show the relationship between the text's content and the techniques used to create it. You also have a systematic means of gathering material in appropriate disciplinary categories, and you have worked through a sample analysis of Williams's "This Is Just to Say." Next you need to learn how to use your material effectively to draft your essay on literature, beginning with formulating a thesis statement. (See also Chapter 4 for a discussion on this stage of the writing process.)

STEP 1 Forming an Opinion

In gathering material about a text, as we have demonstrated, you start from an idea of the text's subject, analyze the text's formal elements, and then identify connections between the subject and the formal elements to arrive at an interpretation of the text's theme or thesis. The *opinion* part of the thesis statement in an essay about literature usually states this theme or thesis in a way that is shaped by the demands of the essay topic.

This does not mean, incidentally, that each text has one and only one meaning that you must discover (or borrow from someone else). It simply means that you present an interpretation of theme that you can support.

- The assignment on William Carlos Williams's "This Is Just to Say" focuses on the speaker's attitude or tone toward his subject. Combining this focus with the theme that emerged from the process of connecting textual features might give you the following thesis opinion:

Thesis opinion: Although the speaker of William Carlos Williams's poem "This Is Just to Say" appears to take a casual tone as he writes a note of apology to his lover, he subtly reveals a more complex attitude toward his lover.

STEP 2 Supporting Your Opinion

In any thesis statement, the support for your opinion will come from the categories of material you used to arrive at the opinion. Many assignments on essays about literature require you to go through the categories of analysis, each of which focuses on a formal element of the text. To indicate the support for the thesis opinion, you will refer to the most relevant disciplinary categories or formal elements. The paragraphs of your own essay may take a single formal element—a disciplinary category that you have examined—as their subject. However, they don't have to. You may weave an analysis of the categories into the paragraphs of your essay. Each paragraph will have a specific focus that is related to the thesis statement.

- To add support to your opinion on Williams's "This Is Just to Say," you would look for the categories of material that led you to that opinion. The formal elements that yielded the most material included diction, tone, and point of view. Adding a reference to these elements would give you a thesis statement like the one below.

Tentative thesis statement	Diction, tone, and point of view in William Carlos Williams's "This Is Just to Say" indicate that the speaker's attitude toward his action of eating the plums and toward his lover is more complicated than it initially appears.

Notice that you indicate the support for your opinion by referring to the subject of the categories, not to specific details or to the points you might make. The reason is that the thesis statement sets out a proposition that you will demonstrate in the rest of the essay.

STAGE 4   Drafting

STEP 1   Organizing Your Material

Refer to Chapter 4 on choosing deductive or inductive structure for your essay. Keep in mind that most essays about literature are organized deductively, with the thesis statement in the introduction. The points derived from the thesis statement are developed in order in the middle paragraphs. This structure provides a framework that makes it easier for readers to grasp the significance of specific details. Also see Chapter 4 for a discussion on choosing a method of development and sequencing your points effectively in ascending order of interest.

STEP 2   Making a Draft Outline

Using a draft outline (described in Chapter 4) will help you avoid the problem of storytelling. Make sure your outline consists of paragraph topics and points, not of plot summary and commentary. You can easily turn your draft outline into a revision outline in the next stage of the writing process by leaving space for revision notes on the right.

- In writing a draft of your essay on Williams's "This Is Just to Say," you might decide to make a draft outline from the systems analysis approach, using the formal elements you refer to in your thesis statement as your paragraph topics and following the sequence you have there. Your draft outline, with space for revision notes, might look like this (MP stands for "middle paragraph," a paragraph in the middle of the essay):

DRAFT OUTLINE

PARAGRAPH TOPIC	POINT	REVISION NOTES
Introduction	Thesis: speaker's tone reveals complexity in relationship with lover	
MP 1: Diction	Words such as "this" and "just" have more than one possible meaning	
MP 2: Tone	Multiple meanings of words and sensuous descriptions complicate tone and reveal guilt and retribution	
MP 3: Point of View	Limited point of view reveals speaker's attitude toward his own action of eating the plums and shows that he guesses his lover's reaction to it	
Conclusion	Poem reveals that what appears simple may be more complex and intricate than one thinks	

In writing your draft you would follow this outline, adding details and quotations from the poem to support your points.

STAGE 5   ## Revising the Thesis Statement and Essay Structure

If you have followed the procedures for gathering material and writing a draft, you might think your draft is unlikely to need much revision. Sometimes that is the case, but most of the time you will need to revise. It is always a good idea to review your draft a day or two after you have written it. You will then be better able to see your work with the eyes of your audience and to make any necessary revisions.

Essays on literature present problems that you may need practice in identifying and solving. In this section, we will discuss how to revise thesis statements, essay structure, and individual paragraphs for essays on litera-ture specifically. You can find more general comments on the revising pro-cess in Chapter 5.

STEP 1   Making a Revision Outline

If you made a draft outline as described in Chapter 4 and previously in this chapter, you can easily turn it into a revision outline. See also Chapter 5 for further discussion on making a revision outline.

STEP 2   Revising Your Thesis Statement

To revise your thesis statement, check that you have an opinion and points to support it. Also check that your thesis statement relates to the essay topic. For more details on how to revise thesis statements, see Chapter 5.

Check the tentative thesis statement for the sample topic on William Carlos Williams's "This Is Just to Say":

Writing Sample

Tentative thesis statement for sample topic   Diction, tone, and point of view in William Carlos Williams's "This Is Just to Say" indicate that the speaker's attitude toward his action of eating the plums and toward his lover is more complicated that it initially appears.

Upon reviewing the tentative thesis statement, you conclude that it is weak. The focus of the thesis statement is the tone of the speaker, and yet tone appears as one of your three points. Also, while you note that the speaker's tone is complicated, you don't note what is complicated about it. The thesis statement is thus vague in that regard.

You decide to make your thesis statement less mechanical by refraining from mentioning three points that you will focus on in each of your para-graphs. While not always desirable, this method is open to you. You focus on your argument about the tone of the work. You may go back later and revise the thesis statement again, once you have revised the body paragraphs in the essay.

Revised thesis statement   If we read William Carlos Williams's poem "This Is Just to Say" with scrutiny, we can per-ceive the speaker's tone as vengeful and haughty—the speaker teases his lover by acknowl-edging not only that he can freely eat the plums but also that he can skilfully use rhetoric to justify the act and earn forgiveness.

The revised thesis statement focuses on the formal element of tone and therefore relates to the essay topic. Your interpretation of the speaker's attitude is very clear and specific. The body paragraphs of the essay will provide evidence to show how that tone is achieved.

Problems with thesis statements in essays on literature often arise from focusing on details of the work or a critic's opinion at the expense of *your* supported opinion on these subjects. Since you have not done research for this essay, you will not encounter this problem here. However, be aware of this issue when you are working on other essay assignments on literature and need to do research.

STEP 3 Revising Your Essay Structure

Use the revision column on your draft outline to note any problems with the analytic framework and to mark in a new order of topics and points if you need one. When you check your draft for essay structure, make sure to check that it is your analysis that provides the framework for your essay, rather than the details of the text. As we mentioned earlier in this chapter, falling into a running summary of the text is one of the most common, and most serious, weaknesses seen in essays on literature. If you find that your topic sentences and paragraph divisions correspond to the sequence of the text you are examining, you will likely need to revise your essay structure.

In reviewing the draft of the sample assignment, you discover that the first and second body paragraphs can both address diction in relation to the thesis statement on tone. The first body paragraph could focus on the multiple meanings of the words "this" and "just," and their significance in relation to the tone of the poem. The second body paragraph could focus on the phrase "forgive me"—the admission of guilt—and the sensuous description of the plums. These connotations would also be related to the thesis statement on tone. Since the essay is only to be 500 words, you can eliminate the third point. You have effectively revised your essay structure by expanding your point on diction and eliminating your point on tone (which is redundant) and your point on point of view.

STAGE 6 Revising Individual Paragraphs

STEP 1 Revising Your Introduction

In revising your draft introduction, check that you provide all the details necessary to identify the work(s), such as author/director and title(s), and that these details and any criticism you present are relevant to the subject identified by the assignment and to your thesis statement. Make sure, also, to avoid broad generalizations about literature or life that are intended to be impressive rather than to illuminate the thesis statement. See Chapter 5 for more discussion on how to revise your introduction.

Let's examine how you might revise the introduction to the essay on William Carlos Williams's poem.

- In the introduction to your draft, you focus on the idea that the tone appears simple but is actually complex. You can revise that observation to make it clearer and more specific. You will also revise your focus on the three points, a decision you already made when you revised your thesis statement and the structure of your essay. In revising your introduction, you will focus on tone through the diction of the poem. You will also need to provide a brief context for the poem by providing your interpretation of it as a note one lover leaves to another. You do not need to provide a lot of information about the author and the time period if you are writing a short essay.

Writing Sample

Revised introduction

William Carlos Williams presents his poem "This Is Just to Say" as a casual note of apology most likely written from one lover to another. Although the poem is deceptively simple, Williams leaves it open to different signifying possibilities that complicate the tone. If we read the poem on a simplistic level, we can perceive the speaker's tone as casual yet honest—in an informal manner, the speaker shows his honesty by admitting his wrong. If we read the poem with scrutiny, we can perceive the speaker's tone as vengeful and haughty—the speaker teases his lover by acknowledging not only that he can freely eat the plums but also that he can skilfully use rhetoric to justify the act and earn forgiveness.

STEP 2   Revising Your Middle Paragraphs

As we discussed in Chapter 5, check that you don't slide back into telling "what happens" in the text you are analyzing. Rather, stay with your argument and support it with concrete evidence from the text. Make sure that your middle paragraphs have a clear topic sentence and a main point. Check that the point of each paragraph is supported with examples—quotations and/or paraphrases—and explanations of those examples.

Consider this draft paragraph on tone in William Carlos Williams's "This Is Just to Say":

Draft paragraph

Diction in the poem reveals tone. The word "this" in the title of the poem is open to more than one possible meaning. It can refer to either the note of apology or to the act of eating the plums. The word "just," also in the title, is open to more than one meaning. It can mean *merely*, or it can mean *legally valid* or *fair*. These meanings show that the tone can be casual and honest or haughty and vengeful.

The topic sentence of the draft paragraph indicates the subject of the paragraph, but it is too vague. It should either be removed—if the subject of the paragraph is very clear—or revised. The indication of multiple meanings of the words in the title of the poem shows that you have paid attention to diction and the nuances in the poem. You've attempted to make a connection between diction and tone, but that connection isn't very clear. You haven't provided explanations of the evidence (quotations) you present. You could also make the transition between your discussion of the meanings of the two words more explicit. Finally, work on connecting the paragraph to the thesis statement in the introduction. Upon noting these problems, you revise to create the following middle paragraph:

Writing Sample

Revised middle paragraph

The word "this," in the title of the poem, is open to more than one possible meaning. It can refer either to the note of apology or to the act of eating the plums. If we read "this" as a reference to the note, then the speaker's tone is either honest or haughty: he either leaves the note because he wants to admit his wrong or because he wants to declare his action and thus tease his lover. If we read "this" as a reference to the act of eating the plums, then the speaker's tone is vengeful: he eats the plums as a statement of vengeance toward his lover. Similarly, the word "just," also in the title, is open to more than one possibility. It can mean *merely*, or it can mean *legally valid* or *fair*. If we read "just" as a synonym for *merely*, then the speaker takes a casual tone: he implies that his act and the note are not very important. If we read "just" as *legally valid*, then the speaker is saying "this is fair to say"—the tone is then one of retribution. Hence, the tone of the title alters between honest, haughty, casual, and vengeful according to the way in which we read the words "this" and "just."

The revised paragraph includes clear explanations of your interpretation of the diction and how it relates to the tone of the poem. You have more explicitly connected your discussion to the thesis statement, your overall argument. You have added the transitional word "similarly" to connect how the multiple meanings of the words work in the poem. The revised paragraph is well organized: two meanings of "this," followed by an ordered interpretation of each meaning; two meanings of "just," also followed by an ordered interpretation of each meaning. Finally, the paragraph has a concluding sentence that highlights the importance of multiple meanings of the words discussed.

STEP 3   Revising Your Conclusion

As we pointed out in Chapter 5, your conclusion should restate and extend your thesis, and suggest its broader context or implications. Check that your conclusion expands the original thesis statement by drawing upon the more specific ideas you have developed in the body of the essay and that it briefly discusses the broader implications of your essay.

Let's take a look at the concluding paragraph of the draft essay on Williams's "This Is Just to Say."

Draft conclusion   In conclusion, diction in the poem shows a complex rather than a simple tone. The words "this" and "just" have various meanings that hide the speaker's haughty and vengeful tone. The phrase "forgive me" and the sensuous description of the plums undermine the speaker's apology by relating how good the plums were. Overall, we can see that the speaker has a complex, even troubled, relationship with his lover.

This conclusion restates the thesis, and its general comments are very much in the spirit of Williams's poem and the points you have made in your essay. The draft conclusion is still weak, however. In a short essay assignment such as this one, it is important not to repeat points you've already made. For a more powerful conclusion, think about the broader implications of the poem. This doesn't mean that you will present large generalizations or moral statements about literature and life. Rather, consider why Williams would write such a poem in the first place and who might be his audience. Think about the poem beyond, but in relation to, the speaker and his attitude toward his lover. This kind of revising doesn't just involve editing or proofreading. It involves a second look at the poem itself, and it involves employing your critical thinking skills. Take the time to reflect on what your analysis has led you to discover about the text and the subject of the assignment.

This is the conclusion that might result from these changes:

Writing Sample

Revised conclusion Although Williams presents his poem as a note of apology, he also presents it as a poem that appears in his collection of poems. What is Williams's purpose in presenting this poem as a piece of literature? In order to answer this question, we may view the poet in the same way that we view the speaker. Like the speaker, the poet creates a seemingly simple work that relays a casual and honest tone, as if the poem can precisely depict and justify the meaning of a particular incident. Essentially, however, he creates a complex piece of literature in which the tone is dependent upon the way we read the words. Williams thus comments on the power of language. We accept words as justifications for action, even though "just saying" is only saying. Perhaps "this" poem then, is "just to say" that there is no single truth or ideal justice that language can express.

Note that the revised conclusion includes the third possible reference to "this"—"this" as the poem itself—that you initially identified when gathering material for the essay. You can see how important it is to keep your notes, even very early ones, because you may later incorporate some of the information you gathered. Also, the broader implications in this conclusion subtly refer back to the context of the poem. When gathering material for your essay, you looked up the definition of *modernism* in M. H. Abrams's *A Glossary of Literary Terms*. The notion in your conclusion that "there is no single truth or ideal justice that language can express" is very much in the spirit of modernism's challenge to existing traditions and truths. Once again, the information you came across in the initial stages of gathering material became useful in writing the final draft of your essay.

Working on Your Own Assignment

Your main purpose in writing essays on literature is often to explain the relationship between *what* the work is about (its subject and theme) and *how* the ideas and emotions are conveyed.

- Make notes on the written text or performance in the appropriate disciplinary categories: subject, genre, context, methods of development, structure, style, tone, and point of view.

- Begin formulating your thesis statement by presenting your opinion of the text's theme or thesis, unless the assignment requires your opinion on a different element of the text.

- Complete your thesis statement by adding a reference to relevant formal elements of the text as support.

- Decide how to organize your draft, bearing in mind that presenting the elements of the text as part of a system (systems analysis) will usually work best.

- Make a draft outline to guide your writing. Leave spaces so that you can later insert revision suggestions.

- Write a draft, paying most attention to developing middle paragraphs.

- Change your draft outline into a revision outline by recording what you have actually done in your draft and what needs to be changed.

- Check that your thesis statement is not a description of the theme/thesis or form but rather your supported opinion on the assignment topic.

- Check that your draft is not a running summary of the text but rather is organized around topics of ascending interest.

- Check that the context section of your introduction provides information that directly leads toward your thesis statement.

- Check that textual detail in middle paragraphs does not simply describe a section of the text but rather is used as evidence to support a point.

- Check that the connection between point and detail in middle paragraphs is sufficiently explained, especially in the case of direct quotations.

- Check that your conclusion restates and expands the thesis and suggests broader implications appropriate to the subject of the assignment and the text.

Exercises

A.   Respond to each of the following questions in a sentence or two.

1. If you are analyzing an essay, what is the difference between the writer's thesis and your own?

2. Why does "telling the story" not work as a structure for an essay about literature?

B.   This two-part exercise relates to the paragraphs that appear following these instructions—the introduction and conclusion to an essay showing how three formal elements in director Terrence Malick's *The Thin Red Line* help convey the theme of the film. After completing the exercise, compare your choices with those of other class members.

1. For the introduction, mark the sentences that indicate
   - an appropriate context for the analysis;
   - the principal paragraph topics the essay will cover;
   - the thesis of the essay.

   Cross out all material that does not relate to one of these three areas.

2. For the conclusion, mark the sentences that
   - restate the thesis;
   - summarize the main points of the essay;
   - suggest the wider implications of thesis and points.

   Cross out all other material.

Introduction   There are many levels of conflict in war. Beyond the obvious physical conflict between the armies, there is the more subtle psychological antagonism that rages inside the minds of the soldiers. This is the aspect of warfare that is explored in Terrence Malick's Second World War film, *The Thin Red Line*. Malick's reputation as a film genius, along with the fact that he had not directed a movie for twenty years, caused Hollywood stars to line up for a chance to act in this project. The result was a film that has only enhanced Malick's illustrious reputation. The film claims that war is as much psychological as it is physical, and it achieves its focus on the psychology of war by using images, structure, and characterization in a very distinctive way. It is a challenging film to watch, but well worth the effort.

Conclusion   Even though it was soundly beaten at the box office and the Academy Awards by *Saving Private Ryan* and many other films that were released in the same year, I believe that *The Thin Red Line* will stand the test of time. It is an extraordinarily powerful film about a topic mankind will never grow weary of analyzing. The innovative use of disjointed images, the very slow pace of the narrative, and the emphasis on collective characterization rather than individual heroism all serve to focus our attention on the psychology of the soldiers rather than their behaviour. There have been many anti-war films about war, obviously, but their messages have been undermined because they have adopted the same conventions as the heroic war film. Malick's film challenges these conventions and makes us question war in a very profound way. I think this focus will make *The Thin Red Line* widely recognized as one of the best films ever made about war. Perhaps if there were more films like this, those Academy Awards judges would start to realize that the times really are changing.

Writing Comparison Essays

(7)

Sample Topic: Comparing Views of Addiction in Maté and Alexander/Shaler

The comparison essay is a special type of analysis essay that you may be asked to write in many college and university courses. You could be asked to compare two poems, two models of moral development, two views of a social problem, or social organization in two tribal societies. Comparison assignments help you and your reader to better understand both the things you are comparing—the *objects of comparison*—and the more general subject, concept, or focus that is the *basis of comparison*.

To illustrate how basic the process of comparison is, let's consider this question: Is someone with an income of twenty thousand dollars a year a wealthy person? In comparison to most of the planet's inhabitants, the answer would be yes; in comparison to the average North American, however, the answer would be no. Without comparison, the term *wealthy* is virtually meaningless.

Our understanding of the concept of wealth will remain fairly superficial, however, unless we take the comparison further. As we work through the similarities and differences between the situations of people with different incomes, we are forced to think not only about those specific instances, but also, and perhaps more significantly, about our own ideas of what constitutes wealth. What standard of living does each person's income provide? How many people does it support? How much of it is disposable income—that is, money that does not have to be spent on necessities such as food, clothing, and housing? Comparing the economic positions of people with different incomes would thus help us to understand both the concept of wealth (the basis of comparison) and these different economic positions (the objects of comparison).

This chapter emphasizes the most problematic aspects of making comparisons: choosing a basis of comparison, arriving at a thesis, and organizing your material. You will also find general guidelines for clarifying topics, gathering material, formulating a thesis statement, and drafting and revising comparison essays. To illustrate these stages of writing, we will focus on a comparison between two essays on addiction that appear in Part 2, Readings: Gabor Maté's "Embraced by the Needle" and Bruce Alexander and Stefa Shaler's "Addiction in Free Markets." You will follow this discussion more easily if you read the essays first.

STAGE 1   Clarifying Comparison Topics

Imagine you have been given the following choices for a comparison essay:

- Compare the explanations of addiction in Gabor Maté's essay "Embraced by the Needle" and Bruce Alexander and Stefa Shaler's essay "Addiction in Free Markets."
- Compare any two similar short stories from your class anthology.

STEP 1   ## Checking for a Basis of Comparison

Comparison essay assignments will indicate, at least generally, the objects of comparison, the two (or more) things you are to compare. Assignments that can be stated as "Compare X and Y in terms of Z" also indicate the basis of comparison, the common element you are to focus on. The first topic above gives the basis of comparison:

> Compare Gabor Maté's essay "Embraced by the Needle" (X) and
> Bruce Alexander and Shefa Shaler's essay "Addiction in Free Markets"
> (Y) in terms of their explanations of addiction (Z).

This is the sample topic we will use for the rest of the chapter.

The second topic does not indicate a basis of comparison. To write successfully on this kind of topic, you will first need to choose objects that share a significant similarity. You might, for example, pick short stories with similar subjects, settings, or main characters. You could use one of these elements as your basis of comparison, or you might discover a more interesting basis of comparison in the process of gathering material.

STEP 2   ## Looking for Similarities and Differences

Remember that "compare" always means "compare and contrast." Look for both similarities and differences in the objects of comparison.

STAGE 2   ## Gathering Material

STEP 1   ## Using Matching Methods of Analysis and Analytic Categories

Before you can compare two things, you need to analyze each separately. To make sure you *can* compare them, you need to use the same methods of analysis for each one. The first step in gathering material, therefore, is to find appropriate methods of analysis. For example, you might use methods of analysis such as cause/effect, process analysis, or systems analysis (see Chapter 3). You will then consider the analytic or disciplinary categories to use. If you are writing a comparison essay on literature, you will consider the disciplinary categories for English discussed in Chapter 6. You will perceive similarities and differences more easily if you set out your material in matching columns.

- In the sample assignment, the phrase "explanations of addiction" indicates that you should focus on the content of the two essays, not on their literary qualities. In Chapter 2, Reading Analytically and Writing Summaries, we discussed how to figure out the basic ideas in a text. Using the categories of analysis discussed in Chapter 2, and drawing upon the methods of analysis discussed in Chapter 3, here is what you come up with:

CATGORIES	MATÉ'S ESSAY	ALEXANDER AND SHALER'S ESSAY
Subject	Causes of addiction	Causes of addiction, then solutions
Main idea	Emotional pain in childhood changes brain chemistry, leading to addiction	Social dislocations in free-market societies lead to "mass addiction"; integration into real communities is the only cure
Development	Cause and effect analysis framed by narratives	Cause and effect analysis. Free-market societies create dislocation; dislocation creates addiction
Detail	Stories of addicts; theories of effects of stress on brain chemistry	Historical examples: present day; 16th- to 19th-century England; the history of Native Canadians
Context/ Perspective	Maté is a physician; perspective more psychological than medical	Alexander teaches in a psychology department, but the essay is concerned more with social trends than with individuals
Purpose	To gain sympathy for addicts' emotional suffering	To explore causes as a prompt to political action for change

Besides helping you focus on similarities and differences, a set of matching categories can reveal imbalances in your material. Occasionally you may find that a category contains a lot of material on one object of comparison, but little or none on the other. In this case you must decide whether to drop the category, find more material, or explain the imbalance.

- In the matching categories for the sample assignment, there are no major imbalances of material. But let's suppose you discovered that you had much more material in the development category for Maté's essay than for Alexander and Shaler's. You would have three options: review Alexander and Shaler's essay and take more notes on its methods of development; drop this category as not relevant to your thesis; or find a reason for the imbalance. You might decide, for instance, that you have more notes on structure in the Maté essay because it is loose and unsystematic, whereas Alexander and Shaler set out the problem and its solution in a straightforward manner.

STEP 2   Clarifying the Basis of Comparison

Creating a set of matching categories will also help you clarify or decide upon a basis of comparison.

If your assignment has indicated a basis of comparison, this basis should be the focus of one set of matching categories. If the assignment has not indicated a basis, you can choose a key area of similarity and/or difference from your list of matching categories.

- The basis of comparison given in the sample assignment on addiction is "explanations of addiction." Under the category of subject, you note that both essays deal with the causes of addiction. You can thus make the basis of comparison more precise by identifying it as "explanations of the causes of addiction."

- If you had chosen the assignment asking you to compare two short stories, your matching disciplinary categories would offer you a number of possibilities to try out as a basis of comparison, such as subject, characterization, setting, style, and theme. You would choose the best basis of comparison by seeing which of these connected with the pattern of material in most other categories.

- If you chose setting, for example, could you compare not only the settings themselves, but also characters' attitudes toward the settings? The figurative language used to describe each setting? The relation between setting and theme?

STAGE 3   Formulating a Comparison Thesis Statement

STEP 1   Forming an Opinion about Each Set of Material

You arrive at a comparison thesis opinion much as you do for other analysis essays, that is, by scanning the material in your categories to see how it is linked and what point it suggests. You begin by considering what point the material in each set of categories, considered separately, makes about the basis of comparison. (We say "considered separately," but putting the columns side by side will sharpen your sense of the qualities of each object.)

- Scanning the material on "Embraced by the Needle," you may notice that Maté's point about emotional pain in childhood causing addiction is reinforced by the narrative framework and details of individual addicts' lives. The material in several categories confirms that Maté's perspective is psychological rather than medical.

- In the Alexander and Shaler essay, several factors indicate a sociological perspective: the point about the social causes of addiction, the systematic cause and effect analysis, and the historical examples.

STEP 2 Forming an Opinion about Overall Similarities and Differences

The next step is to consider the relationship between the two points you came up with in the previous step. Are the objects of comparison similar or different in relation to the basis of comparison? What generalization can you make about the similarities and/or differences? Your answer to these questions becomes the *opinion* part of your thesis statement.

- "Embraced by the Needle" and "Addiction in Free Markets" seem to embody quite different perspectives on the causes of addiction. You might write the opinion part of your thesis statement as follows:

Tentative thesis opinion

In "Embraced by the Needle," Gabor Maté explains the causes of addiction from a psychological perspective, whereas Bruce Alexander and Stefa Shaler offer a sociological perspective in "Addiction in Free Markets."

STEP 3 Supporting Your Opinion about Similarities and Differences

As in any analysis essay, the support for your opinion comes from the categories of material you used to arrive at the opinion. The only difference in formulating a thesis statement for a comparison essay is that you draw the support from the matching categories, not from one set alone. Problems with comparison thesis statements most often come from one-sidedness, where one of the objects of comparison receives unequal treatment either in the opinion or in the support. Take care to make the thesis statement even-handed.

- In the sample assignment, the opinion part of the thesis statement focuses on perspectives, but the perspective of each essay was confirmed by the categories of main idea, development, detail, and purpose. These categories therefore provide support for the thesis opinion.

Tentative thesis statement	In "Embraced by the Needle," Gabor Maté explains the causes of addiction from a psychological perspective, whereas Bruce Alexander and Stefa Shaler offer a sociological perspective in "Addiction in Free Markets." These different perspectives are evident in the writers' points and purposes, and in their handling of development and detail.

A tentative thesis statement like this gives you a starting point for exploring the similarities and differences between the things you are comparing. The process of drafting and revising often leads to deeper insights into your material.

- As you will see with the sample topic, there are important differences between a psychological and a sociological perspective. Through drafting, a better thesis emerges that explains the relationship between these two perspectives on addiction.

STAGE 4   Drafting

STEP 1   Selecting Material

As with other analysis essays, the categories of material that you found relevant in working out your thesis will become the basis for your middle paragraphs. There are two points you need to keep in mind, however.

- Because your matching categories will give you a great deal of material, you may need to limit the number of categories you use. Drop categories where your material is skimpy, imbalanced, or not relevant to your comparison. If, for instance, you were comparing two poems, one a sonnet and one not, you would likely drop the category of structure, since there would not be much point in proving the obvious differences between the two.
- Make sure you include roughly equivalent amounts of material for each of the things you are comparing.

STEP 2   Organizing Comparisons: Block and Point-by-Point Methods

Probably the most common problem in writing comparison essays is finding an effective method of organization. There are two basic methods of organizing comparisons: the *block method* and the *point-by-point method*.

Block method When you use the block method, you say everything you have to say about one subject before you discuss the other. This method can be effective for very short essays in which overall similarities and differences (as you might find, for instance, in a personal essay comparing good teachers and bad teachers) are more important than detailed comparisons. The block method is also useful for in-class essays and essay exams, when you are developing a few main points without extensive quotations or facts and figures as evidence.

Point-by-point method When you use the point-by-point method, you compare things one aspect at a time. The point-by-point method usually works better for essays longer than 500 words because you can explain the significance of similarities and differences as you go along. You don't risk leaving anything unexplained or having to add another section to cover everything.

Making a draft outline is especially valuable when you are using the point-by-point method. Note the point you intend to make about each category so you don't merely repeat the observation that the things you are comparing are similar or different. These points will become the basis for your topic sentences.

- The sample assignment seems too long and complex for the block method, so you would choose the point-by-point method. The draft outline for your middle paragraphs (MPs) might look like this:

DRAFT OUTLINE

MP 1	Thesis and perspective	Addiction is caused by emotional pain in childhood, according to Maté's psychological perspective
		Addiction is caused by social dislocation in Alexander and Shaler's psychological perspective
MP 2	Development	Maté's causal analysis is enclosed in a narrative framework
		Alexander and Shaler's causal analysis is systematic and directly presented
MP 3	Detail	Maté emphasizes the lives of individual addicts
		Alexander and Shaler use non-individual historical examples

STAGE 5 Revising the Thesis Statement and Essay Structure

STEP 1 Revising Your Thesis Statement

In this step you ask yourself the following questions:

- Does your thesis statement present an overall opinion about similarities and differences between two (or more) objects of comparison?
- Does this opinion reflect the relationship between similarities and differences in the material you collected in matching categories?
- Is this opinion based on, and does it indicate, a common basis of comparison?
- Does the thesis statement indicate the support that you are going to present in the body of the essay?

If the answer to any of these questions is no, your thesis statement will need revision.

- Note that the following thesis statements lack some of the necessary components.

Weak thesis statements
- Maté's essay is very different from Alexander and Shaler's, as I shall show by looking at their different forms and purposes. [No basis of comparison indicated]
- "Embraced by the Needle" is a psychological essay, while "Addiction in Free Markets" is more systematic. [No common basis of comparison, no support]

If your thesis statement seems satisfactory, one final question remains:

- Does your draft suggest new ideas that will give you a better thesis?

As we suggested earlier, the tentative thesis statement for the sample assignment seems to have all the components mentioned above. Yet it focuses solely on differences. It does not account for the nagging sense you might have in writing the draft that while the explanations of addiction in the two essays are different, they are not incompatible. There is a link, after all, between the emotional pain suffered by individuals and the social dislocations that give rise to emotional pain. So you might revise your thesis statement to include this idea.

Writing Sample

Revised thesis statement

In "Embraced by the Needle," Gabor Maté explains the causes of addiction from a psychological perspective, whereas Bruce Alexander and Stefa Shaler offer a sociological perspective in "Addiction in Free Markets." While these differences in perspective are evident in the writers' purposes and in their handling of development and detail, the main ideas expressed in the two essays are complementary rather than contradictory, for social dislocations give rise to the emotional pain experienced by individual addicts in childhood.

STEP 2 Revising Your Essay Structure

Use your draft outline, if you made one, or make a revision outline showing the points in each paragraph of your draft to check whether

- your choice of either block or point-by-point organization still seems appropriate. If your outline reveals that each block paragraph is crammed with a variety of ideas, for example, then you should probably decide to adopt the more systematic point-by-point method. On the other hand, if your paragraphs switch back and forth like a Ping-Pong ball, you may need to gather your material into larger blocks.

- your discussion includes matching points about the things you are comparing. Have you inadvertently failed to cover some aspect of one object of comparison? Have you devoted much more space to one object of comparison than another? Identify problems for correction in the next stage of revision.

- your sequence of paragraphs still seems effective. In a comparison essay, your paragraphs should lead toward the point that best illustrates the most important similarity or difference. Thus if your thesis statement suggests that differences are more important than similarities, you would discuss similarities first and then differences, ending with the most significant one. If similarities are more important, you would end with the most significant similarity.

In the sample assignment, for example, the revised thesis statement requires a rethinking of the structure. It indicates you are going to move from showing differences to showing the compatibility of psychological and sociological perspectives. You would therefore start from the most obvious difference—detail—and lead toward your comparison of these perspectives. You will see the results of this reorganization in the sample essay. See C. Jones, "Perspectives on Addictions" (Readings: Sample Essays).

STAGE 6 Revising Individual Paragraphs

Now that you have identified areas where your draft needs revising, it is time to tackle individual paragraphs.

STEP 1 Revising Your Introduction

If you have followed our advice not to worry about your introduction until the structure of the whole essay is clear, you may find that you need to fill out the statement of context that precedes your thesis statement. (See Chapters 5 and 6, Revising Your Introduction.)

Does your statement of context

- indicate your basis of comparison and establish its importance or relevance?
- provide matching information about the objects you are comparing?

In drafting your essay on the explanations of addiction, you might have begun with a statement of context like this:

Draft introduction Understanding the causes of addiction is an important project and few people are better quali-fied for it than Dr. Gabor Maté. Dr. Maté works on Vancouver's Eastside, sometimes called the drug capital of North America, and his writing shows he has on-the-ground knowledge of what he is talking about. I will compare his essay entitled "Embraced by the Needle" with an essay called "Addiction in Free Markets" by Bruce Alexander and Stefa Shaler.

This statement of context successfully indicates the basis of comparison, "understanding the causes of addiction," and provides good information about Gabor Maté. It does not explain why this is an important subject, however, or give matching information on Alexander and Shaler. For the revised version of this introduction, see the sample essay by C. Jones, "Perspectives on Addictions" (Readings: Sample Essays).

STEP 2 Revising Your Middle Paragraphs

Check to see whether

- you use topic sentences that clearly indicate your method of organization;
- you use "umbrella" topic sentences when necessary to indicate the major divisions in your material;
- you give roughly the same amount of space to developing points about each object, text, or concept you are comparing.

Problems in developing comparison paragraphs usually come from imbalance and one-sidedness.

- In reviewing the draft for the sample assignment, for example, you might find a paragraph like the one below.

Draft middle paragraph

The most obvious contrast between "Embraced by the Needle" and "Addiction in Free Markets" is in the type of detail used. In "Embraced," the detail we remember is the detail of individuals: of Anna, who "wasn't wanted"; of Carl, who "had dishwashing liquid poured down his throat"; of Wayne, a tough man, who at the end of the essay "looks away and wipes tears from his eyes." No one cries in "Addiction." In that essay, the language is abstract, the kind argumentative social scientists use.

- This paragraph was intended to compare the use of detail in the two essays. There are no examples to show the kinds of detail used in "Addiction," however, so the point of the comparison is not clear. In revising, you would both clarify the point and provide examples from "Addiction."

STEP 3   Revising Your Conclusion

It may be tempting to conclude by simply repeating what you have said about similarities and differences. Readers expect more than this, however; they want you to step back from the specific objects you have compared and explore what your essay has revealed about your subject.

You will need to check not only that your conclusion summarizes your thesis statement and main points, but also that the development of these points leads to a deeper understanding of both the basis of comparison and the objects you have compared. If either summary or development is missing, you will need to revise.

- Consider the draft conclusion to the sample assignment:

Draft conclusion

"Embraced by the Needle" and "Addiction in Free Markets" are very different because their authors' handling of detail, development, and points are so different. Gabor Maté has a psychological perspective on the causes of addiction, while Bruce Alexander and Stefa Shaler take a sociological point of view on the issue. These are very different perspectives on this important issue, but they may be more complementary than contradictory.

- This conclusion restates the thesis but adds nothing to it. In revising, you would want to stress what you and your readers have learned from considering the causes of addiction from both a psychological and a sociological perspective.
- You will find the complete revised essay, C. Jones, "Perspectives on Addictions," in Part 2, Readings: Sample Essays.

Working on Your Own Assignment

Your purpose in comparing is to illuminate the similarities and differences between two (or more) objects of comparison in reference to a basis of comparison.

- Check your essay topics to make sure you know which ones ask you to compare. Are you given a basis of comparison or will you need to work one out?

- Gather material on both objects of comparison by using the appropriate questions for analysis essays or essays on literature. Analyze the objects separately so that you don't distort them by trying to find similarities too soon.

- Arrange your material in matching categories that contain equivalent amounts of material, focusing on the categories most relevant to your topic.

- Examine your material to determine the overall relationship between similarity and difference in reference to your basis of comparison.

- Formulate a thesis statement by making a general point about this overall relationship and giving reasons to support it.

- Organize your material by the block method or the point-by-point method, depending upon the length and complexity of your essay. Your topic sentences should make clear which method you are using.

- When you revise your draft, check to see whether your paragraphs lead toward the most important similarity or difference, and whether you have given equal attention to both objects of comparison in your thesis statement, your points and detail, and your introduction and conclusion.

Exercises

A. Work out a basis of comparison for a short essay on each of the following subjects. Compare your responses with those of other class members.

1. The celebration of Thanksgiving in your family and another family

2. Canadian and American television programs of a specific type (such as lawyer shows, family dramas, talk shows)

3. Different ways of looking at a local environmental or educational issue

B. Read the essays by Tim Bowling ("Na Na Na Na, Hey Hey Hey, Goodbye") and Kofi Annan ("Football Envy at the UN") in the Readings. What would be a workable basis of comparison for these two essays? Try several possibilities. Compare your responses with those of other class members.

C. Decide whether each of the following is a good thesis statement for a comparison essay and explain your decision.

1. For an essay comparing Sigmund Freud's view of dreams with C. G. Jung's:

> In developing a theory of dreams that emphasizes their prophetic and compensatory functions, Jung departed from the view of the unconscious upon which his mentor, Freud, had built his theory of dreams.

2. For an essay comparing the principles of solar and geothermal heating systems:

> Although solar and geothermal heating systems are similar in some respects, in others they are different.

D. Choose one of the following topics. Use the appropriate questions to gather material and formulate a thesis. Then make an outline showing how you would organize your middle paragraphs. Compare your work with the work of other class members. The essays mentioned are reprinted in Part 2, Readings.

1. Compare the significance of fathers and fatherhood in the essays by Lenore Keeshig-Tobias and Scott Russell Sanders.

2. Compare the authors' views of sports in relation to culture and society in the essays by Tim Bowling, Kofi Annan, and/or Laura Robinson.

3. Choose two other essays from the Readings to compare. You will need to work out your own basis of comparison.

E. David Suzuki's essay "Food Connections" (Readings) is organized in a mixture of the block and point-by-point methods. Make an outline showing how you would organize this essay wholly in the point-by-point method.

Evaluating Arguments and Writing Critiques (8)

There is an important difference between *analysis*—identifying the causes of downtown parking problems, for example—and *evaluation*—judging whether arguments for a new downtown parking lot are logical or illogical, or whether the proposed lot will be beautiful or ugly. As this example suggests, analysis usually precedes evaluation. This does not mean, however, that evaluation is less significant than analysis. Whether you are arguing with a friend about a movie or campaigning for a political candidate, judging the value of things is an important human activity.

Making evaluations is equally important in academic disciplines, as you learn how to determine the worth of theories, experiments, technological innovations, or works of art. When you write evaluative essays in an academic setting, you need to be conscious of and express the criteria you use in making judgments. Although specific criteria will vary, there are four common *standards of evaluation* that provide a broad framework for making judgments. These are the *logical, aesthetic, practical*, and *ethical* standards.

In the persuasive essay, you use one or more of these standards to present your own position on a subject. You will find guidelines for writing this kind of essay in Chapter 9. In the critique, you use one or more of these standards to evaluate someone else's work, such as the methodology of a scientific experiment or the interpretation of a poem.

This chapter will show you how to write a critique that evaluates the logic of stated or implied arguments. We focus on this type of critique for two reasons: to demonstrate how to separate considerations of logic from aesthetic, practical, and ethical concerns; and to give you the tools you need to evaluate your own arguments when you write persuasive essays.

We will first outline the gathering, drafting, and revising process for this kind of essay, and then show the process at work in a sample assignment: evaluating the logic of an essay from Part 2, Readings.

STAGE 1   Clarifying Evaluation Topics: Checking for the Logical Standard

The first stage in tackling any evaluation assignment is to check what standard(s) of evaluation the assignment asks you to use. You will know to use the logical standard of evaluation if the assignment uses words like *logical, reasonable, credible, plausible*, or *valid*, and/or asks you to assess reasoning, evidence, a case, arguments, methodologies, or strategies of argumentation, as in the following:

- Does David Suzuki's "It Always Costs" present a credible case for distrusting technological innovation?
- Assess the plausibility of the evidence Dan Gardner presents in "The Missing Piece to the Gang-Violence Debate."

STAGE 2   Gathering Material: Arguments and Evidence

Most of us have strong emotional responses, positive or negative, to a writer's position on a subject we care about. This emotional response can get in the way of a fair-minded assessment. If we disagree with a writer's views, for instance, we may be tempted to dismiss the argument without giving it serious attention. The best way to avoid this problem is to analyze the reasoning and evidence first, and only then assess the strengths and weaknesses.

STEP 1   Analyzing the Writer's Reasoning and Evidence

In Chapter 2 we introduced categories for analyzing the content of nonfiction writing: subject, main idea/thesis, development, evidence/detail, purpose, and context. You use the same categories to analyze reasoning and evidence when you evaluate a piece of writing according to the standard of logic, except that you pay closer attention to types of argument (development) and kinds of evidence (detail). The discussion that follows will explain what to look for.

Identifying types of argument The important term *argument* may be used for the writer's overall case, for the structure of this case, and for individual points. Usually the context indicates which meaning is involved. The main types of argument are as follows.

Deductive argument Any argument that moves from one or more general principles to make a judgment about one or more particular cases could be called a deductive argument. The most rigorous kind of deductive argument is the *syllogism*, where a general statement (called the *major premise*) is linked to a specific case (called the *minor premise*) to produce a conclusion.

- Historians view history objectively (major premise).
- Joan is a historian (minor premise).
- Therefore Joan views history objectively (conclusion).

On a larger scale, a deductively organized essay moves from an overall point to a series of individual points that serve to confirm and develop it.

Inductive argument Any argument that moves from one or more particular cases toward a general point could be called an inductive argument. An inductive essay is structured around the movement from individual points to a more general thesis.

Causal and other types of argument Reasoning from step to step in a process and from part to part in a system are both relatively rare, but reasoning from cause to effect is an important form of logical reasoning. Causal reasoning becomes causal argument when a writer claims that the cause and effect sequence creates something good or bad.

- In "Na Na Na Na . . . " Tim Bowling moves from causal analysis to causal argument when, near the end of his essay, he claims that the origins of hockey in "blood and beer" and the consequent "empty rhetoric around outdated and destructive notions of patriotism and manhood" (215 Readings) mean that neither he nor the reader should follow the sport any longer.

Identifying kinds of evidence Anything used to show that a statement is true or false is considered evidence. The following list explains the most common types.

Examples An example is a small, detailed, and specific piece of evidence intended to support a point about a larger whole. For instance, a line from a poem may support a statement about the poem's theme, or an anecdote about one mugging may support a case about the causes of street crime. Examples are sometimes called "soft" evidence because they rarely prove a point; it is usually possible to find counter-examples. Nevertheless, examples can be vivid and compelling.

Facts and figures Another kind of evidence is sometimes called "hard" evidence: statistics, research studies, scientific observation, and the like. Hard evidence is widely used in formal scientific and applied research papers, but is also frequently found in popular scientific essays, like David Suzuki's "It Always Costs" (Readings), and in persuasive essays, such as Ted Byfield's essay on population (Readings).

Reference to authorities The opinion of someone who is knowledgeable about a subject is a valid kind of evidence. Within academic disciplines you are often expected to locate your ideas within a tradition of thinking about your subject. Argument by authority is thus important in academic essays, especially research essays.

Analogies An analogy is a comparison based on a partial similarity between the features of two unlike things. If you say that the heart is like a pump, for instance, you are using an analogy that emphasizes the similarity between the functions of the heart and the pump and ignores the differences. When you use an analogy as part of an argument, you are arguing that one situation is like another situation and will have the same outcome, good or bad.

- In "The Voyagers" (Readings), Linda Hogan uses an unmanned space probe carrying greetings from Earth as an analogy for the voyage of our planet itself. This analogy emphasizes the fragility and hopefulness of the great experiment represented by life on Earth.

- Political arguments are often based on historical analogies: "A war in the Middle East would be another Vietnam."

Emotional appeals Emotional appeals are comments or language designed to elicit strong feelings. An emotional appeal conveys a distinct attitude and invites the reader to share that attitude. Thus emotional appeals are often used in propaganda: written, visual, or spoken texts designed to persuade an audience to form a political or religious group, participate in particular social actions, or adopt a particular ideology. The feelings aroused by emotional appeals may be incompatible with a rational consideration of the subject. Thus emotional appeals are not really evidence in the logical sense at all. However, you need to be able to tell when a writer supports a position by emotional appeals rather than reasoned arguments.

You can most reliably identify emotional appeals by their diction and tone. The words used in emotional appeals often reflect extreme feeling: things are *unthinkable, dreadful, inarguable, utterly obvious, unquestionably valuable*. The tone of these appeals may be ridiculing, satiric, or humorous.

- In "Globalisation's Time Is Up," J. H. Kunstler uses an emotional appeal when he claims that "the sunset of the current phase of globalisation seems dreadfully close to the horizon" (256 Readings).

STEP 2   Identifying Strengths and Weaknesses (Fallacies) in Logic

After you have analyzed a writer's reasoning and evidence, the next step is to evaluate the argument to determine its strengths and weaknesses. It is important to look for both strengths and weaknesses, however much you may agree or disagree with the writer's position, because your readers are more likely to be convinced when your critique seems fair-minded.

The following guidelines will help you determine strengths and weaknesses in reasoning and evidence. Note that problems in logic are often called *logical fallacies.*

Evaluating arguments

Deductive argument Deductive arguments are strong if the general principle is valid and supportable, and if the points that follow can be derived from that principle. Similarly, deductively organized essays work when the main points demonstrate the initial thesis.

Problems in deductive arguments occur when the general principle is not valid or the points do not follow from the principle. Earlier we spoke of the syllogism as the purest form of deduction. A syllogism is not valid if the major premise is untrue, the minor premise is missing, or the conclusion does not follow.

- Our earlier example of a syllogism was this: Historians view history objectively; Joan is a historian; therefore Joan views history objectively. This syllogism will not be valid if some historians do not view history objectively; if no proof is offered that Joan is a historian; or if the argument reached the conclusion that because Joan is a historian, she would make a good politician.

You are most likely to find problems in deductive arguments when the major premise is a sweeping generalization that is either unverifiable (cannot be proved to be true or false) or untrue.

- Throughout history humans have struggled for perfection. [Unverifiable]
- Hard work always leads to success. [Untrue]

This is the fallacy of *over-generalization,* a fallacy also involved when you make large conclusions from limited major or minor premises:

- Some historians are objective. [limited major premise] Joan is a historian. Therefore Joan is objective.

Another common deductive problem is the fallacy of *circular reasoning,* or begging the question, where a point that should be proved is assumed to begin with.

- "I will show that this dreadful practice of abortion, child murder, is morally wrong" is a thesis statement flawed by circular reasoning; it assumes that abortion involves murder. This point would have to be part of the essay's moral argument.

Inductive arguments An inductive argument is considered strong if the particulars are connected and if they lead plausibly to some larger conclusion. Similarly, an inductive essay works if the paragraph points are connected with each other and lead toward the concluding thesis.

Problems in inductive arguments most often occur when there is a gap between the particulars and the conclusion that the essay intends to draw from them. This gap is often called the fallacy of *hasty generalization.*

- "My neighbours never cut their lawns and the man across the street leaves his porch light on all night; these are symptoms of the moral decay of the modern world" is an ineffective inductive argument. The concluding point is too broad to emerge convincingly from these particulars.

Causal arguments Causal arguments are valid when the effect is clearly shown to follow from the cause.

- Many families with children have moved into the neighbourhood; therefore, enrolment in local schools is likely to rise.

Problems in causal reasoning arise when the cause-effect relationship is unconvincing. Many ineffective causal arguments suffer from what is called the *post hoc fallacy.* The full phrase in Latin is *post hoc ergo propter hoc,* meaning "after this, therefore because of this." In this fallacy, because a second event follows a first, the first is taken to be the cause of the second.

- The team ate Mighty Bites before the game; no wonder they won.

A special version of *post hoc* is sometimes called the fallacy of *single cause/single outcome,* where a likely multiplicity of causes is reduced to one.

- The claim that "the increase in murders is a direct result of the suspension of the death penalty" is flawed unless further evidence is presented, since many factors are known to affect the homicide rate.

A fallacy common to several kinds of argument and evidence is the *straw man fallacy,* where an opponent's arguments are exaggerated or selectively presented to make them appear insubstantial. This tactic is particularly common in fallacious causal reasoning. In a straw man argument, the possible consequences of an opponent's position are misleadingly exaggerated:

- If funding is increased for daycare centres, more children will attend them; as a result, children will cease to spend any significant time with their mothers.

Evaluating evidence

Examples Examples are valid when they are representative of the larger point or situation they are intended to support. Examples do not prove a point, however.

Problems in handling examples arise when there is a questionable relationship between the particular example and the general point it is intended to prove. Examples can be irrelevant to the point they are supposed to support, or, more commonly, generalizations can be based on too few examples, committing what we earlier called the fallacy of hasty generalization.

- There is a flood of books being published in North America on men's problems. I saw two new titles from Australia only last week. [Irrelevant example]
- Clearly consideration for others is disappearing in today's society; my neighbour's parties have kept me awake three nights in a row. [Inadequate example]

Facts and figures Facts and figures are potentially the most convincing kinds of evidence a writer can present.

Problems result because statistics and other "facts" can be manipulated. Problems in "hard" evidence arise when the sources of the evidence are not current, when the evidence does not come from a reliable and appropriate source (as when statistics about the United States are assumed to apply to Canada), or when the evidence cited is extremely selective.

Reference to authorities Argument by authority is used well when the writer shows a critical awareness of the orientation and expertise of the authorities cited, the authorities have real expertise in the subject, and their ideas do not overshadow the writer's own ideas.

Problems result from citing authorities not relevant to the subject. A famous chemist is a valid authority for an essay on chemistry, but not for an essay on juvenile delinquency. Other problems include vague and unsupported references ("experts claim," "research shows"), unbalanced citation of authorities (where they are all on one side of a case, for example), and general over-reliance on authorities. All these could be called the fallacy of *inappropriate authority*, occasionally referred to as the fallacy of the *argumentum ad verecundiam* (literally, the "argument appealing to respect").

Analogies Analogies often have strong emotional appeal, but they are effective support for an argument only when they are used with other kinds of evidence.

Problems come from the fact that analogies are essentially metaphoric and emphasize similarities; when readers are aware of significant differences between the two objects being compared or see the objects through the lens of a different metaphor, they will consider that the writer has committed the fallacy of *false analogy*.

- For example, readers who value individualism over interdependence will not be convinced by Linda Hogan's vision in "The Voyagers" (Readings) of Earth as a spaceship in which we are all travelling together.

Historical analogies are especially liable to fallacy, since historical situations are complex and often differ from one another substantially.

Emotional appeals Emotional appeals are strong in that they touch the level where beliefs are formed; they are used well when they reinforce logical arguments.

Problems with emotional appeals come when they are used instead of logical argument or when they are excessive. We tend to consider emotional appeals that have come unmoored from logical support as sentimental or manipulative. The common fallacy of *ad hominem* (literally "to the man") arguments—arguments directed against the arguer, not against his or her arguments—reflects a misuse of emotional appeals. So does the fallacy of *ad populum* (literally "to the populace") appeals, those designed to arouse popular unthinking sentiments.

- In Jean-Jacques Rousseau we see the kind of confused thinking about family and education we would expect from a man who put his own children into an orphanage. [*Ad hominem* argument]
- No one who values our pioneer past can deny that the real role for women is in the home, whether that home is a cabin in Northern Quebec or a house in suburban North York. [*Ad populum* argument]

This table summarizes the most common types of argument and evidence, along with their potential problems.

KINDS OF ARGUMENT AND EVIDENCE	FALLACIES
Deductive argument	Over-generalization, circular reasoning (begging the question)
Inductive argument	Hasty generalization
Causal argument	*Post hoc*, single cause/single outcome, straw man
Examples	Hasty generalization
Facts and figures	Outdated, inappropriate, or misleading facts and figures
Reference to authorities	Appeal to inappropriate authority (*ad verecundiam*)
Analogies	False analogy
Emotional appeals	*Ad hominem, ad populum*

Note that this is a partial list of fallacies; for a more complete list, consult a textbook on logic or persuasive writing.

STEP 3   Categorizing and Charting Strengths and Weaknesses

Because of the complexity of evaluating reasoning and evidence, you may find it helpful to make an evaluation chart with one column for the analytic aspects of the writing, a second column for strengths, and a third column for weaknesses. If there is no key strength or weakness for a particular aspect, leave the space blank.

- If you were to analyze and evaluate "Globalisation's Time Is Up" (Readings), for example, you might decide that J. H. Kunstler's analysis of historical periods (aspects column) supports his thesis (strengths column) but his points are rather oversimplified (weaknesses column).

You will find a complete evaluation chart in the Sample Topic section of this chapter. An evaluation chart is useful for summing up the results of gathering material; it also streamlines the process of formulating a thesis statement, as you will subsequently see.

STAGE 3 Formulating an Evaluative Thesis Statement

An evaluative thesis statement for a critique essay should include an opinion about the relationship between strengths and weaknesses in the piece of writing, an indication of the main support for this opinion, and an indication of the standard(s) of evaluation you are using. Let us look at each of these components in turn.

STEP 1 Forming an Opinion about the Relationship between Strengths and Weaknesses

The opinion part of the thesis statement focuses on the overall relationship between strengths and weaknesses. This means you must decide whether, in general, strengths outweigh weaknesses, weaknesses outweigh strengths, or strengths and weaknesses are equally balanced. An evaluative chart makes this decision easier because you can see at a glance where you have noted strengths and weaknesses and where you have left blanks. You must still decide, of course, whether each analytic category you have used is equally important to your overall assessment.

Although you may find it difficult at first, deciding on the overall relationship between strengths and weaknesses is a skill you can acquire with practice. Simply listing some strengths and some weaknesses may be easier, but it won't give you a good thesis opinion. Neither will claiming that there are only strengths or only weaknesses; you would have to work hard to overcome your readers' skepticism, since few arguments are either flawless or totally flawed. Similarly, you cannot avoid making up your mind by using the judgment that strengths and weaknesses are equally balanced. If you claim they are balanced, you will need to demonstrate the balance throughout your essay.

STEP 2 Supporting Your Opinion

An evaluation chart will also reveal the most important support for your thesis opinion, since the fullest categories will likely become the topics you use to organize the body of your essay.

STEP 3 Indicating the Standard of Evaluation

Indicating the standard of evaluation in the thesis statement is more important than you might realize. You know what standard of evaluation you are using, but unless you tell your readers, they may apply their own favoured standard and then be upset when your judgments differ from theirs. You may indicate the standard directly, by referring to logic, or indirectly, by referring to arguments or cases or by using words like *credible* or *convincing*, whichever is more suitable for your audience.

Below are examples of effective and weak thesis statements that evaluate an essay according to the logical standard.

Writing Sample

Weak thesis statements evaluating logic

- David Suzuki's "It Always Costs" is not Suzuki's typical argument about caring for the environment: it's a case against technology. [No identification of strengths or weaknesses]
- David Suzuki's "It Always Costs" provides some valid reasons for refraining from embracing technology too readily, but the argument has weaknesses. [Overall relationship of strengths and weaknesses is not clear; weaknesses are not specified; the standard of evaluation is not clear.]

Effective thesis statements evaluating logic

- Although some of his examples seem stereotyped [weakness], the use of appropriate evidence and a clear process structure [strengths supporting thesis opinion] make David Suzuki's "It Always Costs" a logically credible [standard of evaluation] essay on the costs of technology. [Putting the weakness in a dependent clause indicates that it is less important than the strengths]
- The strength of David Suzuki's argument in "It Always Costs," its clear process structure, is more than offset [overall relationship] by its weaknesses: its stereotypical examples and excessive emotional appeals.
- Stereotypical examples and excessive emotional appeals in David Suzuki's "It Always Costs" are balanced by logical strengths in the use of appropriate evidence and a clear process structure.

STAGE 4   Drafting: Sequencing Strengths and Weaknesses

In critique essays, the relationship between strengths and weaknesses—as expressed in the thesis statement—determines the order of ascending interest. If weaknesses outweigh strengths, you begin with strengths and then move to weaknesses; if strengths outweigh weaknesses, then vice versa.

Once you have decided whether strengths or weaknesses come first, you will also need to decide on the order of points within each category. If you have written the support component of your thesis statement carefully, you should be able to use the sequence of topics it indicates. As for other essays, a draft outline is often helpful. For a critique essay, make sure the draft outline indicates strengths and weaknesses as well as paragraph topics and points. You can find a sample draft outline for a critique essay in Stage 4 Drafting of the sample topic assignment later in this chapter.

STAGE 5 Revising the Thesis Statement and Essay Structure: Reasoning

The key principle to remember in revising is that your reader will judge your reasoning and evidence by the same standard you are using to evaluate someone else's writing. Thus you will need to review your draft to decide whether your argument as a whole is satisfactory.

STEP 1 Revising Your Thesis Statement: Checking for Evaluative Point

If you are not satisfied with your argument as a whole, the problem may lie in your thesis statement.

- Does it contain an opinion about the relationship between strengths and weaknesses?

- Does it mention the specific strengths and weaknesses you discuss in your middle paragraphs, in the order you discuss them?

- Does it make clear that you are using the logical standard of evaluation?

- Has writing your draft given you new ideas about your argument?

You may have a good thesis statement and yet your argument may have changed during the writing of the draft. You may have come to a different understanding of the relationship between strengths and weaknesses or made changes in the specific strengths and weaknesses you discuss. If so, you will need to revise your thesis statement to reflect these changes.

STEP 2 Revising Your Essay Structure: Argument

Problems with the overall argument may lie not in the thesis statement but in the way the argument unfolds. To check essay structure, ask yourself these questions:

- Does the sequence of topics make clear the relationship between strengths and weaknesses set out in the thesis statement?

- Is the topic for each paragraph an item of support indicated in the thesis statement?

- Does the topic sentence of each paragraph make a point about one aspect of the logical standard of evaluation, such as the weaknesses of a deductive argument or the effective use of facts and figures?

If your answer to any of these questions is no, you will need to revise accordingly. You may also discover that writing the draft has revealed flaws in the argument that you planned. If so, you will need to make a revision outline to guide you as you rewrite. For a sample revision outline, see Stage 5, Step 2 in the sample topic assignment in this chapter.

STAGE 6   Revising Individual Paragraphs: *Ethos*, Argument, and Evidence

Just as you review your draft to evaluate the effectiveness of your argument as a whole, so you will need to review each paragraph to see whether you have been fair-minded and argued your points effectively with good evidence to support them.

STEP 1   Revising Your Introduction: *Ethos*

As we will discuss more extensively in Chapter 9, readers are likely to respond more strongly when values are an issue. Therefore, you need to consider your readers carefully when you write any kind of evaluative essay. When you are writing a critique of logic, you want to present yourself as reasonable and fair-minded. This is especially important in the introduction. If the introduction offends their values, readers may proceed no further.

To ensure that readers keep reading, check your introduction for what the ancient rhetoricians like Aristotle called *ethos,* the image of himself or herself the writer projects to the reader. If you can answer yes to the following questions, your introduction is likely to seem reasonable and fair-minded.

- Do you begin by providing a clear summary of the context, subject, and thesis of the piece you are evaluating, rather than praise or critical comments?

- Have you chosen language that is as neutral as possible, rather than language that is biased in favour of or against the piece you are evaluating?

- Is the tone of the introduction as a whole that of a fair-minded, reasonable person?

If the answer to any of these questions is no, you will need to revise. The following examples will show you how.

Writing Sample

Draft introduction Environmentalists are *always complaining* about the technology their very lives depend on. Prominent among these environmentalist *whiners* is David Suzuki, and his essay "It Always Costs" presents the *usual* illogical mixture of *prejudice* and out-of-date science for which he is becoming *notorious.*

Revised introduction The technology we are surrounded by—from toasters to cruise missiles—has been created both by scientists' expertise and by politicians' choices. Is this technology a boon or a curse? We can perhaps help answer this question by evaluating the work of David Suzuki, a commentator on technology who is both a scientist and an environmental activist. Evaluating the logical credibility of his essay "It Always Costs" provides insights into the environmentalist view of the value of technology. [Add thesis statement.]

STEP 2 Revising Your Middle Paragraphs: Arguments and Evidence

Using the list in Stage 2, Step 2 above as a guide, check each middle paragraph to see

- which type(s) of argument and kind(s) of evidence you have used;
- whether you have explained your argument fully enough;
- whether you have provided enough evidence;
- whether you have avoided common problems and fallacies.

Suppose, for example, you had written the following paragraph in an essay on Suzuki's "It Always Costs":

Draft middle paragraph The way David Suzuki develops his argument is particularly impressive because he demonstrates that he can change his mind. Changing one's mind really demonstrates mental flexibility because nothing is more difficult than this. Mentioning DDT, thalidomide, and DES piles up the examples of scientific errors in a very compelling way.

This paragraph comments on Suzuki's argument, but what about your own? You may have intended to write a deductively organized paragraph to show how Suzuki develops his argument and to offer examples as evidence that this development is effective. The draft paragraph is flawed by circular reasoning, however. It asserts that Suzuki changes his mind and claims that is a good thing, but it does not explain what the change is or why it is good. The evidence is flawed by irrelevant examples, since examples concerning scientific error demonstrate nothing about change of mind. In revising the paragraph, you would present examples to show that Suzuki's essay is organized around the movement from one set of beliefs about technology to another, different set.

STEP 3   Revising Your Conclusion

In the conclusion, the emphasis shifts from the piece you have evaluated to your summation of strengths and weaknesses. You still need to leave readers with an image of yourself as fair-minded, however. One way you achieve this image is by mentioning both strengths and weaknesses. If the tone of some of your earlier comments has been sharp, now is the time to return to a more neutral, inclusive tone.

Writing Sample

Draft conclusion   If the environmental movement believes that the world is clogged up with paper products due to the pervasiveness of computer technology, perhaps some radically new decisions are called for. Stopping essays like "It Always Costs" from being printed could be the first step in this new direction. [No summary of strengths and weaknesses; biased tone]

Revised conclusion   David Suzuki's choice of obvious targets like DDT for his examples does encourage a stereotyped response, no question about that. However, this evidence is effective even if it is obvious, and the change-of-mind structure of the essay powerfully counteracts the effect of stereotyping, giving the essay finally a great deal of credibility.

Sample Topic: Critiquing the Logic of Ted Byfield's Essay "Health Canada . . ."

In this section we will work through the essay writing process of gathering material, drafting, and revising an essay that critiques the logic of Ted Byfield's essay "Health Canada Inadvertently Discloses Facts Planned Parenthood Would Like to Suppress" (Readings). You will follow the process more easily if you read Byfield's piece first.

STAGE 1   Clarifying Evaluation Topics: Checking for the Logical Standard

Imagine you have been given the following assignment.

> Does Ted Byfield's essay "Health Canada . . . " present a credible case about current developments in world population? Write an essay evaluating his argument.

By using "credible case" and "argument," the assignment indicates that you should use the logical standard of evaluation. To put the essay in context, you might check on its source and currency, noting that it appeared in March 2002 in the Alberta-based magazine *The Report,* of which Byfield was a founder.

STAGE 2   Gathering Material: Arguments and Evidence

STEP 1   Analyzing the Writer's Reasoning and Evidence

Before you can evaluate the essay, you will need to understand its main ideas and strategies of argumentation. To collect material on these, you use the relevant categories of analysis essays (see Chapter 2), with the analytic categories of development and detail adapted for the analysis of logic:

Subject   Your reading of the essay confirms the subject suggested by the assignment: current developments in world population.

Main idea/thesis   Byfield's thesis seems hard to find until you realize that he presents parts of it in three different places, mostly as the opinion of various authorities. (This is a common tactic in controversial writing.) Put together, his thesis becomes

a)   Canadians are working more and having fewer children.

b)   As a consequence, there is a "serious population decline."

c)   This "decline" will have very negative economic consequences in the Western world and the world in general.

Types of argument   As the thesis indicates, the method of development used to organize this essay is cause and effect.

Kinds of evidence   Byfield brings in statistics (facts and figures) to support his points, his analytic categories, about work and population decline. Various countries—Canada, Italy, India, Egypt, Mexico, and Thailand—serve as examples to support these points. He also uses many references to authorities, both those who support his position and those he criticizes.

His description of the authorities he criticizes creates emotional appeal through satire.

STEP 2   Identifying Strengths and Weaknesses (Fallacies) in Logic

Now that you have *analyzed* Byfield's argument and evidence, you are ready to *evaluate* this material.

Types of argument Your analysis showed that "Health Canada" presents a cause and effect argument organized into three steps. The strength of this argument is that it is systematic: one step follows another. This argument suffers, however, from the fallacy of single cause/single outcome. Byfield does not discuss or refute other explanations of the cause of declining birth rates. It does not seem credible that obsession with work is the only cause. Similarly, since Byfield does not address other arguments about the effects of current developments in population, you question whether a decline, if it were true, would have economic "havoc" as its main effect.

Kinds of evidence

Examples How relevant are Byfield's examples? Do they support his generalizations? There is no evidence that a Canadian obsession with work is also a worldwide obsession. How representative are Byfield's other examples? You will need to look at the use of facts and figures in the essay to answer this question.

Facts and figures The specific statistics Byfield gives as evidence for "population decline" or "absence of kids" may at first seem quite impressive. When you look more closely, however, you realize that even if Europe's birth rate is running at 1.4, this rate is more than balanced by the rates of India (3.5), Egypt (3.9), and Mexico (3). Clearly, though the birth rate is declining in some countries, the world's population is increasing.

Then you note that there are no birth rate statistics for Canada and the United States, only a casual comment implying that their birth rates are more than Thailand's (2). This means their birth rates must be above replacement. Quoting these rates would have weakened Byfield's case about "decline."

Thus the figures quoted seem to be selectively chosen and do not support the claim about "serious population decline." Furthermore, the essay contains neither examples nor facts and figures as evidence of economic "havoc," only a half-sentence assertion that "government welfare programs depend upon a steady inflow of tax money."

Reference to authorities Although Byfield refers to authorities he agrees with and to those he disagrees with, he uses them very differently. He endorses as fact both the American Enterprise Institute's interpretation of the statistics it uses and Tom Bethell's comments in the *American Spectator* about there being "too few people." On the other hand, he dismisses authorities on the other side of the case—Paul Ehrlich, Planned Parenthood, the United Nations—with no summary of their actual arguments.

You decide that including authorities from both sides is a strength but that the one-sided treatment of authorities is a weakness.

Emotional appeals Your evaluation of the treatment of authorities is echoed in your evaluation of emotional appeals. Byfield treats authorities he agrees with objectively, whereas he describes those who perceive serious dangers in population growth in emotionally laden satiric terms as "prophets of doom," "zealous preacher[s]," and the like. This use of emotional appeals decreases the credibility of Byfield's argument.

STEP 3   Categorizing and Charting Strengths and Weaknesses

As an aid to seeing how strengths and weaknesses compare, you set them out briefly in an *evaluation chart*.

EVALUATION CHART

ASPECTS	STRENGTHS	WEAKNESSES
Argument	Systematic argument	Fallacy of single cause/single outcome
Examples		Not representative, don't support generalization
Facts/Figures	Statistics present	Statistics flawed, don't prove thesis
Authorities	Authorities presented	Authorities treated differently
Appeals		Satiric dismissal of authorities on other side

STAGE 3   Formulating an Evaluative Thesis Statement

Looking at this chart, you decide that the strength of the essay "Health Canada . . . " is that it presents the appearance of a cause and effect argument supported by statistics and authorities. Its weakness is that its logic is in appearance, not in substance: its cause and effect argument is fallacious, its treatment of authorities is one-sided, and the statistics and examples do not prove its thesis. As the chart indicates, the weaknesses outweigh the strengths. To express this relationship between strengths and weaknesses and to mention the categories that support this opinion, you come up with the following thesis statement:

Tentative thesis statement	"Health Canada . . . " seems to have strengths: a cause and effect argument, support by statistics, and the presentation of authorities who oppose, as well as those who support, Byfield's thesis. While the statistics he quotes should make us think, they do not actually support his argument, and the essay is very one-sided in the way it deals with authorities.

STAGE 4   Drafting: Sequencing Strengths and Weaknesses

Because you will argue that Byfield's essay has fewer strengths than weaknesses, you will start with strengths and move to weaknesses. Your thesis seems to suggest a workable series of paragraph topics, so you make a draft outline as a guide to writing.

DRAFT OUTLINE

PARAGRAPH TOPIC	POINT
Strength: Cause and effect argument	Byfield's essay does have a causal structure
Strength: Facts and figures	Statistics presented to support two of these steps
Strength: Authorities	Most of thesis taken from authorities; essay refers to authorities on both sides of case
Weakness: Facts and figures	Figures do not support thesis
Weakness: Authorities	Authorities actually very one-sided

You then draft your essay, sketching an introduction and conclusion, and developing each of these points in a middle paragraph.

STAGE 5   Revising the Thesis Statement and
Essay Structure: Reasoning

STEP 1   **Revising Your Thesis Statement:
Checking for Evaluative Point**

At this point, you take a critical look at each of the three components of
your tentative thesis statement.

Relationship Writing your draft did not change your mind about the
overall relationship between strengths and weaknesses, but this relationship is not stated clearly enough. You decide to insert a sentence to make
the relationship explicit.

Support You realize that you have not included the weakness in the cause
and effect argument in your thesis statement. This is an important point,
so you cannot omit it. This change will lead to a change in the structure
of your essay.

Indication of standard The word *logical* does not appear anywhere in
your tentative thesis statement. You decide to add it to make your standard of evaluation clear.

The thesis statement that results from these changes appears below.

Writing Sample

Revised
thesis
statement

"Health Canada . . . " seems to have logical strengths: a cause and effect argument supported by statistics and references to authorities on both sides of the case. These strengths
are more apparent than real, however. Byfield's treatment of authorities is one-sided and
his statistics, while thought-provoking, do not support his point. As a result, his causal
argument fails to be logically convincing.

STEP 2   **Revising Your Essay Structure: Argument**

In reviewing your draft, you note that your paragraphs move from strengths
to weaknesses but that there are more strengths than weaknesses, and the
weaknesses do not follow an order of ascending interest. The essay also
seems to need a more deliberate transition from strengths to weaknesses.

Since the logical strengths of the essay are more apparent than real,
your paragraphs on these topics are skimpy. You decide to discuss all the
strengths in one paragraph, add a transition paragraph, and then change

the order to reflect the movement from least important to most important weakness. These changes will mean adjusting the order of support in your thesis statement. You make the following revision outline for the middle paragraphs (MPs):

REVISION OUTLINE

PARAGRAPH TOPIC	POINT
MP 1 Apparent strengths	Apparent strengths in argument and evidence
MP 2 Transition	These strengths are apparent, not real
MP 3 Weakness: Authorities	Use of authorities is one-sided
MP 4 Weakness: Evidence	Statistics don't prove point
MP 5 Weakness: Causal argument	Failure to deal with alternative cause and effect explanations

For the middle paragraphs written from this outline, see D. Jones, "Reflecting on Population," in Part 2, Readings: Sample Essays.

STAGE 6   Revising Individual Paragraphs: *Ethos*, Argument, and Evidence

STEP 1   **Revising Your Introduction: *Ethos***

In writing your draft, you scribbled the following sentences to lead up to your thesis statement:

Draft introduction
Ted Byfield's essay "Health Canada Inadvertently Discloses Facts Planned Parenthood Would Like to Suppress" appeared in *The Report*, the Alberta-based newsmagazine that Byfield also edited, in March 2002. "Health Canada" is an essay on population that makes claims that sound incredible, and they turn out to be just that, incredible.

Considered logically, these sentences creating a context for your thesis statement have both strengths and weaknesses. The strength is that they provide details of author, title, currency, and location, as well as suggesting Byfield's subject. The main weakness is in *ethos*. The second sentence does not give the impression of fair-mindedness. You decide to replace it with a summary of Byfield's main idea.

STEP 2   Revising Your Middle Paragraphs: Arguments and Evidence

In checking individual paragraphs for effective argument and evidence, you find that your paragraph on Byfield's weakness in using authorities lacks sufficient evidence.

Draft middle paragraph   For a start, it is true that "Health Canada" uses authorities from both sides of the argument about population, but the fact is that they are used very differently. Authorities who argue the dangers of population growth do not have their arguments described, but instead are dismissed in a series of satiric caricatures. The opinions of the American Enterprise Institute and of a journalist writing in the *American Spectator* are, on the other hand, directly quoted and treated as fact. This one-sided handling of authorities diminishes credibility.

Added examples Your comment about treating opinion as fact is supported elsewhere, but your comment on satiric caricature needs examples, so you add the following sentence:

Writing Sample

Byfield calls Paul Ehrlich one of the "prophets of doom," refers to Planned Parenthood as the "zealous preacher of the Save-the-World-with-Smaller-Families message," and states that the United Nations disseminates "don't-have-kids" propaganda.

STEP 3   Revising Your Conclusion

Short of time, you wrote a one-sentence summary as your conclusion:

Draft conclusion   Because of its one-sided use of authorities, failure to link evidence to point, and flawed causal argument, Ted Byfield's "Health Canada . . ." does not achieve logical credibility.

This sentence reflects the sequence of topics you have used. It does not seem fair-minded, however, because it does not refer to the strengths of Byfield's essay. You have claimed that they are strengths of appearance, so you decide to start the conclusion by conceding that giving his essay the appearance of logic contributes to the recognition that logic is needed on this issue. You can then finish with the comment that we do, however, need the substance rather than the appearance of logic.

To read the finished version of this essay, see D. Jones, "Reflecting on Population," in Part 2, Readings: Sample Essays.

Working on Your Own Assignment

Your main goal in a logical critique essay is to assess another writer's handling of logic in writing that is itself logical and balanced.

- Check significant terms to make sure that your assignment requires the logical standard of evaluation.

- Analyze the piece of writing for subject, main idea, argument, and evidence.

- Evaluate the strengths and weaknesses of the argument and evidence.

- Formulate a thesis statement that states an opinion about the relationship between logical strengths and weaknesses in the writing, provides support for that opinion, and indicates, indirectly or directly, that you are using the logical standard of evaluation.

- Write a draft, sequencing the topics to reflect the relationship between strengths and weaknesses indicated in the thesis statement. Use a draft outline if possible.

- With the help of your draft outline or a revision outline, revise the thesis statement and overall essay structure to ensure that your argument is logical and effective.

- Check that you begin your introduction by providing a context for the writing you will discuss rather than by immediately evaluating it, so that you convey the image of yourself as fair-minded.

- Check that your middle paragraphs make strong arguments and give effective evidence.

- Check that your conclusion presents both the strengths and weaknesses of the writing you have discussed and reflects, if possible, a development of the thesis statement.

- For an example of a logical critique essay, see D. Jones, "Reflecting on Population" in Part 2, Readings: Sample Essays.

Exercises

A.   Write a sentence evaluating the following as thesis statements for logical critique essays.

1. Although there is a lunatic fringe that opposes a woman's right to abortion, this right is self-evident and I will examine some key books on the issue to show that it is rationally justified.

2. In *The Hazards of Being Male*, Herb Goldberg argues that pressures to conform to a stereotyped image of masculinity force many men to live like emotional zombies. Goldberg's thesis may be correct, but there is a problem with the arguments he uses and with his narrow range of examples.

3. Charles Taylor's *The Malaise of Modernity* is one of the most rational books I have ever come across. If you want a well-reasoned book on what's wrong with the modern world, look no further.

B.   Read Polly Toynbee's "Inequality Is the Real Enemy" (Readings). Then evaluate the use of argument and evidence in the following paragraph. First, state the main idea of the paragraph. Next, identify any common fallacies. Then revise the paragraph so that it uses argument and evidence effectively:

> Polly Toynbee is reviewing a book by Richard Wilkinson on inequality. She echoes and supports Wilkinson's illogical arguments on equality, and this makes her views illogical too. Inequality arises from some people's lack of commitment to hard work. It is probably the fact that Toynbee comes from a family of celebrated writers and academics that makes her miss this. However, Toynbee does choose good examples from Wilkinson's book, notably the comparison between life expectancies in Harlem and in Bangladesh, and Wilkinson's comments on the irrelevance of diet to the survival of orphanage children in postwar Germany. Examples like these do support the claim that inequality is a relative not an absolute term.

Writing Persuasive Essays (9)

Sample Topic: Same-Sex Marriages

Stage 1	**Clarifying Evaluation Topics**
	Step 1 Defining Key Terms
	Step 2 Finding a Standard of Evaluation

Stage 2	**Gathering Material**
	Step 1 Analyzing
	Step 2 Categorizing Strengths and Weaknesses

Stage 3   **Formulating an Evaluative Thesis Statement**

Stage 4   **Drafting: Working Out a Pro-Con Outline**

Stage 5	**Revising Thesis Statement and Essay Structure**
	Step 1 Revising Your Thesis Statement: Checking for an Evaluative Point
	Step 2 Revising Essay Structure: Checking Sequence and Pro-Con Transitions

Stage 6	**Revising Individual Paragraphs**
	Step 1 Revising Your Introduction: *Ethos*
	Step 2 Revising Middle Paragraphs: Logic and Transitions
	Step 3 Revising Your Conclusion: Achieving Balance

In Chapter 8, you learned how to assess the strengths and weaknesses in someone else's argument in order to write a critique essay. In this chapter, you will learn how to discover and argue your own position on a subject. Essays of this type are called *persuasive* essays because their purpose is to persuade readers to agree with your position. The following are typical assignments for persuasive essays:

1. How should Canadian institutions respond to pressure to sanction same-sex marriages?

2. Should the summer holidays for schoolchildren be reduced to one month?

3. Is the original *Star Wars* trilogy better than the more recent *Star Wars* trilogy?

This chapter will take you through all the steps of planning, writing, and revising a persuasive essay, using the first assignment above as the sample topic, but drawing examples from the second and third topics as well.

In the planning stages, you focus on analysis and evaluation. First you analyze your subject to determine its good and bad points, its advantages and disadvantages, its strengths and weaknesses. This analysis gives you the material you need to arrive at a considered judgment: your evaluation of overall strengths and weaknesses.

In drafting and revising, you focus on persuasion: how to present your position so that your readers are most likely to take your arguments seriously. The strategies you use depend to some extent on your audience. You may be writing for readers who are *hostile* (unlikely to agree with your position), *neutral* (likely to have an open mind), or *friendly* (likely to agree with your position). Academic writing generally assumes a neutral reader, but we will comment briefly on techniques of persuasion for hostile and friendly readers.

STAGE 1   Clarifying Evaluation Topics

STEP 1   Defining Key Terms

Understanding the key terms of the assignment and the subject is particularly important in writing persuasive essays. You will often need to define terms in your essay. Otherwise your readers may misunderstand or disagree because they do not understand the terms in the same way.

- For an essay on legalizing marijuana, for example, you would need to be sure your readers understood the big difference between legalizing the use of marijuana (making it available for sale under controlled circumstances, like liquor) and decriminalizing it (not prosecuting people who use it).

- For the sample topic on same-sex marriage that we are focusing on in this chapter, it would be essential for you and your readers to understand the difference between marriage as a social or religious commitment and marriage as a legal contract. You would need to define these terms for your readers.

In many cases, one or more key terms may depend on the context of the subject you are writing about, and you will need to define that context in your essay.

- For example, a key term in the topic on same-sex marriages is *institution*. Because you researched the issue, you are aware that the institution of the state was involved both in legalizing same-sex marriage through the Civil Marriage Act in 2005 and in subsequent opposition to legalization focused on Stephen Harper's 2005 campaign promise to organize a free vote in the Commons on the issue. You are aware that in 2006 the House of Commons voted not to re-open the issue, so the Conservative opposition to the legalization of same-sex marriage failed. You are also aware that a second institution, namely the church, was involved in the debate. The church comprises both those who oppose the legalization (for example, the hierarchy and many of the congregations of the Roman Catholic Church) and those who support it (for example, the hierarchy and many congregations of the United Church of Canada). Thus you will need to define the term *institution* in this assignment as comprising church and state.

You may also need to clarify key terms, at least for yourself, by determining exactly what you are being asked to evaluate.

- For example, in the sample topic, you are being asked "How should Canadian institutions respond" (note the key term) to same-sex marriages. You are not being asked directly how you would respond to this subject; rather, you are being asked to analyze the responses of institutions and then evaluate these responses, that is, decide which ones represent the way institutions, in your view, should respond.

On what basis will you make this evaluation? The answer: by finding one or more standards of evaluation, either ones indicated by the assignment or ones of your own choosing.

STEP 2   Finding a Standard of Evaluation

When you evaluate, as we pointed out in Chapter 8, you use one or more standards of evaluation as a basis for judging things. Your essay topic might explicitly ask you to consider the moral arguments for and against same-sex marriages, the practical advantages and disadvantages of reducing summer holidays, or the artistic merits of the films. More often, your essay topic will imply the standard(s) or expect you to figure out which ones to use. For example, if you chose the third assignment, you would need to ponder what "better" might mean. More artistically satisfying? A better money-maker? Conveying a more moral view of life?

Whether you are given the standards of evaluation or have to figure them out, you will need to know how to use them. We discussed the logical standard in Chapter 8. Here is a brief discussion of the three other most useful standards of evaluation: the *aesthetic*, the *practical*, and the *ethical*.

Aesthetic standard   Aesthetics is literally the study of beauty. The aesthetic standard is commonly used to judge works of art or the performance aspect of any activity, such as a political candidate's speaking skills or a figure skater's technique. When you use an aesthetic standard, you ask one or more of these questions:

- Is it well constructed, beautiful, pleasing to the senses?
- Is it well performed?
- Is it a good example of its kind?

Behind these questions are judgments based on two key criteria for aesthetic judgments: *coherence* and *comparison*.

If something is coherent, then the parts work together to create a satisfying whole. For example, you might decide that the original *Star Wars* trilogy is good filmmaking because it has interesting characters, a suspenseful plot, and a compelling, original musical score that all combine to make definitive science fiction movies.

The judgment that something is a good example of its kind or is better than another of its kind obviously depends on comparison with typical features of the genre or with others of its kind. If you think that the original trilogy is a better, more challenging set of movies about "a galaxy far, far away" than the later trilogy, for example, you are comparing these films not just to each other but also to an ideal model of the good science fiction films as allegories of humanity, a model that values complexity over, say, entertainment and special effects.

Your evaluation of aesthetic strengths and weaknesses will be most effective when you use both comparison and coherence as your criteria.

Practical standard When you use the practical standard of evaluation, your main criteria are feasibility and usefulness. These are the key questions:

- Will this work?
- Will it be useful?
- Does it have a relevant application?

In "The Missing Piece to the Gang-Violence Debate" (Readings), Dan Gardner argues that the Conservative and Liberal proposals "to deal with gang crime by, yet again, increasing law enforcement and boosting sentences" (235) will simply fail, and thus make the situation worse. This argument uses the practical standard of evaluation: we may support more enforcement for moral reasons, but this method does not work.

Practical judgments connect the thing being evaluated (such as a school board, a law, a product, or a proposed action) with the social situation or context in which it will be applied or the purpose it will serve. You will produce the most effective practical evaluations by considering as many aspects of the context as possible. Ask yourself questions like these: Who benefits? In what ways? What will this help us to do? How much will it cost? How long will it take? What are the long-term and short-term effects?

- For example, if you were evaluating a plan to reduce summer holidays for schoolchildren to one month, you might note that the shortened vacation period could make it difficult for working parents to take holidays at the same time. On the other hand, the shorter holiday would decrease the amount of time teachers need to spend reviewing what students have forgotten and would use schools' physical plants more efficiently. Weighing these practical advantages and disadvantages against each other could lead you to a very effective judgment.

Ethical standard When you use the ethical standard, you judge an object's worth according to *moral, ideological,* or *religious* values. Ask questions like these:

- Is this right or wrong?
- Is this a position worth believing in?
- Is this a course of action worth following?

When you evaluate from a moral perspective, you judge whether something is right or wrong according to a set of principles about the values that should govern behaviour. Sometimes moral principles conflict. For one person, telling a lie may be good if the lie benefits more people than it hurts; for another, telling a lie is always bad because lying damages a person's integrity.

When you evaluate from an ideological perspective, you judge by a set of social principles. Social principles, like moral principles, can conflict. For example, an environmentally conscious person might argue that shopping at big-box stores is socially destructive. From a practical point of view, shopping at such stores might be convenient, but her argument is based on the ideological conviction that healthy societies are based on local production and distribution.

When you evaluate from a religious perspective, you base your judgments on the doctrines of a particular religious group. Many Roman Catholics, for example, would argue against abortion on religious grounds, just as many Jehovah's Witnesses would object to blood transfusions for religious reasons. Religious principles, like moral and social principles, may conflict over particular issues.

Values may conflict not only within each of these perspectives, but also between perspectives. For example, a person may download music from the internet, knowing that it is morally wrong to acquire copyrighted material in a way that does not benefit the artists who produced the music. The person may justify or rationalize this act by arguing that the internet represents a new kind of information sharing where copyright is less important than exposure. Therefore, the person privileges an ideological perspective (the internet benefits artists through exposure) over a moral viewpoint (it is wrong to download copyrighted materials).

Because of the wide range of values people hold, you need to take special care when you evaluate issues from an ethical perspective. Few readers are likely to accept your judgment of strengths and weaknesses simply because your system of values supports it ("Big-box stores are wrong because environmentalists say so"). Try to be aware of your own system of values and make sure those values are appropriate to your subject. Your argument will be stronger if you acknowledge ethical positions that differ from your own.

Using more than one standard of evaluation Many issues invite evaluation from more than one standard of evaluation. Some could be evaluated from all four standards that we have discussed—logical, aesthetic, practical, and ethical. You will be able to give a more balanced assessment if you gather material using all relevant standards. Your decision about which of these to include in your final essay will depend on the assignment, the subject, your own position, and the audience. It may also depend on how confident you are about handling several standards.

- If you were evaluating a film script for possible production, you might begin with its artistic merits (aesthetic standard), but you would also need to consider its audience appeal and the production costs (practical standard). If the content was potentially objectionable or offensive, you might also assess its moral strengths and weaknesses (ethical standard).

- The sample topic on same-sex marriage does not indicate a standard of evaluation. Logical and aesthetic standards are not relevant to the subject. You decide to try ethical and practical standards. Your decision to try these standards is strengthened by your defining of context in Step 1, where you noted that the institutions involved in this topic include the church, usually associated with the ethical standard, and the state, usually associated with the practical standard.

STAGE 2   Gathering Material

STEP 1   Analyzing

If you are clear on your standard of evaluation and think you know your position on an issue, you may be tempted to skip analysis and plunge straight into evaluation. We advise you not to skip the earlier step. The process of analysis will lead you to examine more aspects of your subject, which will give you stronger arguments for your position and a greater awareness of the counter-arguments. It will also provide you with the details to make your arguments convincing.

To analyze, you need to find appropriate categories for dividing your subject into parts. The methods of analysis described in Chapter 3 (cause/effect, process, and systems analysis) will provide appropriate categories for analyzing a broad range of issues. The disciplinary categories of analysis for English described in Chapter 6, Writing Essays on Literature, will help you analyze subjects that you will evaluate by the aesthetic standard.

You can also use the standards of evaluation themselves to gather material by asking questions such as these:

- What ethical issues does this subject raise? For whom?
- What practical issues does this subject raise? For whom?

- What aesthetic issues does this subject raise? For whom?
- How valid are the arguments given about this issue? (See Chapter 8 for detailed guidelines on evaluating arguments and evidence.)

To see how you would choose categories of analysis and put them to use, let's consider the sample topic on same-sex marriage.

- The sample topic asks, "How should Canadian institutions respond to same-sex marriages?" Institutions could respond in three possible ways: by continuing to support legal same-sex marriage; by seeking to reverse legalization; or by seeking a compromise (to do nothing would have the same result as accepting the legality of same-sex marriage). As a result of defining the key terms, you would be aware that the institutions involved in questions of marriage are the federal and provincial governments (the lawmakers) and the churches. To these categories you might add the category of society, since social views often influence the actions of church and state. If you were to brainstorm about the ethical and practical issues raised for each of these groups, you might come up with the following list:

CHURCH	Opposes because of literal reading of scriptures
	Supports because progressive positions draw younger people in
	Supports because all churchgoers are "children of God"
	Supports so as not to alienate gay and lesbian churchgoers
	Opposes so as not to alienate backbone members of church and traditionalist clergy
SOCIETY	Opposition from traditionalists who value traditional two-parent family
	Support from pluralists who recognize present diversity of Canadian society and/or support value of pluralism
STATE	Support indicated by current legislation
	Opposition indicated by proposal for free vote in 2005

STEP 2   Categorizing Strengths and Weaknesses

After you have gathered material through analytic categories, you are ready to evaluate it using the appropriate standard(s) of evaluation. You first organize the material you have gathered into appropriate evaluative categories (such as strengths and weaknesses, advantages and disadvantages, arguments for and against) and then group entries within each category according to the standard of evaluation they represent.

- For the sample topic, you could categorize the points that indicate support for same-sex marriages as *arguments for* and points that indicate opposition as *arguments against*. You would group points within each category according to the ethical and practical standards you used in brainstorming. You would come up with the following table:

CATEGORIZING ARGUMENTS	ARGUMENTS FOR	ARGUMENTS AGAINST
CHURCH	Ethical: acceptance of all as "children of God"	Ethical: condemnation through literal reading of scriptures
	Practical: value of attracting young people	Practical: value of not alienating traditionalist members and clergy
	Practical: value of not alienating gay and lesbian members	
SOCIETY	Ethical: value of pluralism	Ethical: traditionalist value of two-parent families
	Practical: accepting Canadian reality as pluralistic	
STATE	Practical: Civil Marriage Act now in place	Practical: some political opposition exists
	Practical: legalization reflects social consensus	

STAGE 3 Formulating an Evaluative Thesis Statement

The general procedure in formulating a thesis is to identify the pattern created by the material in your categories, considered as a response to a specific essay assignment. As we pointed out in Chapter 8, the distinctive components of an evaluation thesis are an opinion about the relationship between strengths and weaknesses, an outlining of the support for this opinion, and an indication of the standard(s) of evaluation you have used.

If you are evaluating a subject about which you have an open mind, you may arrive at your opinion about the relationship between strengths and weaknesses by simply noting which category contains more points.

- Looking at the pattern of arguments for the sample topic on same-sex marriage, for instance, you might conclude that though ethical issues are fairly well balanced, the practical arguments for church and state to support same-sex marriage outweigh the practical arguments against that position. So you would write a tentative thesis statement that reflects this judgment.

Tentative thesis statement (sample topic)	Though there are serious reasons why voices in the state and especially the church resist same-sex marriages, there are better reasons to endorse not only the practical legal solution represented by the Civil Marriage Act, but also the value of church marriage for same-sex couples, a value that is social and ethical as well as practical.

As we mentioned earlier, our thinking about evaluative questions is shaped by our own values. Underlying this seemingly disinterested weighing of arguments, as you will see by reading the relevant persuasive sample essay (E. Jones, "Same-Sex Marriages: Tradition and Change" [Readings: Sample Essays]), is an ideological belief in the value of pluralism. Nevertheless, this thesis statement lays the foundation for an effective persuasive essay because it takes opposing points of view into account. This is a key consideration when you are writing for a hostile audience or, as in most academic situations, a neutral audience. These readers will be more likely to consider your position if you are fair-minded in the way you present it.

The process of analysis may lead you to change your ideas about an issue by forcing you to consider positions different from your own. On the other hand, what happens if the opposing arguments seem stronger or more numerous than your deeply held beliefs about an issue? What do you do then? If you were writing for a friendly audience, one that shared your views, you might downplay or ignore other points of view. This tactic is not an option when you write in an academic situation, where the burden of proof is on you. You must take other positions into account while putting forward the strongest possible case for your own.

- Let's consider how you might formulate an evaluative thesis statement for the sample topic if you were opposed to same-sex marriage on religious grounds. You might, for example, concede that there are strong practical arguments for institutions to support same-sex unions, even as you argue that ethical considerations are more important. Furthermore, you might conclude that within the ethical standard, religious arguments outweigh ideological arguments. That would leave you with two opposing religious views: the belief that all human beings are "children of God," and therefore to be treated equally, as an argument for; and the belief that scripture condemns same-sex relationships, and therefore sanctioning same-sex unions would be morally wrong, as an argument against. In trying to balance these opposing views, you might formulate a tentative thesis statement like this:

Tentative thesis statement (countering strong opposing arguments)	While there are strong practical arguments for allowing same-sex marriages, practical considerations should not persuade church and government officials to sanction behaviour that is morally wrong, as is currently the case. We may all be "children of God," but God has laid down the kind of behaviour He expects from His children in the Bible, and the Bible explicitly condemns same-sex relationships.

This thesis statement takes other views into account, but you would have great difficulty in making the argument convincing to neutral or hostile readers because many of them would not agree with the basic premise that the Bible is an appropriate guide to human behaviour.

You may also need to give special attention to formulating a thesis statement when you are both comparing and evaluating, and to presenting the relationship between strengths and weaknesses when both are relatively strong. The following example, using the third assignment from the list at the beginning of the chapter, shows how you might achieve both goals:

Tentative thesis statement (comparative and balanced evaluation)	Although the more recent *Star Wars* trilogy has dazzling special effects and exciting action sequences, the original trilogy has superior acting, character development, and ideological critique to demonstrate the conflicts of power between good and evil as a commentary on national, political, and religious interests in our own world.

STAGE 4 Drafting: Working Out a Pro-Con Outline

Formulating a thesis statement completes the work of clarifying your own position on the subject you are examining. In writing your draft you shift your focus more fully to persuasion, finding strategies that will help to convince your readers to agree with your position. The most powerful tool for achieving this goal is known as *pro–con structure*.

Pro and *con* are the Latin words for *for* and *against*. The side you have decided is stronger (whether strengths or weaknesses, arguments for or arguments against) becomes the pro argument; the weaker side becomes the con argument.

- For example, if you had formulated a thesis statement asserting that the film you were reviewing had more weaknesses than strengths, your pro argument would be something like "This is a poorly written film," and your list of weaknesses would support this position. The con argument would be "This film has some strengths," an opinion supported by your list of strengths.

The principle of pro–con structure is that you systematically present the arguments against your case, conceding (admitting) their validity or refuting (arguing against) them, and then present the arguments for your case. The idea is that readers hostile to your case, or predisposed against any particular argument (likely even for neutral readers), will be more persuaded by seeing their views taken seriously before you develop your own position.

Pro–con structure may be unnecessary or inadvisable when your purpose is to reinforce the values of a friendly audience rather than to discuss them, such as when you are writing articles for your own political party. Academic writing, as we said earlier, always assumes readers need to be convinced.

There are two main ways to organize a pro–con essay:

1. State all the con arguments in a paragraph or two at the beginning of your essay, deal with these arguments, and then devote the rest of the essay to the pro arguments. This method works best for neutral (academic) readers or when strengths outweigh weaknesses, or vice versa.

   - If you were reviewing the original *Star Wars* trilogy, for example, you might concede that the special effects are not as compelling as those of the contemporary films and then go on to discuss the many strengths of the films.

2. Answer the arguments against your position point by point throughout your essay. This method is a better choice when your readers may be hostile or when there are strong arguments on both sides.

Taking con arguments into account does not mean you have to refute them all. If you concede the validity of some of the points—admit they are right or reasonable—you show more maturity and are therefore likely to be more persuasive.

You will find a draft outline invaluable for working out pro–con structure. Follow the sequence of topics and points indicated in your thesis statement. To help you keep track of your overall argument, note whether points are pro or con and what standard of evaluation they are based on. Leave spaces to record any changes you decide to make when you revise.

- The draft outline for the sample topic would look something like this (MP stands for middle paragraph):

DRAFT OUTLINE

TOPIC	POINT	REVISION NOTES
INTRODUCTION		
MP1 SOCIETY	**Con** (ETH): Traditionalists value two-parent families **Pro** (ETH): Value of pluralism	
MP2 STATE	**Pro** (PRAC): Legislation provides needed legal protection and helps society **Pro** (ETH): Legal protection has an ethical dimension	
MP3 CHURCH	**Con** (ETH): Historical scriptures condemn same-sex relations **Pro** (ETH): Progressive valuation of equality also part of doctrines	
MP4 CHURCH	**Con** (PRAC): Danger of outraging traditionalists **Pro** (PRAC): Danger of outraging gay and lesbian churchgoers; value of attracting younger generation and dealing with the changed world	
CONCLUSION		

STAGE 5   Revising Thesis Statement and Essay Structure

**STEP 1   Revising Your Thesis Statement: Checking
for an Evaluative Point**

If you have followed all the steps in gathering material and formulating a thesis, your thesis statement should present, in a reasonable and fair-minded way,

- your opinion about the relationship between strengths and weaknesses;
- your support for this opinion;
- an indication of the standards of evaluation you have used.

If your thesis statement is weak, you may have allowed strong opinions to carry you away, as in the first example below, or you may have ignored evidence contrary to your position, as in the second example.

Weak thesis statements
- The reasons people give for resisting same-sex marriages are nonsense; if they had any sense, they would endorse not only the current legislation but also church marriages for same-sex couples. [No relationship between strengths and weaknesses, no support, no standard of evaluation]
- Though there are just as many ethical reasons to support same-sex marriages as to oppose them, the institutionalization of such marriages is simply unacceptable. [Support contradicts opinion]

The tentative thesis statement for the sample topic that you formulated earlier, however, meets all the requirements for an effective evaluative thesis. But when you check your indication of standards of evaluation, you notice that in your last outline you have come up with an ethical standard linked to the state. You also believe you can make your case more sympathetic to a neutral audience by eliminating the formality of referring to "voices in the state" and to the Civil Marriage Act. Rewritten, the thesis runs as follows:

Writing Sample

Effective thesis statement (sample topic)
Though there are serious reasons behind the resistance to same-sex marriage, there are better practical and ethical reasons for both church and state to endorse not only legal marriages but also church ceremonies for same-sex couples.

STEP 2 ## Revising Essay Structure: Checking Sequence and Pro-Con Transitions

You will find it useful in revising essay structure to turn your draft outline into a revision outline by identifying the points you made, as opposed to those you intended to make, and then checking for these key elements of persuasive structure:

- Have you presented your arguments in an *order of ascending interest*, ending with the most important?

- If you have used a *pro–con structure*, have you dealt with con points first and then presented the pro points, either in the essay as a whole or paragraph by paragraph?

- Do you need to *add paragraphs* in order to define terms or to make transitions from one section of your argument to another?

- Are the *transitions* between strengths and weaknesses clear in the movement *between* paragraphs?

- Do individual paragraphs reveal problems with *internal transitions* or other problems that you will need to address in the next stage of revision?

Problems in persuasive structure generally come from the difficulties writers have in distinguishing strengths from weaknesses or pro arguments from con arguments. The solution lies in learning to make the multiple transitions a good persuasive essay requires. Let us look at this issue of transitions in more detail.

In a sense, your whole essay is in transition toward your most important argument. You end with this point so that its impact is greatest on your readers. This movement will be impeded and the impact lessened if you have not dealt with the con points you have raised—or if readers are aware of points you should have raised but have not. Check to make sure you have put con points first, and responded to them, before you present your pro points.

The placement of points is not the only issue, however. The movement between paragraphs must be clearly marked by transitions so that readers know when they are moving to a paragraph beginning with a con argument, or a paragraph of definition, or a paragraph offering another aspect of the issue. (You will find additional information on this subject in Part 3, D Writing Better Paragraphs.)

- In reviewing the draft for the sample assignment, you might find that the biggest problem is the lack of transition between sections of your argument. You might decide to add both a paragraph of definition and a transition paragraph to ensure a more deliberate movement between state and church. You would note these changes in the revision column of your draft outline. The abbreviated outline below illustrates the revised essay structure (MP stands for middle paragraph).

DRAFT OUTLINE

TOPIC	REVISION NOTES
INTRODUCTION	
MP 1 SOCIETY	Definitions
MP 2 STATE	SOCIETY
MP 3 CHURCH	STATE
MP 4 CHURCH	Transition
MP 5	CHURCH
MP 6	CHURCH
CONCLUSION	

STAGE 6   Revising Individual Paragraphs

STEP 1   Revising Your Introduction: *Ethos*

If *ethos*—the image a writer projects of him or herself—is important in writing introductions to critique essays, as we suggested in Chapter 8, it is even more important in persuasive essays, where readers' responses are likely to be governed by deep beliefs and emotions. The goal is to present yourself as committed but fair-minded. If you present yourself as so dogmatic that you have no sympathy for or understanding of other views, then you are unlikely to convince readers who disagree with you.

In an academic situation, where open-minded critical thinking is valued, introductory sentences like the examples below may bias the reader against your essay.

Weak introductory sentences

- Things have changed. These days both marriage partners may be wearing a tuxedo. This is the new reality. Better get used to it.

- The bureaucratic mind is known for its selfishness and stupidity, and recently it has come up with a proposal with just these qualities, the proposal to reduce school holidays to a month and force hard-working teachers to work twice as hard as before.

- I like the more recent *Star Wars* trilogy. It has great action sequences and killer special effects. I know you will like it too. I have not met anyone who disliked these films.

The need to avoid obviously biased comments does not mean you should use deceit or conceal your position. It means that you should precede your thesis statement either with something likely to appeal to all readers or with something that establishes neutral ground, such as questions about the subject that you do not immediately answer.

- In the draft for the sample assignment, the thesis statement is preceded merely with a question:

Draft introductory comment

How do you think Canadian institutions should respond to the current status of same-sex marriages in Canada?

This is a good question to establish neutral ground, but since there is still a good deal of prejudice in certain circles against same-sex couples, hostile readers might have an immediate negative answer. So you might decide to open with a neutral explanation of what the current status of same-sex marriage actually is, in terms of institutional response.

You can read the resulting introduction in E. Jones, "Same-Sex Marriages: Tradition and Change" (Readings: Sample Essays)—an essay that was written shortly after the passing of the Civil Marriage Act in Canada.

STEP 2   Revising Middle Paragraphs: Logic and Transitions

You may have identified problematic middle paragraphs in your review of essay structure. If not, now is the time to evaluate each middle paragraph and revise as necessary.

When you check middle paragraphs, make sure that

- each paragraph contains topic, point, and detail that support your thesis;
- you have used words, phrases, and sentences to identify pro and con arguments and to create clear transitions between these

arguments, and between the arguments and the detail that supports them;

- your arguments and evidence are valid.

Earlier we mentioned that problems in middle paragraphs arise from the difficulty of handling transitions within a pro–con structure. This statement is true, but often problems in transitions stem from problems in logic. We have said little about the logical standard in this chapter, but of course many persuasive essays use the logical standard in combination with aesthetic, ethical, or practical standards. Whether you have used the logical standard or not, your readers will expect your own arguments and evidence to be free of errors in logic (see Chapter 8, Stage 2, Step 2: Identifying Strengths and Weaknesses [Fallacies] in Logic).

- The following paragraph from the sample assignment exhibits typical problems with logic and transitions:

Draft middle paragraph
There is an ethical difficulty churches face in marrying same-sex couples. Their scriptures teach love and respect, though, and the spirit of inclusiveness. This is a time of sectarianism, and the spirit of inclusiveness is exactly what we need. The churches should speak out. Churches that make same-sex couples fully participating members of their own congregations send a powerful message of inclusion to society as a whole.

This paragraph meets some of the logical requirements for arguments and evidence: most church scriptures do teach love and respect, and the final argument seems reasonable. The paragraph has significant omissions, however: our era is not just a sectarian one; church scriptures teach other things besides love and respect; and the con argument announced by the topic sentence (which does not sum up the paragraph) is never developed. You could revise by first presenting the con argument about scriptures denouncing same-sex unions, then presenting a balanced statement about the literal versus the "spirit" interpretation of scripture as transition, and concluding with your pro argument about the message inclusiveness would send. The resulting paragraph is the sixth paragraph in E. Jones, "Same-Sex Marriages: Tradition and Change" (Readings: Sample Essays).

STEP 3   Revising Your Conclusion: Achieving Balance

As we pointed out in Chapter 8, you should have the same concern for *ethos* in your conclusion as in your introduction. To demonstrate your fair-mindedness in the conclusion, you include the con position as well as the

pro position, though you do so in a way that reinforces rather than under-
mines your argument. Thus in revising your conclusion you check for

- a summary and expansion of your thesis statement that refers to
  both strengths and weaknesses, to the relationship between them,
  and to the supporting topics;
- a statement of broader implications that does not dismiss the weak
  side of the case but emphasizes the implications of the strong side.

To see how you might achieve this kind of balance, consider the draft
conclusion for the sample assignment:

Draft conclusion   If true leadership involves finding the best way to promote ongoing virtues in changing
circumstances, then it seems valid to urge church and state to exercise leadership by recognizing the ethical and practical value of not only legal marriages but also church weddings
for same-sex couples.

This conclusion provides a good summary of the pro argument and
expands its implications into the domain of leadership. It does not refer to
the weak side of the case, however; nor does it incorporate this weak side
into a clear statement of broader implications. In looking back over your
essay, you might realize that the desire of gays and lesbians for an institutional recognition of love and commitment represents a continuation of
a traditional value. This point, which balances your case that leadership
involves the recognition of change, would make a good starting place for
your conclusion. For the revised version, see the final paragraph of E. Jones,
"Same-Sex Marriages: Tradition and Change" (Readings: Sample Essays).

For other examples of student-written persuasive essays, see James Ash,
"To Peacekeep or Not to Peacekeep" and Joyce MacDonald, "The Problem
of Environmental Costs: Suzuki vs. Merwin" in Part 2, Readings: Sample
Essays.

Working on Your Own Assignment

Your main goal in writing and revising a persuasive essay is to work out
your position and then persuade your readers to agree with it.

- Find a standard or standards of evaluation either in the assignment
  or in the process of gathering material.
- Analyze your subject by choosing appropriate categories and gathering material in them.

- Identify strengths and weaknesses by applying the appropriate standard(s) of evaluation to the material in your categories.
- Formulate a thesis that states an opinion about the relationship between strengths and weaknesses, gives reasons to support your opinion, and indicates your standard(s) of evaluation.
- Construct a draft outline according to the principle of pro–con structure and write the draft.
- Check the draft by means of a revision outline for problems in thesis statement, pro–con structure, and transitions.
- Check the introduction and conclusion for fair-mindedness; check middle paragraphs for problems in transition and logic.

Exercises

A. Identify the standard(s) of evaluation implied or stated in each of the following essay topics.

1. James Thurber's "The Catbird Seat" and Ernest Hemingway's "The Short Happy Life of Francis Macomber" are both stories about manhood. Which uses setting and characterization more effectively in conveying a theme about this subject?
2. Choose one of the educational theories we have discussed this term and evaluate whether or not it could be successfully used in either science or arts classes in your local high school.
3. Is the term *sustainable growth* an oxymoron in the twenty-first century?
4. Discuss whether feminism still remains a reasonable system of beliefs for contemporary women to adopt.

B. Write a sentence or two evaluating the following as thesis statements for persuasive essays.

1. People describe terrorism as a complex issue. What's complex about it? You have to fight terrorism by every means available; force is the only language terrorists understand.
2. It is clear that, on moral grounds, we should have the right to interfere with customs and practices of other cultures when these customs clearly degrade one or more classes of people. Other cultures have important reasons for their customs, though; these customs are often central to their religious beliefs.
3. Lenore Keeshig-Tobias's essay "He Was a Boxer When I Was Small" (Readings) is really effective in conveying the complexities of a father-daughter relationship. It's nice to read something written by an Aboriginal writer.

C.   Decide what point the writer of the following paragraph is trying to prove. State that point in a topic sentence. Then reorganize the paragraph, putting the con arguments first and the pro arguments second. Compare your paragraph with the paragraphs of other class members.

> Cellphones can save lives in emergencies. If your car breaks down at 3:00 a.m. on an isolated road, you can phone for help and let your family know that you will be late. Loud conversations by people using cellphones drive restaurant customers sitting at nearby tables crazy. The ringing of cellphones can destroy the climax of any movie. Cellphones are a great way to give a teenager both safety and more freedom. Drivers who talk or text on their cellphones while making a left turn are a menace on the roads.

D.   Choose a controversial issue and work out your own position on this issue by following the steps in this chapter for finding a standard of evaluation, gathering material, and formulating a thesis statement. Then make a draft outline indicating the sequence in which you would present the arguments for and against your position.

Gathering Material for Research Essays (10)

Sample Topic: Margaret Laurence's "The Loons"

While different academic disciplines may have their own methods for conducting research and presenting their findings, the creation of new knowledge through research is a central activity of every discipline. Within each discipline, primary research may range from field work to laboratory work to textual work such as analyzing, interpreting, and synthesizing information. For example, sociologists can study daily workplace behaviour, or they can run controlled experiments that alter variables in the workplace environment. Furthermore, they can study all the published research on past experiments and methods, and develop new models for learning about workplace behaviour. The results of all these different kinds of research are made known to other researchers and to the general public through scholarly books and articles, the professional forms of research essays.

It is important to understand the difference between a survey of research and a research essay. In disciplines such as psychology and sociology, a research assignment may ask you to do a literature survey on a particular topic, such as depression among the elderly or youth unemployment. A literature survey requires you to examine the available scholarly publications and report on their scope and content, often without offering an interpretation or synthesis of those materials. By contrast, a research essay requires you to work out a thesis about the topic in relation to the available materials.

Although research projects may seem intimidating, research essays are quite similar to analysis, comparison, and persuasive essays. The basic principles of essay structure remain the same. The main difference is that in writing a research essay, you use secondary materials to complement the essay's overall purpose.

Research and research essays have three main purposes. They allow you

- to acquire information about a particular subject;
- to become familiar with the current conventions and knowledge base of a discipline;
- to add to existing knowledge by offering your own opinion or ideas.

Each successive purpose builds on the preceding one. For example, if your philosophy instructor asked you to write a six-page research essay on violence, you would begin by acquiring information. In your library, you would find numerous books and articles addressing this topic from different perspectives. Since your assignment is for a philosophy course, you select materials on violence primarily from within that discipline. In reviewing these books and articles, you realize that the authors have different, if not conflicting, viewpoints and arguments about violence. You agree with some and disagree with others. You then think through the different perspectives and offer your own interpretation, opinion, or understanding of violence.

This is the basic process of research that we examine in this chapter. The next chapter will focus on writing and revising the research essay. Both chapters refer to a sample topic on Margaret Laurence's short story "The Loons" (Readings). You will better understand the procedures outlined here if you read the story first.

STAGE 1   Clarifying Research Topics

Research assignments are generally handed out at least a month before the assignment is due for good reason: research takes time. Allow at least two to three weeks to think about your topic, find material, write a draft, and revise it.

STEP 1   Understanding Directions

As soon as you receive a research assignment, make sure you understand the meaning of each possible topic, your instructor's particular requirements, and the relation between primary and secondary sources.

Specialized terms Since research assignments are usually on specialized topics, you should be alert to the specialized use of terms. For example, *narcissism* in a psychology assignment means something more specific than its popular meaning of egotism or self-absorption.

Specific requirements The way instructors phrase assignments can vary considerably. Some instructors offer broad research questions such as "Write a research essay on the debates about AIDS drugs in African countries." Other instructors give narrowly defined topics with precise guidelines about research materials, essay structure, and documentation. Some instructors may ask for a preliminary report before the final copy of the essay is due in order to ensure that you are on the right track. Take careful note of any instructions.

Primary and secondary sources Most instructors will expect you to integrate *your* views about your subject with the commentary of other writers. If your subject is something you know little or nothing about, such as, perhaps, "the debates about AIDS drugs in African countries," you would arrive at your own view by analyzing and evaluating the arguments you find in *secondary sources* (such as books and articles about the subject). On the other hand, if your subject is a *primary source* (such as a literary work you have read or a performance you have seen), you would work out your own ideas before consulting secondary sources.

Sample Topic

To demonstrate how you might work through the above aspects of Step 1, we will consider the following assignments for a 1500 word research essay on Margaret Laurence's short story "The Loons" for a first-year English class:

1. Write a research essay that examines how Margaret Laurence develops the relationship between Vanessa and Piquette in her short story "The Loons."

2. In Margaret Laurence's short story "The Loons," Vanessa says that Piquette and her family "were actually Indians, or as near as made no difference." Write a research essay that explores how Laurence treats race and race relations through the characters of Vanessa and Piquette.

3. Near the end of Margaret Laurence's short story "The Loons," Vanessa learns of Piquette's death and thinks that "As so often with Piquette, there did not seem to be anything to say." Earlier in the story, when Jules or Lazarus would get into conflict in the town, the Mounties would put them in jail "and the next morning they would be quiet again." Both the Tonnerre and MacLeod families experience silence. Write a research essay that analyzes the different types of silence in this story. You must incorporate at least three secondary sources into your essay. All quotations and citations must be in MLA format.

Notice that the primary material in each assignment is the same: Margaret Laurence's story "The Loons." The subjects are different, however; subjects vary from the depiction of a relationship to the treatment of race to the meanings of silence in the story. While only the third assignment outlines the number of secondary sources and the documentation style, you would need to use and document secondary sources in the other assignments as well. Instructors may cover this material in class or in supplementary handouts rather than in the initial assignment.

STEP 2   Choosing a Topic

It is important to think through the demands of an assignment rather than choose a topic on the basis of surface impressions. The topic that looks the easiest will not necessarily be the easiest one for you to write about. You will have a better experience writing about something you find enjoyable rather than something you find a bore. So if your assignment has different options for research, select the topic that most interests you. If your assignment does not have options but has a broad scope, ask yourself which particular area of the subject you would like to know more about. If the topic interests you, you will find yourself thinking about it even when you are not directly working on your project.

Sample Topic

In the list of sample assignments above, the first assignment about the "relationship" between Vanessa and Piquette may appear to be the easiest because you are required to write about only one thing, not several things. However, even one thing can be quite complicated. How many factors enter into a relationship? Race is mentioned in the second assignment (Vanessa is white, Piquette is Métis), and so you begin to think about how race might influence the relationship. There are also differences in age, social status, and family composition. You begin to see that this topic requires you to consider different types of relationships in the same way that the third topic requires you to consider "different types of silence."

STEP 3   Defining a Preliminary Research Question

The number and variety of secondary materials available on almost any topic make researching and writing a research essay a challenge. Both tasks will be easier if you make sure your topic is manageable within the specified length of the assignment. One good strategy is to brainstorm by asking questions about your subject. From these questions, choose one that seems central to the subject (and that interests you) as your preliminary research question. We call this a *preliminary question* because it comes before you have systematically analyzed either your primary material or your secondary sources. Focusing on your preliminary research question will help you decide which secondary sources are most relevant; it will also guide you toward a clear position about one important area of your subject.

For example, if you received a political science assignment to research the conflict in the Darfur region of Sudan, you might ask questions like these: Was the conflict religiously motivated? Was the conflict racially motivated? What was the response of the international community? What were the effects on families and children? While you could conceivably try to answer all these questions in a research essay, taking one as your preliminary research question and searching for an answer would produce a more focused essay.

Sample Topic

To see how you would define a preliminary research question, let us suppose you choose the first of the sample assignments on "The Loons."

Brainstorming, you come up with the following questions: What is the relationship between Vanessa and Piquette? Is there much actual relationship when Piquette's presence in Vanessa's life is so minimal? Is it the relationship in Vanessa's head that is most important? If so, does this relationship change?

This last question in particular interests you because you notice that Laurence shows Vanessa's views of Piquette at three different ages, creating a passage of time that is unusually long for a short story. It seems reasonable to assume that as Vanessa grows up, she gains a greater understanding both of Piquette and of their relationship, an assumption you can test against the textual evidence of the story. Thus you decide to make this assumption into your preliminary research question: "Does Laurence portray Vanessa as attaining a more mature understanding of Piquette and of their relationship?"

STAGE 2   Finding and Gathering Materials

Once you have defined your preliminary research question, you are ready for the second stage of the research process: analyzing your primary source(s), if any; acquiring information and ideas from secondary sources; and then developing your own point of view by analyzing the relationship among your source materials.

STEP 1   Gathering Material from Primary Sources

If the starting point for your research essay is one or more primary sources (such as literary works and other written documents, or performances, experiments, or interviews), you need to know what you think about the primary source(s) before you can deal effectively with secondary sources. Working out your ideas requires choosing a method of analysis (usually systems analysis for essays on literature) and choosing disciplinary or analytic categories. We explain methods of analysis in Chapter 3, and disciplinary and analytic categories in Chapters 3 through 6. Remember that disciplinary categories are terms specific to the field of study. In English, you might consider categories such as genre, figurative language, or a specific kind of figurative language, such as metaphor. Analytic categories are your own, based on your analysis of the text. We will use the sample topic to show how a preliminary research question can lead you to the categories you need.

Sample Topic

Your preliminary research question for your assignment on "The Loons" asks whether Margaret Laurence portrays her main character, Vanessa, as achieving a more mature understanding of Piquette and of their relationship. This is a question about characterization, and so a disciplinary category such as characterization will be useful. That Vanessa achieves greater maturity seems possible because of Laurence's use of time in the story, an aspect of narrative structure. When you ask yourself whether Laurence endorses Vanessa's understanding of Piquette, however, you find it hard to be sure because of the point of view: the story is written from the first-person point of view, with detail and judgment coming entirely from Vanessa. Finally, the title emphasizes the significance of the loons on the lake outside the MacLeods' summer cabin, so you add the disciplinary category of figurative language.

Analyzing the story in terms of these categories, you come up with the following chart:

ANALYSIS OF "THE LOONS"

Narrative structure:

Organized around Vanessa's understanding of Piquette at different ages:

- at 11, seeing Piquette as "spr[u]ng from the people of Big Bear and Poundmaker" (261)
- at 15, feeling embarrassment, distance, and a moment of empathy
- at 19, seeing Piquette as perhaps "the only one, after all, who had heard the crying of the loons" (266)

Characterization:

- Vanessa as dynamic character, with changing perceptions of Piquette (we learn little of Piquette's own desires)
- white, middle-class background, educated, daughter of doctor, Scots ancestry
- imaginative, close to father, feels guilty about not befriending Piquette as he wished

Point of view:

- first-person
- enclosed within Vanessa's own perceptions; no authorial comment

Figurative language:

- loons identified by Dr. MacLeod with unpeopled land
- loons identified by Piquette as "squawkin' birds"
- by end of story, loons identified by Vanessa with suffering; Piquette; victims of white development

STEP 2   Forming a Preliminary Opinion

It may be helpful, once you have analyzed any primary material, to see if this material suggests an answer to your preliminary question. This answer will be an opinion on the subject of the assignment that reflects your response to the primary material. It is a preliminary opinion, however, not a tentative thesis: a thesis statement for a research essay also needs to incorporate a response to the range of secondary material. However, having an opinion on the primary material will usually keep you from feeling overwhelmed by the range of opinions in the secondary sources. Keep in mind that you may have to change your opinion substantially once you consider this material.

Sample Topic

Does Laurence portray Vanessa as achieving a more mature understanding of Piquette and of her relationship with the young Métis woman? When you look at your categories of primary material, it concerns you that the point of view makes it hard to assess Laurence's attitude toward Vanessa's perceptions. Nevertheless, your other categories seem to suggest that by the end of the story, Vanessa does develop a more realistic and empathetic understanding. So far, your analysis of the story suggests an affirmative answer to your preliminary research question.

STEP 3   Finding Secondary Sources

When you are writing on topics that do not require analysis of a primary source, such as current political events, topics of general interest, and some academic subjects, you will rely on secondary sources for information and ideas. When your starting point is the analysis of primary material, secondary sources will provide additional information and allow you to test your understanding of your material against the opinions of other writers. What exactly is a secondary source? A secondary source may be an encyclopedia entry, a specialized handbook or dictionary, CD-ROM materials, a book, or an article—in short, anything that is not a primary source but is related to your research question in a meaningful way.

Not all of these types of material are equally useful when you are writing a research essay. Perhaps the most important distinction is between *scholarly* (or **peer-reviewed**) and *non-scholarly* (or non–peer-reviewed) secondary sources. Scholarly sources, which have been reviewed by experts in the field, generally contain more accurate and more reliable information than non-scholarly sources, which have not been reviewed by experts. Using a scholarly source is one way of making an appeal to authority, as discussed in Chapter 8.

There are two main formats for scholarly sources: books and journal articles. A scholarly book may focus on a single subject, or it may address several smaller topics that fall within another category of classification. For example, a literary scholar may publish an entire book on the works of Margaret Laurence or a book on Canadian short stories that includes only one chapter on Margaret Laurence. A collection of scholarly articles, which contains multiple chapters authored by different people on a common subject, may also contain useful information about your subject even if the title does not directly indicate it.

Scholarly journals (often called *periodicals* because they appear periodically, usually between one and four times per year) consist of articles or essays that make public the research findings of experts in a field of study. They are much like magazines; however, where magazines appeal to a general audience, scholarly journals appeal to an expert audience. Because journals are published regularly and quickly, compared to books, they often contain the most up-to-date research in any given field.

Many journals also publish reviews that may help you decide whether a book is relevant to your purpose. If you want to refer to the content of the book in your essay, however, you should generally consult the original, since a review is shaped by the perspective of the reviewer and omits a great deal. Ask your instructor whether or not reviews are acceptable materials for your research essay.

Compiling a working bibliography A working bibliography is a list of potentially useful books, articles, and other material that you put together as you search for secondary sources. You are likely to discover that some of the material is not relevant after all, and that some of it is not available, so you should aim for a working bibliography of fifteen to twenty items. From a preliminary list this size, you are almost sure to find enough good references for your essay. When you encounter a book or article that looks useful, get into the habit of printing, cutting and pasting, or copying down the bibliographic details as well as the library call number. This information will enable you to find the book or journal easily and to complete your Works Cited or References page for your essay. You may also want to make a few notes about why you think the book or article is relevant.

For most books you will require the author, the title, the city of publication, the publisher, and the year of publication. Include the editor(s) for edited books. For most journal articles you will require the author, the title of the article, the title of the journal, the volume (and issue) number of the journal, the year of publication, and the page numbers of the article. To find out exactly what bibliographic information you need for different sources, consult Part 3, H3 Documentation.

There are two main places to locate secondary sources:

- your library catalogue
- online database services

We will also discuss the advantages and disadvantages of internet sources and interlibrary loans.

The library catalogue You may find all the information you need on current events and topics of general interest in the holdings of your local public library. Your school library, which is designed to help students and instructors, will contain much more scholarly information about academic topics. If you want to find single- or multi-author books, your library catalogue is the first place to go.

You can access your school's library catalogue through a computer in the library or from your home computer via the internet. The searchable library catalogue lists all the materials your library physically contains, including books, journals, newspapers, microfilms, microfiches, CDs, CD-ROMs, and so forth.

Searching Although library catalogues vary, most allow you to search by keywords, subjects, and authors. Many also allow you to search by titles, periodical titles, call numbers, or other categories. Keyword and subject searches are probably the most useful for beginning researchers. Knowing what terms to use will help you find relevant materials. This is why it is a good idea to think about your topic *before* you begin to research, as you will have a number of key terms or key ideas to use as search strings. Often, the difficulty is not finding information but finding the right information.

Depending on the size of your school's library, any given search term will return a number of results. Some of the materials may not be relevant to your assignment, however. Rather than working your way through the whole list to find out, you can narrow your search by combining search terms. In Chapter 3, we introduced disciplinary categories as a set of terms that help to define the scope of materials in a particular field of study. The library catalogue is based upon many of these disciplinary categories to allow you to search the catalogue more quickly and easily.

Some catalogues also allow you to truncate or shorten search terms so you can search numerous terms simultaneously. For example, instead of searching separately, you are able to use a term like "Canad*" to search for both "Canada" and "Canadian" or "wom?n" to search for both "women" and "woman." Consult your instructor or the reference librarian for more tips on how to better search the catalogue.

For a demonstration of how to use search terms and narrow your search, see the sample topic at the end of this section.

Online database services Academic journals are excellent research resources because they publish scholarly arguments on precise topics. If you want to find journal articles, the first place to look is the online database services. These services index scholarly and non-scholarly journals and allow you to search the contents of those journals, as well as newspapers and magazines. Some databases index journals for a specific discipline or a few related disciplines: an example is the *MLA International Bibliography,* which includes journals related to literature and literary criticism. Other databases can be very comprehensive. *Academic Search Complete,* for example, covers fields as diverse as chemistry, psychology, and the humanities. Ask your instructor or librarian to tell you what databases are available to you.

- Database searching is similar to searching a library catalogue. You rely on relevant names, concepts, keywords, and disciplinary categories to help you find articles related to your topic. You may need to search multiple databases to find the right information for your topic. Ask your instructor or reference librarian about which databases are most suitable for your research topic.

- The results for database searches may take a number of forms: citation, abstract, full-text HTML, or full-text PDF. Essentially, some databases give you the full text of a journal article, which you can print off, download, save, or email to yourself. Full-text databases are quick and easy to use.

- Non–full-text databases return only a citation (reference) or an abstract (a brief summary) of an article. These databases usually give you details of journal, issue, and page numbers; then you must physically retrieve the journal from your library shelf and read or photocopy the article. Therefore, when searching a non–full-text database, it is important to realize that you need to check the title of the journal in your school's library catalogue to know if your school subscribes to the print journal. If your school does subscribe, you can retrieve the journal from the shelves; if the library does not subscribe, you will need to order the article through interlibrary loan.

- Some databases provide you with both full-text articles and non–full-text articles. As we will explain, it is worth considering both kinds of articles.

Library catalogue and online database searches: advantages and disadvantages At this point you may be tempted to conclude that collecting books and journals is too time-consuming, so you should forget about searching the library catalogue and non–full-text databases. Why can't you just search full-text databases? Consider the strengths and weaknesses of these different methods of research:

- Many online databases include journals only from the 1990s and later; therefore, they do not include any information prior to the first year of indexing. Clearly, every discipline has important research materials prior to the digitalization of knowledge.

- For financial reasons, some journals withhold online access to the most recent months or years of the print version of the journal. Consequently, the most recent information is only available in print form.

- Non–full-text databases can refer you to important information that is not available online. Many important print journals are not included in full-text online databases. Therefore, you should consider print articles as well.

- Most of your library's book holdings are not available in full-text online versions. Books contain some of the best information, so it is important to search through the books in your library. To ignore your library stacks is to ignore one of the most significant sources of information at your disposal. It is becoming increasingly common for books, as well as articles, to be online and available electronically through your school library. Even so, it is important to consider those books that are not available electronically and to look them up in your school's library stacks.

- Some databases include non-scholarly sources. Newspapers and magazines can be valuable resources if you are writing on a subject of general interest. If you are writing on an academic subject, however, you should draw your secondary sources primarily from scholarly books and articles. Some databases allow you to limit your searches to scholarly sources; some do not. In either case, you are ultimately responsible for determining the value and reliability of your secondary sources.

The internet The internet is becoming an increasingly valuable tool for researchers and the general public. For many people, it is the starting point to find information. When using the internet (as with any source of information), it is important to consider the source or origin of the information you find. Many academic, professional, and governmental organizations are publishing their materials online for public use, and these are very useful resources. Other sources, probably like your school's library and its database subscriptions, offer online access limited to members within the institution who have exclusive access to helpful resources. Generally speaking, pages like *Wikipedia* or personal blogs are not the most reliable sources of information, as just about anyone can contribute to them. They may or may not be accurate. If you are not sure about a source, consult with your instructor.

Interlibrary loan If you don't find the secondary sources you need by searching your library catalogue and online databases, you may be able to access materials through interlibrary loan. Most college and university libraries are accessible online, and you can search other library catalogues quite easily. Be aware, however, that it may take a week or a few weeks to receive materials through interlibrary loan services. For more information on interlibrary searching, consult your librarian.

Sample Topic

The first step in looking for scholarly secondary materials on Margaret Laurence is searching the library catalogue. If we conducted an author search using Laurence's name, the search would return the titles of books *by* Laurence, not *about* Laurence. Luckily, most catalogues allow you to search a person's name as a *subject* of study rather than as an *author* of the text. For example, searching a college catalogue using "Laurence, Margaret" as the subject (not author) search term returned twelve results. One of these, you discover when you visit the library stacks, is a collection of articles that includes a chapter on "The Loons" by Laurence herself, entitled "Time and the Narrative Voice" (included in Readings). This material will likely prove useful because the author is discussing her own method of composition, and so you photocopy the article and take down the relevant bibliographic information. Provide the information from the source that you are viewing, as information may be available in several places—such as original publications, reprints, or online reproductions. If the source is in print, for example, your citation should specify that medium.

> Laurence, Margaret. "Time and the Narrative Voice." *Margaret Laurence.* Ed. W. H. New. Toronto: McGraw-Hill Ryerson, 1977. 156-60. Print.

Using Laurence's name as a subject on a major university catalogue returned 124 items, far too many to wade through. You can narrow the results by combining search terms. If we think about Margaret Laurence as a writer, she is Canadian, a woman, from Manitoba, writing in the 1960s and 1970s. By combining the terms relevant to Laurence, terms from your class notes, and categories suggested by the story, you might come up with the following chart of possible search terms.

LITERATURE	RACE	AGE	CHARACTER
"The Loons"	Métis	adolescent	development
Laurence, Margaret	Native	youth	narrative
short story	Indian	child	narrator
short fiction	First Nations	maturity	authorial intent
Canada/Canadian	Aboriginal	family	voice
genre	Indigenous	school	point of view
women	white		
A Bird in the House	cultural assimilation		

Let's see what results you might get by combining some of these search terms.

- The four-word search string "Native and women and literature and Canada" yields eight results. Writing down the call numbers of several books, you find one in the stacks that has a whole chapter on "The Loons." This book did not turn up on your subject search of Laurence's name in the library catalogue. You take down the following bibliographic information:

  Acoose, Janice. *Iskwewak—Kah' Ki Yaw Ni Wahkomakanak: Neither Indian Princesses nor Easy Squaws.* Toronto: Women's Press, 1995. Print.

- The three-term string "Native and cultural assimilation and Canada" also yields eight items, one of which offers some interesting historical material about residential schools and the abduction or forced adoption of Aboriginal children in the 1960s and 1970s, the time when Laurence was writing this story. You add this book to your working bibliography:

  Fournier, Suzanne, and Ernie Crey. *Stolen from Our Embrace: The Abduction of First Nations Children and the Restoration of Aboriginal Communities.* Vancouver: Douglas & McIntyre, 1997. Print.

You would follow the same process for searching online databases.

You won't need to search every possible combination of terms to find materials for your project. Choose the most likely. As this last example shows, even material that does not deal directly with your subject may prove useful. It is up to you to make the connections between your secondary sources and your ideas about your primary source.

STEP 4   Evaluating Secondary Sources and Taking Notes

Once you have a significant working bibliography (fifteen to twenty entries), you are ready to read, evaluate, and take notes on your secondary sources. However, you do not have to read the whole of every book and article. Rather, begin by skimming over some of the materials. For example, read the introductory chapter of a book or the abstract or first paragraph of a scholarly essay. If the material looks promising, keep reading. If it looks irrelevant, briefly skim another section or two and then discard the material if it does not suit your essay. Make a note on why you discarded the material in case your research direction changes at a later date and the material becomes relevant.

How do you decide which secondary materials are relevant? Material is relevant if it helps answer your preliminary question. It is relevant if it agrees with your preliminary opinion; it is equally if not more relevant if it expresses different opinions. You are looking for a range of perspectives, not simply opinions that echo your own. From your initial list, choose six to eight of the most relevant sources for closer attention. You may not end up including all of them in your essay, but you should work with as many sources as possible when developing your thesis. Remember as well that you can use secondary sources to address general questions related to your specific area of research and to provide contextual material.

Once you have selected your best sources, read through the materials and isolate the key points that will help you support your ideas or answer your questions. Does this book or article support your opinion? Does it contradict your opinion? Does it necessitate a shift in your thinking? As you read further in any field, you should think about connections between secondary sources. Do you notice any trends? Are there common approaches or common assumptions? Do certain names keep appearing as major figures in the field? Furthermore, as you continue to read, you may find a book or article that makes more or less exactly the case you had in mind. Do not despair. View this as a strength because it demonstrates that you identified an important idea or argument in the field. It is likely that there are different answers to your preliminary question and that you now must recast it in terms of the research.

Occasionally you may find that none of your secondary sources answers exactly the question you are asking. This does not mean that you ask it anyway and dismiss all the secondary commentary as irrelevant. Nor does it mean that you throw away your question and settle for one that has been fully discussed already. Instead, consider whether you could broaden or alter the focus of your question in a way that will allow you to use your secondary material.

One strategy for coming to grips with your secondary sources is to read each book (or, more practically, each relevant chapter) or article once through, reasonably closely but not too slowly. If working from your own print copy, underline or highlight sections you find particularly illuminating. Upon completion, write down what you think is the author's thesis or main point. Also write down your response to this point as well as how you think it might relate to your own opinion.

Then, do a second reading that is much more meticulous. You may come across numerous discipline-specific terms that are unfamiliar to you; as a result, your research materials may seem overly wordy and unnecessarily difficult. It is your responsibility as a good researcher to look up unfamiliar terms either in a standard dictionary or in a specialized dictionary specific to the particular research field. Although this work can be time-consuming, you will find that your research materials will be more useful to you when you understand their complexities and nuances.

As you progress through the reading, keep in mind your idea about the thesis of the work. This focus will help you follow the author's argument in close detail, to understand how he or she arrives at the conclusion. As you work through the second reading, take detailed notes of relevant sections.

- Make sure that your notes are both accurate and precise. In order to avoid plagiarism, you need to distinguish between your ideas and the ideas you use from secondary sources. As you take notes, either summarize the author's ideas in your own words (see Chapter 2) or quote directly from the secondary source (see Part 3, H2 Quotations). When quoting, you must quote materials *exactly* as they appear in the original text. For both summary and quotation, you must include the relevant page number(s) of the materials. You should also include, in square brackets, your evaluation of this material: why is it relevant to your essay? When you begin to write your essay, this approach will help you separate your ideas from the ideas of others.

Sample Topic

Out of the fifteen or so items in your working bibliography, half a dozen present various opinions about Vanessa's relationship with Piquette, so you don't need to modify your preliminary research question. You take more extensive notes on these sources, being particularly careful to be accurate about publication details, quotations, and summaries. You are also careful about adding your own notes on how each critic's thesis relates to your preliminary opinion, putting them in square brackets to distinguish them from the material directly from the critic. Notes on one of these items might look like this:

Acoose, Janice. "Fenced In and Forced to Give Up: Images of Indigenous Women in Selected Non-Indigenous Writers' Fiction." *Iskwewak—Kah' Ki Yaw Ni Wahkomakanak: Neither Indian Princesses nor Easy Squaws.* Toronto: Women's Press, 1995. 69-88. Print.

Thesis: that indigenous women are "misrepresented in non-Indigenous writers' texts" (70) and that W. P. Kinsella and Margaret Laurence participate in this misrepresentation.

[contradicts my claim that Laurence portrays a more mature understanding]

Development of argument: Acoose starts with the case of a young Aboriginal woman being assaulted and murdered, then shows that works by Kinsella and Laurence portray Aboriginal women as either empty and wanton (Kinsella) or worthwhile but helpless victims (Laurence). She then returns to the case of murdered Aboriginal women, suggesting that they are victims of this kind of stereotyping, and urges writers and others to see Aboriginal women as having "strength, determination, and beauty" (88).

Important quotations:

(1) "I urge readers to consider the white constructs of Indigenous women who have been variously portrayed as creatures of nature, temptresses, or femme fatales, Indian princesses easy squaws, or suffering, helpless victims." (74)

[Does the comparison of Piquette to the loons perpetuate this idea of her as a creature of nature and as a helpless victim?]

(2) "In Margaret Laurence's 'The Loons,' protagonist Vanessa MacLeod . . . is a young white christian lower-middle-class girl whose understanding of reality is filtered through a racist, classist, and male-privileged ideological value system. Vanessa is represented as a somewhat autonomous subject, whereas Piquette Tonnerre is represented as a victim who is consistently victimized." (79)

[Contradicts my opinion, suggests Vanessa's viewpoint is static and deluded]

When you have taken detailed notes on all of the secondary sources you have selected for extensive treatment, you are ready to see how these items relate to each other and to your primary material.

STEP 5 Comparing Source Material

Since opinions vary wildly on almost every subject under the sun, your research has likely yielded relevant but differing opinions about your research question. In order to formulate a full research thesis statement, you will need to bring these opinions into relationship with each other and, if you have also analyzed a primary source (or sources), with your preliminary opinion.

If you are working solely with secondary sources, your essential task is that of comparing the opinions expressed in your sources and then figuring out how and why you agree or disagree with each one. You will find this task easier if you make a chart to show matching categories of analysis, like the chart comparing two essays on addiction (see page 103 in Chapter 7).

If you began by analyzing a primary source or sources, you can simply add the secondary source material to the categories you found for the primary material. If you have altered the preliminary question or changed your opinion in the course of your research, you may have to adjust the categories accordingly.

Putting your source material into common categories is the last step in gathering material. We will show how this technique works by referring to the sample topic.

Sample Topic

Among the items you chose for detailed notes was a book on Laurence in which Jon Kertzer argues that "In [Vanessa's] memoir she succeeds in making contact, at least in the sense of understanding and feeling compassion for Piquette's plight, but only after her friend is dead and the loons have vanished"(Kertzer 68) and an article by Peter Easingwood that speaks of Vanessa's "psychological compulsion to question [given] reality" and the "older narrator's . . . recogni[tion of this] compulsion"(Easingwood 126). You also found an article by Laurence herself that claims that Vanessa, hearing of Piquette's death, realizes that "she, too, like the entire town, is in part responsible" ("Time," 271 Readings). These claims for Vanessa's increasing maturation are contradicted by Janice Acoose, whose work we summarized in Step 4. You found support for Acoose's position in a non-literary source, *Stolen from Our Embrace*, a book on the "abduction" of Aboriginal children in which Suzanne Fournier and Ernie Crey argue that the taking away of children was based on the belief that Aboriginal people did not have the strength to be responsible for their own communities. Remembering that articles in academic periodicals often contain the most specific criticism, you have included an article in which Tracy Ware reviews criticism of

"The Loons" and argues that Acoose is correct; while "The Loons" does contain social criticism, he maintains, it also follows a "debased master narrative that regards Natives as victims" (Ware 71). When you map these different opinions onto the categories you devised for the primary material, you come up with the following chart:

"THE LOONS"

Narrative structure

PRIMARY:

Story organized around Vanessa's understanding of Piquette at different ages: at 11, seeing Piquette as "spr[u]ng from the people of Big Bear and Poundmaker," "a daughter of the forest" (261); at 15, feeling embarrassment, distance, and a moment of empathy; at 19, seeing Piquette as perhaps "the only one, after all, who had heard the crying of the loons" (266)

SECONDARY:

Acoose—does not see change in Vanessa's viewpoint

Laurence, Kertzer, Easingwood—Vanessa arrives at responsibility (L), compassion (K), recognition (E)

Ware—Vanessa does change; her "distance from her youthful excesses is the source of most of the [story's] irony" (76)

Characterization

PRIMARY:

Vanessa as middle class, doctor's daughter; also as dynamic character, with changing perceptions of Piquette

SECONDARY:

Acoose—Vanessa as static, transmitter of ideology

Laurence, Kertzer, Easingwood—Vanessa as developing more mature understanding, within limits

Point of view

PRIMARY:

Story told from first-person point of view. Effect: enclosure within Vanessa's own perceptions; no authorial comment.

SECONDARY:

Acoose, Ware: Laurence sees beyond Vanessa's viewpoint, but not far enough to repudiate stereotype of indigenous woman as victim. Fournier and Crey: stereotype of Indian as victim is destructive.

Figurative language

PRIMARY:

Loons identified with unpeopled land (Dr. MacLeod); "squawkin' birds" (Piquette 263); suffering, Piquette, victims of white development (Vanessa at end of story)

SECONDARY:

Acoose's critique of "princess of nature" vision could apply to this identification (81)

Ware: Critics identify Indian and Métis with loons, but so does Laurence

Gadpaille: Identification of Métis with nature makes story a "helpless lament" (qtd. in Ware 80)

This chart allows you to see major similarities and differences among your sources at a glance, and therefore lays the groundwork for formulating your research thesis statement.

Working on Your Own Assignment

Preliminary thinking and writing about your research topic will help you plan and carry out an efficient strategy for gathering material.

- Consider each possible topic carefully to clarify its demands.
- Choose a topic that interests you and narrow your focus to one or two specific research questions.
- Use appropriate methods of analysis and disciplinary or analytic categories (see Chapter 3 and Chapter 6) to gather primary material or explore your topic.
- Compile a working bibliography of secondary sources by using your library's online catalogue and online database services.
- For each secondary source, take down complete bibliographic information.
- For the sources you select to use in your research essay, make detailed notes in point form with short, carefully selected quotations for key ideas. Include page numbers for both quoted and paraphrased material.
- Make a chart that allows you to compare notes from all your research material (primary source[s], if used, as well as secondary sources) within appropriate categories.

Exercises

A. Suppose that you were writing a research paper using one or both of David Suzuki's essays "Food Connections" and "It Always Costs" (Readings) as your primary source material. Write brief responses to each of the following questions. Save your material for possible use in the exercises for Chapter 11.

1. Formulate three different preliminary research questions you might ask in response to one or both of these essays. Then choose the one that most interests you and brainstorm for five minutes about that question.

2. How would you go about searching your library catalogue for material by David Suzuki? For material about David Suzuki?

3. Which online databases in your school library would be most appropriate for finding secondary material on your research question?

4. List five to ten methods of analysis relevant to your research question. Use disciplinary and/or analytic categories as appropriate.

5. List five strings of search terms likely to yield relevant material on your research question. These strings may consist of terms from the methods of analysis you listed above as well as biographic material on David Suzuki (see the opening pages of his two essays in Readings).

B. Suppose that you were writing a research paper using E. B. White's "Once More to the Lake" (Readings) as your primary source. Write brief responses to each of the following questions. Save your material for possible use in the exercises for Chapter 11.

1. Formulate three different preliminary research questions about the literary essay. Then choose the one that most interests you and brainstorm for five minutes about that question.

2. How would you go about searching your library catalogue for material by E. B. White? For material about E. B. White?

3. Which online databases in your school library would be most appropriate for finding secondary material on your research question?

4. List five to ten methods of analysis relevant to your research question. Use disciplinary or analytic categories as appropriate.

5. List five strings of search terms likely to yield relevant material on your research question. These strings may consist of terms from the methods of analysis you listed above as well as biographic material on E. B. White.

C. Make research notes on Margaret Laurence's essay "Time and the Narrative Voice" (Readings) that would be appropriate for the sample research topic.

Works Cited

Acoose, Janice. "Fenced In and Forced to Give Up: Images of Indigenous Women in Selected Non-Indigenous Writers' Fiction." *Iskwewak–Kah' Ki Yaw Ni Wahkomakanak: Neither Indian Princesses nor Easy Squaws*. Toronto: Women's Press, 1995. 69-88. Print.

Easingwood, Peter. "The Realism of Laurence's Semi-Autobiographical Fiction." *Critical Approaches to the Fiction of Margaret Laurence.* Ed. Colin Nicholson. Vancouver: U of British Columbia P, 1990. 119–32. Print.

Fournier, Suzanne, and Ernie Crey. *Stolen from Our Embrace: The Abduction of First Nations Children and the Restoration of Aboriginal Communities.* Vancouver: Douglas & McIntyre, 1997.

Kertzer, Jon. *"That House in Manawaka": Margaret Laurence's* A Bird in the House. Toronto: ECW P, 1992. Print.

Laurence, Margaret. "Time and the Narrative Voice." *Margaret Laurence.* Ed. W. H. New. Toronto: McGraw-Hill Ryerson, 1977. 156–60. Print.

Ware, Tracy. "Race and Conflict in Garner's 'One-Two-Three Little Indians' and Laurence's 'The Loons.'" *Studies in Canadian Literature* 23.2 (1998): 71–84. Print.

Writing Research Essays (11)

Sample Topic: Margaret Laurence's "The Loons"

When you have completed the preliminary stages outlined in Chapter 10, you are ready to compose your research essay. If you have made initial efforts to clarify your own thinking and have taken good notes on the secondary materials, the writing process will be easier than if you have attempted to keep everything in your own mind without writing things down.

This chapter highlights the importance of synthesizing your materials as you formulate a thesis, and as you draft and revise your essay. Synthesis is the combination of different elements into a complex whole. Weak research essays often result from a lack of meaningful connections between ideas or sources, leading to a fragmented or disconnected line of argument. Good research essays, in contrast, establish and develop meaningful links between the research materials, the subject of study, and the writer's viewpoint. As you draft and revise, however, your thinking may change, requiring changes in your thesis statement and essay structure, as the sample topic on Margaret Laurence's "The Loons" will demonstrate. So you also need to have the mental flexibility to make substantial revisions when they are called for.

STAGE 3   Formulating a Research Thesis Statement

Like other essays, a research essay is built upon a thesis statement: your opinion on your subject, supported by reasons. As you work out your draft research thesis statement, you must do so in relation to the research materials you have gathered. Your thesis may be similar to positions outlined in the secondary materials or different from them all. It should not simply echo any of them, however. Even if you agree with one of these positions, you will support your opinion by your own set of reasons. Then your essay will become one voice in a discussion among informed people.

STEP 1   Forming a Research Opinion

Before you formulate the opinion part of your thesis statement, check to see whether your preliminary research question still seems valid or whether it needs adjusting in light of your secondary sources. Then examine the categories you have used to compare your sources. What patterns of response to your research question do you find?

After analyzing case studies of addiction (primary material), for example, you may have decided on the following research question: Is a cognitive model sufficient to explain the causes of addiction? When you review the secondary sources, however, you find few references to cognitive causes and many references to physiological causes, so you change your question to the following: Is a disease model sufficient to explain the causes of addiction? Comparing your primary and secondary material leads you to this research opinion:

Draft research opinion	Academics in medical disciplines find the disease model sufficient, while substance abuse counsellors find this model insufficient, an opinion I share.

STEP 2   Supporting Your Opinion

The support for a thesis opinion usually comes from your own ideas about your subject or your analysis of primary material, along with the secondary sources that confirm your opinion. Since it is hard to combine so much in a single sentence, writers commonly refer to secondary material in a sentence or two preceding the thesis statement. Then they give their own reasons, which represent their distinctive contribution to the discussion, after the thesis opinion.

Remember that this version is not necessarily a final thesis statement. Although you arrived at this thesis statement in a systematic way, you may change your mind or discover new ideas as you draft your research essay and revise it.

Sample Topic

For an example of how you would form a research opinion and support it, let us look at the sample topic on Margaret Laurence's "The Loons" (Readings).

You found secondary sources on "The Loons" that addressed the issue of whether Laurence portrays her main character, Vanessa MacLeod, as gaining a more mature understanding of the young Métis woman, Piquette Tonnerre, so this still seems a valid research question. Your answer has changed, however. On reviewing the patterns in the materials in your chart, you find yourself convinced by the critical positions developed by Janice Acoose, Tracy Ware, and Suzanne Fournier and Ernie Crey. You are persuaded that "The Loons" presents an Aboriginal person as a victim and in doing so reinforces a destructive stereotype. So you revise your preliminary opinion to reflect this change. In a sentence or two leading into this opinion, you summarize the differences among critics as you would for a pro–con argument (see Formulating an Evaluative Thesis Statement in Chapter 9), beginning with the critics you disagree with and ending with the critics you agree with. You then add to your thesis opinion a reference to the disciplinary categories you used in analyzing the story that best supports your position. Your tentative thesis statement would look something like this:

Tentative thesis statement   While critics like Kertzer and Easingwood agree that Vanessa MacLeod grows in understanding, critics like Acoose and Ware lay more emphasis on the persistence of destructive racial stereotypes in Vanessa's views and in the story as a whole. In this essay I will examine issues in narrative structure, characterization, point of view, and figurative language in "The Loons" to show that, while it initially appears that Margaret Laurence portrays Vanessa as achieving a more mature understanding of Piquette, in some ways this understanding is not mature at all, a fact Laurence does not appear to recognize.

This thesis statement contains all the elements it needs. Nevertheless, as you will see later, it does not reflect the writer's final thoughts on the subject, nor is it in a final polished form.

STAGE 4   Drafting

STEP 1   Sequencing Topics and Points

The basic principle for sequencing research essays, as for any other essay, is to try to maintain an order of ascending interest, beginning with topics that contradict or offer only weak support for your thesis and ending with topics that give the strongest evidence in its favour. Achieving this order may be complicated by the need to integrate your own analysis with your responses to secondary material. There is not one way to meet this need. You may discuss your responses to secondary material early in the essay and then move to your analysis; or, more often, you may have a mixture of your analysis and references to secondary material in most of your paragraphs. In every case, you will have to clarify the topics you plan to cover and the point you intend to make about each topic before you can figure out an effective sequence.

STEP 2   Making a Formal Outline

Making an outline is particularly valuable for the research essay, as the complexity of research material makes it easy to lose sight of paragraph topics. Although a regular draft outline will work for this purpose, you may be asked to hand in a *formal outline* as a guide for your reader. Some writers finish the essay first and then write an outline. Others make an outline before they draft the essay in order to work out the relationship among major points, minor points, and supporting evidence. An outline will help you maintain a balance between your own analysis and the material you have found in your sources.

To make a formal outline, write your thesis statement at the top of a page. Then list your major points with Roman numerals, your subpoints under each heading with capital letters, and evidence to support each subpoint with Arabic numerals. If you need a fourth level, use lowercase letters. For an example, see the sample topic below.

Sample Topic

To work out an order of ascending interest for your topics and points, you consider the categories you've used for your chart comparing primary and secondary material. The categories of characterization and narrative structure offer most support for the idea of Vanessa's maturation, an idea you no longer support. You therefore decide to start with these paragraph topics and to follow them with paragraphs on point of view and figurative language, topics that directly support your case. You then make the following formal outline as a guide for writing your draft:

Writing Sample

Thesis statement In this essay I will examine issues in narrative structure, characterization, point of view, and figurative language in "The Loons" to show that, while it initially appears that Margaret Laurence portrays Vanessa as achieving a more mature understanding of Piquette, in some ways this understanding is not mature at all, a fact Laurence does not appear to recognize.

Major point
Subpoint
Evidence

I.   **Characterization**
  A. Some critics suggest that Vanessa gains a more mature understanding, within limits.
      1. Quotation from Kertzer and analysis
      2. Quotation from Easingwood and analysis
  B. Another critic implies that Vanessa is a static character.
      1. Quotation from Acoose and analysis
  C. My own reading suggests that Vanessa is a dynamic, changing character, with increasing awareness.
      1. Quotation from story and analsyis

Additional points to be expanded

II. **Narrative Structure**
  A. The story's stages are based around Vanessa's developing viewpoint.
  B. Evidence shows that her changes in understanding do structure the story.
  C. Some critics confirm this point.

III. **Point of View**
  A. The first-person point of view raises problems.
  B. Some critics argue that these problems reflect the limits of Laurence's vision.
  C. The destructive effects of the victim stereotype are well documented.

IV. **Figurative Language**
  A. The loons are associated with suffering and helplessness, both in the story and in the criticism.
  B. Some critics comment on the identification of Aboriginal peoples with "creatures of nature."
  C. The limits of Vanessa's vision and maturity are evident in this metaphor.

Remember that each section of the outline corresponds not to a single paragraph but to a topic; you may need more than one paragraph to discuss a topic fully.

STEP 3   Sketching the Introduction and Conclusion

Although it's generally best not to spend much time on introductions and conclusions when you are drafting, some writers cannot proceed effectively until they have written a good introduction. We will therefore give you some guidelines that you can use while you are drafting your introduction and conclusion or when you revise.

An *introduction* for a research essay will usually need the following:

- an explanation of the primary material (if any) and/or the subject that provides the context for your research question;

- an indication of your research question;

- a reference to the secondary material, providing an indication of its range and highlighting any point(s) of difference relevant to answering your research question;

- a thesis statement that responds to primary material and/or subject in the context of the secondary material.

A research essay conclusion will usually contain the following:

- a summary of the way in which the body of the essay has confirmed and extended the thesis statement;

- a statement of the further implications of your project, which might include the call for more research or suggest ways your research applies to a broader area.

So that you can see these checklists in use, in the following pages we have included a draft introduction and conclusion for the sample topic at the revision stage of the writing process.

STEP 4   Writing the Draft

Your main goal in writing a first draft is to get your ideas on paper, however rough the form. At this point you are still exploring your subject and working out the connections among your sources. Your draft may be much shorter than your final essay, for in revising you may expand your discussion of your sources, add details, or even develop a whole new line of argument. Remember that *revision* means "seeing again," rethinking every part of your essay, not merely correcting errors in grammar and spelling. If you are a writer who likes to craft each paragraph before moving on, you may want to consult the checklists on revising middle paragraphs (Stage 6, Step 2) before you write your draft.

STAGE 5   Revising Thesis Statement and Essay Structure: Relating to Your Sources

As you drafted your essay, you may have had the sense that you were wandering off-topic or developing new ideas. Now is the time to take a broad overview of your essay. Are you satisfied with your thesis statement? If not, how does it need to change? If your thesis statement still seems satisfactory, does the overall structure of the essay develop your reasons in a logical way? If not, how does it need to change?

You may find that, like many students struggling with research material, you have relied too heavily on particular sources or, alternatively, failed to use them enough.

You can tell that you have depended too much on your sources when your entire essay completely agrees with one of them or perhaps agrees consecutively with sources that turn out to disagree with each other. It is true that your opinion about your subject may not differ from the views of other writers you have consulted. If you were researching Britain's entry into the First World War, for example, you might conclude, along with the historians you had consulted, that the British were initially disorganized and inefficient. The historians might identify different causes for this inefficiency. One source might argue that the main cause was Prime Minister Herbert Asquith's indecisiveness; another might blame the arrogance of Field Marshal Earl Kitchener; a third might blame the British class system and capitalist economics. You would be relying too heavily on your sources if you merely adopted the views of one historian and followed the same line of argument, or if you presented each historian's view without evaluating them all. You would need to backtrack, analyze the strengths and weaknesses of each historian's position, and then work out a revised thesis statement and essay structure.

The second problem arises from a failure to use research material in an integrated way. The thesis statement might take no account of the secondary material, or the secondary material might be used at random rather than to answer the research question. If your draft makes little use of your sources, you may need to make sure you understand each writer's main ideas or gather material that is more relevant.

When you have reviewed your draft, revise your thesis statement, if necessary. Then make note of any changes required to your essay structure on a revision outline (see Making a Revision Outline in Chapter 5).

Sample Topic

Revising the thesis statement In drafting your research essay on "The Loons," you had the increasing sense that you were presenting too simple a case. When you review your thesis and the development of your points, you realize that you have essentially endorsed the positions developed by Janice Acoose and Tracy Ware. You wonder, though, whether the evidence in the story confirms their position: that Laurence is misguidedly endorsing Vanessa's identification of Piquette with the loons, and thus Aboriginal people with helpless victimhood. If, as Ware points out, Laurence treats the younger Vanessa's positions ironically, why should we assume that this irony disappears in the treatment of the older Vanessa's views? When consulting the story as you drafted, you became aware of the voice of an older narrator, introduced at the beginning and present at the end. When you reread the details of the ending in light of this older, ironic voice and Laurence's comments on time in "Time and the Narrative Voice," you decide that Laurence is not endorsing Vanessa's identification of Piquette with the loons but critiquing it.

When you revise your thesis statement, then, you indicate this more independent perspective and your deeper understanding of the story by moving the category of point of view to a more emphatic position, by making your opinion and reasons more precise, and by removing the claim that Laurence is not aware of the limitations of Vanessa's understanding.

Writing Sample

Revised thesis statement

Critics Jon Kertzer and Peter Easingwood agree that Vanessa MacLeod grows in understanding, whereas critics Janice Acoose and Tracy Ware lay more emphasis on the persistence of destructive racial stereotypes in Vanessa's views and in the story as a whole. An analysis of characterization, narrative structure, figurative language, and point of view in "The Loons" suggests that, while Laurence shows Vanessa struggling with her conceptions of Piquette and maturing in certain ways, she also demonstrates Vanessa's inability to escape the historical and social limits of her understanding.

Revising essay structure The changes in the thesis statement will mean changes in essay structure. You also realized as you wrote your draft that characterization and narrative structure are inseparable because each stage of the narrative focuses on a stage in Vanessa's development. In the revision column of your outline you make notes to expand your discussion of narrative structure, to examine the metaphor of the loons before discussing point of view, which has become a more significant topic, and to add a point about the link between the figurative language at the end of the story and Laurence's conception of time. For the results of these changes, see F. Smith's research essay "Laurence's 'The Loons': Insight or Stereotype?" (Readings: Sample Essays).

STAGE 6   Revising Individual Paragraphs: Integrating and Documenting

STEP 1   Revising the Introduction

Even if you used the checklist for research introductions (see Stage 4, Step 3) for drafting your essay, you will find it a helpful guide to revision. Assuming that you have already revised your presentation of secondary sources and your thesis statement itself, you may find that you have not succeeded in giving the context for your subject and/or primary material in a compact way, or that you have forgotten to mention your research question. We will demonstrate the revision of these elements through the sample topic.

Sample Topic

The first half of the introductory paragraph of the draft research essay on "The Loons" reads as follows:

> In her short story "The Loons," Margaret Laurence uses the memories of Vanessa at different stages of her life to create a unique and dynamic relationship between Vanessa and Piquette. Their relationship moves through certain stages as Vanessa grows up and comes to realize certain truths. As an eleven-year-old, Vanessa sees Piquette "in terms of romanticized notions of Indians" ("Time" 271); at fifteen, she remembers feeling "embarrassment and pity" ("Time" 271); at eighteen, Vanessa realizes that she is somewhat responsible for Piquette's demise.

These introductory sentences present one important aspect of the story's context, Vanessa's process of development; however, they do not explain who Vanessa and Piquette are, mention the research question, or identify the source of the quotations.

You might revise like this:

Writing Sample

Revised introductory sentences

Following the main character Vanessa MacLeod's development from the age of eleven to eighteen, Margaret Laurence's short story "The Loons" focuses on the white girl's relationship with a Métis girl named Piquette Tonnerre. Vanessa's attitudes change during the story—from naive romanticism to "embarrassment and pity" (Laurence, "Time" 271) to accepting her share of collective responsibility for Piquette's death. This final change allows the reader to think that Vanessa gains insight into her would-be friend's life, what Laurence herself called "the pain and bewilderment of one's knowledge of other people" (270). But does Laurence actually portray Vanessa as achieving a mature understanding of Piquette and of their relationship by the end of the story? Laurence critics provide a range of answers to this question.

You can read the whole of the revised introduction in the finished research essay, F. Smith's "Laurence's 'The Loons': Insight or Stereotype?" (Readings: Sample Essays).

STEP 2   Revising Middle Paragraphs: Integrating Sources

In drafting your essay, you probably used your research material in each of your middle paragraphs, to varying degrees. One paragraph may present a key writer's position on your subject and your response; another paragraph may draw equally upon several secondary sources; a third may be devoted to your analysis of a primary source, with little reference to secondary sources. When you are ready to revise, you may discover that you have given too much or too little attention to your sources. Or, in trying to juggle your sources, you may have lost sight of the overall point or structure of your paragraph. Use the following checklist to help you identify where you need to revise.

CHECKLIST FOR REVISING MIDDLE PARAGRAPHS: INTEGRATING SOURCES

- Are the topic of the paragraph and your own point about it clearly set out in your topic sentence? Do the topic sentences, when read sequentially, guide the reader through each step of your analysis or argument?
- Does the order of points within the paragraph develop the analysis or argument in a logical way?

(Continued)

(Continued)

- Have you provided your own evidence to explain why you agree or disagree with points made by other writers? Don't rely on quotations from secondary sources to make important points for you.

- Have you made clear distinctions between your ideas and those of your sources? Introduce quotations and paraphrases by briefly mentioning the idea you wish to highlight, using appropriate transitional words and phrases, such as "Wong's study provides further support . . . ; on the other hand, Friedman argues . . ." (for more on this topic, see Part 3, H2 Quotations).

- Have you provided enough details from primary and/or secondary sources to support your point? Have you included explanations that make the significance of those details apparent to your reader?

When you are trying to pull together material from a wide variety of sources, it's easy to get caught up in details and lose sight of the points those details are meant to support. In the following paragraph, for instance, the writer draws on three sources: J. M. Bynner, *The Young Smoker* (London: Her Majesty's Stationery Office, 1969); Bernard Mausner and Ellen S. Platt, *Smoking: A Behavioral Analysis* (New York: Pergamon, 1971); and Richard Olshavsky, *No More Butts: A Psychologist's Approach to Quitting Smoking* (Bloomington: Indiana UP, 1977). Although the paragraph provides adequate *details* in a mixture of summary and quotation, it does not provide enough *explanation* of the relationship between the topic sentence and the various studies; indeed, one of the studies seems to contradict the others.

Draft middle paragraph

The social causes of smoking have been established in a number of studies. According to B. Mausner and E. Platt, many smokers reported that they thought of smokers as daring and sophisticated and of non-smokers as sensible and careful (7). According to Richard Olshavsky, advertising does not seem either to inhibit or to promote cigarette smoking (98). In his study of the smoking habits of British schoolboys, J. M. Bynner discovered that "Boys who smoke thought of themselves as being fairly tough but not as tough as they would like to be. They, more than any other group, saw non-smokers as completely lacking in toughness and thus the act of giving up smoking involved identification with a group which had a very unattractive characteristic" (93).

Notice how the revised version links the topic sentence with the research details, explains the apparent contradiction in the studies, and maintains the mixture of summary and quotation:

Revised middle paragraph

The social causes of smoking have been established in a number of studies. Although the image of smokers conveyed by advertising may not be important, since, as Richard Olshavsky points out, advertising does not seem either to inhibit or to promote cigarette smoking (98), there is good evidence that the image smokers have of themselves is very important. In his study of the smoking habits of British schoolboys, J. M. Bynner discovered that "Boys who smoke thought of themselves as being fairly tough but not as tough as they would like to be. They, more than any other group, saw non-smokers as completely lacking in toughness and thus the act of giving up smoking involved identification with a group which had a very unattractive characteristic" (93). Adults seem to share this kind of thinking. According to B. Mausner and E. Platt, many smokers reported that they thought of smokers as daring and sophisticated and of non-smokers as sensible and careful (7).

In this instance, the paragraph could be revised effectively by merely rearranging its parts and rewriting a few sentences. More often, middle paragraphs need to be revised substantially, a process that can be quite time-consuming. Be prepared to reread your sources, rework the points you've made, and add new material.

STEP 3   Revising Middle Paragraphs: Documenting Sources

Learning how to integrate source material is a key step in learning to write a research essay. The next step is learning how to identify or *document* the sources you have used in a clear and unambiguous way. When you document sources, you tell readers exactly where you found quotations and paraphrased material so that, if they wish, they can locate each item for themselves. Using quotations and paraphrased material without identifying the source is called *plagiarism*. More exactly, plagiarism is the act, intentional or otherwise, of copying or borrowing words or ideas without properly acknowledging the original source. Plagiarism carries serious consequences, ranging from a failing grade to expulsion, so it's important to understand the different forms that plagiarism can take. Plagiarism occurs when

- a student hands in work done wholly or in part by another person;
- portions of a submitted work are taken from another source without proper reference to that source;

- a student paraphrases sections of another work without acknowledging the source;
- ideas in a work are borrowed, derived, or developed from another source without reference to that source (for example, "checking a few internet sites for ideas").

Last-minute panic or a lack of ideas leads some students into *intentional plagiarism*—deliberately copying large sections of a published work, stringing together unacknowledged quotations from several works, or handing in an essay written by someone else. If you give yourself plenty of time and follow the guidelines we have suggested for gathering material, you won't find yourself tempted to plagiarize.

Unintentional plagiarism, on the other hand, generally results from losing track of your sources as you take notes and draft your essay. The surest way to avoid unintentional plagiarism is to learn how to document research materials properly. That means giving in-text references in addition to including full bibliographic information for each source in a Works Cited or References page at the end. The examples of plagiarism that follow will demonstrate how to use your source material without plagiarizing.

First, imagine writing an essay on Michael Ondaatje's novel *Coming through Slaughter.* You might come across a published article—a hypothetical example by S. Smith—that is relevant to your essay topic.

EXCERPT OF PUBLISHED WRITING

Michael Ondaatje's fragmented writing in *Coming through Slaughter* stylistically echoes the improvised, unpredictable music and actions of the main character, Buddy Bolden.

Plagiarized words

In *Coming through Slaughter,* Ondaatje's fragmented writing stylistically echoes Buddy Bolden's music.

Revision

S. Smith has argued that Ondaatje's "fragmented writing . . . stylistically echoes" (32) Buddy Bolden's music.

Here the point is attributed to the author, quotation marks and ellipses indicate the words quoted, and the page reference ensures that readers could find the quotation.

Plagiarized idea

> Michael Ondaatje writes in a style similar to Buddy Bolden's jazz music.

Revision

> Michael Ondaatje writes in a style similar to Buddy Bolden's jazz (Smith 32).

As you can see, the only difference between the plagiarized idea and the revision is the inclusion of the parenthetical reference giving the source of the idea. While it is generally better to introduce quotations and paraphrases by at least mentioning the author's name, the writer is no longer guilty of plagiarism. If you have kept track of your sources while you are gathering material, you can easily supply any missing information when you revise. You will find it difficult to document your sources accurately, however, if your notes do not distinguish quotations from paraphrases as well as paraphrases from your own ideas.

When you revise, use the following checklist to help you identify problems with documentation.

CHECKLIST FOR REVISING MIDDLE PARAGRAPHS: DOCUMENTING SOURCES

- Have you put quotation marks around all quoted material and identified the source, including page number, in the style required for your assignment?
- Are quotations accurate? Are they used effectively?
- Have you identified the source of all paraphrased material in the style required for your assignment?
- Have you documented the origin of any ideas that you borrowed, developed, or derived from another source?
- Have you given full bibliographic details for each source you used, primary or secondary, in a Works Cited or References list, in the style required?
- Does your Works Cited or References list contain *all* the works mentioned in your research essay? Does it contain *only* the works mentioned in your essay?

You will find further information on quotations and on MLA and APA documentation styles in Part 3, H3 Documentation).

Sample Topic

Let us suppose that your draft research essay on Laurence's story includes the following paragraph on the metaphor of the loons. How well are the research materials used to present the various interpretations of this metaphor and to advance the thesis? Are sources appropriately introduced and documented? Keep the checklists for integrating and documenting sources in mind as you read.

The expectations imposed on Piquette along with Vanessa's "white" version of history make it nearly impossible for the two girls to see eye to eye and become friends. Vanessa's "understanding of reality is filtered through a racist, classist, and male-privileged ideological value system" (Acoose p. 79 Fenced). She does not seem to realize that Aboriginal peoples have been among the most disadvantaged people in Canada (Fournier and Crey, p. 82), so little regarded that white people have found it justified to take away large numbers of their children for adoption. Laurence uses the loons, whose "voices belonged to a world separated by aeons from [Vanessa's] neat world" (p. 263), as a metaphor for the First Nations people of Canada. Dr. MacLeod remarks that the loons must have sounded plaintive and pitiful before any person, meaning any white person, ever set foot here. In saying this, it is understood that the MacLeods believe the Aboriginal peoples of Canada to have always been as they are: destitute and powerless victims. This is a misrecognition of such people. Tracy Ware says this misrecognition is also Laurence's. Critics like Michelle Gadpaille say the story is a lament for the passing of a way of life.

These are some of the problems you might identify:

Integrating sources

- Topic sentence about loons buried in the middle of the paragraph
- No clear line of argument through the paragraph; need to reorganize
- Little use of own evidence; most points made by critics
- Not clear whose point it is in sentence beginning "In saying this, it is understood . . . "; not clear whose term "misrecognition" is
- A brief explanation of loon metaphor and details of its first occurrence, but no discussion of the metaphor at the end of the story

Documenting sources

- Quotations from the character Dr. MacLeod and the critics Gadpaille and Ware not in quotation marks; parenthetical citations not in MLA style
- Need to replace Acoose quotation with quotation more relevant to loons

- First paraphrase from Fournier and Crey documented; second paraphrase not documented
- "The Loons," Acoose, Fournier and Crey, Ware should appear in Works Cited
- Gadpaille is quoted in Ware, which should be acknowledged, but Gadpaille should not appear as an entry in Works Cited

Revised along these lines, this paragraph expands into three, as you will see in paragraphs 10, 11, and 12 of the sample research essay by F. Smith, "Laurence's 'The Loons': Insight or Stereotype?" (Readings: Sample Essays).

STEP 4 Revising the Conclusion

You may have used the checklist for research essay conclusions (Stage 4, Step 3) in drafting your essay; you should certainly use it in revising. Does your conclusion summarize and draw together the major points of your essay? Does it show whether your research question has been answered in the way that you claimed it would? Does it sound mechanical?

You can avoid a simple repetition of your thesis by making reference to the way some of your initial ideas have been developed. You can also suggest the larger implications for your thesis; that is, you can explain how, if you had more time and space to write, you would develop your ideas in a wider context. In this way you will show that you have thought about not only the details of your subject but also the larger scope of the project.

Sample Topic

Let us suppose that you have written the following conclusion to your draft:

Draft conclusion

Vanessa was raised with certain ideals and her reality has been filtered in such a way that her world has been processed to give her an inherently stereotypical view of indigenous people. As they are, they do not fit into Vanessa's little world, therefore she has an idea of what they should be like so that they will fit. This in turn affects the way she treats Piquette. Laurence works through the steps, first by making Vanessa assume that Piquette is like a historical Native, familiar with the forests and the lands of Canada. Vanessa then realizes Piquette's need to fit in, but cannot allow her to because of who she is. Finally, Piquette dies and Vanessa can only think of how uncomfortable Piquette made her, and she wants to forget the look she saw in Piquette's eyes the moment she really saw her. In her short story, Laurence has used stereotypical images of Aboriginal Canadians and their history to create an adverse relationship between Vanessa and Piquette.

This conclusion neither makes an effective summary nor develops the implications of the research. It does refer to the research question and reaffirm the thesis about Vanessa's maturation, but it presents this view in a way that does not sum up the actual analysis. This is a common mistake, springing from the desire not to repeat what has already been said.

Your aim in revising is to summarize the analysis in a way that presents the argument in an overall—and thus new—light, especially when you add a statement of implications. So you reinstate the categories you used as paragraph topics and show how your points about them have answered your research question. Then you review your judgments about the secondary sources and their contribution to the question of stereotyping. You decide that a point about the way Laurence critiques stereotyping can be your statement of the broader implications of your essay. The conclusion that results from these revisions is the final paragraph in F. Smith, "Laurence's 'The Loons': Insight or Stereotype?" (Readings: Sample Essays).

Working on Your Own Assignment

In writing and revising a research essay, your goal is to integrate your own ideas about your subject with information and ideas drawn from secondary sources.

- Formulate a thesis statement by reviewing your notes to find (a) the connections between the material you have gathered and your research question, and (b) the most important similarities and differences between your ideas and the ideas expressed in your secondary sources.

- Organize your material by making a formal outline that sets out the main ideas in your essay. Indicate in the outline where you want to bring in secondary material and the point you want to make about it.

- As you write your draft, keep track of your sources by putting the author and page number in parentheses after each quotation and after any paraphrased material (for APA style, include the year of publication).

- Check the thesis statement and overall structure of your draft against your formal outline. Watch for paragraphs that are too long. You may need to subdivide them, to shorten quotations, or to delete unimportant or irrelevant material. Make a note of any necessary changes.

- As you read through each middle paragraph, ask yourself two questions: What is the main point? How does this material support my thesis? If your topic sentence does not answer these questions, revise it. Put all the important points in your own words and include quotations, references, and other evidence to support them. Make clear why you agree or disagree with the opinions of other writers.

- In both your introduction and your conclusion, connect your own thinking with your research material.

- Make sure that you have documented all your sources, both by using parenthetical references in the essay and by giving complete bibliographical details in a list of Works Cited or References.

Exercises

A. Make a formal outline of the sample research essay, "Laurence's 'The Loons': Insight or Stereotype?" (Readings: Sample Essays). Compare this outline with the outline used in writing the draft (Stage 4, Step 2). What changes do you observe? Consider such things as the topics covered, the points made, and the secondary sources used.

B. Write a paragraph evaluating the strengths and weaknesses of the following introduction to a research essay on computers and learning. Use the checklist for sketching introductions (Stage 4, Step 3) as a guide. Focus on content rather than correctness.

> In the last fifteen years, our education system has changed. It now advocates the use of computers as tools for enhancing the education of students. Computers are viewed as machines that link us universally and consequently offer endless information to children. This technology is gaining major publicity, as people assume that computers will give future generations of children an advantage; they will have more knowledge and problem-solving skills. Whether or not this change is positive and necessary is still a topic for debate. In "It Always Costs," Suzuki boldly states that "we must understand that there is no such thing as a problem-free technology. However beneficent, technology always has a cost" (310).

C. Review the checklist for integrating secondary sources (Stage 6, Step 2), the checklist on documenting (Stage 6, Step 3), and the analysis of the sample paragraph (Stage 6, Step 3). Then read the following middle paragraph of an essay on computers and learning. Underline the writer's paragraph topic, main point, and explanations of details. Circle transitions and citation details. Then make a list similar to that in Stage 6, Step 2 to show what changes you would make to create a more effective middle paragraph.

Without motivation or stimulation, any task becomes boring or difficult to achieve. It is postulated that computers motivate children, as they can be simple and exciting. In Schleter's *Problems and Promises of Computer-Based Training,* he asserts that "as advertisements for CBI [computer-based instruction] products have claimed, learner motivation is high for a particular CBI program because the system is easy and fun to use" (11). Science teachers, apparently, see students are able to learn just as much through computer simulations as through hands-on laboratory procedures. Motivation may indeed be lost through lengthy hands-on procedures. There is speculation that motivation may be lost through the physical stagnation involved in using a computer. Armstrong and Casement researched this field in *The Child and the Machine* and discovered that "even if computer use instills a positive attitude towards the technology, there is no proof that this enthusiasm spills into other areas of learning." A child may be fascinated by the technology but still not have the motivation to learn on her own.

D.   Janice Acoose argues that Canadian literature needs more positive representations of indigenous characters by indigenous writers. Find a short story by an indigenous Canadian writer that includes positive images of indigenous characters. To find a suitable story, consult anthologies of Aboriginal writers or search the library catalogue for books by writers such as Thomas King, Lee Maracle, and Jeannette Armstrong. Find secondary sources to inform your reading of the story. Then write a research essay comparing the story you found with "The Loons." Use the material on "The Loons" in this text, including the research essay by F. Smith, in any way that suits your comparison.

E.   Draft and revise a research essay on the topic you chose from Exercise A or B, Chapter 10.

Readings

Published Writings

(Part 2)

Sample Essays

Published Writings

Addiction in Free Markets

Bruce K. Alexander and Stefa Shaler

Although any person in any society can become addicted, free market 1
societies universally dislocate their members, leading to mass addiction. This simple proposition can profoundly change the way that we deal with addictions in ourselves and others. Although often overlooked by addiction professionals, the evidence for this proposition fills our history and our everyday life.

In order for a "free market" to be "free," the exchange of labour, land, 2
currency and consumer goods must be controlled by the laws of supply and demand, and must not be "distorted" by personal loyalties, village or neighbourhood responsibilities, guild or union rights, charity, family obligations, ethnic tastes and aversions, social roles, or religious values. . . .

Disastrously, today's free market 3
fundamentalists ignore all previously understood limits, including Adam Smith's[1] warning that national governments must resist the power of manufacturers to "become formidable to the government and . . . intimidate the legislature." Smith also feared excessive profits and considered "private luxury and extravagance" to be "ruinous taxes." We've gone too far toward the free market extreme, and one of those consequences is mass dislocation and, in its train, mass addiction.

At the beginning of the 21st century, for rich and poor alike, jobs disappear on short notice, communities are 4

Bruce K. Alexander is a professor emeritus of psychology at Simon Fraser University and a research associate with the Canadian Centre for Policy Alternatives. His research interests include the causes of addiction, the effects of globalization on psychological functioning, and the history of psychology.

Stefa Shaler describes herself as a freelance social worker who volunteers for numerous peace initiatives, including recent travels to the Middle East to try to prevent violence against Iraqi people.

"Addiction in Free Markets" was published in Bruce Alexander's *Peaceful Measures* (University of Toronto Press, 1990). Reprinted with permission of University of Toronto Press. This is a shortened version, with references omitted. For the complete text, see the original publication.

weak and unstable, people routinely change lovers, families, occupations, co-workers, technical skills, languages, nationalities, therapists, spiritual beliefs and ideologies as they navigate the shopping malls, real estate markets, and employment agencies. Prices and incomes are no more stable than social life. Even the continued viability of ecological systems is in question. For rich and poor alike, dislocation plays havoc with delicate ties between people and society that comprise psychosocial integration.

What is the relationship between dislocation and addiction? Most people 5 who cannot achieve a reasonable degree of psychosocial integration find that they must develop "substitute" lifestyles in order to endure. Substitute lifestyles entail excessive habits intended to fill the painful void of dislocation. These habits include drug use and many other activities that do not center on drug use. They also include social relationships that provide some satisfaction although they are not sufficiently close, stable or socially acceptable to comprise real psychosocial integration. People in this predicament—whether barroom drunks, internet sex surfers or needle-using junkies—cling to their substitute lifestyles with a tenacity that is properly called addiction. . . .

Examples of forced dislocation and consequent addiction fill the his- 6 tory of free market society. For example, by a series of increments, England moved to a full-blown free market system between the late 16th and the early 19th centuries. This was achieved in part through massive evictions of the rural poor from their farms, commons, and villages and their absorption into urban slums and a brutal, export oriented manufacturing system. Those who resisted these new realities too strenuously were further dislocated by forced apprenticeship of their children, destruction of their unions and other associations, elimination of local charity to the "undeserving poor," and by confinement in "houses of correction" where unruly behaviour was corrected with whips and branding irons.

Forced dislocation spread from England to the rest of the British 7 Isles, e.g., the "clearances" of the clan society of the Scottish Highlands, and spread to English colonies abroad, e.g., the settlement of Australia by "transportation" of convict labour. Dislocated British emigrants reproduced their own condition by dislocating aboriginal peoples wherever they landed, including Vancouver, with the support and encouragement of the imperial government.

The historical correlation between severe dislocation and addiction is 8 strong. Although alcohol consumption and drunkenness on festive occasions was widespread in Europe during the middle ages, and although a few people became "inebriates" and "drunkards," mass alcoholism was not a problem. However, alcoholism gradually spread with the beginnings of the free markets after 1500 and eventually became a raging epidemic with the dominance of free market society after 1800. . . .

The predictable relationship between free market society, dislocation, and addiction is clearly visible in the history of Native Canadians. Although murder, adultery and insanity sometimes occurred within Canadian aboriginal culture, anthropologists have found no evidence of large-scale addiction, despite the fact that activities were available that have proven addictive in free market societies, such as eating, sex, gambling, psychedelic mushrooms, etc. 9

Canadian aboriginal society did not have access to alcohol, but natives in what is now called Mexico and the American southwest did. In those societies where alcohol was readily available, it was used moderately, often ceremonially, rather than addictively, prior to the destruction of native culture. 10

The popular explanation for rampant alcoholism among Canadian natives is that they have a racial inability to control alcohol. But this is unlikely, since addiction was not a ruinous problem among natives until assimilation subjected them to extreme dislocation. Moreover, if natives were handicapped by the "gene of alcoholism," the same must be said of Europeans since those subjected to conditions of extreme dislocation also fell into addiction almost universally. Even the Orkney Islanders who were brought to Canada from Scotland by the Hudson's Bay Company specifically because of their characteristic sobriety and obedience and because they were accustomed to extreme northern weather and life at sea, fell prey to rampant alcoholism under the stresses of dislocation. . . . 11

Members of free market societies generally still cherish the hope that free markets will create universal well being. Therefore, it is only polite to overlook connections between free markets, dislocation and addiction. Print and electronic media help us to maintain this civil inattention, celebrating free market achievements with blinding fireworks and deafening fanfare. They endlessly publicize new medical explanations for the puzzling epidemic of "drug" addiction and hopeful new solutions. They continue decades of futile debate about whether addiction is a "criminal" or a "medical" problem whereas, in fact, it is neither. In free market society, the spread of addiction is primarily a political and spiritual problem. If we do not find wellsprings of psychosocial integration, society, with its ever-freer markets, will manifest even more dislocation and addiction. 12

The key to controlling addiction is maintaining a society in which every member is included in a larger community with a sense of meaning and belonging. People need to belong within their society, not just trade in its markets. . . . 13

Changing the terms of the familiar debates on addiction is necessary if   14
political action is to become possible. This is a huge task since the current
manner of speaking about addiction as an individual drug-using disease
enjoys the support of free market leaders. People endure this chronic barrage
of misinformation because it complements a deeply rooted North American
"temperance mentality" which makes it natural to blame social problems on
drugs and alcohol, and also because it profits many institutions and professions
that treat, police, prevent and "harm reduce" the putative disease. Those who
launch the misinformation campaigns prosper financially because the "War on
Drugs," which has drawn its justification from them, serves vital commercial
and geopolitical purposes for vested interests with very deep pockets.

Authoritative voices around the world are raising a mighty chorus of   15
warnings against the psychological, ecological and social devastation engen-
dered by free market extremism. Careful reflection on addiction can add
a new counterpoint to this chorus, stressing the relationship between free
markets, dislocation and addiction. Needless to say, a healthier society ultimately leads to a healthier economic system as well.

An alternative to the extreme free market orthodoxy must begin with a   16
sense that all of us are participants in a sacred trust to nurture, protect and
promote delicate and intricate bonds with every aspect of the biosphere and
the invisible forces of spirit and humanitarianism.

NOTE

[1] Adam Smith (1723–1790) was a Scottish economist whose book *The Wealth of Nations* (1776) contains the famous claim that the invisible hand of the market translates self-interest into public benefit.

VOCABULARY

biosphere—the part of the Earth's crust, waters, and atmosphere where living organisms
can subsist

geopolitical—based on the interrelation of geography and politics

psychosocial integration—to be "included in a larger community with a sense of meaning
and belonging" (par. 13)

QUESTIONS

1. Alexander and Shaler take addiction to include "drug use and many other activities that
   do not center on drug use." What definition of addiction do you think they are using in
   this essay?

2. Alexander and Shaler refer extensively to three centuries of English history and to the
   history of Native Canadians. How do they link these examples with the effects of free
   market society in the present? Is this argument convincing to you?

3. "Addiction in Free Markets" contains both neutral and evaluative diction. Identify three to five examples of each kind. How is the use of diction linked to the essay's purpose, as you understand it?

4. In this essay an explanation of the causes of addiction leads to a proposal for solutions. How effective is this problem–solution structure? To what extent would this structure be useful in your own writing?

SUGGESTION FOR WRITING

Alexander and Shaler describe the beginning of the twenty-first century as a time of weak communities, rapid change, and instability in work, relationships, beliefs, and places of residence. Write a short essay exploring to what extent your own experience of the beginning of the twenty-first century echoes this view.

Football Envy at the UN

Kofi Annan

The World Cup[1] makes us at the UN green with envy. As the pinnacle of the only truly global game, played in every country by every race and religion, it is one of the few phenomena as universal as the UN. You could say it's more universal. Fifa[2] has 207 members; we have only 191. But there are better reasons for our envy.

This is an event in which everybody knows where their team stands, and what it did to get there. They know who scored and how and in what minute of the game; they know who saved the penalty. I wish we had more of that sort of competition in the family of nations. Countries vying for the best standing in the table of respect for human rights, and trying to outdo one another in child survival rates or enrolment in secondary education. States parading their performance for all the world to see. Governments being held accountable.

Millions of people around the planet love talking about the World Cup. In Paraguay fans will be picking over that own goal; in Japan they will be debating strategies for today's contest with Australia.[3] Everywhere people are dissecting the games, revealing an intimate knowledge of their own teams and many others. Tongue-tied teenagers suddenly become eloquent and dazzlingly analytical. I wish we had more of that sort of conversation in the world at large: citizens consumed by the topic of how their country could do better on the Human Development Index,[4] or exercised about how to reduce carbon emissions or HIV infections.

The competition takes place on a level playing field, where every country has a chance to participate on equal terms. Only two commodities matter: talent and teamwork. I wish we had more levellers like that in the global arena. Free and fair exchanges without the interference of subsidies, barriers or tariffs. Every country getting a real chance to field its strengths on the world stage.

The World Cup illustrates the benefits of cross-pollination between peoples and countries. More and more national teams now welcome coaches from other countries, who bring new ways of thinking

Kofi Annan (b. 1938) is a Ghanaian diplomat who served two terms as the first black African Secretary General of the United Nations (1997–2006). Winner of the Nobel Peace Prize jointly with the UN in 2001, he opposed the US and British invasion of Iraq in the absence of UN support.

"Football Envy at the UN" appeared in the My Two Cents column of *The Guardian* on June 12, 2006, and is reprinted with permission of Kofi A. Annan.

and playing. The same goes for the players who represent clubs away from home. They inject fresh qualities into their new team and are able to contribute more to their home side when they return. In the process, they often become heroes in their adopted countries—helping to open hearts and minds.

I wish it were equally plain for all to see that human migration in general can create triple wins—for migrants, for their countries of origin, and for the societies that receive them. Migrants not only build better lives for themselves and their families, but are also agents of development—economic, social, and cultural—in the countries they go and work in, while they inspire with new-won ideas and knowhow when they return.

Playing in the World Cup brings profound national pride. For countries qualifying for the first time—such as my native Ghana—it is a badge of honour. For those doing so after years of adversity—such as Angola[5]—it provides a sense of national renewal. And for those who are currently riven by conflict, but whose World Cup team is a unique and powerful symbol of national unity—such as Ivory Coast[6]—it inspires nothing less than the hope of national rebirth.

Which brings me to what is perhaps most enviable of all for us in the UN: the World Cup is an event in which we see goals being reached. I'm not talking only about the goals a country scores; I also mean the most important goal of all—being there, part of the family of nations and peoples, celebrating our common humanity. I'll try to remember that today as Ghana plays Italy in Hanover. Of course, I can't promise I'll succeed.

NOTES

[1] Games among the thirty-two national soccer teams qualifying for the 2006 World Cup were played at various sites in Germany during June and July 2006.

[2] "Fifa" stands for the *Federation Internationale de Football Association,* the regulatory body for international soccer.

[3] In the first round of the World Cup tournament, Paraguay lost to England 1–0 on a goal inadvertently put into his own net by a Paraguay player; Japan lost to Australia 3–1.

[4] The Human Development Index is an instrument developed in 1992 to measure countries' achievements in three basic areas: life expectancy, literacy, and standard of living.

[5] The armed wing of the Angola rebel movement was disbanded in 2002, ending twenty-seven years of civil war.

[6] Voting reforms that would have disenfranchised most of the predominantly Muslim northern region, exacerbated by an economic downturn and ethnic tensions, led to the outbreak of civil war in Ivory Coast in 2002. Under a UN mandate, French troops were dispatched as peacekeepers in the former French colony.

VOCABULARY

riven—torn apart

QUESTIONS

1. An analogy is a comparison between unlike things that emphasizes similarities and downplays differences. Kofi Annan develops his essay by means of an extended analogy between the World Cup and the UN.

   a. List the specific points of comparison paragraph by paragraph. Which aspects of this analogy do you find most effective? Least effective? (See Chapter 8, Analogies [118, 122].) Why do you think Annan chose analogy to make his case?

   b. Can you think of aspects of the game of soccer not mentioned by Annan that would complicate his argument? For example, Annan does not mention the role or influence of soccer referees in games. Who enforces rules on the world stage? In 2011, bribery was alleged around Qatar's successful bid for the 2022 World Cup, and there were allegations of rampant game fixing in professional soccer by organized crime. Are there similar scandals on the world stage?

2. Sum up in a sentence or two Annan's vision of how countries should operate. Do you agree or disagree with this vision? Why?

3. How does Annan's view of equality among nations, as presented in paragraph 4, compare with the view Polly Toynbee presents in "Inequality Is the Real Enemy" (Readings)?

SUGGESTIONS FOR WRITING

1. Kofi Annan, like Tim Bowling in "Na Na Na Na, Hey Hey Hey, Goodbye" (Readings), captures the allure of sports. Is there a sport that attracts you in a similar way? If so, write a one-page essay that conveys its special qualities. Or, in the light of the estimates that well over one billion people watched the final game of the 2006 World Cup, write an essay that argues the merits and/or drawbacks of our enthusiasm for sports.

2. Use Annan's piece as a model for writing an extended analogy comparing some aspect of everyday life with an institution such as a school, a hospital, a business, or a political party.

Na Na Na Na, Hey Hey Hey, Goodbye

Tim Bowling

I t's late spring, 1993. Millions of Canadians are tuned in to Game 7 of the Stanley Cup semifinals between the Toronto Maple Leafs and the Los Angeles Kings. It's an event of operatic drama. The Leafs have not won the Stanley Cup since 1967, while the Kings, in uncharted territory, are led by none other than the Great One, Wayne Gretzky, whose 1988 trade from Edmonton to Hollywood shocked those same millions of Canadians now frozen before their TV sets. [1]

I'm not one of those millions. It is true I have been a hockey fan as long as I can remember. In fact, one of my earliest memories is from the late sixties, not long after the Leafs' last Cup raising, when I'd play with hockey cards on the linoleum floor of the kitchen, passing a marble back and forth and re-enacting great goals and saves as my mother clattered dishes in the sink nearby. The NHL has always been my primary source of spectator entertainment. [2]

But I'm not watching Game 7 between the Leafs and the Kings. I can't. The tension is too much for me. I *care* too much. I so loathe the Kings—representatives of everything glitzy, shallow, crass and American—and so want an all-Canadian dream final between the Leafs and Montreal Canadiens, that I'm hiding out from the game. This is not an easy thing to do when nearly the whole country is tuned in. I'm so well versed in watching televised hockey that even the faintest sound emanating from a TV set or someone watching a TV set will tip me off to developments in the game. So I have to get away. But to where? Fortunately, I'm old enough and smart enough to be resourceful. [3]

While Gretzky dipsy-doodles behind the Leafs' net, I sit in a dark, nearly empty Vancouver theatre, watching *Howards End.* It's a long movie, long enough to cover three periods and at least one period of overtime. With luck, the drama, NHL style, will be over before the credits roll. [4]

Tim Bowling, who now lives in Edmonton, was born in Vancouver and has worked as a deckhand on a salmon-fishing boat. He is the author of many novels and books of poetry. Of these, *Dying Scarlet* won the 1998 Stephan G. Stephansson Award for Poetry, and both *The Witness Ghost* (2003) and *The Memory Orchard* (2004) were shortlisted for the Governor General's Literary Award for Poetry. Bowling was the recipient of a Guggenheim Fellowship in 2008. He has recently published a new collection of poetry, *Tenderman* (2011).

"Na Na Na Na, Hey Hey Hey, Goodbye" was first published in *Alberta Views,* December 2005/January 2006. Thank you to *Alberta Views.*

As humiliating as it is to recall this memory, I mention it for two rea-   5
sons. One, it highlights the bizarre Canadian fact that many so-called sensitive, cultured men (the sort who happily watch Ivory/Merchant films) are
nonetheless fervent fans of a brutal, bone-breaking, blood-spattering sport.
And two, it marks my nadir as a professional hockey fan. In the spring of
1993, something had to give. Either I was going to remain a "fanatic," or I
was going to put away childish things. For God's sake, I had even read several E.M. Forster novels! What the hell was I doing caring so much about
professional hockey, a game so violent that its rules include penalties for
drawing blood and instigating fights? I abhorred violence and even cited it
as a reason why I so disliked the United States. Yet I was drawn to the NHL
like a bear to a campsite, like a politician to graft, like Simone de Beauvoir
to Jean-Paul Sartre. I just couldn't turn away. Only when I walked out of
that theatre into the street and hailed a group of teenaged boys (obviously
they'd know the result of the game), and saw them shrug and heard one say
"I have no idea," did I begin the process of cultural de-programming that
would find me, a decade later, completely indifferent to the labour dispute
between the NHL team owners and players.

However, indifference to the business side of professional hockey, and to   6
the NHL, whose games have so declined in quality over the past decade that
a breakaway merits a mention on the national news, doesn't quite translate
into disinterest. The truth is, like so many non-violent Canadian men, alter-
nately bored and disgusted by the game's outdated machismo code, I always
have one ear cocked for news of the NHL. This remains true despite the
fact that I no longer watch the games or care who wins, and that I actively
scorn the corporate and boorishly patriotic culture that has grown up around
professional hockey in Canada. Why? What is it about the NHL that retains
even a slight grip on my imagination?

The most compelling answer concerns the primal pull of narrative. The   7
NHL, for better or worse, is the Great Canadian Novel, a tale replete with
villains and heroes, prima donnas and blue collar types, triumph and failure, hope and revenge, all played out at high speed over generations. Like
millions of Canadians, I grew up on the lore of the game, everything from
Conn Smythe's infamous remark that "if you can't beat 'em in the alley,
you can't beat 'em on the ice" to Paul Henderson's famous series-winning
goal against the Soviets in 1972. When the Tragically Hip uncovered a
great rock song in the tragic death of the Leafs' Bill Barilko—"Bill Barilko
disappeared / that summer (in 1951) / he was on a fishing trip (in a plane) /
The last goal he ever scored (in overtime) / won the Leafs the Cup / They
didn't win another until 1962 / the year he was discovered"—I understood.

When the internationally acclaimed Canadian filmmaker Atom Egoyan directed a TV movie about Brian "Spinner" Spencer's descent from NHL tough guy to drug gang shooting victim, I understood. When ex-Maple Leafs defenceman Tim Horton's doughnut chain became a Canadian cultural icon, I understood. The NHL, in short, is the book most Canadians have been reading all their lives. What other is there?

Just as King Shahryar put off killing Scheherazade[1] because he wanted   8 to hear how the story she was telling would turn out, I can't quite kill off my interest in the NHL. Northrop Frye[2] maintained that narrative was the common denominator between high and low culture, which explains our interest in everything from opera to soap opera. That makes eminent sense to this disillusioned NHL follower—why else should I carry around ridiculous facts such as six out of seven Sutter brothers from Viking, Alberta, made the big time and Bobby Clarke overcame diabetes to realize his professional dreams, or smile with goofy fondness at the common graffiti of my childhood—"Jesus Saves, Esposito Scores on the Rebound"?

Canadian poet Al Purdy described hockey as a combination of ballet   9 and murder. Certainly the grace and beauty of the game when played well remains a major reason why I'm still mildly attracted to the NHL. After all, the players are the most skilled in the world, even if expansion and relentless marketing (just how many jerseys can one team have?) have conspired to water down the talent and glaciate the pace of play. Besides, hockey requires a special skill that takes years to master. Most people can imagine doing the running and jumping and catching required by baseball, football and basketball, but if you can't skate (and many Canadians can't), you can't even take to the playing surface. Hockey is uniquely demanding at its most basic level, and therefore its beauty is all the more impressive. Even so, would a ballet lover, in expectation of a rare graceful step, put up with the prima ballerina being slammed into the scenery every few minutes?

This question leads directly to the most worrying explanation for my   10 ongoing interest in the NHL: I'm not nearly as sensitive and enlightened as I think I am. When Thomas Hobbes[3] wrote that life is "nasty, brutish and short," he wasn't referring to hockey, but, like most Canadian men, I've absorbed a Hobbesian philosophy as a way to justify my imaginative commitment to a machismo culture in which 14-year-old boys are sent away from home to play junior hockey and, as in the case of Sheldon Kennedy and others, sexually abused by their coaches in the process; and in which a star player like Todd Bertuzzi can jump an opponent from behind, breaking his neck, and not be universally vilified for his actions, but rather become the particular hero of Vancouver Canucks hockey fans. In fact, Don Cherry, the wildly popular spokesman for everything bigoted and "traditional" in hockey culture, is a sort of combination Thomas Hobbes/ Don Rickles/ Buffalo Bill Cody, exploiting a dog-eat-dog philosophy to garner laughs at others' expense while travelling around the country in his garish huckster's clothes. Perhaps following the NHL, and watching *Coach's Corner,* is simply akin to slowing down on the highway to gawk at an accident. We don't like what we see, but we're drawn to it in some primal way.

But that's too harsh an indictment of our fascination with the NHL.   11
A more likely reason for it is political. It's perhaps a cliché by now to point out the importance of hockey to Canada's national identity, but it's a cliché with undeniable truth. When the Canadian icemakers at the 2002 Winter Olympic games in Salt Lake City placed a loonie under the ice as good luck for Team Canada in its gold medal game with Team USA, most Canadians were delighted. And a major part of that delight lies in our undefeatable conviction that, no matter what else the world beats us at, it can't beat us at hockey. This particular form of patriotism has deep roots for my generation of hockey fans, of course. Explaining the tension of the 1972 Summit Series between Canada and the USSR, in which Team Canada won the final three games behind the Iron Curtain to retain global hockey supremacy, Phil Esposito, with no sense of embarrassment or irony, remarked, "It wasn't hockey, it was war."

Well, Phil, I was happy Canada won, and at one time I even under-   12
stood Bobby Clarke's vicious slash of Valeri Kharlamov, which knocked the Soviets' star player out of the series, as a patriotic act. But the summit series was not Vimy Ridge or Dieppe. Yet the link between hockey and nationhood, as currently promoted even more vociferously by media coverage of the game in Canada, is not easily broken. That Don Cherry can use his few minutes of nationally televised screen-time every week to lobby for increased support of Canada's armed forces proves just how powerfully the hockey/nationhood link is forged (and don't forget Jean Chrétien dubbed his globe-trotting trade missions Team Canada, in a desperate attempt to benefit from reflected hockey glory). One day, perhaps, our soldiers will wear their names on their backs and UN peacekeeping missions will end with the announcement of first, second and third stars.

A more honourable connection between the NHL and Canadian politi-   13
cal life does exist, however. Because professional hockey is a shared national story, it affords us a kind of grassroots democracy. Everyone is entitled to participate in the tangled discourse of finance, politics and entertainment spawned by the modern NHL. Your background doesn't matter (unless you're an American), your education and income don't matter, not even your annual beer consumption matters. If you have an opinion on salary

caps or on refereeing or on the superiority of Edmonton over Calgary as a hockey city, you're welcome to share it. Whether you're in Glace Bay or Nanaimo, Guelph or Banff (or any other place that sounds like two players colliding), you can walk into a bar where *Hockey Night in Canada* is showing and feel that your opinions are a national birthright, like 5 per cent beer and bilingualism (OK, maybe not bilingualism, but you get the idea).

At this point, no doubt, many Canadians will throw up their hands   14 in frustration and say, "He's taking all this too seriously. It's just a game." Well, let's look at the NHL from the simple perspective of escapist entertainment. Into what are we escaping exactly? When I was a boy, the boards, ice and score clock were free of advertising; goals and assists meant more than salaries; and players and teams had distinct characters. If you attended a game, there was silence after the whistle so you could hear someone in the crowd heckle a ref (one I remember from the seventies, directed at referee Bruce Hood: "Hey, Bruce, take off your hood!" Not exactly Evelyn Waugh level of wit, but appreciated nonetheless). Or perhaps, instead of silence, an organist played "Three Blind Mice." Today at a game, you're so relentlessly bombarded with supersonic noise and flashing lights and company logos that you come away with two conclusions: the NHL is for 20-year-old men who love violent video games, and the games themselves are beside the point, just another way to promote a crass, materialistic, corporatist agenda.

We're deep into the NHL season now, the first in two years. Dozens   15 of players have changed teams, a dozen others have retired. There's a new phenom named Sidney Crosby who's expected to challenge the scoring statistics of Gretzky one day, and the Leafs still haven't won the Cup since 1967 (the Kings beat them back in '93, in case you were dying to know). I haven't watched a game all year, and I don't intend to, just as I didn't miss the NHL at all during its year-long absence—which was, in fact, wonderfully refreshing, like fasting after binging on double-doubles and maple creams down at the local Tim Hortons. Why should I follow a sport whose foundation in this country is made of blood and beer and an empty rhetoric around outdated and destructive notions of patriotism and manhood?

I shouldn't, and neither should you, especially if you're over 40.   16 To everything there is a season, as the Bible says, and the season for the NHL is past. As the league continues to struggle with its dinosaur code of machismo, as it expands into Arkansas and Tijuana, as the players wear jerseys with Wal-Mart and McDonald's logos, I won't be watching.

And yet, if somehow the fates conspire, and two Canadian teams meet   17 in the Stanley Cup Finals, can I resist the lure of nostalgia and the pull of narrative? Can I stop thinking and be entertained?

NOTES

[1] In the *Arabian Nights Entertainment,* Scheherazade is the wife of a Persian king who puts off executing her because he is enthralled by the stories she tells every night.

[2] Northrop Frye was a well-known Canadian literary critic, author of works on Blake, literary criticism, and the mythic imagination, among other topics. See Frye's "Preface to the *Bush Garden*" (229).

[3] Thomas Hobbes (1588–1679) was an English philosopher whose masterwork, *Leviathan,* argued for a materialist view of human motives.

QUESTIONS

1. Bowling begins his essay at a point more than a decade earlier than his time of writing. Why?

2. How can you tell that Bowling is knowledgeable about Canadian hockey? Why is knowledge of hockey important to the essay?

3. Most of Bowling's essay is organized around cause/effect analysis, as he considers the reasons for the NHL's "grip on [his] imagination." Where does he shift to cause/effect analysis (evaluating whether these reasons are worthwhile)?

4. Bowling's references range widely from poets and critics to Canadian bands like the Tragically Hip, from watching *Howards End* to insulting hockey referees. Does this range of reference help Bowling's case or weaken it? Why?

SUGGESTION FOR WRITING

Does something grip your imagination without your really knowing why? If so, use cause/effect analysis to explore this attraction. Consider whether some of Bowling's strategies could be helpful for your essay.

The Persistence of Poetry and the Destruction of the World*

Robert Bringhurst

What it pleases us to call the New World is in fact a very old world— just as old, at any rate, as Asia, Europe, and Africa. It is part of the ancient continent of Pangaea, born from the same geological matrix as Europe. Its rivers and forests, and its ecology and geology, were thoroughly developed long before Columbus. And it has been inhabited by thinking, speaking, knowing human beings for several thousand years.

But an inhabited world, with its own philosophical, artistic, scientific, and literary traditions, is not what the European conquerors and colonists wanted to find. It is therefore not what they saw. They saw instead an empty world, free and ripe for the taking. They saw a gift of God meant for no one but themselves.

This deliberate hallucination is still with us, like the star of a Christmas without end.

The European colonists' arrival in the New World marks the escalation of a war that had been fought in Europe and Asia for more than two millennia and continues even now. It is the war between those who think they belong to the world and those who think that the world belongs to them. It is the war between the pagans, who know they are surrounded and outnumbered by the gods, and all the devotees of the number one—one empire, one history, one market, or one God—and who nowadays insist on the preeminence of everyone for himself: the smallest number one of all.

It is no accident that prophets of monotheism, including Plato[1] and Mohammed, have often banished the poets. These prophets understand that the poet is a pagan and polytheist by nature. In a certain sense, even Dante, Milton,

Robert Bringhurst (b. 1946) is a writer of considerable breadth. He also written poetry consistently since the early 1970s. In 1992, he published *The Elements of Typographic Style*, which greatly influenced the field of typography. He also collaborated with the late Aboriginal artist Bill Reid and has translated works of oral Haida storytellers into written English. Bringhurst lives on Quadra Island, off the coast of British Columbia. This essay was originally a lecture and is collected in his 2006 book, *The Tree of Meaning: Thirteen Talks*.

"The Persistence of Poetry and the Destruction of the World" is dated "Universidad de La Laguna, Tenerife 8 May 1996" and is translated from Spanish. It is taken from *The Tree of Meaning: Thirteen Talks* (Kentville, NS: Gaspereau Press, 2006) 40-45. Reprinted with permission of Gaspereau Press, Printers and Publishers.

San Juan de la Cruz, Teresa of Ávila, Gerard Manley Hopkins, and T. S. Eliot are pagans. Without admitting it, they seem to understand, like the peoples of the Altiplano[2] of Bolivia and Peru, and like many Native Canadians, that it is best to interpret Christianity as one more form of paganism.

But Mohammed and Plato are poets too in their way, monotheistic and tedious at times, but very much livelier and more pluralistic at others.   6

The great danger is single-mindedness: reducing things to one perspective, one idea, one overriding rule.   7

A polytheistic understanding of the world survived in Europe even in the time of the conquistadors, though it was then forced to take a wordless form. Music gave it refuge. It is found in polyphonic music, which is the music of multiple, simultaneous and independent voices. The churches of Europe overflowed with music of this kind in the fifteenth, sixteenth and seventeenth centuries. It did not change the course of history, but it preserved an essential perception of the plurality of being. It preserved the essential, faithful heresy that reality is not of just one mind.   8

European music of more recent centuries is, for the most part, homophonic. It is the music of one voice that speaks in the name of all and of many voices that answer as one voice.   9

In the meantime, the conquest continues—in South America, North America, Asia, Australia, and in Europe too. It continues in Bosnia and Hercegovina, where a tradition of oral epic poetry survived from Homer's time until even a few months ago. Now, at this moment, the villages in which those poets lived are rubble and mass graves.[3]   10

From Alaska to Tierra del Fuego, and from Ireland to Japan, the forests fall and subdivisions replace them. The homes of the gods are supplanted by the houses and garages of human beings. It is hard work, this eviction of the gods and of all the cultures that acknowledge their existence. We keep at it even so.   11

The Haida poet Skaay[4] refers to human beings as *xhaaydla xitiit ghidaay*: "plain, ordinary surface birds." Creatures with more power—killer whales, loons, grebes, sea lions, seals—know how to dive. They pierce the surface, the *xhaaydla* it is called in Haida. If we go with them—if, that is, we are *invited* to go with them—we enter the world of the myths. We come back speaking poetry.   12

Two thousand kilometres south of the country of the poet Skaay, in the Ruby Mountains, the country of the Paiute, now part of the state of Nevada, there are pines of the species *Pinus aristata,* bristlecone pines. These trees live longer than any other creatures on the earth. The oldest individuals—not much taller than I am—are 5,000 years of age or more. A few years ago,   13 a person who called himself a scientist found in these mountains a pine that might, he thought, be the oldest of all. He cut it down to count its rings. He killed what may indeed have been the oldest living being in the world, to convert it into a statistic. Then he published his report, without the least apology, in a scientific journal.[5]

This is not science. It is one more thoughtless manifestation of the conquest, one more step in reducing the world to human terms.   14

The American novelist William Faulkner, when he received the Nobel Prize, concluded his address by saying, "Mankind will not only survive, he will prevail." I am an admirer of Faulkner, but I think that his prediction is logically impossible. I think that if humanity survives, it can only be because it does *not* prevail, and that if we insist, like Ozymandias,[6] on prevailing, we will surely not survive.   15

I have been listening to the world for barely half [a] century. I do not have the wisdom even of a young tree of an ordinary kind. Nevertheless, I have been listening—with eyes, ears, mind, feet, fingertips—and what I hear is poetry.   16

What does this poetry say? It says that what-is is: that the real is real, and that it is alive. It speaks the grammar of being. It sings the polyphonic structure of meaning itself.   17

In the great ceiling of the Sistine Chapel there are readers rather than writers. The prophets and sibyls scrutinize their folios and scrolls. Nothing is written there that we can read. The great pages in their laps and in their hands reflect what happens as if they were mirrors. In front of these blank mirrors the blind prophets are listening. There is only one writer, Jehosaphat[7] the scribe, tucked away in the corner with his scrap of paper, listening to those who really listen.   18

The theme of the ceiling is the poetry of the world, not the glory of the poet.   19

It is true that the face of Michelangelo is there in the midst of the chapel's big back wall. It is rendered, this self-portrait, as a face still attached to a human hide freshly peeled from someone else's living body. The sculptor is subsumed in his own tale. The listener listens to himself. In the midst of his own vision, the visionary can be seen. But he is peeled. In the midst of that most sculptural of paintings, the image of the sculptor is reduced to two dimensions.   20

When I was a youngster in school, someone asked me, "If a tree falls in the forest with no one there to hear it, does it make a sound or not?" The question is demented. If a tree falls in the forest, all the other trees are there to hear it. But if a man cuts down the forest and then cries that he has no food, no firewood, no shade, and that his mind can get no traction, who is going to hear *him?*   21

Poetry is the language of being: the breath, the voice, the song, the   22
speech of being. It does not need us. We are the ones in need of it. If we
haven't learned to hear it, we will also never speak it.

Beings eat one another. This is the fundamental business of the world.   23
It is the whole, not any of its parts, that must prevail, and this whole is
always changing. There is no indispensable species, and no indispensable
culture. Especially not a culture that dreams of eating without being eaten,
and that offers the gods not even the guts or the crumbs.

When he sees his own people destroying the world, what is the poet to   24
say? *Stop?* Or more politely, *Please stop, please?*

All the poets of all times can only say one thing. They can say that   25
what-is is. When he sees his people destroying the world, the poet can say,
"we're destroying the world." He can say it in narrative or lyric or dramatic
or meditative form, tragic or ironic form, short form or long form, in verse
or prose. But he cannot lie, as a poet, and offer himself as the savior. He can
believe or not believe that salvation is possible. He can believe in one God
or in many gods or in none. He can believe or not believe in belief. But he
cannot finally say anything more than the world has told him.

When he sees that, in absolute terms, we human beings are now too   26
numerous —in addition to the fact that we seem too powerful as a species—
what is the poet going to do? Pull the trigger? Sing a song of praise to Herod[8]
or to Hitler? It is hard to say it to other humans, and humans, of course, are
loath to believe it, but this is the fact: human beings have built a world in
which humans need to die more and faster than they do. Yet even in this
condition, murder is not the answer.

Long ago, in a book of poems protesting the war in Vietnam, I read   27
a simple statement that stays with me. I have not in thirty years been able
to find the book again, and I am told that the lines I remember are really
quoted from a speech by Martin Luther King. I remember seeing them in a
poem, but perhaps the book in which I saw them was published only in my
dreams. The lines as I remember them, in any case, are these:

> *When one is guided by conscience only,*
> *there is no other side*
> *to which one can cross.*

There is no other earth to cross to either. There are no new worlds.   28
Paradise will not be our asylum, and our hell will not be anywhere other
than here. The world is one, at the same time that it is plural, inherently plural, like the mind. The proof of this plurality is the persistence
of poetry in our time. It is extraordinary but true, in the present day, that
poetry survives in the voices of humans, just as it does in the voices of all
the other species in the world.

NOTES

The following notes are editors' notes, except where "Author's note" is indicated in parentheses.

1 Plato in Book X of *The Republic* banishes the poets from the ideal city because Plato views poetry as imitation and, therefore, removed from reality, or truth.

2 Altiplano refers to the high plains of South America.

3 Bringhurst delivered this talk in 1996, shortly after Bosnia and Hercegovina experienced the Bosnian war (1992–1995).

4 Skaay is a Haida oral poet whom Bringhurst has translated into written English.

5 The first-person account of this event is in Donald R. Currey, "An Ancient Bristlecone Pine Stand in Eastern Nevada." *Ecology* 46.4 (Durham, North Carolina, 1965): 564-6. Galen Rowell retells the story well in *High and Wild* (San Francisco: Sierra Club, 1979): 99-105. (Author's note)

6 Ozymandias is the name of an Egyptian Pharaoh made famous in English literature by Percy Bysshe Shelley in a sonnet that warns against the arrogance of powerful individuals desiring immortality.

7 Jehosaphat was a Biblical figure who was a recorder (historian) of events. He is referenced in 1 Kings 4.3 and elsewhere.

8 Herod was a Roman leader of the first century BCE in Jerusalem, who is known for ruling by terror.

VOCABULARY

homophonic—music that has a single melodic line

Pangaea—the supercontinent that existed between the Paleozoic and Mesozoic periods, roughly 250 million years ago

polyphonic—music that has multiple melodic lines, often called contrapuntal

QUESTIONS

1. Bringhurst draws on very long views of history and geography in order to make his point. Do you think these kinds of generalizations help or hinder his argument?

2. Bringhurst claims that poetry "does not need us. We are the ones in need of it." Do you think poetry today is as important as Bringhurst suggests it is?

3. Near its conclusion, the essay states that "murder is not the answer." The essay does not specifically state an alternative answer. What do you think Bringhurst might suggest as a solution to humanity's challenges?

SUGGESTION FOR WRITING

Part of the purpose of this essay is to define poetry. Bringhurst utilizes several unusual examples to make his argument, such as trees listening to each other and sea animals diving below the surface of the ocean. Using one of Bringhurst's examples or one of your own choosing, define the inherent poetic qualities of the reality of an area of study. For example, define the poetic qualities of engineering or environmentalism.

Health Canada Inadvertently Discloses Facts Planned Parenthood Would Like to Suppress

Ted Byfield

C anadians, says a recent study, are working too hard—too hard for their health, too hard for their sanity, and above all too hard to have children. The study, released last month[1] at a meeting sponsored by Calgary United Way, is the largest of its kind in Canada, involving some 31,000 workers. It found that in the struggle to balance the demands of work and family, work continually wins. Consequently, women put off having children and many young people opt to have none. 1

The research, conducted by Professors Linda Duxbury of Carleton University and Chris Higgins of the University of Western Ontario, showed that 40% of women in professional jobs have not started a family because of work; 30% of men said they wanted no children, for the same reason. This has profound implications, of course. If many of the best potential parents of any society won't produce offspring, or perhaps only one child late in life, the intelligence level of the next generation will surely decline. Some achievement. 2

What is most unusual about this study, however, is not so much what it found as who paid for it, namely Health Canada. For by making note of our failure to have children, the federal government has inadvertently called attention to one of the better kept secrets of current demographic sociology, which is this: The much ballyhooed "population explosion," which for years we were assured would soon crowd the world with wall-to-wall people, was dead wrong. By the 1980s, predicted Paul Ehrlich[2] back in the 1960s (he being one of the century's most prominent prophets of doom), 65 million Americans would die of starvation. Well, they didn't. 3

What actually threatens us instead is serious population decline, a "birth dearth" that will wreak great havoc on the economies of much of the western world. So, at any rate, we are now told by the American Enterprise Institute[3] in 4

Ted Byfield is a Western Canadian journalist whose articles can be seen in the *Edmonton Sun* and other Canadian newspapers. Byfield was one of the founders of the *Alberta Report* magazine, later called *The Report*. He was also connected with the creation of the Reform Party of Canada.

Washington, which makes a point of talking about a situation most other foundations and government agencies seem reluctant to discuss.

The reason for this reticence is explained by journalist Tom Bethell in a recent issue of *The American Spectator* magazine.[4] "Government officials no doubt realize," writes Mr. Bethell, "that saying there are too few people, so soon after the hue and cry about there being too many, would destroy their own credibility." Other governments are in a similar case, since pretty well everybody bought into the Ehrlich "population bomb" expectations. Indeed, even now "hardly a year goes by when Ehrlich does not receive another award or prize" for his alarming predictions. Small wonder few care to acknowledge the alarms were false.

The American Enterprise Institute does, however, and its numbers—all taken from official census and other demographic records—leave the factual case beyond doubt. To maintain zero population growth in developed countries, each woman must have an average of 2.1 children. This will replace the male and female involved, and allow for the fact that some female children will die before reaching child-bearing age. The European average 15 years ago had fallen to 1.7, and is now running at 1.4. In Italy, where about one million babies were born in 1964, only about 500,000 were born last year. This amounts to a birth rate of 1.2, an impending economic disaster.

The effects of such a decline do not appear immediately; a generation must grow up for them to be fully felt. But even if European fertility rates were to return to 2.1 tomorrow—a virtual impossibility—Europe's current population of 727 million would still drop by 171 million by 2050. Since government welfare programs depend upon a steady inflow of tax money, few countries will have enough people by then to support such programs.

Even more surprising, the drop is not confined to developed countries. India's birth rate has fallen from about 5.6 in 1960 to 3.5 and is still dropping. Egypt, whose rate in 1960 at something over 7.0 was the world's highest, is down to 3.9. Mexico has dropped from 6.8 down to 3, Thailand from 6.5 to 2, less than replacement level. Thailand's is even lower than the American and Canadian levels—whose populations are being sustained by massive immigration, most of it from the Third World.

All this, needless to say, is bad news for an organization like Planned Parenthood, zealous preacher of the Save-the-World-with-Smaller-Families message (by abortion if necessary). Will PP now turn around and urge us to save it with bigger ones? Not very likely, when most of its funding is predicated on the need to reduce population. At the same time, the United Nations has been so successful in its don't-have-kids propaganda that it is rapidly making the absence of kids the world's No. 1 economic problem.

Meanwhile in Europe, where one government after another experi-   10
ments with costly child-bearing incentives, the universal experience is that
bribes don't work. Women must *want* to have children. So why don't they?
And why do men readily concur? Because, the Canadian study finds, they
both make their work more important. And this, we may discover, is a very
difficult mindset to change.

NOTES

[1] The study was released in February 2002.

[2] Paul Ehrlich is President, Center for Conservation Biology and Bing Professor of Population Studies
at Stanford University. He is author of *The Population Bomb* (1968) and many other books.

[3] The American Enterprise Institute, located in Washington, D.C., is a policy research institute that
announces itself as devoted to "strengthening the foundations of freedom." Its strongest supporter
was former president Ronald Reagan.

[4] *The American Spectator* is a monthly magazine devoted to exposing the fallacies of Democratic and
left-wing policies.

VOCABULARY

demographic sociology—the branch of social science concerned with vital and social statistics, such as births, deaths, marriages, disease rates

QUESTIONS

1. Why is it "unusual" that Health Canada would pay for the study Byfield describes?
    What assumptions about the federal government, and about governments in general,
    does Byfield make in this essay?

2. If it is true that Canadians prioritize work over starting a family, what do you think are
    the reasons? Do you think Byfield answers this question in the essay? If so, what is his
    answer? If not, why does he leave the question unanswered?

3. According to Byfield, American and Canadian populations "are being sustained by mas-
    sive immigration, most of it from the Third World." Does the essay present such immi-
    gration as a good way of maintaining replacement levels of population?

4. What kind of audience—hostile, neutral, friendly, or mixed—does Byfield seem to be
    writing for in this essay? What in the essay helps you identify its intended audience?

SUGGESTION FOR WRITING

There are likely many statements in Byfield's essay with which you strongly agree or disagree. Take any one statement and write a paragraph explaining why you agree or disagree
for either practical or ethical reasons. Then rewrite the paragraph as a letter to Byfield. How
does the change in audience affect the way you express your opinion? (For a discussion of
standards of evaluation and their relation to audience, see Chapter 8.)

My Wood

E. M. Forster

A few years ago I wrote a book which dealt in part with the difficulties of the English in India. Feeling that they would have had no difficulties in India themselves, the Americans read the book freely. The more they read it the better it made them feel, and a cheque to the author was the result. I bought a wood with the cheque. It is not a large wood—it contains scarcely any trees, and it is intersected, blast it, by a public footpath. Still, it is the first property that I have owned, so it is right that other people should participate in my shame, and should ask themselves, in accents that will vary in horror, this very important question: What is the effect of property on the character? Don't let's touch economics; the effect of private ownership upon the community as a whole is another question—a more important question, perhaps, but another one. Let's keep to psychology. If you own things, what's their effect on you? What's the effect on me of my wood?

In the first place, it makes me feel heavy. Property does have this effect. Property produces men of weight, and it was a man of weight who failed to get into the Kingdom of Heaven. He was not wicked, that unfortunate millionaire in the parable, he was only stout; he stuck out in front, not to mention behind, and as he wedged himself this way and that in the crystalline entrance and bruised his well-fed flanks, he saw beneath him a comparatively slim camel passing through the eye of a needle and being woven into the robe of God. The Gospels all through couple stoutness and slowness. They point out what is perfectly obvious, yet seldom realized: that if you have a lot of things you cannot move about a lot, that furniture requires dusting, dusters require servants, servants require insurance stamps,[1] and the whole tangle of them makes you think twice before you accept an invitation to dinner or go for a bathe in the Jordan.[2] Sometimes the Gospels proceed further and say with Tolstoy[3] that property is sinful; they approach the difficult ground of asceticism here, where I cannot follow them. But as to the immediate

The opening sentence of "My Wood" refers to the success of Edward Morgan Forster's most famous novel, *A Passage to India* (1924). Besides novels and short stories, Forster (1879–1970) wrote *Aspects of the Novel* (1927), a work of literary criticism; biography; travel literature; and two collections of essays: *Abinger Harvest* (1936), from which "My Wood" is taken, and *Two Cheers for Democracy* (1951).

"My Wood" is reprinted with permission of the Provost and Scholars of King's College, Cambridge, and The Society of Authors as the Literary Representatives of the Estate of E. M. Forster.

1

2

effects of property on people they just show straightforward logic. It produces men of weight. Men of weight cannot, by definition, move like the lightning from the East unto the West, and the ascent of a fourteen-stone[4] bishop into a pulpit is thus the exact antithesis of the coming of the Son of Man. My wood makes me feel heavy.

In the second place, it makes me feel it ought to be larger.   3

The other day I heard a twig snap in it. I was annoyed at first, for I   4 thought that someone was blackberrying, and depreciating the value of the undergrowth. On coming nearer, I saw it was not a man who had trodden on the twig and snapped it, but a bird, and I felt pleased. My bird. The bird was not equally pleased. Ignoring the relation between us, it took fright as soon as it saw the shape of my face, and flew straight over the boundary hedge into a field, the property of Mrs. Henessy, where it sat down with a loud squawk. It had become Mrs. Henessy's bird. Something seemed grossly amiss here, something that would not have occurred had the wood been larger. I could not afford to buy Mrs. Henessy out, I dared not murder her, and limitations of this sort beset me on every side. Ahab[5] did not want that vineyard—he only needed it to round off his property, preparatory to plotting a new curve—and all the land around my wood has become necessary to me in order to round off the wood. A boundary protects. But—poor little thing—the boundary ought in its turn to be protected. Noises on the edge of it. Children throw stones. A little more, and then a little more, until we reach the sea. Happy Canute![6] Happier Alexander![7] And after all, why should even the world be the limit of possession? A rocket containing a Union Jack, will, it is hoped, be shortly fired at the moon. Mars. Sirius. Beyond which . . . But these immensities ended by saddening me. I could not suppose that my wood was the destined nucleus of universal dominion—it is so very small and contains no mineral wealth beyond the blackberries. Nor was I comforted when Mrs. Henessy's bird took alarm for the second time and flew clean away from us all, under the belief that it belonged to itself.

In the third place, property makes its owner feel that he ought to do   5 something to it. Yet he isn't sure what. A restlessness comes over him, a vague sense that he has a personality to express—the same sense which, without any vagueness, leads the artist to an act of creation. Sometimes I think I will cut down such trees as remain in the wood, at other times I want to fill up the gaps between them with new trees. Both impulses are pretentious and empty. They are not honest movements towards money-making or beauty. They spring from a foolish desire to express myself and from an inability to enjoy what I have got. Creation, property, enjoyment form a sinister trinity in the human mind. Creation and enjoyment are both very very good, yet they are often unattainable without a material basis, and at such moments property pushes itself in as a substitute, saying, 'Accept me instead—I'm good enough for all three.' It is not enough. It is, as Shakespeare said of lust, 'The expense of spirit in a waste of shame': it is 'Before, a joy proposed; behind, a dream.'[8] Yet we don't know how to shun it. It is forced on us by our economic system as the alternative to starvation. It is also forced on us by an internal defect in the soul, by the feeling that in property may lie the germs of self-development and of exquisite or heroic deeds. Our life on earth is, and ought to be, material and carnal.[9] But we have not yet learned to manage our materialism and carnality properly; they are still entangled with the desire for ownership, where (in the words of Dante) 'Possession is one with loss.'

And this brings us to our fourth and final point: the blackberries.   6

Blackberries are not plentiful in this meagre grove, but they are easily   7 seen from the public footpath which traverses it, and all too easily gathered. Foxgloves, too—people will pull up the foxgloves, and ladies of an educational tendency even grub for toadstools to show them on the Monday in class. Other ladies, less educated, roll down the bracken in the arms of their gentlemen friends. There is paper, there are tins. Pray, does my wood belong to me or doesn't it? And, if it does, should I not own it best by allowing no one else to walk there? There is a wood near Lyme Regis,[10] also cursed by a public footpath, where the owner has not hesitated on this point. He has built high stone walls each side of the path, and has spanned it by bridges, so that the public circulate like termites while he gorges on the blackberries unseen. He really does own his wood, this able chap. Dives[11] in Hell did pretty well, but the gulf dividing him from Lazarus could be traversed by vision, and nothing traverses it here. And perhaps I shall come to this in time. I shall wall in and fence out until I really taste the sweets of property. Enormously stout, endlessly avaricious, pseudo-creative, intensely selfish, I shall weave upon my forehead the quadruple crown of possession until those nasty Bolshies[12] come and take it off again and thrust me aside into the outer darkness.

NOTES

[1] Insurance stamps: required in the UK to validate health and disability insurance benefits.

[2] The Jordan River flows between the Sea of Galilee and the Dead Sea.

[3] A Russian writer, author of *War and Peace* (1869) and *Anna Karenina* (1877), Leo Tolstoy (1828–1910) believed that possession of private property was an evil and practised severe asceticism.

[4] A stone equals fourteen pounds.

[5] Ahab was the seventh king of Israel from 874 to 853 BC. His wife, Jezebel, coveting a fine vineyard adjoining the palace grounds, arranged that its owner, Naboth, be convicted of blasphemy and executed. Ahab then became legal owner of the vineyard.

[6] Canute, or C'nut, was an ambitious conqueror of the eleventh century who was simultaneously King of England (1016–1035), Denmark (1018–1035), and Norway (1028–1035).

[7] Alexander the Great, King of Macedonia, sought to conquer the entire world to satisfy his desire for power and glory.

[8] The phrases are from Shakespeare's Sonnet 129. The single quotation marks are British usage.

[9] In Forster's day the word *carnal* referred to the body as the seat of all appetites. Also, archaically, *carnal* was used as the opposite of *spiritual.*

[10] Lyme Regis: a coastal town in England chartered as a royal borough in 1284 that eventually became known, in Forster's time, as a beach resort of some notoriety.

[11] Dives and Lazarus figure in a biblical story. Dives, a rich man, takes no notice of Lazarus, a beggar. Dives ends up in Hades and Lazarus in heaven (Luke 16:19–31).

[12] The Bolsheviks ("Bolshies") were the majority group of the Russian Social Democratic Party. They favoured revolutionary tactics to achieve socialism and seized power during the Russian Revolution to set up a workers' state.

QUESTIONS

1. In the first paragraph of "My Wood," Forster announces that his essay is concerned with the effects of owning something on a person's character. What does he mean by "character"? Does Forster confine his essay to the effects of ownership on the individual?

2. Does Forster list these effects in an order of increasing importance? In some other order? Explain.

3. Forster introduces the first three effects with similar topic sentences beginning "It [or "property"] makes me [or "its owner"] feel. . . ." Why does he abandon this formula when he introduces the fourth effect?

4. Forster's novel *A Passage to India* (1924) is about the corrupting effects of property and imperialism on the British in India. Thus it is ironic that the proceeds of this novel allowed Forster himself to buy property. Can you find other instances of irony, or an ironic tone, in the essay? Do you think irony, rather than direct statement, makes this essay more persuasive? Explain.

5. Throughout this essay, Forster makes a number of allusions to figures in religion, history, and literature. Why does Forster include these allusions? How do they affect you as a reader?

6. "My Wood" was first published in England in 1936. Does this context illuminate any of the attitudes and concerns in this essay?

SUGGESTION FOR WRITING

Using "My Wood" as a model, write an essay explaining how owning something (a house, a car, a CD collection) corrupted your character. Organize your essay in the same way Forster does, with an introduction and three or four middle paragraphs. Deal with one effect in each paragraph. Like Forster, you can add a separate conclusion. Include allusions if you think they will strengthen your rapport with your reader.

Preface to *The Bush Garden: Essays on the Canadian Imagination*

Northrop Frye

. . . [T]he question of Canadian identity, so far as it affects the creative 1
imagination, is not a "Canadian" question at all, but a regional question.
An environment turned outward to the sea, like so much of Newfoundland,
and one turned towards inland seas, like so much of the Maritimes, are
an imaginative contrast: anyone who has been conditioned by one in his
earliest years can hardly become conditioned by the other in the same way.
Anyone brought up on the urban plain of southern Ontario or the gentle
pays farmland along the south shore of the St. Lawrence may become fascinated by the great sprawling wilderness of Northern Ontario or Ungava,
may move there and live with its people and become accepted as one of
them, but if he paints or writes about it he will paint or write as an imaginative foreigner. And what can there be in common between an imagination nurtured on the prairies, where it is a centre of consciousness diffusing
itself over a vast flat expanse stretching to the remote horizon, and one
nurtured in British Columbia, where it is in the midst of gigantic trees and
mountains leaping into the sky all around it, and obliterating the horizon
everywhere?

Thus when the CBC is instructed by Parliament to do what it can to 2
promote Canadian unity and identity, it is not always realized that unity
and identity are quite different things to be promoting, and that in Canada
they are perhaps more different than they are anywhere else. Identity is local
and regional, rooted in the imagination and in works of culture; unity is
national in reference, international in perspective, and rooted in a political
feeling. There are, of course, containing imaginative forms which are common to the whole country, even if not
peculiar to Canada. I remember seeing
an exhibition of undergraduate painting,
mostly of landscapes, at a Maritime university. The students had come from all
over Canada, and one was from Ghana.
The Ghana student had imaginative qualities that the Canadians did not have, but
they had something that he did not have,
and it puzzled me to place it. I finally

Northrop Frye (1912–1991) is an internationally
renowned Canadian literary scholar. His influential works include *Fearful Symmetry* (1947),
a study of William Blake, and *Anatomy of
Criticism: Four Essays* (1957). This excerpt is
from the Preface to *The Bush Garden: Essays
on the Canadian Imagination* (1971).

realized what it was: he had lived, in his impressionable years, in a world where colour was a constant datum: he had never seen colour as a cycle that got born in spring, matured in a burst of autumn flame, and then died out into a largely abstract, black and white world. But that is a factor of latitude rather than region, and most of the imaginative factors common to the country as a whole are negative influences.

Negative, because in our world the sense of a specific environment as   3 something that provides a circumference for an imagination has to contend with a global civilization of jet planes, international hotels, and disappearing landmarks—that is, an obliterated environment. The obliterated environment produces an imaginative dystrophy that one sees all over the world, most dramatically perhaps in architecture and town planning (as it is ironically called), but in the other arts as well. Canada, with its empty spaces, its largely unknown lakes and rivers and islands, its division of language, its dependence on immense railways to hold it physically together, has had this peculiar problem of an obliterated environment throughout most of its history. The effects of this are clear in the curiously abortive cultural developments of Canada, as is said later in this book. They are shown even more clearly in its present lack of will to resist its own disintegration, in the fact that it is practically the only country left in the world which is a pure colony, colonial in psychology as well as in mercantile economics.

The essential element in the national sense of unity is the east-west   4 feeling, developed historically along the St. Lawrence-Great Lakes axis, and expressed in the national motto, *a mari usque ad mare.* The tension between this political sense of unity and the imaginative sense of locality is the essence of whatever the word "Canadian" means. Once the tension is given up, and the two elements of unity and identity are confused or assimilated to each other, we get the two endemic diseases of Canadian life. Assimilating identity to unity produces the empty gestures of cultural nationalism; assimilating unity to identity produces the kind of provincial isolation which is now called separatism.

The imaginative Canadian stance, so to speak, facing east and west, has   5 on one side one of the most powerful nations in the world; on the other there is the vast hinterland of the north, with its sense of mystery and fear of the unknown, and the curious guilt feelings that its uninhabited loneliness seems to inspire in this exploiting age. If the Canadian faces south, he becomes either hypnotized or repelled by the United States: either he tries to think up unconvincing reasons for being different and somehow superior to Americans, or he accepts being "swallowed up by" the United States as inevitable. What is resented in Canada about annexation to the United

States is not annexation itself, but the feeling that Canada would disappear into a larger entity without having anything of any real distinctiveness to contribute to that entity: that, in short, if the United States did annex Canada it would notice nothing except an increase in natural resources. If we face north, much the same result evidently occurs: this happened to the Diefenbaker campaign of 1956, which has been chronicled in books with such words as "lament" and "renegade" in their titles.[1]

Whenever the east-west context of the Canadian outlook begins to   6 weaken, separatism, which is always there, emerges as a political force. Every part of Canada has strong separatist feelings: there is a separatism of the Pacific Coast, of the Prairies, of the Maritimes, of Newfoundland, as well as of Quebec. Ontario, of course, began with a separatist movement from the American Revolution. But since the rise of the great ideological revolutionary movements of our time, whether communist, fascist, imperialist, Islamic or what not, separatism has been an almost wholly destructive force. The successful separatings, like that of Norway and Sweden in 1905, took place before the rise of these movements. In India and Pakistan, in the Arab-Jewish world, and in many other centres divided by language, colour or religion, separatism has seldom if ever stabilized the prejudices which gave rise to it, but has steadily increased them. Even where there is no political affiliation, the separation of Cuba from the American sphere of influence, or of Yugoslavia from the Russian one, cannot be a politically neutral act. Quebec in particular has gone through an exhilarating and, for the most part, emancipating social revolution. Separatism is the reactionary side of this revolution: what it really aims at is a return to the introverted malaise in which it began, when Quebec's motto was *je me souviens* and its symbols were those of the habitant rooted to his land with his mother church over his head, and all the rest of the blood-and-soil bit. One cannot go back to the past historically, but the squalid neo-fascism of the FLQ[2] terrorists indicates that one can always do so psychologically. . . .

I grew up in two towns, Sherbrooke and Moncton, where the popula-   7 tion was half English and half French, divided by language, education and religion, and living in a state of more or less amiable Apartheid. In the Eastern Townships the English-speaking group formed a northern spur of New England, and had at a much earlier time almost annexed themselves to New England, feeling much more akin to it than to Quebec. The English-speaking Maritimers, also, had most of their cultural and economic ties with New England, but their political connexion was with New France, so that culturally, from their point of view, Canada stopped at Fredericton and started again at Westmount. There were also a good many Maritime

French families whose native language was English, and so had the same cultural dislocation in reverse.

As a student going to the University of Toronto, I would take the train to Montreal, sitting up overnight in the coach, and looking forward to the moment in the early morning when the train came into Levis, on the south side of the St. Lawrence, and the great fortress of Quebec loomed out of the bleak dawn mists. I knew that much of the panorama was created by a modern railway hotel, but distance and fog lent enchantment even to that. Here was one of the imaginative and emotional centres of my own country and my own people, yet a people with whom I found it difficult to identify, what was different being not so much language as cultural memory. But the effort of making the identification was crucial: it helped me to see that a sense of unity is the opposite of a sense of uniformity. Uniformity, where everyone "belongs," uses the same clichés, thinks alike and behaves alike, produces a society which seems comfortable at first but is totally lacking in human dignity. Real unity tolerates dissent and rejoices in variety of outlook and tradition, recognizes that it is man's destiny to unite and not divide, and understands that creating proletariats and scapegoats and second-class citizens is a mean and contemptible activity. Unity, so understood, is the extra dimension that raises the sense of belonging into genuine human life. Nobody of any intelligence has any business being loyal to an ideal of uniformity: what one owes one's loyalty to is an ideal of unity, and a distrust of such a loyalty is rooted in a distrust of life itself. . . . 8

NOTES

[1] Frye is referring to George S. Grant's *Lament for a Nation: The Defeat of Canadian Nationalism* (1965) and Peter C. Newman's *Renegade in Power: The Diefenbaker Years* (1963).

[2] The FLQ stands for the *Front de libération du Québec* (Quebec Liberation Front). The FLQ was a terrorist group that claimed to support a sovereign Quebec. They were responsible for the October Crisis in 1970 when they kidnapped two government officials.

VOCABULARY

a mari usque ad mare—a Latin phrase that translates as "from sea to sea"

dystrophy—a wasting away, usually of organ or tissue

je me souviens—the provincial motto of Quebec, which means "I remember"

pays—Frye is using this French term in its historical sense, where the *pays* is a kind of community or county that is controlled by a medieval count

QUESTIONS

1. Frye, writing in 1971, claims that if the US were to annex Canada, "Canada would disappear into a larger entity without having anything of any real distinctiveness to contribute to that entity." In the present day, do you think this anxiety about annexation still exists? Does the anxiety about a non-distinct Canadian identity still persist? In other words, are Canadians better able to define themselves now in terms of a distinct nationalism? What are the distinct features?

2. Toward the end of this writing, Frye refers to Sherbrooke, Moncton, Fredericton, and Westmount. Depending on where you live, do you find these geographical references familiar or unfamiliar? How does your response fit in with Frye's thesis that Canadian identity is a "regional question"?

3. Frye argues that a culture of uniformity "is totally lacking in human dignity." With the apparent increase in big-box stores and chain stores in many cities and countries, do you agree or disagree with Frye's assertion?

SUGGESTION FOR WRITING

Write an essay that compares and contrasts Frye's arguments with Charles Taylor's arguments in "All for One, and One for All" (Readings).

The Missing Piece to the Gang-Violence Debate

Dan Gardner

1   Now that politicians and the public have finally started to discuss guns, gangs and murder, countless explanations have been offered. It's about fatherless families, weak immigration rules and a soft-touch criminal justice system, one side says. No, it's about racism and poverty, the other side counters, and too many guns.

2   All these points are important and worthy of discussion, but there's something missing. Most gang-related murders have one thing in common, one motivation, and yet scarcely a word has been said about this missing piece. But it is the key. Take it out of the equation and most of the killing stops.

3   To see this missing element in all its bloody glory, take a look at recent events in Mexico, a country embroiled in a gang war that makes the violence in Toronto look like a high-school debate.

4   The gun battles erupted in March 2003, in Nuevo Laredo, a city on the border with the United States. The federal government flooded the city with officers but that only displaced the fighting. Now the bullets are flying all over Mexico. About 1,000 people have died so far. And the war continues.

5   The fight is over control of the mammoth trade in marijuana, methamphetamine,[1] cocaine and heroin. Some of the drugs are produced in Mexico, others are imported from South America, but almost all are sold to willing buyers in the United States.

6   That the illicit drug trade is violent is no surprise to anyone, but what most people don't know is that violence in black markets tends to be cyclical. A mature market, with established networks and powerful figures in place, tends to minimize bloodshed. It's when the status quo is disrupted that all hell breaks loose.

Dan Gardner has worked as policy adviser for the Ontario Minister of Education and for the Premier of Ontario. Since 1997 he has been on the editorial board of the *Ottawa Citizen*. His writing has won numerous awards, including a Justicia Award, the National Newspaper Award, the Edward M. Brecher Award, and two Amnesty International Canadian Media Awards. He recently published *Future Babble: Why Expert Predictions Fail—and Why We Believe Them Anyway* (2010).

"The Missing Piece to the Gang-Violence Debate" was first published in the *Ottawa Citizen* on December 14, 2005. Material reprinted with the express permission of the Ottawa Citizen Group Inc., a division of Postmedia Network Inc.

That's exactly what happened in Mexico in March 2003, when Mexican 7
authorities arrested the drug lord who controlled the Nuevo Laredo smug-
gling conduit. President Vicente Fox praised the arrest as a great victory and
proof his country was making progress in the fight against the drug trade.

It doesn't look like such a triumph now. "Why are we in this situa- 8
tion?" Mexico's deputy attorney general told the *New York Times*. "Because
the only leaders who can contain the violence are the ones in jail."

That's the thing about drug enforcement: Even when you win, you 9
lose.

Yes, drugs are the missing piece in Canada's guns-and-gangs debate. 10
Why are gangsters shooting up Toronto and Winnipeg and Vancouver? It's
true that gang culture, fatherless homes, poverty and other factors people
are talking about may play a role. But in almost every case, the drug trade
is the reason the trigger is squeezed. If the black market didn't exist, neither
would most of the bloodshed.

Homicide studies in many countries have repeatedly confirmed this 11
fact. One review of murders in New York City in 1988 found 39 per cent
of killings—all killings, not just those involving gangs—involved a drug-
trade business dispute. If you can't sue, you shoot.

Now, one could say that the answer is tough enforcement. Wipe out 12
the drug trade and the violence goes with it.

Of course anyone who even points a gun at another human being must be 13
caught and punished. But it is a mistake to think law enforcement can eliminate the drug trade and the violence swirling around it. As every economist
knows, markets are self-correcting mechanisms. Even if the police took down
every drug dealer in Toronto tomorrow, the unsatisfied demand for drugs
would drive the price up and that higher price would entice new traders into
the market. It's the law of supply and demand and it trumps any law passed
by Parliament.

Of course politicians don't like to admit they aren't omnipotent. And 14
they really don't want to say unpopular things in public, particularly during
an election. And so both the Liberals and the Conservatives have prom-
ised to deal with gang crime by, yet again, increasing law enforcement and
boosting sentences.

This will fail. And worse. 15

Jeffrey Miron, an economist at Boston University, has studied the links 16
between violence and prohibition, of both alcohol and other drugs, over
the last century. His research found a strong correlation not only between
violence and a drug's legal status—the moment it's banned, violence goes
up—but also between violence and the amount of money spent trying to
enforce the ban.[2]

After controlling for other factors that might be influencing the result,   17
Miron came to a clear conclusion: "Higher enforcement is associated with
higher homicide."

I'm sure Mexicans are starting to get Miron's point. And if politicians   18
in this country ignore the evidence of almost a century of failure and greatly
ratchet up law enforcement, so will Canadians.

NOTES

[1] Methamphetamine is a very addictive stimulant drug known on the streets as "meth," or as methamphetamine hydrochloride, "crystal meth."

[2] Dr. Jeffrey A. Miron has developed his case concerning drug policy in several articles and studies, including *Drug War Crimes: The Consequences of Prohibition* (Oakland, CA: The Independent
Institute, 2004).

VOCABULARY

correlation—a reciprocal relationship, especially in statistical or scientific studies

omnipotent—all-powerful

QUESTIONS

1. Gardner claims one cause is always ignored in explanations of gang-related murders, but
   does not explicitly reveal this cause until the middle of his essay. Why?

2. In this essay, Gardner is not just identifying causes of violence (cause/effect analysis) but
   also arguing for the importance of one particular cause (cause/effect argument). What is
   the standard of evaluation he uses for this argument?

3. Much of Gardner's evidence consists of a comparison between events in Mexico and
   more recent events in Canada. Do you find this comparison convincing? Why or why
   not?

SUGGESTION FOR WRITING

Write an essay comparing Gardner's views on drugs with those either of Bruce Alexander
and Stefa Shaler or of Gabor Maté (see Readings). You can either make a point about the
similarities and differences in the views developed by the essays (analysis essays) or you can
judge the value of the different positions.

Kiddy Thinks

Alison Gopnik

When my son was a toddler his first question about a meal was always: "What's for dessert?" One day we had pineapple in kirsch. He spat it out, then looked at the adults devouring the stuff, and said: "Pineapple: it's yucky for me but it's yummy for you." For weeks afterwards, he would stop suddenly in the middle of a game and say: "Pineapple: yucky for me but yummy for you," as if he had discovered the most extraordinary fact of life. And in a sense he had: the realization that people think and feel differently is a profound one. 1

When we look around a room full of people, we don't see bags of skin and cloth draped over the furniture. We see other people, people with thoughts and emotions, desires and beliefs, sometimes like our own, sometimes not. And by the time they are 18 months old, this is what toddlers see as well. But how do such tiny children get from bags of skin to "other minds"? 2

In the past 30 years we have learned more about what young children know and how they learn than we did in the preceding 2,500 years. And this has revolutionised our view of children. For centuries, psychologists and philosophers agreed that babies were the opposite of adults. They were emotional and passive, dominated by perception and incapable of rational thought. John Locke[1] said they were "blank slates". 3

Today, scientists have only recently begun to appreciate just how much even the youngest babies know—and how much and how quickly they learn. There are three elements to this new picture. First, that children know a great deal, literally from the moment they are born. Second, that they are born with extremely powerful learning abilities. And, finally, that adults appear to be "programmed" to unconsciously teach babies and young children just the things they need to know. 4

In *How Babies Think,* my co-authors and I argue that very young children use the same strategies as scientists. They think, observe, formulate theories, make predictions, and do experiments. They also change their theories as they accumulate counter-evidence to their predictions. 5

Alison Gopnik is a professor of developmental psychology at the University of California, Berkeley, and a researcher for the Institute of Human Development (IHD), an organized research unit at Berkeley since 1927. Gopnik's specialties in the area of psychology include cognition and language development and children's theories of mind.

"Kiddy Thinks," published in the *Guardian Weekly,* February 3-9, 2000, was adapted from a chapter in *The Scientist in the Crib.* © Alison Gopnik, co-author of *The Scientist in the Crib,* HarperCollins, 2000.

But where scientists focus their attention on distant stars and invisible   6
microbes, babies concentrate on everyday things: blocks, pet dogs, words
and, most important: Mum and Dad and Aunt Ethel. In fact understanding other people seems to be one of the most crucial items in the scientific
agenda of childhood, and it's a good illustration of how early learning takes
place.

To begin with, children are born knowing that people are special.   7
Newborn babies (the youngest tested was only 42 minutes old) can imitate
facial expressions. There are no mirrors in the womb; newborns have never
seen their own face. These tiny babies must somehow already understand the
similarity between their own internal feeling (of, say, sticking out their tongue)
and the external face they see (a round shape from which something pink pro-
trudes). Newborn babies not only prefer faces to things but also recognise that
those faces are *like their own face.* Nature, it seems, gives human beings a jump
start on the Other Minds problem.

And what a jump start. By the time they are nine months old, babies   8
can tell the difference between expressions of happiness, sadness and anger,
and understand something about the emotions that produce those expressions. By the time they are one, they know that they will see something by
looking where other people point; they know that they should do something by watching what others do; and they know how they should feel
about something by seeing how others feel.

For instance, an adult can look in two boxes. She looks into one with   9
an expression of joy and into the other with disgust. The baby will happily reach into the box that made her happy, but won't touch the box that
disgusted her. The baby has discovered that its initial emotional rapport
with other people extends to joint attitudes towards the world. In a simple
way, one-year-olds already participate in a culture. But as babies learn that
people usually have the same attitudes towards objects as they do, they are
setting themselves up to learn something else, something more disturbing:
they discover that sometimes people *don't* have the same attitudes.

Observe what happens when a baby reaches for a forbidden object—a   10
lamp cord, say. It must seem perverse to the one-year-old: the more clearly
she indicates her desire, the more adamantly her carer keeps it away. Even
though the baby and the grown-up are reacting to the same object, their
attitudes toward the object seem to be different.

By the time babies are about one-and-a-half, they start to understand   11
the nature of these differences between people and become fascinated. If
you offer a baby two bowls, one of biscuits, the other of raw broccoli, all
the babies prefer the biscuits. But if the researcher indicates to the baby that
she hates biscuits and loves broccoli, then hands the bowls to the baby and

says: "Could you give me some?" something interesting happens. Fourteen-month-olds, with their innocent assumption that we all want the same thing, give her biscuits. But the wiser 18-month-olds give her broccoli, even though they themselves despise it. These tiny children have learned that other people's desires may conflict with their own.

This is also dramatically apparent in everyday life. Parents all know, and dread, the "terrible twos." While one-year-olds seem irresistibly drawn to forbidden objects (that lamp cord again), the two-year-olds seem deliberately bloody-minded. She doesn't even look at the lamp cord. Instead, her hand goes out to touch it as she looks, steadily, gravely, at you.   12

This demonic behaviour is quite rational, though. Our broccoli experiments show that children only begin to understand the differences in desires at 18 months. The terrible twos seem to involve a systematic exploration of that idea, like an experimental research programme. Toddlers are testing the extent to which their desires and those of others may conflict. The grave look is directed at you because you and your reaction, rather than the lamp cord, are the interesting thing. The terrible twos reflect a clash between children's need to understand other people and their need to live happily with them. If the child is a budding scientist, we parents are the laboratory rats.   13

Two-year-olds also have to learn how visual perception works. Toddlers love hide and seek but aren't very good at it—a toddler will bury his head under the table with his bottom in view. In our lab, we explored when children learn how to hide things. Suppose I put a child on one side of a table and sit on the other. Then I put a screen and a toy on the table and ask the child to hide the toy from me. At 24 months, a toddler will put the toy on *my* side of the screen, so that it is actually hidden from them, but not from me. But 36-month-olds get this right. In fact, they'll often tell me they can see the toy but I can't. In the months in between, we observed many children experimenting. They would switch the toy from one side to the other, or come around to my side of the screen to make sure the toy really was hidden.   14

But this isn't the end of the story. Three-year-olds still have trouble with another important fact about people. They know that we can see different things, but not that what we think about the world may be wrong.   15

In a classic experiment, you can give three-year-olds a shut chocolate box. They open it and it turns out to have pencils inside. Then you ask them about another child in the nursery: "What will Nicky think is in the box: pencils or chocolates?" Three-year-olds report that Nicky will say there are pencils inside. They don't understand that Nicky will probably make the same mistake they made. Four-year-olds know that Nicky will be misled by the picture on the box.   16

Like scientists, children change their theories precisely because they   17
make the wrong predictions. In "mistaken belief" experiments, simply telling children the right answer makes no difference. Like scientists, children
at first resist counter-evidence. Virginia Slaughter and I visited three-year-
olds over several weeks and gave them examples of mistaken beliefs: a golf
ball that turned out to be soap, a yellow duck that looked green when put
behind blue plastic. Each time the child made the wrong prediction, we
presented them with counter-evidence. After two weeks these three-year-
olds understood a brand-new "mistaken belief" task, one they had never
seen before, much better than a control group.

This experiment shows that even very young children are naturally   18
able to alter their predictions in the light of new evidence. But it also shows
how important other people can be: our adult behaviour had helped the
children to work out the correct answer. Of course, we're developmental
psychologists.

Do grown-ups naturally help children learn in their everyday lives? The   19
new research suggests they do. One of the most dramatic examples of this
is the sing-song voice adults use when they talk to babies. This speech style
helps children sort out the sounds of language.

Similarly, the way that parents talk about the mind seems to influence   20
their children's everyday psychology. What are the consequences of this new
view? The research *doesn't* mean there is some set of flashcards that will help
babies be brighter. Babies are already as bright as can be. They learn through
everyday play, and through the care and attention of adults around them.
It also *doesn't* mean there is some "critical period" for learning in the first
three years or some set of experiences children must have. Children and
even adults keep learning throughout life. It definitely *doesn't* mean mothers
should quit their jobs. Anyone who cares for small children and is sensitive
to what interests them can teach them what they need to know.

On the other hand, the research does suggest that the everyday, unre-   21
munerated, unremarkable work of caring for babies and young children
is extremely important. Humans have managed to learn so much because
generations of adults put effort into caring for children.

Ironically, this new scientific perspective comes when young children   22
and parents are under enormous pressure. We still penalise parents for taking time off work to be with their children, instead of rewarding them.
Most parents face agonising dilemmas as they balance jobs and children. If
we really want babies to learn, we should ditch the videotapes and flashcards
and work for paid parental leave, flexible work arrangements and publicly
supported, high-quality childcare.

NOTE

[1] English philosopher John Locke (1632–1704) believed that all of our knowledge comes from our senses. He thought that children were "blank slates" (that is, clean sheets of paper), passively acquiring knowledge through sensory impressions from the world around them.

VOCABULARY

adamantly—strongly, stubbornly

unremunerated—not paid to do

QUESTIONS

1. Gopnik begins this essay by telling a story about her own child. Is this narrative introduction effective? Why or why not?

2. Where does Gopnik first indicate her subject? Where does she present her thesis? State her thesis in your own words.

3. Gopnik uses process analysis as her main method for developing her material, but she also includes lots of specific examples. Are these examples effective in clarifying her point? How does Gopnik make an example of what one child does representative of what all children do?

4. How does Gopnik blend analysis and persuasion in this essay? Do you find the assertions she makes in the final paragraph convincing?

SUGGESTION FOR WRITING

You can use process analysis as Gopnik does in this article to explain how something happens, but you can also use process analysis to give your reader directions on how to carry out a procedure. For both kinds of writing, you need an introduction that makes the subject of your essay seem interesting and important. Choose either kind of analysis and write an introductory paragraph. Possible topics include the following: how to burn a CD, how to give a cat a bath, how diabetes can trigger mood swings, how films are made. You might consider treating your subject ironically, as W. S. Merwin does in "Unchopping a Tree" (Readings).

The Voyagers

Linda Hogan

I remember one night, lying on the moist spring earth beside my mother. The fire of stars stretched away from us, and the mysterious darkness traveled without limit beyond where we lay on the turning earth. I could smell the damp new grass that night, but I could not touch or hold such black immensity that lived above our world, could not contain within myself even a small corner of the universe.

There seemed to be two kinds of people: earth people and those others, the sky people, who stumbled over pebbles while they walked around with their heads in clouds. Sky people loved different worlds than I loved; they looked at nests in treetops and followed the long white snake of vapor trails. But I was an earth person, and while I loved to gaze up at night and stars, I investigated the treasures at my feet, the veined wing of a dragonfly opening a delicate blue window to secrets of earth, a luster-less beetle that drank water thirstily from the tip of my finger and was transformed into sudden green and metallic brilliance. It was enough mystery for me to ponder the bones inside our human flesh, bones that through some incredible blueprint of life grow from a moment's sexual passion between a woman and a man, walk upright a short while, then walk themselves back to dust.

Years later, lost in the woods one New Year's eve, a friend found the way home by following the north star, and I began to think that learning the sky might be a practical thing. But it was the image of earth from out in space that gave me upward-gazing eyes. It was the same image that gave the sky people an anchor in the world, for it returned us to our planet in a new and loving way.

To dream of the universe is to know that we are small and brief as insects, born in a flash of rain and gone a moment

Linda Hogan (b. 1947), a retired associate professor of creative writing and Native American literature at the University of Colorado, is a Chickasaw poet, novelist, and essayist. Her works include *Walk Gently Upon the Earth* (2010), *The Inner Journey: Views from Native Traditions* (2009), *Sightings: The Gray Whales' Mysterious Journey* (2002), *The Woman Who Watches over the World: A Native Memoir* (2001), *The Sweet Breathing of Plants: Women and the Green World* (2000), and *Power* (1998). She has won many literary awards, including the Mountains and Plains Booksellers Spirit of the West Literary Achievement Award (2007). "The Voyagers" appears in *Dwellings: A Spiritual History of the Living World* (1995), essays exploring Hogan's ideas about the interconnections between humans and nature.

later. We are delicate and our world is fragile. It was the transgression of Galileo[1] to tell us that we were not the center of the universe, and now, even in our own time, the news of our small being here is treacherous enough that early in the space program, the photographs of Earth were classified as secret documents by the government. It was thought, and rightfully so, that the image of our small blue earth would forever change how we see ourselves in context with the world we inhabit.

When we saw the deep blue and swirling white turbulence of our earth   5 reflected back to us, says photographer Steven Meyers,[2] we also saw "the visual evidence of creative and destructive forces moving around its surface, we saw for the first time the deep blackness of that which surrounds it, we sensed directly, and probably for the first time, our incredibly profound isolation, and the special fact of our being here." It was a world whose intricately linked-together ecosystem could not survive the continuing blows of exploitation.

In 1977, when the Voyagers[3] were launched, one of these spacecraft   6 carried the Interstellar Record, a hoped-for link between earth and space that is filled with the sounds and images of the world around us. It carries parts of our lives all the way out to the great Forever. It is destined to travel out of our vast solar system, out to the far, unexplored regions of space in hopes that somewhere, millions of years from now, someone will find it like a note sealed in a bottle carrying our history across the black ocean of space. This message is intended for the year 8,000,000.

One greeting onboard from Western India says: "Greetings from a   7 human being of the Earth. Please contact." Another, from Eastern China, but resembling one that could have been sent by my own Chickasaw[4] people, says: "Friends of space, how are you all? Have you eaten yet? Come visit us if you have time."

There is so much hope in those greetings, such sweetness. If found,   8 these messages will play our world to a world that's far away. They will sing out the strangely beautiful sounds of Earth, sounds that in all likelihood exist on no other planet in the universe. By the time the record is found, if ever, it is probable that the trumpeting bellows of elephants, the peaceful chirping of frogs and crickets, the wild dogs baying out from the golden needle and record, will be nothing more than a gone history of what once lived on this tiny planet in the curving tail of a spiral galaxy. The undeciphered language of whales will speak to a world not our own, to people who are not us. They will speak of what we value the most on our planet, things that in reality we are almost missing.

A small and perfect world is traveling there, with psalms journeying   9 past Saturn's icy rings, all our treasured life flying through darkness, going its way alone back through the universe. There is the recorded snapping of fire, the song of a river traveling the continent, the living wind passing through dry grasses, all the world that burns and pulses around us, even the comforting sound of a heartbeat taking us back to the first red house of our mothers' bodies, all that, floating through the universe.

The Voyager carries music. A Peruvian wedding song is waiting to be heard in the far, distant regions of space. The Navajo Night Chant[5] travels through darkness like medicine for healing another broken world. Blind Willie Johnson's[6] slide guitar and deep down blues are on that record, in night's long territory.   10

The visual records aboard the Voyager depict a nearly perfect world, showing us our place within the whole; in the image of a snow-covered forest, trees are so large that human figures standing at their base are almost invisible. In the corner of this image is a close-up of a snow crystal's elegant architecture of ice and air. Long-necked geese fly across another picture, a soaring eagle. Three dolphins, sun bright on their silver sides, leap from a great ocean wave. Beneath them are underwater blue reefs with a shimmering school of fish. It is an abundant, peaceful world, one where a man eats from a vine heavy with grapes, an old man walks through a field of white daisies, and children lovingly touch a globe in a classroom. To think that the precious images of what lives on earth beside us, the lives we share with earth, some endangered, are now tumbling through time and space, more permanent than we are, and speaking the sacred language of life that we ourselves have only just begun to remember.   11

We have sent a message that states what we most value here on earth: respect for all life and ways. It is a sealed world, a seed of what we may become. What an amazing document is flying above the clouds, holding Utopia.[7] It is more magical and heavy with meaning than the cave paintings of Lascaux,[8] more wise than the language of any holy book. These are images that could sustain us through any cold season of ice or hatred or pain.   12

In *Murmurs of Earth,*[9] written by members of the committee who selected the images and recordings, the records themselves are described in a way that attests to their luminous quality of being: "They glisten, golden, in the sunlight, encased in aluminum cocoons." It sounds as though, through some magical metamorphosis, this chrysalis of life will emerge in another part of infinity, will grow to a wholeness of its own, and return to us alive, full-winged, red, and brilliant.   13

There is so much hope there that it takes us away from the dark times of horror we live in, a time when the most cruel aspects of our natures have been revealed to us in regions of earth named Auschwitz, Hiroshima,   14

My Lai, and Rwanda,[10] a time when televised death is the primary amusement of our children, when our children are killing one another on the streets.

At second glance, this vision for a new civilization, by its very presence, shows us what is wrong with our world. Defining Utopia, we see what we could be now, on earth, at this time, and next to the images of a better world, that which is absent begins to cry out. The underside of our lives grows in proportion to what is denied. The darkness is made darker by the record of light. A screaming silence falls between the stars of space. Held inside that silence are the sounds of gunfire, the wailings of grief and hunger, the last, extinct song of a bird. The dammed river goes dry, along with its valleys. Illnesses that plague our bodies live in this crack of absence. The broken link between us and the rest of our world grows too large, and the material of nightmares grows deeper while the promises for peace and equality are empty, are merely dreams without reality.   15

But how we want it, how we want that half-faced, one-sided God.   16

In earlier American days, when Catholic missions were being erected in Indian country, a European woman, who was one of the first white contacts for a northern tribe of people, showed sacred paintings to an Indian woman. The darker woman smiled when she saw a picture of Jesus and Mary encircled in their haloes of light. A picture of the three kings with their crowns and gifts held her interest. But when she saw a picture of the crucifixion, the Indian woman hurried away to warn others that these were dangerous people, people to fear, who did horrible things to one another. This picture is not carried by the Voyager, for fear we earth people would "look" cruel. There is no image of this man nailed to a cross, no saving violence. There are no political messages, no photographs of Hiroshima. This is to say that we know our own wrongdoings.   17

Nor is there a true biology of our species onboard because NASA[11] officials vetoed the picture of a naked man and pregnant woman standing side by side, calling it "smut." They allowed only silhouettes to be sent, as if our own origins, the divine flux of creation that passes between a man and a woman, are unacceptable, something to hide. Even picture diagrams of the human organs, musculature, and skeletal system depict no sexual organs, and a photograph showing the birth of an infant portrays only the masked, gloved physician lifting the new life from a mass of sheets, the mother's body hidden. While we might ask if they could not have sent the carved stone gods and goddesses in acts of beautiful sexual intimacy on temple walls in India, this embarrassment about our own carriage of life and act of creative generation nevertheless reveals our feelings of physical vulnerability and discomfort with our own life force.   18

From an American Indian perspective, there are other problems here.   19
Even the language used in the selection process bespeaks many of the failings
of an entire system of thought and education. From this record, we learn
about our relationships, not only with people, but with everything on earth.
For example, a small gold-eyed frog seen in a human hand might have been
a photograph that bridges species, a statement of our kinship with other
lives on earth, but the hand is described, almost apologetically, as having "a
dirty fingernail." Even the clay of creation has ceased to be the rich element
from which life grows. I recall that the Chilean poet Pablo Neruda wrote
"What can I say without touching the earth with my hands?"[12] We must
wonder what of value can ever be spoken from lives that are lived outside of
life, without a love or respect for the land and other lives.

In *Murmurs of Earth,* one of the coauthors writes about hearing dol-   20
phins from his room, "breathing, playing with one another. Somehow,"
he says, "one had the feeling that they weren't just some sea creatures
but some very witty and intelligent beings living in the next room." This
revealing choice of words places us above and beyond the rest of the world,
as though we have stepped out of our natural cycles in our very existence
here on earth. And isn't our world full of those rooms? We inhabit only a
small space in the house of life. In another is a field of corn. In one more is
the jungle world of the macaw. Down the hall, a zebra is moving. Beneath
the foundation is the world of snakes and the five beating hearts of the
earthworm.

In so many ways, the underside of our lives is here. Even the metals   21
used in the record tell a story about the spoils of inner earth, the laborers in
the hot mines. Their sweat is in that record, hurtling away from our own
galaxy.

What are the possibilities, we wonder, that our time capsule will be   22
found? What is the possibility that there are lives other than our own in
the universe? Our small galaxy, the way of the milk, the way of sustenance,
is only one of billions of galaxies, but there is also the possibility that we
are the only planet where life opens, blooms, is gone, and then turns over
again. We hope this is not the case. We are so young we hardly know what
it means to be a human being, to have natures that allow for war. We
barely even know our human histories, so much having unraveled before
our time, and while we know that our history creates us, we hope there is
another place, another world we can fly to when ours is running out. We
have come so far away from wisdom, a wisdom that is the heritage of all
people, an old kind of knowing that respects a community of land, animals, plants, and other people as equal to ourselves. Where we know the
meaning of relationship.

As individuals, we are not faring much better. We are young. We hardly   23
know who we are. We face the search for ourselves alone. In spite of our
search through the universe, we do not know our own personal journeys.
We still wonder if the soul weighs half an ounce, if it goes into the sky at
the time of our death, if it also reaches out, turning, through the universe.

But still, this innocent reaching out is a form of ceremony, as if the   24
Voyager were a sacred space, a ritual enclosure that contains our dreaming
the way a cathedral holds the bones of saints.

The people of earth are reaching out. We are having a collective vision.   25
Like young women and men on a vision quest, we seek a way to live out the
peace of the vision we have sent to the world of stars. We want to live as if
there is no other place, as if we will always be here. We want to live with
devotion to the world of waters and the universe of life that dwells above
our thin roofs.

I remember that night with my mother, looking up at the black sky   26
with its turning stars. It was a mystery, beautiful and distant. Her body I
came from, but our common ancestor is the earth, and the ancestor of earth
is space. That night we were small, my mother and I, and we were innocent.
We were children of the universe. In the gas and dust of life, we are voyagers. Wait. Stop here a moment. Have you eaten? Come in. Eat.

NOTES

[1] Galileo (1564–1642) was an Italian physicist and astronomer who supported Copernicus's theory
that the earth and planets moved around the sun. He developed the astronomical telescope, which
enabled him to discover craters on the moon, and showed that the Milky Way is composed of stars.

[2] Steven Meyers, photographer, is the author of *On Seeing Nature* (Golden, CO: Fulcrum, 1987).

[3] Voyagers: unmanned interplanetary probes designed to send information about the outer planetary
system back to Earth.

[4] Chickasaw: a tribe now based in Oklahoma, in the United States.

[5] The Navajo are located in Arizona and New Mexico, in the United States. The Night Chant is a
sacred ritual.

[6] Blind Willie Johnson (c. 1902–1949) was a Texas-born religious singer-songwriter and guitarist who
gave black people inspiration in difficult times.

[7] Utopia, derived from the title of Thomas More's novel *Utopia* (1516), refers to an imagined ideal
place or state of social or political perfection.

[8] The cave paintings of Lascaux, situated in Dordogne, France, are paintings of animals believed to
date from 15 000 to 13 000 BC. They were discovered in 1940 in a cave believed to be an ancient
centre for the performance of hunting and magical rites.

[9] Carl Sagan et al., *Murmurs of Earth: The Voyager Interstellar Record* (New York: Random House, 1978).

[10] Auschwitz was a Nazi concentration camp in Poland, operational 1940–1945, where up to four million prisoners died. Hiroshima is a city in Japan, the site of the first wartime use of the atomic bomb,

in August 1945, when more than 160 000 people died. My Lai refers to the massacre of civilian elderly, women, and children in a village in Vietnam by US army troops in March 1968. Rwanda is a country in east-central Africa, site of the tribal massacre of half a million Tutsis in 1994.

[11] NASA: National Aeronautics and Space Administration (US).

[12] The quotation is from "Party's End," section XIII of *Ceremonial Songs,* 1961, in Pablo Neruda, *A New Decade: Poems: 1958–1967,* trans. Ben Belitt and Alastair Reid (New York: Grove, 1969).

VOCABULARY

ecosystem—the ecological balance of the Earth's environment

metamorphosis—transformation or change of form by magic or natural development

musculature—the muscular system of the body

QUESTIONS

1. How does Hogan develop her initial distinction between "earth people" and "sky people" in the course of her essay?

2. The selection of sounds and images for the Interstellar Record, as Hogan describes it, suggests both a hopeful desire to communicate with other intelligences and a desire to make ourselves look as good as possible. What, in Hogan's opinion, does the Interstellar Record suggest about what we value on our own planet?

3. What does the decision to omit some aspects of life on Earth from the space capsule reveal about us?

4. How does Hogan develop a variety of possible meanings for the term *voyager*? How, for example, is the Voyager connected with the dream vision?

5. How would you describe the tone of this essay? Try to be specific about Hogan's attitude toward herself, her readers, and her subject.

6. Do you think Hogan presents a distinctively Aboriginal perspective on the issues she discusses in this essay?

SUGGESTION FOR WRITING

Do you think a space capsule should present us as we wish to be seen by strangers, or should we be more honest? If you were in charge of assembling the materials for a space capsule, what aspects of human life and Earth's ecosystems would you include? What would you leave out? Write a short essay on this topic.

He Was a Boxer When I Was Small

Lenore Keeshig-Tobias

His thundering rages are most vivid, his tears subtle. Watching and feeling for them, but unable to bridge the gap, I learned to love, hate him all in the same breath. No one ever knew this. They saw a kid in love with her father. 1

He was a boxer when I was small. People say he was good and would have made it had he started younger, but he had a wife and growing family to provide for. Amateur boxing paid nothing, but he loved it. I think he must have been about twenty-two then. He claims that we were too young to have seen him fight, but I remember. 2

I remember the lights, the ring, my mother shouting "Kill him, Don, kill him!" and my sister eating popcorn. I remember how he'd shadow box at home, punching, dancing lightly, swinging left—left—right, and missing because there was nothing there except air. 3

His prowess in the ring must have cowed my mother during his drunken rages. Or maybe it was his thundering voice, or the way the furniture went flying. Yet, with all his storming and her crying, I couldn't help but think that there was something more, something he couldn't articulate. When his ferocity gave way to tears of exasperation, I would cry with him, my dad, the boxer, the young man out to beat the world. 4

"It's not his fault," I would argue. "It's not all his fault, it's Mom's fault too," I would tell Gramma, even if I didn't know whose fault it was. She would disdainfully look off into the trees whenever I answered with this. Mom had Gramma to stick up for her. Dad had no one, only me. 5

There were, of course, times when things were fine. Dad would have a good job,[1] Mom would be fresh with child,[1] and my sisters and brothers carefree. We would spread a blanket in the front yard, or gather around the kitchen table. Dad would tell stories of Nanabush,[2] stories of long ago when only the Indians and animals lived here. Good ole Nanabush danced before our eyes. We saw his courage, his generosity and love for the animals and our people. We also saw his 6

Lenore Keeshig-Tobias (b. 1950) is an Ojibway poet, playwright, fiction writer, editor, filmmaker, and cultural activist. Her children's book, *Bird Talk* (1991), is a bilingual English/Ojibway story. She has edited *The Ontario Indian, Sweetgrass,* and *The Magazine to Re-establish the Trickster: New Native Writing,* as well as *Into the Moon: Heart, Mind, Body, Soul,* a collection of writings by the Native Women's Writing Circle (1996).

"He Was a Boxer When I was Small" is reprinted with permission of Lenore Keeshig-Tobias.

anger, miserly ways, and blundering practical jokes, but we loved him and would laugh until we cried.

At other times we would play, all of us, seven, eight, nine of us rolling 7 and tumbling while Mom sat back beaming like a big fat sun. We'd pretend box, then race, roll, and tumble again. How I wished those times would go on and on. He would stand shoulders up to the sky, as we climbed. He could carry all of us on his back.

One summer my sides ached with laughter. Then one day, I moved 8 to the edge of the blanket and sat back to watch my sisters and brothers giggle and climb. Dad leaned forward, then down on hands and knees, all those laughing children on his back. That was when I noticed grey hairs hiding in his side-burns. I went to my room, dug out his boxing pictures, and cried.

I was about ten at the time, my dad about twenty-nine, and my 9 mother twenty-eight. After that summer I never again played like that with the others. I felt too old, and instead I stood back and watched. I watched my sisters and brothers grow up. I watched him grow older, fighting all the way.

When he went to school, he tells us, he spoke only Ojibway[3] and a bit 10 of French. His grandmother was French. The only English he knew was yes and no. Indian kids, in those days, were not allowed to speak anything but English in school. So besides being punished for speaking Ojibway, he was also punished for giving the wrong answer which was either yes or no.

He says he eventually learned to read, write, and do arithmetic, and he 11 laughs when he tells us how he would get on the teacher's good side and then steal test answers for the rest of the class. She never had to keep any of them in after class, but then she never realized how they had cheated and helped each other. She never realized what a bunch of stupid kids she graduated.

My dad never graduated. He learned enough to be able to go out and 12 get a job.

Once, Dad was working in Toronto as an industrial painter (Indian 13 men are noted for their surefootedness in high places). Mom, the kids, and I sat around the supper table. We didn't expect him home until the week-end, but there he was, standing in the doorway with his suitcase. Later that evening, I heard him confiding to Mom his reason for coming home.

He had beat up a fellow worker, a wisecracking whiteman, who had 14 been bugging him for weeks. The ambulance was being called for when he left. My dad was afraid, afraid because he was Indian and because he had once been a boxer.

In between the various jobs on the reserve or high-painting and iron-work off in some big city, there were bouts of drinking and bouts of fanatical Christianity with thunderous preaching. We cowered every weekend waiting for him to erupt. 15

"Damn you, goddamn you," I would curse under my breath. "Why do you make our lives so miserable?" 16

We grew up as Christians, something I shall never forgive those Catholic missionaries for, although for a time it was the most settling thing in our lives. Dad made sure, in spite of everything else, his kids went to church. If he couldn't be a good father to us, then God would. But God wasn't an Indian, or a boxer, and my dad was. His visits to the Parish priest taught him fear of the Lord. But we went faithfully to church because of fear of our dad, and fear for our furniture. 17

We should all be good at sports because Indians are known for that. Look at Jim Thorpe, Tom Longboat, George Armstrong.[4] We should all get a good education and not be stupid like him. We should all go to church every Sunday and not drink like him . . . he'd preach. 18

I got fed up with things, eventually. I was no good at sports. School was boring. I stopped going to church and even dared to argue with my dad. Finally, Mom and Dad had the priest come talk to me, to get me to go back to church and school. 19

The old man would listen when I told him that I would like to pray under the trees. He laughed. We argued. He laughed again, shook his head, and said something about excommunication. I told him off, that I would rather go to hell and burn with the rest of my heathen savage ancestors because there would be too few Indians in heaven and I'd probably get lonely. The old missionary wobbled into the house, quite shaken, and told my dad that I was "lost." Dad came out, white-faced, and beat me. He told me to leave, that he had other kids to worry about. 20

I settled into my own life, fighting bouts of my own, but continued hearing of his through letters and phone calls. 21

Was there no end? Mom and the kids kept looking to me for answers, as if I were the referee. I'd listen, but offer no solution. I was beginning to see what was driving him. I was beginning to understand that he was fighting the world, and there was no way I'd turn on him behind his back. 22

Afraid at first, I began to meet him blow for blow. People would say that I was like my dad. I thought I was like myself. I never did learn to box. He always laughed at the way I clenched my fists. I never was really interested in boxing. Being the eldest daughter of a boxer was enough, quite enough. But I can, however, thunder as loud as he can. 23

He's mellowed somewhat. And there have been times in quiet talk 24
when he has acknowledged his weaknesses, his aspirations and exaspera-
tions for all of us in our effort to grow up and become educated. I guess
these talks are what comes with being the oldest of ten.

Thundering rages, subtle tears . . . I have seen him cry with frustration, 25
cry out in anger, and in pride, pride in his beautiful young looking wife and
her accomplishments, his kids and grandchildren. Yet, the tears that touch
me the most are those that roll down his cheeks when he talks of Nanabush.

Good ole Nanabush, the paradox, the son of a mortal woman and the 26
thundering West Wind, a boy raised by his grandmother, the best loved
of all Ojibway spirits. It was through his transgressions as well as his virtue
that Nanabush taught his people. And they never negated or attempted to
cover up his imperfections. Dad cries when he talks of Nanabush.

I dreamed of Dad. This was after he had argued and I told him why 27
I would never go to church and how I could not understand why he still
went. After all, the church, like the government, had set out to break the
Indian, to make him feel less than what he was. I did not hold back that
time and told him everything I had ever felt or thought about concerning
our people. He couldn't answer and politely admitted, "You've got me. But
I can't argue with you now, I'll answer you when I'm not drinking."

This was the first time I had won an argument against him, and it 28
didn't dawn on me until days later. We had talked, sipping our beer and
not shouting. Arguments in our house were usually won by whoever could
shout the loudest.

In my dreams I was fighting. Someone or something evil, disguised, was 29
pushing me the wrong way, trying to make me do something I did not want
to do. Thinking to expose this by disrobing it, I reached out and tugged. It
turned to fend me off and guard its robe fiercely. We struggled until I stood
alone with a bundle of clothes and flesh in my arms, and dread realization
that I had killed another human being. Overwhelmed with guilt, I started
to cry. Who would believe this act was unintentional? Then I saw him off in
the distance, standing alone, his boxer's dressing-gown over his shoulders.

I could tell him. I could tell him everything. But would he listen? 30
Understand? Lowering my burden, covering and folding it carefully I cowered toward him. His head was down, his shoulders slouched. He didn't see
me until I spoke.

"Dad," I sobbed, "I killed someone who was pushing me the wrong 31
way. I didn't mean to do it, Dad, help me."

He put his arms around me, tightly. 32

"I'll beat the world," he said and punched at the air. 33

NOTES

[1] Fresh with child: newly pregnant.

[2] Nanabush is a figure from Ojibway mythology; it is explained later in the story that he is "the son of a mortal woman and the thundering West Wind."

[3] Ojibway is the language of the Ojibway tribe, originally from around Lake Superior.

[4] Jim Thorpe (1887–1953), athlete of the Sauk and Fox tribes, was the winner of the gold medal for pentathlon and decathlon in the 1912 Stockholm Olympics and also a professional baseball player from 1913 to 1919. Tom Longboat (1887–1949) was a distance runner from the Onondaga tribe. George Armstrong (b. 1930), originally from the Six Nations Reserve, was captain of the Toronto Maple Leafs when they won the Stanley Cup in 1967.

VOCABULARY

prowess—skill

QUESTIONS

1. In the opening paragraph, Keeshig-Tobias says that she "learned to love, hate [her father] all in same breath." How does she use specific details to help us understand her ambivalent response to her father?

2. How and why do her feelings about her father change as she grows older?

3. What does boxing mean to Keeshig-Tobias's father? To Keeshig-Tobias herself? Why does she begin and end the essay with boxing?

4. In what ways is her father like Nanabush? How important are these similarities?

5. What prompts Keeshig-Tobias's dream about her father? How does this dream help us to understand her feelings about him when she is an adult?

6. How closely connected are boxing and tears in Keeshig-Tobias's memories of her father?

7. What is the thesis of this essay? Do you think Keeshig-Tobias's decision to imply her thesis rather than state it directly strengthens or weakens her essay?

SUGGESTION FOR WRITING

Sometimes you can get a perspective on a person you want to write about by developing the implications of a particular activity (cooking, gardening, fixing the plumbing, playing soccer) that you associate with him or her. Choose a family member and write an essay that imitates some of the techniques you have observed in "He Was a Boxer When I Was Small." Remember that you will need to work out your thesis even though you may not state it explicitly.

Globalisation's Time Is Up

James Howard Kunstler

The big yammer these days in the United States is to the effect that globalisation[1] is here to stay: it's wonderful, get used to it. The chief cheerleader for this point of view is Thomas Friedman, columnist for the *New York Times* and author of *The World Is Flat*. The seemingly unanimous embrace of this idea in the power circles of America is a marvellous illustration of the madness of crowds, for nothing could be further from the truth than the idea that globalisation is now a permanent fixture of the human condition.   1

Today's transient global economic relations are a product of very special transient circumstances, namely relative world peace and absolutely reliable supplies of cheap energy. Subtract either of these elements from the equation and you will see globalisation evaporate so quickly it will suck the air out of your lungs. It is significant that none of the cheerleaders for globalisation takes this equation into account. In fact, the American power elite is sleepwalking into a crisis so severe that the blowback may put both major political parties out of business.   2

The world saw an earlier phase of robust global trade run from the 1870s to a dead stop in 1914. This was the boom period of railroad construction and the advent of the ocean-going steamship. The great powers had existed in relative peace since Napoleon's last stand. The Crimean war was a minor episode that took place in the backwaters of Eurasia, and the Franco-Prussian war was a comic opera that lasted less than a year. The American civil war hardly affected the rest of the world.[2]   3

This first phase of globalisation then took off under coal-and-steam power. There was no shortage of fuel, the colonial boundaries were stable, and the pipeline of raw materials from them to the factories of western Europe ran smoothly. The rise of a middle class running the many stages of the production process provided markets for all the new production. Innovations in finance gave legitimacy to   4

James Howard Kunstler (b. 1948) lives in Saratoga Springs, NY, and writes extensively on environmental issues. *The Geography of Nowhere* (1993) and *Home from Nowhere* (1996) explore the American urban landscape and the possibilities for its regeneration. *The Long Emergency: Surviving the Converging Catastrophes of the Twenty-First Century* (2005) explores human possibilities in a future shaped by crises in oil supply, global climate change, and other world problems.

"Globalisation's Time Is Up" was originally published in *The Guardian Weekly*, 12–18 Aug. 2005: 3. Reprinted with permission of the author.

all kinds of tradable paper. Life was very good for Europe and America, notwithstanding a few sharp cyclical depressions. Trade boomed between the great powers. The belle époque represented the high tide of hopeful expectations. In America it was called the progressive era.[3] The 20th century looked golden.

It all fell apart in 1914, and a new round of globalisation did not ramp 5 up again until the mid-1960s.

It may be significant that the first collapse of globalisation occurred 6 as the coal economy was transitioning into an oil economy, with deep geopolitical implications for those who had oil (America) and those who might seek to control the other major region closest to Europe that possessed it (then the Caspian,[4] since Arabian oil was as yet undiscovered). The first world war was settled by those nations (Britain and France) that were friendly with the greatest producer of oil most readily accessed. Germany was the loser and again in the reprise for its poor access to oil. Japan suffered similarly.

We are now due for another folding up of the periodic global trade 7 fair as the industrial nations enter the tumultuous era beyond the global oil production peak. The economic perversities that have built up in the current era are not hard to see, though our leaders dread to acknowledge them. The dirty secret of the US economy for at least a decade now is that it has come to be based on the ceaseless elaboration of a car-dependent suburban infrastructure—McHousing[5] estates, eight-lane highways, big-box chain stores, hamburger stands—that has no future as a living arrangement in an oil-short future.

The American suburban juggernaut can be described succinctly as the 8 greatest misallocation of resources in the history of the world. The mortgages, bonds, real estate investment trusts and derivative financial instruments associated with this tragic enterprise must make the judicious goggle with wonder and nausea.

Add to this grim economic picture a far-flung military contest, already 9 under way, really, for control of the world's remaining oil, and the scene grows darker. Two-thirds of that oil is in the possession of people who resent the West (America in particular), many of whom have vowed to destroy it. Both America and Britain have felt the sting of freelance asymmetrical warmakers not associated with a particular state but with a transnational religious cause that uses potent small arms and explosives to unravel western societies and confound their defences.

China, a supposed beneficiary of globalisation, will be as desperate for 10 oil as all the other players, and perhaps more ruthless in seeking control of the supplies, some of which they can walk to. Of course, it is hard to imagine the continuation of American chain stores' manufacturing supply lines with China, given the potential for friction. Even on its own terms, China faces issues of environmental havoc, population overshoot, and political turmoil—orders of magnitude greater than anything known in Europe or America.

Viewed through this lens, the sunset of the current phase of globalisation seems dreadfully close to the horizon. The American public has enjoyed the fiesta, but the blue-light special orgy of easy motoring, limitless air-conditioning, and super-cheap products made by factory slaves far, far away is about to close down. Globalisation is finished. The world is about to become a larger place again.

NOTES

[1] "Globalisation" (British spelling) or "globalization" refers to an increased openness of national borders to the movement of trade, products, and money in the last forty years or so.

[2] The Crimean War was fought between Russia and Britain and its allies in 1853–1856. The Franco-Prussian War was fought between France and Prussia (the core of present-day Germany) in 1870–1871. The American Civil War was fought between the Union North and the Confederate South, largely over the issue of slavery, between 1861 and 1865.

[3] Belle Époque, which could be translated from the French as "the beautiful period," was the period of European history from 1871 to 1914. It was characterized by peace and the development of arts and culture, as was the Progressive era (1890–1913) in the United States.

[4] The Caspian is the area surrounding the Caspian Sea, in the territory of the then Soviet Union.

[5] McHousing is a reference to McDonald's, the hamburger chain; the implication is that suburban housing has as much originality and value as fast food.

VOCABULARY

blowback—significant reaction

colonial—of the colonies, countries, and areas settled during the period of European expansion from the seventeenth to the nineteenth centuries

geopolitical—concerning the interaction between geography and politics

judicious—well-judged, carefully considered

transient—not lasting for long, passing

QUESTIONS

1. This essay appeared in a British newspaper. Is Kunstler addressing a British audience? How can you tell?

2. Why is the continuing development of suburbs in the United States a "tragic enterprise," according to Kunstler? What standard(s) of evaluation does he base this judgment on?

3. Why are the cycles of history so important to Kunstler? How does using these cycles as evidence link with his thesis?

4. Does Kunstler consider counter-arguments to his case? If not, can you think of any?

SUGGESTION FOR WRITING

Does globalization affect your own life or the life of your community in any way? Do you, for example, get products from distant places, but find that local jobs have gone abroad too? If globalization has effects on your local situation, write an essay analyzing (and, if you like, also evaluating) these effects.

The Loons

Margaret Laurence

Just below Manawaka, where the Wachakwa River ran brown and noisy over the pebbles, the scrub oak and grey-green willow and chokecherry bushes grew in a dense thicket. In a clearing at the centre of the thicket stood the Tonnerre family's shack. The basis of this dwelling was a small square cabin made of poplar poles and chinked with mud, which had been built by Jules Tonnerre some fifty years before, when he came back from Batoche with a bullet in his thigh, the year that Riel was hung and the voices of the Metis entered their long silence.[1] Jules had only intended to stay the winter in the Wachakwa Valley, but the family was still there in the thirties, when I was a child. As the Tonnerres had increased, their settlement had been added to, until the clearing at the foot of the town hill was a chaos of lean-tos, wooden packing cases, warped lumber, discarded car tyres, ramshackle chicken coops, tangled strands of barbed wire and rusty tin cans.

The Tonnerres were French half-breeds, and among themselves they spoke a *patois* that was neither Cree nor French. Their English was broken and full of obscenities. They did not belong among the Cree of the Galloping Mountain reservation, further north, and they did not belong among the Scots-Irish and Ukrainians of Manawaka, either. They were, as my Grandmother MacLeod would have put it, neither flesh, fowl, nor good salt herring. When their men were not working at odd jobs or as section hands on the C.P.R., they lived on relief. In the summers, one of the Tonnerre youngsters, with a face that seemed totally unfamiliar with laughter, would knock at the doors of the town's brick houses and offer for sale a lard-pail full of bruised wild strawberries, and if he got as much as a quarter he would grab the coin and run before the customer had time to change her mind. Sometimes old Jules, or his son Lazarus, would get mixed up in a Saturday-night brawl, and would hit out at whoever was nearest, or howl drunkenly among the offended shoppers on Main Street, and then the Mountie would put them for the night in the barred cell underneath the Court House, and the next morning they would be quiet again.

Piquette Tonnerre, the daughter of Lazarus, was in my class at school. 3 She was older than I, but she had failed several grades, perhaps because her attendance had always been sporadic and her interest in schoolwork negligible. Part of the reason she had missed a lot of school was that she had had tuberculosis of the bone, and had once spent many months in hospital. I knew this because my father was the doctor who had looked after her. Her sickness was almost the only thing I knew about her, however. Otherwise, she existed for me only as a vaguely embarrassing presence, with her hoarse voice and her clumsy limping walk and her grimy cotton dresses that were always miles too long. I was neither friendly nor unfriendly towards her. She dwelt and moved somewhere within my scope of vision, but I did not actually notice her very much until that peculiar summer when I was eleven.

"I don't know what to do about that kid," my father said at dinner one 4 evening. "Piquette Tonnerre, I mean. The damn bone's flared up again. I've had her in hospital for quite a while now, and it's under control all right, but I hate like the dickens to send her home again."

"Couldn't you explain to her mother that she has to rest a lot?" my 5 mother said.

"The mother's not there," my father replied. "She took off a few years 6 back. Can't say I blame her. Piquette cooks for them, and she says Lazarus would never do anything for himself as long as she's there. Anyway, I don't think she'd take much care of herself, once she got back. She's only thirteen, after all. Beth, I was thinking—what about taking her up to Diamond Lake with us this summer? A couple of months rest would give that bone a much better chance."

My mother looked stunned. 7

"But Ewen—what about Roddie and Vanessa?" 8

"She's not contagious," my father said. "And it would be company for 9 Vanessa."

"Oh dear," my mother said in distress, "I'll bet anything she has nits in 10 her hair."

"For Pete's sake," my father said crossly, "do you think Matron would 11 let her stay in the hospital for all this time like that? Don't be silly, Beth."

Grandmother MacLeod, her delicately featured face as rigid as a cameo, 12 now brought her mauve-veined hands together as though she were about to begin a prayer.

"Ewen, if that half-breed youngster comes along to Diamond Lake, I'm   13
not going," she announced. "I'll go to Morag's for the summer."

I had trouble in stifling my urge to laugh, for my mother bright-   14
ened visibly and quickly tried to hide it. If it came to a choice between
Grandmother MacLeod and Piquette, Piquette would win hands down,
nits or not.

"It might be quite nice for you, at that," she mused. "You haven't seen   15
Morag for over a year, and you might enjoy being in the city for a while.
Well, Ewen dear, you do what you think best. If you think it would do
Piquette some good, then we'll be glad to have her, as long as she behaves
herself."

So it happened that several weeks later, when we all piled into my   16
father's old Nash, surrounded by suitcases and boxes of provisions and toys
for my ten-month-old brother, Piquette was with us and Grandmother
MacLeod, miraculously, was not. My father would only be staying at the
cottage for a couple of weeks, for he had to get back to his practice, but the
rest of us would stay at Diamond Lake until the end of August.

Our cottage was not named, as many were, "Dew Drop Inn" or "Bide-a-   17
Wee," or "Bonnie Doon." The sign on the roadway bore in austere letters only
our name, MacLeod. It was not a large cottage, but it was on the lakefront. You
could look out the windows and see, through the filigree of the spruce trees, the
water glistening greenly as the sun caught it. All around the cottage were ferns,
and sharp-branched raspberry bushes, and moss that had grown over fallen tree
trunks. If you looked carefully among the weeds and grass, you could find wild
strawberry plants which were in white flower now and in another month would
bear fruit, the fragrant globes hanging like miniature scarlet lanterns on the
thin hairy stems. The two grey squirrels were still there, gossiping at us from
the tall spruce beside the cottage, and by the end of the summer they would
again be tame enough to take pieces of crust from my hands. The broad moose
antlers that hung above the back door were a little more bleached and fissured
after the winter, but otherwise everything was the same. I raced joyfully around
my kingdom, greeting all the places I had not seen for a year. My brother,
Roderick, who had not been born when we were here last summer, sat on
the car rug in the sunshine and examined a brown spruce cone, meticulously
turning it round and round in his small and curious hands. My mother and
father toted the luggage from car to cottage, exclaiming over how well the
place had wintered, no broken windows, thank goodness, no apparent damage
from storm-felled branches or snow.

Only after I had finished looking around did I notice Piquette. She was   18
sitting on the swing, her lame leg held stiffly out, and her other foot scuffing

the ground as she swung slowly back and forth. Her long hair hung black and straight around her shoulders, and her broad coarse-featured face bore no expression—it was blank, as though she no longer dwelt within her own skull, as though she had gone elsewhere. I approached her very hesitantly.

"Want to come and play?" 19

Piquette looked at me with a sudden flash of scorn. 20

"I ain't a kid," she said. 21

Wounded, I stamped angrily away, swearing I would not speak to her for the rest of the summer. In the days that followed, however, Piquette began to interest me, and I began to want to interest her. My reasons did not appear bizarre to me. Unlikely as it may seem, I had only just realised that the Tonnerre family, whom I had always heard called half-breeds, were actually Indians, or as near as made no difference. My acquaintance with Indians was not extensive. I did not remember ever having seen a real Indian, and my new awareness that Piquette sprang from the people of Big Bear[2] and Poundmaker,[3] of Tecumseh,[4] of the Iroquois[5] who had eaten Father Brebeuf's heart[6]—all this gave her an instant attraction in my eyes. I was a devoted reader of Pauline Johnson[7] at this age, and sometimes would orate aloud and in an exalted voice, *West Wind, blow from your prairie nest; Blow from the mountains, blow from the west*—and so on. It seemed to me that Piquette must be in some way a daughter of the forest, a kind of junior prophetess of the wilds, who might impart to me, if I took the right approach, some of the secrets which she undoubtedly knew—where the whippoorwill made her nest, how the coyote reared her young, or whatever it was that it said in Hiawatha.[8] 22

I set about gaining Piquette's trust. She was not allowed to go swimming, with her bad leg, but I managed to lure her down to the beach—or rather, she came because there was nothing else to do. The water was always icy, for the lake was fed by springs, but I swam like a dog, thrashing my arms and legs around at such speed and with such an output of energy that I never grew cold. Finally, when I had had enough, I came out and sat beside Piquette on the sand. When she saw me approaching, her hand squashed flat the sand castle she had been building, and she looked at me sullenly, without speaking. 23

"Do you like this place?" I asked, after a while, intending to lead on from there into the question of forest lore. 24

Piquette shrugged. "It's okay. Good as anywhere." 25

"I love it," I said. "We come here every summer." 26

"So what?" Her voice was distant, and I glanced at her uncertainly, wondering what I could have said wrong. 27

"Do you want to come for a walk?" I asked her. "We wouldn't need to 28 go far. If you walk just around the point there, you come to a bay where great big reeds grow in the water, and all kinds of fish hang around there. Want to? Come on."

She shook her head. 29

"Your dad said I ain't supposed to do no more walking than I got to." 30

I tried another line. 31

"I bet you know a lot about the woods and all that, eh?" I began 32 respectfully.

Piquette looked at me from her large dark unsmiling eyes. 33

"I don't know what in hell you're talkin' about," she replied. "You nuts 34 or somethin'? If you mean where my old man, and me, and all them live, you better shut up, by Jesus, you hear?"

I was startled and my feelings were hurt, but I had a kind of dogged 35 perseverance. I ignored her rebuff.

"You know something, Piquette? There's loons here, on this lake. You 36 can see their nests just up the shore there, behind those logs. At night, you can hear them even from the cottage, but it's better to listen from the beach. My dad says we should listen and try to remember how they sound, because in a few years when more cottages are built at Diamond Lake and more people come in, the loons will go away."

Piquette was picking up stones and snail shells and then dropping them 37 again.

"Who gives a good goddamn?" she said. 38

It became increasingly obvious that, as an Indian, Piquette was a dead 39 loss. That evening I went out by myself, scrambling through the bushes that overhung the steep path, my feet slipping on the fallen spruce needles that covered the ground. When I reached the shore, I walked along the firm damp sand to the small pier that my father had built, and sat down there. I heard someone else crashing through the undergrowth and the bracken, and for a moment I thought Piquette had changed her mind, but it turned out to be my father. He sat beside me on the pier and we waited, without speaking.

At night the lake was like black glass with a streak of amber which was 40 the path of the moon. All around, the spruce trees grew tall and close-set, branches blackly sharp against the sky, which was lightened by a cold flickering of stars. Then the loons began their calling. They rose like phantom birds from the nests on the shore, and flew out onto the dark still surface of the water.

No one can ever describe that ululating sound, the crying of the loons, 41 and no one who has heard it can ever forget it. Plaintive, and yet with a quality of chilling mockery, those voices belonged to a world separated by aeons from our neat world of summer cottages and the lighted lamps of home.

"They must have sounded just like that," my father remarked, "before any person ever set foot here."   42

Then he laughed. "You could say the same, of course, about sparrows, or chipmunks, but somehow it only strikes you that way with the loons."   43

"I know," I said.   44

Neither of us suspected that this would be the last time we would ever sit here together on the shore, listening. We stayed for perhaps half an hour, and then we went back to the cottage. My mother was reading beside the fireplace. Piquette was looking at the burning birch log, and not doing anything.   45

"You should have come along," I said, although in fact I was glad she had not.   46

"Not me," Piquette said. "You wouldn' catch me walkin' way down there jus' for a bunch of squawkin' birds."   47

Piquette and I remained ill at ease with one another. I felt I had somehow failed my father, but I did not know what was the matter, nor why she would not or could not respond when I suggested exploring the woods or playing house. I thought it was probably her slow and difficult walking that held her back. She stayed most of the time in the cottage with my mother, helping her with the dishes or with Roddie, but hardly ever talking. Then the Duncans arrived at their cottage, and I spent my days with Mavis, who was my best friend. I could not reach Piquette at all, and I soon lost interest in trying. But all that summer she remained as both a reproach and a mystery to me.   48

That winter my father died of pneumonia, after less than a week's illness. For some time I saw nothing around me, being completely immersed in my own pain and my mother's. When I looked outward once more, I scarcely noticed that Piquette Tonnerre was no longer at school. I do not remember seeing her at all until four years later, one Saturday night when Mavis and I were having Cokes in the Regal Café. The jukebox was booming like tuneful thunder, and beside it, leaning lightly on its chrome and its rainbow glass, was a girl.   49

Piquette must have been seventeen then, although she looked about twenty. I stared at her, astounded that anyone could have changed so much. Her face, so stolid and expressionless before, was animated now with a gaiety that was almost violent. She laughed and talked very loudly with the boys around her. Her lipstick was bright carmine, and her hair was cut short and frizzily permed. She had not been pretty as a child, and she was   50 not pretty now, for her features were still heavy and blunt. But her dark and slightly slanted eyes were beautiful, and her skin-tight skirt and orange sweater displayed to enviable advantage a soft and slender body.

She saw me, and walked over. She teetered a little, but it was not due to her once-tubercular leg, for her limp was almost gone.   51

"Hi, Vanessa." Her voice still had the same hoarseness. "Long time no see, eh?"   52

"Hi," I said. "Where've you been keeping yourself, Piquette?"   53

"Oh, I been around," she said. "I been away almost two years now. Been all over the place—Winnipeg, Regina, Saskatoon. Jesus, what I could tell you! I come back this summer, but I ain't stayin'. You kids goin' to the dance?"   54

"No," I said abruptly, for this was a sore point with me. I was fifteen, and thought I was old enough to go to the Saturday-night dances at the Flamingo. My mother, however, thought otherwise.   55

"Y'oughta come," Piquette said. "I never miss one. It's just about the on'y thing in this jerkwater town that's any fun. Boy, you couldn' catch me stayin' here. I don' give a shit about this place. It stinks."   56

She sat down beside me, and I caught the harsh over-sweetness of her perfume.   57

"Listen, you wanna know something, Vanessa?" she confided, her voice only slightly blurred. "Your dad was the only person in Manawaka that ever done anything good to me."   58

I nodded speechlessly. I was certain she was speaking the truth. I knew a little more than I had that summer at Diamond Lake, but I could not reach her now any more than I had then. I was ashamed, ashamed of my own timidity, the frightened tendency to look the other way. Yet I felt no real warmth towards her—I only felt that I ought to, because of that distant summer and because my father had hoped she would be company for me, or perhaps that I would be for her, but it had not happened that way. At this moment, meeting her again, I had to admit that she repelled and embarrassed me, and I could not help despising the self-pity in her voice. I wished she would go away. I did not want to see her. I did not know what to say to her. It seemed that we had nothing to say to one another.   59

"I'll tell you something else," Piquette went on. "All the old bitches an' biddies in this town will sure be surprised. I'm gettin' married this fall—my boyfriend, he's an English fella, works in the stockyards in the city there, a very tall guy, got blond wavy hair. Gee, is he ever handsome. Got this real classy name. Alvin Gerald Cummings—some handle, eh? They call him Al."   60

For the merest instant, then, I saw her. I really did see her, for the first   61
and only time in all the years we had both lived in the same town. Her defiant
face, momentarily, became unguarded and unmasked, and in her eyes there
was a terrifying hope.

"Gee, Piquette—" I burst out awkwardly, "that's swell. That's really   62
wonderful. Congratulations—good luck—I hope you'll be happy—"

As I mouthed the conventional phrases, I could only guess how great   63
her need must have been, that she had been forced to seek the very things
she so bitterly rejected.

When I was eighteen, I left Manawaka and went away to college. At the   64
end of my first year, I came back home for the summer. I spent the first few
days in talking non-stop with my mother, as we exchanged all the news that
somehow had not found its way into letters—what had happened in my life
and what had happened here in Manawaka while I was away. My mother
searched her memory for events that concerned people I knew.

"Did I ever write you about Piquette Tonnerre, Vanessa?" she asked   65
one morning.

"No, I don't think so," I replied. "Last I heard of her, she was going to   66
marry some guy in the city. Is she still there?"

My mother looked perturbed, and it was a moment before she spoke,   67
as though she did not know how to express what she had to tell and wished
she did not need to try.

"She's dead," she said at last. Then, as I stared at her, "Oh, Vanessa,   68
when it happened, I couldn't help thinking of her as she was that summer—
so sullen and gauche and badly dressed. I couldn't help wondering if we
could have done something more at that time—but what could we do? She
used to be around in the cottage there with me all day, and honestly, it was
all I could do to get a word out of her. She didn't even talk to your father
very much, although I think she liked him, in her way."

"What happened?" I asked.   69

"Either her husband left her, or she left him," my mother said. "I don't   70
know which. Anyway, she came back here with two youngsters, both only
babies—they must have been born very close together. She kept house, I
guess, for Lazarus and her brothers, down in the valley there, in the old
Tonnerre place. I used to see her on the street sometimes, but she never
spoke to me. She'd put on an awful lot of weight, and she looked a mess, to
tell you the truth, a real slattern, dressed any old how. She was up in court
a couple of times—drunk and disorderly, of course. One Saturday night
last winter, during the coldest weather, Piquette was alone in the shack with
the children. The Tonnerres made home brew all the time, so I've heard,
and Lazarus said later she'd been drinking most of the day when he and the

boys went out that evening. They had an old woodstove there—you know the kind, with exposed pipes. The shack caught fire. Piquette didn't get out, and neither did the children."

I did not say anything. As so often with Piquette, there did not seem to be anything to say. There was a kind of silence around the image in my mind of the fire and the snow, and I wished I could put from my memory the look that I had seen once in Piquette's eyes. 71

I went up to Diamond Lake for a few days that summer, with Mavis and her family. The MacLeod cottage had been sold after my father's death, and I did not even go to look at it, not wanting to witness my long-ago kingdom possessed now by strangers. But one evening I went down to the shore by myself. 72

The small pier which my father had built was gone, and in its place there was a large and solid pier built by the government, for Galloping Mountain was now a national park, and Diamond Lake had been re-named Lake Wapakata, for it was felt that an Indian name would have a greater appeal to tourists. The one store had become several dozen, and the settlement had all the attributes of a flourishing resort—hotels, a dance-hall, cafés with neon signs, the penetrating odours of potato chips and hot dogs. 73

I sat on the government pier and looked out across the water. At night the lake at least was the same as it had always been, darkly shining and bearing within its black glass the streak of amber that was the path of the moon. There was no wind that evening, and everything was quiet all around me. It seemed too quiet, and then I realized that the loons were no longer here. I listened for some time, to make sure, but never once did I hear that long-drawn call, half mocking and half plaintive, spearing through the stillness across the lake. 74

I did not know what had happened to the birds. Perhaps they had gone away to some far place of belonging. Perhaps they had been unable to find such a place, and had simply died out, having ceased to care any longer whether they lived or not. 75

I remembered how Piquette had scorned to come along, when my father and I sat there and listened to the lake birds. It seemed to me now that in some unconscious and totally unrecognised way, Piquette might have been the only one, after all, who had heard the crying of the loons. 76

NOTES

[1] Louis Riel was the leader of the Métis after founding the province of Manitoba. He led the Red River Rebellion (1869–1870) and the North-West Rebellion (1885) against the Canadian government to try to gain rights and independence for the Métis. Riel was defeated at Batoche on May 15, 1885.

² Big Bear (1825–1888) was a chief of the Cree First Nation and, like Louis Riel, resisted the expansion of the Canadian government into the West.

³ Poundmaker (1842–1886) was a chief of the Cree First Nation who participated in the North-West Rebellion.

⁴ Tecumseh (1768–1813), a leader of the Shawnee, helped slow the progress of Americans into Upper Canada during the War of 1812.

⁵ The Iroquois Confederacy expanded into much of the Northeastern United States in the late 1600s; its members were largely pushed back into their original homeland in Ontario, Quebec, and upstate New York after the American Revolution (1775–1776).

⁶ Jean de Brébeuf (1593–1649) was a Jesuit who worked among the Hurons. He and the Hurons were defeated in 1649 by the Iroquois. Iroquois reportedly ate Brébeuf's heart as they killed him.

⁷ Pauline Johnson (1861–1913) was a Canadian writer who celebrated her Aboriginal ancestry. Her most noted work is *Flint and Feather* (1912), a collection of poetry.

⁸ *The Song of Hiawatha* is an epic poem by American Henry Wadsworth Longfellow (1807–1882), loosely based on Ojibwe legends. Although widely criticized later for its romanticism, the poem was immensely popular for many years.

VOCABULARY

patois—a regional dialect that is often considered substandard or vulgar

QUESTIONS

1. After a few days at the cottage, Vanessa says, "Piquette began to interest me, and I began to want to interest her" (261). What do you notice about the way Vanessa phrases this statement?

2. At one point, Vanessa says that Piquette and her family "were actually Indians, or as near as made no difference" (261). To what cultural heritage does Piquette belong? What are the effects of Vanessa erasing this cultural difference?

3. Count the number of times Piquette actually speaks in the story. Is this surprising? Why or why not? What does her relative quietness tell us about the story?

4. In describing Piquette's life, Beth says, "Either her husband left her, or she left him. . . . I don't know which" (265). Do you think these details might be important? What does this statement tell us about Beth?

5. Near the end of the story, Vanessa offers two explanations for the disappearance of the loons. What are they, and which is more realistic?

6. At the end of the story, Vanessa thinks that Piquette really heard the loons' cries and that the birds and Piquette have much in common. Do you agree with this connection? Do you see any problems with it?

Time and the Narrative Voice

Margaret Laurence

The treatment of time and the handling of the narrative voice—these two things are of paramount importance to me in the writing of fiction. Oddly enough, although they might seem to be two quite separate aspects of technique, in fact they are inextricably bound together. When I say "time," I don't mean clock-time, in this context, nor do I mean any kind of absolute time—which I don't believe to exist, in any event. I mean historical time, variable and fluctuating. 1

In any work of fiction, the span of time present in the story is not only as long as the time-span of every character's life and memory; it also represents everything acquired and passed on in a kind of memory-heritage from one generation to another. The time which is present in any story, therefore, must—by implication at least—include not only the totality of the characters' lives but also the inherited time of perhaps two or even three past generations, in terms of parents' and grandparents' recollections, and the much much longer past which has become legend, the past of a collective cultural memory. Obviously, not all of this can be conveyed in a single piece of prose. Some of it can only be hinted at; some of it may not be touched on at all. Nevertheless, it is *there* because it exists in the minds of the characters. How can one even begin to convey this sense of time? What parts of the time-span should be conveyed? These are questions which I always find enormously troubling, and before beginning any piece of writing, I tend to brood for quite a long time (clockwise) on these things. Not that the brooding does very much good, usually, or perhaps it bears fruit at some unrecognized subconscious level, because when the writing begins, a process of selection takes place in a way not consciously chosen, and this is where the long time-span implicit in every story or novel is directly and intimately related to the narrative voice. 2

Most of the fiction I have written in recent years has been written in the first person, with the main character assuming the narrative voice. Even when I have written in the third person, as I did in part of my novel *The Fire-Dwellers,* it is really a first-person narrative which happens to be written in the third person, for the narrative voice even here is essentially that of the main character, and the writer does not enter in as 3

For biographic details, see the previous reading, Laurence, Margaret, "The Loons."

"Time and the Narrative Voice" is reprinted from *The Narrative Voice,* ed. John Metcalf (Toronto: McGraw-Hill Ryerson, 1972) with permission of the estate of Margaret Laurence.

commentator. Some people hold the erroneous belief that this kind of fiction is an evasion—the writer is hiding behind a mask, namely one of the characters. Untrue. The writer is every bit as vulnerable here as in directly autobiographical fiction. The character is not a mask but an individual, separate from the writer. At the same time, the character is one of the writer's voices and selves, and fiction writers tend to have a mental trunk full of these—in writers, this quality is known as richness of imagination; in certain inmates of mental hospitals it has other names, the only significant difference being that writers are creating their private worlds with the ultimate hope of throwing open the doors to other humans. This means of writing fiction, oriented almost totally towards an individual character, is obviously not the only way, but it appears to be the only way I can write.

Once the narrative voice is truly established—that is, once the writer   4 has listened, really listened, to the speech and idiom and outlook of the character—it is then not the writer but the character who, by some process of transferral, bears the responsibility for the treatment of time within the work. It is the character who chooses which parts of the personal past, the family past and the ancestral past have to be revealed in order for the present to be realized and the future to happen. This is not a morbid dwelling on the past on the part of the writer or the character. It is, rather, an expression of the feeling which I strongly hold about time—that the past and the future are both always present, *present* in both senses of the word, always now and always here with us. It is only through the individual presence of the characters that the writer can hope to convey even a fragment of this sense of time, and this is one reason, among others, why it is so desperately important to discover the true narrative voice—which really means knowing the characters so well that one can take on their past, their thoughts, their responses, can in effect for a while *become* them. It has sometimes occurred to me that I must be a kind of Method[1] writer, in the same way that some actors become the characters they play for the moments when they are portraying these characters. I didn't plan it this way, and possibly it sounds like gibberish, but this is how it appears to take place.

Theorizing, by itself, is meaningless in connection with fiction, just as   5 any concept of form is meaningless in isolation from the flesh and blood of content and personality, just as a skeleton is only dry bone by itself but when it exists inside a living being it provides the support for the whole creature. I'll try to show something of what I mean about time and voice by reference to . . . two stories of mine. . . .

These stories are part of a collection called *A Bird in the House,* eight in   6 all, published separately before they were collected in a single volume, but conceived from the beginning as a related group. Each story is self-contained in the sense that it is definitely a short story and not a chapter from a novel, but the net effect is not unlike that of a novel. Structurally, however, these stories as a group are totally unlike a novel. I think the outlines of a novel (mine, anyway) and those of a group of stories such as these interrelated ones may be approximately represented in visual terms. In a novel, one might perhaps imagine the various themes and experiences and the interaction of characters with one another and with themselves as a series of wavy lines, converging, separating, touching, drawing apart, but moving in a *horizontal* direction. The short stories have flow-lines which are different. They move very close together but parallel and in a *vertical* direction. Each story takes the girl Vanessa along some specific course of her life and each follows that particular thread closely, but the threads are presented separately and not simultaneously. To this extent, the structure of these stories is a good deal simpler than that of a novel. Nevertheless, the relationship of time and the narrative voice can be seen just as plainly in the stories as in a novel.

"To Set Our House in Order" takes place when Vanessa is ten years old.   7 Her age remains constant throughout the story. The actual time-span of the story itself is short, a few days in her life, immediately before, during and after the birth of her brother. The things which happen on the surface are simple, but the things that happen inside Vanessa's head are more complex.

The narrative voice is, of course, that of Vanessa herself, but an older   8 Vanessa, herself grown up, remembering how it was when she was ten. When I was trying to write this story, I felt as I did with all the stories in *A Bird in the House,* that this particular narrative device was a tricky one, and I cannot even now personally judge how well it succeeds. What I tried to do was definitely *not* to tell the story as though it were being narrated by a child. This would have been impossible for me and also would have meant denying the story one of its dimensions, a time-dimension, the viewing from a distance of events which had happened in childhood. The narrative voice had to be that of an older Vanessa, but at the same time the narration had to be done in such a way that the ten-year-old would be conveyed. The narrative voice, therefore, had to speak as though from two points in time, simultaneously.

Given this double sense of time-present, Vanessa herself had to recol-   9 lect those things which were most meaningful to her, and in doing so, she reveals (at least I hope she does to the reader as she does to me) what the story is really about. It is actually a story about the generations, about the pain and bewilderment of one's knowledge of other people, about the reality of other people which is one way of realizing one's own reality, about the fluctuating and accidental quality of life (God really doesn't love Order), and perhaps more than anything, about the strangeness and mystery of the very concepts of *past, present and future.* Who is Vanessa's father? The doctor who is struggling to support his family during the depression and who seems a pillar of strength to the little girl? Or the man who has collected dozens of travel books because once he passionately wanted to go far beyond Manawaka and now knows he won't? Or the boy who long ago half-blinded his brother accidentally with an air-rifle? Or the nineteen-year-old soldier who watched his brother die in the First World War? Ewen is all of these, and many many more, and in the story Vanessa has the sudden painful knowledge of his reality and his intricacy as a person, bearing with him the mental baggage of a lifetime, as all people do, and as she will have to do. The events of the story will become (and have become, to the older Vanessa) part of her mental baggage, part of her own spiritual fabric. Similarly, her father passes on to her some actual sense of her grandparents, his parents—the adamant Grandmother MacLeod, whose need it has been to appear a lady in her own image of herself; the dead Grandfather MacLeod, who momentarily lives for his granddaughter when she sees for the first time the loneliness of a man who could read the Greek tragedies in their original language and who never knew anyone in the small prairie town with whom he could communicate.

In "The Loons," the narrative voice is also that of the older Vanessa, but in her portrayal of herself in past years, she ranges in age from eleven to eighteen. This meant, of course, that the tone of the narration had to change as Vanessa recalled herself at different ages, and this meant, for me, trying to feel my way into her mind at each age. Here again, the narrative voice chooses what will be recalled, and here again, the element of time is of great importance in the story. The eleven-year-old Vanessa sees the Métis girl, Piquette Tonnerre, in terms of romanticized notions of Indians, and is hurt when Piquette does not respond in the expected way. That summer lies submerged in Vanessa's mind until she encounters Piquette at a later time, but even then her reaction is one mainly of embarrassment and pity, not any real touching, and Piquette's long experience of hurt precludes anything except self-protectiveness on her part. It is only when Vanessa hears of Piquette's death that she realizes that she, too, like the entire town, is in part responsible. But the harm and alienation started a long way back, longer even than the semimythical figure of Piquette's grandfather, Jules Tonnerre, who fought with Riel at Batoche. The loons, recurring in the story both in their presence and in their absence, are connected to an ancestral past which belongs to Piquette, and the older Vanessa can see the irony of the only way in which Piquette's people are recognized by the community, in the changing of the name Diamond Lake to the more tourist-appealing Lake Wapakata.

10

What I said earlier may perhaps be more clearly seen now to show a   11
little of the relationship between the narrative voice and the treatment of
time—it is the character who chooses which parts of the personal past, the
family past and the ancestral past have to be revealed in order for the present to be realized and the future to happen.

NOTE

[1] Developed in the 1940s, Method acting is an approach to character where actors draw upon their
own emotions and imagination in order to become the character they are playing. Actors seek to
represent lifelike, realistic emotional responses through the characters.

QUESTIONS

1. Laurence mentions three different types of time in the introduction. Define each of
   these different meanings of time.

2. Many readers and critics consider Laurence's writing to be largely autobiographical.
   How does Laurence respond to this idea in this essay?

3. For Laurence, what distinguishing features separate a novel from a collection of related
   short stories?

4. To what extent are Piquette and Métis history part of Vanessa's personal, family, and
   ancestral pasts? To what extent are Vanessa and white history part of Piquette's personal, family, and ancestral pasts?

5. Laurence ends the piece by claiming that both the present and the future require the
   past in order to happen at all. To what extent do you think the past determines the
   future?

SUGGESTION FOR WRITING

Laurence states that in writing the character of Vanessa, "The tone of the narration had to
change as Vanessa recalled herself at different ages, and this meant, for me, trying to feel my
way into her mind at each age." Select an event or situation from your childhood, and write
two different versions of that event: one from the narrative point of view of your past self
as a child, the other from the narrative point of view of your present self as an adult. Try to
use diction that is appropriate to each age or point of view.

Embraced by the Needle

Gabor Maté

Addictions always originate in unhappiness, even if hidden. They are emotional anesthetics; they numb pain. The first question—always—is not "Why the addiction?" but "Why the pain?" The answer, ever the same, is scrawled with crude eloquence on the wall of my patient Anna's room at the Portland Hotel in the heart of Vancouver's Downtown Eastside: "Any place I went to, I wasn't wanted. And that bites large."

The Downtown Eastside is considered to be Canada's drug capital, with an addict population of 3,000 to 5,000 individuals. I am a staff physician at the Portland, a non-profit harm-reduction facility where most of the clients are addicted to cocaine, to alcohol, to opiates like heroin, or to tranquilizers—or to any combination of these things. Many also suffer from mental illness. Like Anna, a 32-year-old poet, many are HIV positive or have full-blown AIDS. The methadone[1] I prescribe for their opiate dependence does little for the emotional anguish compressed in every heartbeat of these driven souls.

Gabor Maté is a Vancouver family physician and counsellor with a special interest in counselling adults, parents, and children with attention deficit hyperactivity disorder (ADHD). He is widely known for his expertise on addictions, mental health, and parenting. His most recent book is *In the Realm of Hungry Ghosts: Close Encounters with Addiction* (2009), for which he won the Hubert Evans Non-Fiction Prize. A long-time medical columnist for the *Vancouver Sun* and the *Globe and Mail*, he is also the author of *When the Body Says No: The Cost of Hidden Stress* (2004), *Hold On to Your Kids: Why Parents Need to Matter More than Peers* (2004), and *Scattered Minds: A New Look at the Origins and Healing of Attention Deficit Disorder* (1999).

"Embraced by the Needle" was first published in the *Globe and Mail*, August 27, 2001.

Methadone staves off the torment of opiate withdrawal, but, unlike heroin, it does not create a "high" for regular users. The essence of that high was best expressed by a 27-year-old sex-trade worker. "The first time I did heroin," she said, "it felt like a warm, soft hug." In a phrase, she summed up the psychological and chemical cravings that make some people vulnerable to substance dependence.

No drug is, in itself, addictive. Only about 8 per cent to 15 per cent of people who try, say alcohol or marijuana, go on to addictive use. What makes them vulnerable? Neither physiological predispositions nor individual moral failures explain drug addictions. Chemical and emotional vulnerability are the products of life experience, according to current brain research and developmental psychology.

Most human brain growth occurs following birth; physical and emotional interactions determine much of our brain development. Each brain's circuitry and chemistry reflects individual life experiences as much as inherited tendencies.   5

For any drug to work in the brain, the nerve cells have to have receptors—sites where the drug can bind. We have opiate receptors because our brain has natural opiate-like substances, called endorphins, chemicals that participate in many functions, including the regulation of pain and mood. Similarly, tranquilizers of the benzodiazepine[2] class, such as Valium, exert their effect at the brain's natural benzodiazepine receptors.   6

Infant rats who get less grooming from their mothers have fewer natural benzo receptors in the part of the brain that controls anxiety. Brains of infant monkeys separated from their mothers for only a few days are measurably deficient in the key neuro-chemical, dopamine.   7

It is the same with human beings. Endorphins are released in the infant's brain when there are warm, non-stressed, calm interactions with the parenting figures. Endorphins, in turn, promote the growth of receptors and nerve cells, and the discharge of other important brain chemicals. The fewer endorphin-enhancing experiences in infancy and early childhood, the greater the need for external sources. Hence, the greater vulnerability to addictions.   8

Distinguishing skid row addicts is the extreme degree of stress they had to endure early in life. Almost all women now inhabiting Canada's addiction capital suffered sexual assaults in childhood, as did many of the males. Childhood memories of serial abandonment or severe physical and psychological abuse are common. The histories of my Portland patients tell of pain upon pain.   9

Carl, a 36-year-old native, was banished from one foster home after another, had dishwashing liquid poured down his throat for using foul language at age 5, and was tied to a chair in a dark room to control his hyperactivity. When angry at himself—as he was recently, for using cocaine—he gouges his foot with a knife as punishment. His facial expression was that of a terrorized urchin who had just broken some family law and feared draconian retribution. I reassured him I wasn't his foster parent, and that he didn't owe it to me not to screw up.   10

But what of families where there was not abuse, but love, where parents did their best to provide their children with a secure nurturing home? One also sees addictions arising in such families. The unseen factor here is the stress the parents themselves lived under even if they did not recognize it. That stress could come from relationship problems, or from outside circumstances such as   11 economic pressure or political disruption. The most frequent source of hidden stress is the parents' own childhood histories that saddled them with emotional baggage they had never become conscious of. What we are not aware of in ourselves, we pass on to our children.

Stressed, anxious, or depressed parents have great difficulty initiating   12
enough of those emotionally rewarding, endorphin-liberating interactions with their children. Later in life such children may experience a hit of heroin as the "warm, soft hug" my patient described: What they didn't get enough of before, they can now inject.

Feeling alone, feeling there has never been anyone with whom to share   13
their deepest emotions, is universal among drug addicts. That is what Anna had lamented on her wall. No matter how much love a parent has, the child does not experience being wanted unless he or she is made absolutely safe to express exactly how unhappy, or angry, or hate-filled he or she may feel at times. The sense of unconditional love, of being fully accepted even when most ornery, is what no addict ever experienced in childhood—often not because the parents did not have it to give, simply because they did not know how to transmit it to the child.

Addicts rarely make the connection between troubled childhood experi-   14
ences and self-harming habits. They blame themselves—and that is the greatest wound of all, being cut off from their natural self-compassion. "I was hit a lot," 40-year-old Wayne says, "but I asked for it. Then I made some stupid decisions." And would he hit a child, no matter how much that child "asked for it"? Would he blame that child for "stupid decisions"?

Wayne looks away. "I don't want to talk about that crap," says this tough   15
man, who has worked on oil rigs and construction sites and served 15 years in jail for robbery. He looks away and wipes tears from his eyes.

NOTES

[1] Methadone is a synthetic narcotic used in the treatment of drug addictions.

[2] Benzodiazepines (BZDs) are sedative-hypnotic agents widely used to treat conditions like anxiety and insomnia, and also to induce pre-operative relaxation.

VOCABULARY

hyperactivity—the state of being unusually or excessively active, sometimes identified as a childhood disorder

neuro-chemical—chemical element found in the brain

opiate—a medicine or substance containing opium

physiological—pertaining to the body

QUESTIONS

1. Maté uses several direct quotations from addicts, some in street language. Does this technique increase or decrease the credibility of his statements?

2. Maté discusses addicts' feelings, the workings of endorphins and other chemicals in the brain, and the dynamics of stressed and dysfunctional families. Can we assume that he, as a physician, has the authority to speak on these topics? Are there any places in the essay where Maté seems to lack authority for his comments?

3. How does the diction of the essay convey Maté's attitude to the drug addicts he treats? List some key words or phrases that convey his attitude.

4. The essay ends with a story about "40-year-old Wayne" rather than with a conclusion summarizing the development of the thesis. Why do you think Maté chooses to conclude in this way? Is the conclusion effective?

SUGGESTION FOR WRITING

Interview a classmate about his or her experience or views of a current social issue. Then write a one-page essay using direct quotations from the interview that support your thesis or argue against it. For guidelines on using quotations effectively, see Part 3, H2 Quotations.

Unchopping a Tree

W. S. Merwin

Start with the leaves, the small twigs, and the nests that have been shaken, ripped, or broken off by the fall; these must be gathered and attached once again to their respective places. It is not arduous work, unless major limbs have been smashed or mutilated. If the fall was carefully and correctly planned, the chances of anything of the kind happening will have been reduced. Again, much depends upon the size, age, shape, and species of the tree. Still, you will be lucky if you can get through this stage without having to use machinery. Even in the best of circumstances it is a labor that will make you wish often that you had won the favor of the universe of ants, the empire of mice, or at least a local tribe of squirrels, and could enlist their labors and their talents. But no, they leave you to it. They have learned, with time. This is men's work. It goes without saying that if the tree was hollow in whole or in part, and contained old nests of bird or mammal or insect, or hoards of nuts or such structures as wasps or bees build for their survival, the contents will have to be repaired where necessary, and reassembled, insofar as possible, in their original order, including the shells of nuts already opened. With spiders' webs you must simply do the best you can. We do not have the spider's weaving equipment, nor any substitute for the leaf's living bond with its point of attachment and nourishment. It is even harder to simulate the latter when the leaves have once become dry—as they are bound to do, for this is not the labor of a moment. Also it hardly needs saying that this is the time for repairing any neighboring trees or bushes or other growth that may have been damaged by the fall. The same rules apply. Where neighboring trees were of the same species it is difficult not to waste time conveying a detached leaf back to the wrong tree. Practice, practice. Put your hope in that.

W. S. Merwin was born in New York in 1927 and is principally known for his poetry, though he won the PEN Translation Prize in 1969 for his book *Selected Translations 1948-1968*. He won the Pulitzer Prize in 1971 for his book of poetry *The Carrier of Ladders* and gave the Pulitzer Prize money to the draft resistance movement opposing the Vietnam War. He also won the Pulizer Prize in 2009. Recent titles include *The Ends of the Earth* (2004), *Migration: New & Selected Poems* (2005), and a memoir of his childhood, *Summer Doorways* (2006). He has also published numerous books of translation. Merwin was appointed the seventeenth Poet Laureate Consultant in Poetry to the Library of Congress for 2010-2011. He lives and writes in Hawaii.

Now the tackle must be put into place or the scaffolding, depending on   2
the surroundings and the dimensions of the tree. It is ticklish work. Almost
always it involves, in itself, further damage to the area, which will have to
be corrected later. But as you've heard, it can't be helped. And care now
is likely to save you considerable trouble later. Be careful to grind nothing
into the ground.

At last the time comes for the erecting of the trunk. By now it will   3
scarcely be necessary to remind you of the delicacy of this huge skeleton.
Every motion of the tackle, every slight upward heave of the trunk, the
branches, their elaborately re-assembled panoply of leaves (now dead) will
draw from you an involuntary gasp. You will watch for a leaf or a twig to
be snapped off yet again. You will listen for the nuts to shift in the hollow
limb and you will hear whether they are indeed falling into place or are
spilling in disorder—in which case, or in the event of anything else of the
kind—operations will have to cease, of course, while you correct the matter.
The raising itself is no small enterprise, from the moment when the chains
tighten around the old bandages until the bole hangs vertical above the
stump, splinter above splinter. Now the final straightening of the splinters
themselves can take place (the preliminary work is best done while the wood
is still green and soft, but at times when the splinters are not badly twisted
most of the straightening is left until now, when the torn ends are face to
face with each other). When the splinters are perfectly complementary the
appropriate fixative is applied. Again we have no duplicate of the original
substance. Ours is extremely strong, but it is rigid. It is limited to surfaces,
and there is no play in it. However the core is not the part of the trunk that
conducted life from the roots up into the branches and back again. It was
relatively inert. The fixative for this part is not the same as the one for the
outer layers and the bark, and if either of these is involved in the splintered
section they must receive applications of the appropriate adhesives. Apart
from being incorrect and probably ineffective, the core fixative would leave
a scar on the bark.

When all is ready the splintered trunk is lowered onto the splinters of   4
the stump. This, one might say, is only the skeleton of the resurrection.
Now the chips must be gathered, and the sawdust, and returned to their
former positions. The fixative for the wood layers will be applied to chips
and sawdust consisting only of wood. Chips and sawdust consisting of several substances will receive applications of the correct adhesives. It is as well,
where possible, to shelter the materials from the elements while working.
Weathering makes it harder to identify the smaller fragments. Bark sawdust
in particular the earth lays claim to very quickly. You must find your own

ways of coping with this problem. There is a certain beauty, you will notice at moments, in the pattern of the chips as they are fitted back into place. You will wonder to what extent it should be described as natural, to what extent man-made. It will lead you on to speculations about the parentage of beauty itself, to which you will return.

The adhesive for the chips is translucent, and not so rigid as that for the   5
splinters. That for the bark and its subcutaneous layers is transparent and runs into the fibers on either side, partially dissolving them into each other. It does not set the sap flowing again but it does pay a kind of tribute to the preoccupations of the ancient thoroughfares. You could not roll an egg over the joints but some of the mine-shafts would still be passable, no doubt. For the first exploring insect who raises its head in the tight echoless passages. The day comes when it is all restored, even to the moss (now dead) over the wound. You will sleep badly, thinking of the removal of the scaffolding that must begin the next morning. How you will hope for sun and a still day!

The removal of the scaffolding or tackle is not so dangerous, perhaps,   6
to the surroundings, as its installation, but it presents problems. It should be taken from the spot piece by piece as it is detached, and stored at a distance. You have come to accept it there, around the tree. The sky begins to look naked as the chains and struts one by one vacate their positions. Finally the moment arrives when the last sustaining piece is removed and the tree stands again on its own. It is as though its weight for a moment stood on your heart. You listen for a thud of settlement, a warning creak deep in the intricate joinery. You cannot believe it will hold. How like something dreamed it is, standing there all by itself. How long will it stand there now? The first breeze that touches its dead leaves all seems to flow into your mouth. You are afraid the motion of the clouds will be enough to push it over. What more can you do? What more can you do?

But there is nothing more you can do.   7

Others are waiting.   8

Everything is going to have to be put back.   9

QUESTIONS

1. How well does "Unchopping a Tree" satisfy the requirements for step-by-step instructions and precise, easy-to-visualize detail in the "how-to" process analysis essay?

2. At what point did you first realize that these instructions are, in fact, impossible to carry out? Is process analysis an effective way to make this point? Why?

3. Reread the first paragraph and analyze the rhythm Merwin creates through his use of sentence lengths and sentence patterns. How does this rhythm help to establish the tone of the essay?

4. Note Merwin's use of figurative language throughout this essay (for more on this, see Joyce MacDonald's essay on Merwin and Suzuki in Readings: Sample Essays). How does this language develop and strengthen Merwin's thesis?

5. Throughout the essay, Merwin adopts the persona of a teacher instructing the reader-student. Where is this persona most evident? What purposes does it serve?

6. Merwin creates irony by leaving the obvious unsaid: that it is impossible to unchop a tree. How similar is Merwin's irony to Swift's in "A Modest Proposal" (Readings)? Do you think irony is an effective strategy for persuasion? Is irony ever risky?

SUGGESTION FOR WRITING

Using "Unchopping a Tree" as a model, write an essay in which the impossibility of carrying out your instructions makes a persuasive point. Remember that in an ironic essay, your real thesis is the opposite of what you seem to be saying. You will find this irony easier to create and sustain if, like Merwin, you adopt the persona of the teacher who encourages the students but who provides impossibly complex instructions. Like Merwin, you should develop your essay as a process analysis, so be sure to include transitions that help your readers to follow the steps in your procedure.

Shooting an Elephant

George Orwell

In Moulmein, in lower Burma,[1] I was hated by large numbers of people— the only time in my life that I have been important enough for this to happen to me. I was sub-divisional police officer of the town, and in an aimless, petty kind of way anti-European feeling was very bitter. No one had the guts to raise a riot, but if a European woman went through the bazaars alone somebody would probably spit betel juice[2] over her dress. As a police officer[3] I was an obvious target and was baited whenever it seemed safe to do so. When a nimble Burman tripped me up on the football field and the referee (another Burman) looked the other way, the crowd yelled with hideous laughter. This happened more than once. In the end the sneering yellow faces of young men that met me everywhere, the insults hooted after me when I was at a safe distance, got badly on my nerves. The young Buddhist priests were the worst of all. There were several thousands of them in the town and none of them seemed to have anything to do except stand on street corners and jeer at Europeans.

All this was perplexing and upsetting. For at that time I had already made up my mind that imperialism was an evil thing and the sooner I chucked up my job and got out of it the better. Theoretically—and secretly, of course—I was all for the Burmese and all against their oppressors, the British. As for the job I was doing, I hated it more bitterly than I can perhaps make clear. In a job like that you see the dirty work of Empire at close quarters. The wretched prisoners huddling in the stinking cages of the lock-ups, the gray, cowed faces of the long-term convicts, the scarred buttocks of the men who had been flogged with bamboos—all these oppressed me with an intolerable sense of guilt. But I could get nothing into perspective. I was young and ill educated and I had had to think out my problems in the utter silence that is imposed on every Englishman in the East. I did not even know that the British Empire is dying, still less did I

George Orwell (1903–1950) was born in India as Eric Arthur Blair. Primarily a journalist, he worked as a police officer for the Indian Imperial Police in Burma from 1922 to 1927. His fiction includes *Animal Farm* (1945) and *Nineteen Eighty-Four* (1949). He also wrote many essays, often exploring his ideas about democracy and socialism; collections include *Inside the Whale and Other Essays* (1940) and *Shooting an Elephant and Other Essays* (1950).

know that it is a great deal better than the younger empires that are going to supplant it. All I knew was that I was stuck between my hatred of the empire I served and my rage against the evil-spirited little beasts who tried to make my job impossible. With one part of my mind I thought of the British Raj[4] as an unbreakable tyranny, as something clamped down, in *saecula saeculorum,*[5] upon the will of prostrate peoples; with another part I thought that the greatest joy in the world would be to drive a bayonet into a Buddhist priest's guts. Feelings like these are the normal by-products of imperialism; ask any Anglo-Indian official, if you can catch him off duty.

One day something happened which in a roundabout way was enlight- 3 ening. It was a tiny incident in itself; but it gave me a better glimpse than I had had before of the real nature of imperialism—the real motives for which despotic governments act. Early one morning the sub-inspector at a police station the other end of the town rang me up on the 'phone and said that an elephant was ravaging the bazaar. Would I please come and do something about it? I did not know what I could do, but I wanted to see what was happening and I got on to a pony and started out. I took my rifle, an old .44 Winchester and much too small to kill an elephant, but I thought the noise might be useful *in terrorem.*[6] Various Burmans stopped me on the way and told me about the elephant's doings. It was not, of course, a wild elephant, but a tame one which had gone "must."[7] It had been chained up, as tame elephants always are when their attack of "must" is due, but on the previous night it had broken its chain and escaped. Its mahout,[8] the only person who could manage it when it was in that state, had set out in pursuit, but had taken the wrong direction and was now twelve hours' journey away, and in the morning the elephant had suddenly reappeared in the town. The Burmese population had no weapons and were quite helpless against it. It had already destroyed somebody's bamboo hut, killed a cow and raided some fruitstalls and devoured the stock; also it had met the municipal rubbish van and, when the driver jumped out and took to his heels, had turned the van over and inflicted violences upon it.

The Burmese sub-inspector and some Indian constables were waiting 4 for me in the quarter where the elephant had been seen. It was a very poor quarter, a labyrinth of squalid bamboo huts, thatched with palm-leaf, winding all over a steep hillside. I remember that it was a cloudy, stuffy morning at the beginning of the rains.[9] We began questioning the people as to where the elephant had gone and, as usual, failed to get any definite information. That is invariably the case in the East; a story always sounds clear enough at a distance, but the nearer you get to the scene of events the vaguer it becomes. Some of the people said that the elephant had gone in one direction, some said that he had gone in another, some professed not even to have heard of any elephant. I had almost made up my mind that the whole story was a pack of lies, when we heard yells a little distance away. There was a loud, scandalized cry of "Go away, child! Go away this instant!" and an old woman with a switch in her hand came round the corner of a hut, violently shooing away a crowd of naked children. Some more women followed, clicking their tongues and exclaiming; evidently there was something that the children ought not to have seen. I rounded the hut and saw a man's dead body sprawling in the mud. He was an Indian, a black Dravidian coolie,[10] almost naked, and he could not have been dead many minutes. The people said that the elephant had come suddenly upon him round the corner of the hut, caught him with its trunk, put its foot on his back and ground him into the earth. This was the rainy season and the ground was soft, and his face had scored a trench a foot deep and a couple of yards long. He was lying on his belly with arms crucified and head sharply twisted to one side. His face was coated with mud, the eyes wide open, the teeth bared and grinning with an expression of unendurable agony. (Never tell me, by the way, that the dead look peaceful. Most of the corpses I have seen looked devilish.) The friction of the great beast's foot had stripped the skin from his back as neatly as one skins a rabbit. As soon as I saw the dead man I sent an orderly to a friend's house nearby to borrow an elephant rifle. I had already sent back the pony, not wanting it to go mad with fright and throw me if it smelt the elephant.

The orderly came back in a few minutes with a rifle and five cartridges, and meanwhile some Burmans had arrived and told us that the elephant was in the paddy fields[11] below, only a few hundred yards away. As I started forward practically the whole population of the quarter flocked out of the houses and followed me. They had seen the rifle and were all shouting excitedly that I was going to shoot the elephant. They had not shown much interest in the elephant when he was merely ravaging their homes, but it was different now that he was going to be shot. It was a bit of fun to them, as it would be to an English crowd; besides they wanted the meat. It made me vaguely uneasy. I had no intention of shooting the elephant—I had merely sent for the rifle to defend myself if necessary—and it is always unnerving to have a crowd following you. I marched down the hill, looking and feeling a fool, with the rifle over my shoulder and an ever-growing army of people jostling at my heels. At the bottom, when you got away from the huts, there was a metalled road and beyond that a miry waste of paddy fields a thousand yards across, not yet ploughed but soggy from the first rains and dotted with coarse grass. The elephant was standing eight yards from the road, his left side toward us. He took not the slightest notice

5

of the crowd's approach. He was tearing up bunches of grass, beating them against his knees to clean them, and stuffing them into his mouth.

I had halted on the road. As soon as I saw the elephant I knew with   6
perfect certainty that I ought not to shoot him. It is a serious matter to shoot a working elephant—it is comparable to destroying a huge and costly piece of machinery—and obviously one ought not to do it if it can possibly be avoided. And at that distance, peacefully eating, the elephant looked no more dangerous than a cow. I thought then and I think now that his attack of "must" was already passing off; in which case he would merely wander harmlessly about until the mahout came back and caught him. Moreover, I did not in the least want to shoot him. I decided that I would watch him for a little while to make sure that he did not turn savage again, and then go home.

But at that moment I glanced round at the crowd that had followed   7
me. It was an immense crowd, two thousand at the least and growing every minute. It blocked the road for a long distance on either side. I looked at the sea of yellow faces above the garish clothes—faces all happy and excited over this bit of fun, all certain that the elephant was going to be shot. They were watching me as they would watch a conjurer about to perform a trick. They did not like me, but with the magical rifle in my hands I was momentarily worth watching. And suddenly I realized that I should have to shoot the elephant after all. The people expected it of me and I had got to do it; I could feel their two thousand wills pressing me forward, irresistibly. And it was at this moment, as I stood there with the rifle in my hands, that I first grasped the hollowness, the futility of the white man's dominion in the East. Here was I, the white man with his gun, standing in front of the unarmed native crowd—seemingly the leading actor of the piece; but in reality I was only an absurd puppet pushed to and fro by the will of those yellow faces behind. I perceived in this moment that when the white man turns tyrant it is his own freedom that he destroys. He becomes a sort of hollow, posing dummy, the conventionalized figure of a sahib.[12] For it is the condition of his rule that he shall spend his life in trying to impress the "natives," and so in every crisis he has got to do what the "natives" expect of him. He wears a mask, and his face grows to fit it. I had got to shoot the elephant. I had committed myself to doing it when I sent for the rifle. A sahib has got to act like a sahib; he has got to appear resolute, to know his own mind and do definite things. To come all that way, rifle in hand, with two thousand people marching at my heels, and then to trail feebly away, having done nothing—no, that was impossible. The crowd would laugh at me. And my whole life, every white man's life in the East, was one long struggle not to be laughed at.

But I did not want to shoot the elephant. I watched him beating his   8
bunch of grass against his knees with that preoccupied grandmotherly air
that elephants have. It seemed to me that it would be murder to shoot him.
At that age I was not squeamish about killing animals, but I had never
shot an elephant and never wanted to. (Somehow it always seems worse to
kill a *large* animal.) Besides, there was the beast's owner to be considered.
Alive, the elephant was worth at least a hundred pounds; dead, he would
only be worth the value of his tusks, five pounds, possibly. But I had got to
act quickly. I turned to some experienced-looking Burmans who had been
there when we arrived, and asked them how the elephant had been behav-
ing. They all said the same thing: he took no notice of you if you left him
alone, but he might charge if you went too close to him.

It was perfectly clear to me what I ought to do. I ought to walk up to   9
within, say, twenty-five yards of the elephant and test his behavior. If he
charged, I could shoot; if he took no notice of me, it would be safe to leave
him until the mahout came back. But also I knew that I was going to do no
such thing. I was a poor shot with a rifle and the ground was soft mud into
which one would sink at every step. If the elephant charged and I missed
him, I should have about as much chance as a toad under a steam-roller.
But even then I was not thinking particularly of my own skin, only of the
watchful yellow faces behind. For at that moment, with the crowd watching me, I was not afraid in the ordinary sense, as I would have been if I
had been alone. A white man mustn't be frightened in front of "natives";
and so, in general, he isn't frightened. The sole thought in my mind was
that if anything went wrong those two thousand Burmans would see me
pursued, caught, trampled on, and reduced to a grinning corpse like that
Indian up the hill. And if that happened it was quite probable that some of
them would laugh. That would never do. There was only one alternative. I
shoved the cartridges into the magazine and lay down on the road to get a
better aim.

The crowd grew very still, and a deep, low, happy sigh, as of people who   10
see the theater curtain go up at last, breathed from innumerable throats.
They were going to have their bit of fun after all. The rifle was a beautiful
German thing with cross-hair sights. I did not then know that in shooting
an elephant one would shoot to cut an imaginary bar running from ear-hole
to ear-hole. I ought, therefore, as the elephant was sideways on, to have
aimed straight at his ear-hole; actually I aimed several inches in front of this,
thinking the brain would be further forward.

When I pulled the trigger I did not hear the bang or feel the kick—one   11
never does when a shot goes home—but I heard the devilish roar of glee
that went up from the crowd. In that instant, in too short a time, one would

have thought, even for the bullet to get there, a mysterious, terrible change had come over the elephant. He neither stirred, nor fell, but every line of his body had altered. He looked suddenly stricken, shrunken, immensely old, as though the frightful impact of the bullet had paralyzed him without knocking him down. At last, after what seemed a long time—it might have been five seconds, I dare say—he sagged flabbily to his knees. His mouth slobbered. An enormous senility seemed to have settled upon him. One could have imagined him thousands of years old. I fired again into the same spot. At the second shot he did not collapse but climbed with desperate slowness to his feet and stood weakly upright, with legs sagging and head drooping. I fired a third time. That was the shot that did for him. You could see the agony of it jolt his whole body and knock the last remnant of strength from his legs. But in falling he seemed for a moment to rise, for as his hind legs collapsed beneath him he seemed to tower upward like a huge rock toppling, his trunk reaching skyward like a tree. He trumpeted, for the first and only time. And then down he came, his belly toward me, with a crash that seemed to shake the ground even where I lay.

I got up. The Burmans were already racing past me across the mud. It   12
was obvious that the elephant would never rise again, but he was not dead. He was breathing very rhythmically with long rattling gasps, his great mound of a side painfully rising and falling. His mouth was wide open—I could see far down into caverns of pale pink throat. I waited for a long time for him to die, but his breathing did not weaken. Finally I fired my two remaining shots into the spot where I thought his heart must be. The thick blood welled out of him like red velvet, but still he did not die. His body did not even jerk when the shots hit him, the tortured breathing continued without a pause. He was dying, very slowly and in great agony, but in some world remote from me where not even a bullet could damage him further. I felt that I had got to put an end to that dreadful noise. It seemed dreadful to see the great beast lying there, powerless to move and yet powerless to die, and not even to be able to finish him. I sent back for my small rifle and poured shot after shot into his heart and down his throat. They seemed to make no impression. The tortured gasps continued as steadily as the ticking of a clock.

In the end I could not stand it any longer and went away. I heard later   13
that it took him half an hour to die. Burmans were bringing dahs[13] and baskets even before I left, and I was told they had stripped his body almost to the bones by the afternoon.

Afterward, of course, there were endless discussions about the shoot-   14
ing of the elephant. The owner was furious, but he was only an Indian and could do nothing. Besides, legally I had done the right thing, for a mad elephant has to be killed, like a mad dog, if its owner fails to control it.

Among the Europeans opinion was divided. The older men said I was right, the younger men said it was a damn shame to shoot an elephant for killing a coolie, because an elephant was worth more than any damn Coringhee coolie.[14] And afterward I was very glad that the coolie had been killed; it put me legally in the right and it gave me a sufficient pretext for shooting the elephant. I often wondered whether any of the others grasped that I had done it solely to avoid looking a fool.

NOTES

[1] Burma (Union of Myanmar) is a country in Southeast Asia, and was part of the British Empire at the time to which Orwell is referring.

[2] Betel juice is produced by chewing the leaf of the betel plant wrapped around parings of the areca nut.

[3] As an officer in the Indian Imperial Police, Orwell was an agent of the Empire, and thus often resented by the local population.

[4] British Raj: British rule in the Indian subcontinent prior to 1947.

[5] For ever and ever.

[6] As a warning.

[7] *Must* is a state of dangerous frenzy to which certain male animals, especially elephants and camels, are subject at infrequent intervals.

[8] A *mahout* is an elephant driver.

[9] The rainy season.

[10] *Coolie* is a European word used to describe natives in India and elsewhere who are hired as labourers or burden carriers. Dravidians, so called because they speak one of the Dravidian family of languages, live in southern India and northern Sri Lanka.

[11] Paddy fields are fields of rice.

[12] *Sahib* is a respectful term of address used by Indians and Asians to Europeans, equivalent to "Sir."

[13] A *dah* is a short heavy sword, also used as a knife.

[14] A Coringhee coolie is from Coringa, a small town in southern India.

VOCABULARY

despotic—oppressive or tyrannical

imperialism—the principle, spirit, or ideology by which the existence of an empire, or the extension of territory in the name of protection of existing trading or economic interests, is justified

QUESTIONS

1. Reread the first two paragraphs of "Shooting an Elephant." What are Orwell's attitudes toward the Burmese, the British, and his own position in Burma? How does Orwell use descriptive details and diction to establish his perspective and create the tone of this essay?

2. Note the description of the man killed by the elephant (fourth paragraph). What purposes does this description serve in the essay as a whole?

3. Make a list of Orwell's reasons for not shooting the elephant. Then make a list of the reasons he gives for shooting the elephant. Are you convinced that Orwell was justified in shooting the elephant? What would you have done if you had been in his situation?

4. Note the detailed and graphic description of the elephant's death. What purposes does this description serve? What does the elephant symbolize?

5. Where does Orwell indicate his subject? What insights into the real motives for which imperialist governments act does Orwell actually gain from his experience? What is his thesis?

6. Do you think Orwell uses narration effectively as a persuasive strategy in this essay?

SUGGESTION FOR WRITING

Like Orwell, most of us have done something we are rather ashamed of but have never forgotten because it taught us something important. Using Orwell's essay as a model, write a narrative essay in which you tell a story about a single incident. Be sure this incident has a definite beginning, middle, and end. Try to begin by establishing the context of the incident (how old you were, where it happened, why it was especially important). Include plenty of vivid, precise descriptive details. You can imitate the structure of "Shooting an Elephant" by leading up to your thesis, which you may choose to imply rather than state explicitly.

Girl Unprotected

Laura Robinson

I t is the winter of 1996–97 and your daughter's boyfriend is a junior 1
hockey player. He lives with a bunch of other players and their coach in
a hotel suite in Deseronto, Ontario.[1] The relationship does not venture
outside the hockey rink or the hotel but the coach is always there and he
has a reputation of ensuring players go to school, do their homework, keep
their grades up and observe a curfew.

The coach and the players he brought with him have turned the team 2
around. Once it could never win, now it seems never to lose and everybody
loves a winner. Your daughter must be safe.

In 2004 you and the rest of Canada are shocked when Michael Jefferson, 3
one of those star players who had since remade himself into Mike Danton
in the NHL, pleads guilty to conspiracy to murder charges in St. Louis, and
you learn it was David Frost, his coach back in Deseronto, now his agent,
whom he conspired to have murdered. Both Danton and Frost deny a conspiracy or intent of any kind, but at least with a guilty plea there will be no
investigation. Danton commences his jail term in New Jersey.

Your daughter and her best friend are now young women, removed from 4
Deseronto and the near zero options small towns offer girls. There were no
chances for them to become great junior players, because, like every other
small town in Canada, Deseronto did not
provide "professional" junior hockey teams
for girls. In this highly gendered equation,
girls were only allowed to be adjectives
that helped describe boys, much as hockey
scores do. Shortly after the Danton story
broke they went to the police.

With distance and maturity the girls 5
understood that the limited sexual opportunities offered by their ex-boyfriends
weren't about loving the female body at
all; rather they were twisted relationships
that revolved around their all powerful
coach. The coach Danton wanted dead.

In a Napanee courtroom this week one 6
young woman said, "I felt uncomfortable

Laura Robinson is a freelance journalist who
writes primarily about issues in sport. Her
book *Crossing the Line: Violence and Sexual
Assault in Canada's National Sport* (1998) was
one of the earlier examinations of the negative downsides of hockey culture in Canada.
She has also written extensively about women
in sport, including *She Shoots, She Scores:
Canadian Perspectives on Women in Sport*
(1997) and *Black Tights: Women, Sport and
Sexuality* (2002). She is also a former member of Canada's national cycling team and a
former Canadian rowing champion.

"Girl Unprotected" is published on
www.playthegame.org.

with it, but . . . I felt kind of pressured to do it" referring to having to have sex with Mr. Frost. She added that she "didn't want to do it again, but finally I got persuaded into it" after her boyfriend continued to pressure her to have sex once more with him and Mr. Frost.

Robin Warshaw wrote the groundbreaking book *I Never Called It Rape*   7 in 1988. She went to university campuses across the United States and asked girls and young women if they had ever been raped. Almost exclusively they responded in the negative. Then she asked them if they had ever been pressured to have sex by someone who was much larger, who held power over them, who used intimidating or coercive tactics physically, psychologically or emotionally? Had they ever been brow-beaten into sex; simply worn down by a guy who wouldn't take "no"? Had they ever agreed to have sex because it seemed to be the only way out of the situation? The answers came back in the affirmative.

The girls in Deseronto cooperated with police for over two years, but   8 on March 6, 2007, Crown Attorney Adam Zegouras dropped the charges that concerned the alleged assaults against the girls, declaring there was insufficient evidence.

It was at this point that one of the girls finally gave the police her   9 diary where she kept her most intimate and embarrassing recollections of what went on in the hotel room. Too late: the charges had been dropped and eventually her name, which I will not use, was disclosed to the media as everyone pretended she was a willing participant in acts that sexually exploited and degraded her in a situation she was coerced into.

Somehow, though, the charges involving hockey players who were   10 allegedly abused in the exact same incidents at exactly the same time as the girls moved forward. These were the young men who the girls say colluded with Mr. Frost and persuaded them to have sex with their coach. Obviously Mr. Zegouras does not understand what acquaintance rape is, and how was Judge Geoffrey Griffin understanding it when he lifted the publication ban on the girls' names?

These girls are all of our daughters. While writing *Crossing the Line:*   11 *Violence and Sexual Assault in Canada's National Sport* I found too many cases where the "justice" system propped up the hockey mythology and abandoned girls, blind to the cyclical nature of sexual abuse because such ugliness could not be part of hockey. In a subculture presided over with an iron fist, where garbage and garbage cans were thrown over players who didn't play well, where Frost was convicted of assault after he punched a player in the face, everyone became a victim.

Girls' bodies were objectified in the most absolute meaning of the word,   12 becoming the surface on which and in which the real relationship—that between the coach and players—took place. Abusive sex was a stand-in for hockey; the female body a stand-in for ice as Mr. Frost's players did as they were told. Like the Swift Current Broncos, who were paid $50.00 to bring a girl back to their coach Graham James' house so he could videotape them having sex, these allegedly victimized players became victimizers.[2] James pled guilty to 350 counts of sexual assault at the exact same time Frost started his fiefdom in Deseronto. Plus ça change.

Girls, in a subculture where Frost told players they were "pussies" and to put their skirts back on and go home, were not human beings. One ex-girlfriend testified she only came to the hotel when "invited." Determining when she saw her boyfriend and when and with whom she would have sexual activity was not her right; another tragic chapter in a litany of many that the hockey myth continues to deny.

13

NOTES

[1] Deseronto is a town on the northern shore of Lake Ontario, west of Kingston.

[2] Graham James coached junior hockey and was the subject of controversy when Sheldon Kennedy made allegations of sexual abuse against James. In 1997, James pleaded guilty to sexual assault charges and served jail time until his parole in 2001. In October 2010, James faced a new set of charges for sexual assault against the former NHL player Theoren Fleury. Fleury discusses his abuse by James in his autobiographical book, *Playing with Fire* (2009).

VOCABULARY

acquaintance rape—sexual assault where the victim knows the perpetrator

QUESTIONS

1. After reading what Robinson has to say about the dark side of hockey culture in Canada, do you think hockey should be a national symbol for Canada? Can Canada reconcile its pride in hockey (or should it), when hockey is revealed to be entrenched in such violence?

2. Robinson specifically introduces gender in this essay to highlight the limited opportunities that girls and women have in the hockey world. How do you see gender differences in hockey or in sport as a whole? While star athletes are generally held in high regard, what does this say about female role models for girls?

3. Robinson states that the girls are mere "adjectives that helped describe boys." Can you think of any scenarios where these gender roles might be reversed?

SUGGESTION FOR WRITING

Define the myth of hockey and write about which elements you believe are true and which elements you believe are false.

The Men We Carry in Our Minds

Scott Russell Sanders

"This must be a hard time for women," I say to my friend Anneke. 1
"They have so many paths to choose from, and so many voices calling them."

"I think it's a lot harder for men," she replies. 2

"How do you figure that?" 3

"The women I know feel excited, innocent, like crusaders in a just 4
cause. The men I know are eaten up with guilt."

We are sitting at the kitchen table drinking sassafras tea,[1] our hands 5
wrapped around the mugs because this April morning is cool and drizzly.
"Like a Dutch morning," Anneke told me earlier. She is Dutch herself, a
writer and midwife and peacemaker, with the round face and sad eyes of a
woman in a Vermeer painting[2] who might be waiting for the rain to stop,
for a door to open. She leans over to sniff a sprig of lilac, pale lavender, that
rises from a vase of cobalt blue.

"Women feel such pressure to be everything, do everything," I say. 6
"Career, kids, art, politics. Have their babies and get back to the office a
week later. It's as if they're trying to overcome a million years' worth of
evolution in one lifetime."

"But we help one another. We don't try to lumber on alone, like so 7
many wounded grizzly bears, the way men do." Anneke sips her tea. I gave
her the mug with the owls on it, for wisdom. "And we have this deep-down sense
that we're in the *right*—we've been held
back, passed over, used—while men feel
they're in the wrong. Men are the ones
who've been discredited, who have to
search their souls."

I search my soul. I discover guilty 8
feelings aplenty—towards the poor, the
Vietnamese, Native Americans, the whales,
an endless list of debts—a guilt in each
case that is as bright and unambiguous as a
neon sign. But toward women I feel something
more confused, a snarl of shame,
envy, wary tenderness, and amazement.

Scott Russell Sanders (b. 1945) is a fiction
writer, essayist, critic, and former professor of
English at Indiana University. His publications
include *The Country of Language* (1999), *The
Force of Spirit* (2000), and *A Private History
of Awe* (2006). He was named winner of the
Mark Twain Award in 2009, National Winner of
the Eugene and Marilyn Glick Indiana Authors
Award in 2010, and winner of the Cecil Woods
Jr. Award in Nonfiction in 2011.

This muddle troubles me. To hide my unease I say, "You're right, it's tough being a man these days."

"Don't laugh." Anneke frowns at me, mournful-eyed, through the   9
sassafras steam. "I wouldn't be a man for anything. It's much easier being the victim. All the victim has to do is break free. The persecutor has to live with his past."

How deep is that past? I find myself wondering after Anneke has left.   10
How much of an inheritance do I have to throw off? Is it just the beliefs I breathed in as a child? Do I have to scour memory back through father and grandfather? Through St. Paul?[3] Beyond Stonehenge[4] and into the twilit caves? I'm convinced the past we must contend with is deeper even than speech. When I think back on my childhood, on how I learned to see men and women, I have a sense of ancient, dizzying depths. The back roads of Tennessee and Ohio where I grew up were probably closer, in their sexual patterns, to the campsites of Stone Age hunters than to the genderless cities of the future into which we are rushing.

The first men, besides my father, I remember seeing were black con-   11
victs and white guards, in the cottonfield across the road from our farm on the outskirts of Memphis. I must have been three or four. The prisoners wore dingy gray-and-black zebra suits, heavy as canvas, sodden with sweat. Hatless, stooped, they chopped weeds in the fierce heat, row after row, breathing the acrid dust of boll-weevil poison.[5] The overseers wore dazzling white shirts and broad shadowy hats. The oiled barrels of their shotguns flashed in the sunlight. Their faces in memory are utterly blank. Of course those men, white and black, have become for me an emblem of racial hatred. But they have also come to stand for the twin poles of my early vision of manhood—the brute toiling animal and the boss.

When I was a boy, the men I knew labored with their bodies. They   12
were marginal farmers, just scraping by, or welders, steel-workers, carpenters; they swept floors, dug ditches, mined coal, or drove trucks, their forearms ropy with muscle; they trained horses, stoked furnaces, built tires, stood on assembly lines wrestling parts onto cars and refrigerators. They got up before light, worked all day long whatever the weather, and when they came home at night they looked as though somebody had been whipping them. In the evenings and on weekends they worked on their own places, tilling gardens that were lumpy with clay, fixing broken-down cars, hammering on houses that were always too drafty, too leaky, too small.

The bodies of the men I knew were twisted and maimed in ways vis-   13
ible and invisible. The nails of their hands were black and split, the hands tattooed with scars. Some had lost fingers. Heavy lifting had given many of

them finicky backs and guts weak from hernias. Racing against conveyor belts had given them ulcers. Their ankles and knees ached from years of standing on concrete. Anyone who had worked for long around machines was hard of hearing. They squinted, and the skin of their faces was creased like the leather of old work gloves. There were times, studying them, when I dreaded growing up. Most of them coughed, from dust or cigarettes, and most of them drank cheap wine or whiskey, so their eyes looked bloodshot and bruised. The fathers of my friends always seemed older than the mothers. Men wore out sooner. Only women lived into old age.

As a boy I also knew another sort of men, who did not sweat and break   14
down like mules. They were soldiers, and so far as I could tell they scarcely worked at all. During my early school years we lived on a military base, an arsenal in Ohio, and every day I saw GIs in the guardshacks, on the stoops of barracks, at the wheels of olive drab Chevrolets. The chief fact of their lives was boredom. Long after I left the Arsenal I came to recognize the sour smell the soldiers gave off as that of souls in limbo. They were all waiting—for wars, for transfers, for leaves, for promotions, for the end of their hitch—like so many braves waiting for the hunt to begin. Unlike the warriors of older tribes, however, they would have no say about when the battle would start or how it would be waged. Their waiting was broken only when they practiced for war. They fired guns at targets, drove tanks across the churned-up fields of the military reservation, set off bombs in the wrecks of old fighter planes. I knew this was all play. But I also felt certain that when the hour for killing arrived, they would kill. When the real shooting started, many of them would die. This was what soldiers were *for,* just as a hammer was for driving nails.

Warriors and toilers: those seemed, in my boyhood vision, to be the   15
chief destinies for men. They weren't the only destinies, as I learned from having a few male teachers, from reading books, and from watching television. But the men on television—the politicians, the astronauts, the generals, the savvy lawyers, the philosophical doctors, the bosses who gave orders to both soldiers and laborers—seemed as remote and unreal to me as the figures in tapestries. I could no more imagine growing up to become one of these cool, potent creatures than I could imagine becoming a prince.

A nearer and more hopeful example was that of my father, who had   16
escaped from a red-dirt farm to a tire factory, and from the assembly line to the front office. Eventually he dressed in a white shirt and tie. He carried himself as if he had been born to work with his mind. But his body, remembering the earlier years of slogging work, began to give out on him in his fifties, and it quit on him entirely before he turned sixty-five. Even such

a partial escape from man's fate as he had accomplished did not seem possible for most of the boys I knew. They joined the army, stood in line for jobs in the smoky plants, helped build highways. They were bound to work as their fathers had worked, killing themselves or preparing to kill others.

A scholarship enabled me not only to attend college, a rare enough feat   17
in my circle, but even to study in a university meant for the children of the rich. Here I met for the first time young men who had assumed from birth that they would lead lives of comfort and power. And for the first time I met women who told me that men were guilty of having kept all the joys and privileges of the earth for themselves. I was baffled. What privileges? What joys? I thought about the maimed, dismal lives of most of the men back home. What had they stolen from their wives and daughters? The right to go five days a week, twelve months a year, for thirty or forty years to a steel mill or a coal mine? The right to drop bombs and die in war? The right to feel every leak in the roof, every gap in the fence, every cough in the engine, as a wound they must mend? The right to feel, when the lay-off comes or the plant shuts down, not only afraid but ashamed?

I was slow to understand the deep grievances of women. This was   18
because, as a boy, I had envied them. Before college, the only people I had ever known who were interested in art or music or literature, the only ones who read books, the only ones who ever seemed to enjoy a sense of ease and grace were the mothers and daughters. Like the menfolk, they fretted about money, they scrimped and made-do. But, when the pay stopped coming in, they were not the ones who had failed. Nor did they have to go to war, and that seemed to me a blessed fact. By comparison with the narrow, ironclad days of fathers, there was an expansiveness, I thought, in the days of mothers. They went to see neighbors, to shop in town, to run errands at school, at the library, at church. No doubt, had I looked harder at their lives, I would have envied them less. It was not my fate to become a woman, so it was easier for me to see the graces. Few of them held jobs outside the home, and those who did filled thankless roles as clerks and waitresses. I didn't see, then, what a prison a house could be, since houses seemed to me brighter, handsomer places than any factory. I did not realize—because such things were never spoken of—how often women suffered from men's bullying. I did learn about the wretchedness of abandoned wives, single mothers, widows; but I also learned about the wretchedness of lone men. Even then I could see how exhausting it was for a mother to cater all day to the needs of young children. But if I had been asked, as a boy, to choose between tending a baby and tending a machine, I think I would have chosen the baby. (Having now tended both, I know I would choose the baby.)

So I was baffled when the women at college accused me and my sex of   19
having cornered the world's pleasures. I think something like my baffle-
ment has been felt by other boys (and by girls as well) who grew up in
dirt-poor farm country, in mining country, in black ghettos, in Hispanic
barrios,[6] in the shadows of factories, in Third World nations—any place
where the fate of men is as grim and bleak as the fate of women. Toilers
and warriors. I realize now how ancient these identities are, how deep
the tug they exert on men, the undertone of a thousand generations.
The miseries I saw, as a boy, in the lives of nearly all men I continue to
see in the lives of many—the body-breaking toil, the tedium, the call to
be tough, the humiliating powerlessness, the battle for a living and for
territory.

When the women I met at college thought about the joys and privileges   20
of men, they did not carry in their minds the sort of men I had known in
my childhood. They thought of their fathers, who were bankers, physi-
cians, architects, stockbrokers, the big wheels of the big cities. These fathers
rode the train to work or drove cars that cost more than any of my childhood houses. They were attended from morning to night by female helpers,
wives, and nurses and secretaries. They were never laid off, never short of
cash at month's end, never lined up for welfare. These fathers made decisions that mattered. They ran the world.

The daughters of such men wanted to share in this power, this glory.   21
So did I. They yearned for a say over their future, for jobs worthy of their
abilities, for the right to live at peace, unmolested, whole. Yes, I thought,
yes yes. The difference between me and these daughters was that they saw
me, because of my sex, as destined from birth to become like their fathers,
and therefore as an enemy to their desires. But I knew better. I wasn't an
enemy, in fact or in feeling. I was an ally. If I had known, then, how to tell
them so, would they have believed me? Would they now?

NOTES

[1] Sassafras tea is made from the root of the sassafras tree, a small tree native to North America.

[2] Jan Vermeer (1632–1675) was a Dutch painter known in particular for his depiction of peaceful
domestic scenes.

[3] St. Paul, author of a number of biblical Epistles, is known for his stern views on Christian belief and
behaviour.

[4] Stonehenge is a prehistoric circle of stones on Salisbury Plain in England.

[5] The boll weevil is a beetle that attacks the seed vessels of cotton, a major crop in the American South.

[6] Barrios are Spanish-speaking districts of cities or towns in the United States, especially poor neigh-
bourhoods populated by immigrants.

VOCABULARY

arsenal—an arms repository or store

limbo—a place between heaven and hell, where the souls of the unbaptized are supposed to reside

QUESTIONS

1. How does Sanders's account of his conversation with his friend Anneke create a framework for the rest of the essay?

2. What do the men Sanders carries in his mind—convicts and guards, marginal farmers, factory workers, labourers, soldiers—have in common? How have these men shaped Sanders's attitudes toward gender issues?

3. How does Sanders use comparison as a strategy to develop and organize his ideas in this essay?

4. Do you think Sanders makes effective use of descriptive detail?

5. If you are a female reader, did Sanders's essay make you more willing to believe that men have problems? If you are a male reader, can you identify with Sanders's account of men's lives?

SUGGESTION FOR WRITING

What men or women do you carry in your mind? How have they influenced your attitudes toward whether men or women have easier lives? Write an essay in which you describe the appearance of the men or women you grew up with and the work they did. Be sure to include a range of specific sensory details.

Systems: Open or Closed?

Virginia Satir

I want to discuss something that at first you might not think has much   1
to do with your family and peoplemaking.[1] Stay with me. The concept of *systems* was borrowed from the world of industry and com-
merce. It has become a way of understanding how human beings in
groups work.

Any system consists of several individual parts. Each part is essential   2
and related to each other part to attain a certain outcome; each acts as a
stimulus to other parts. The system has an order and a sequence which
is determined through the actions, reactions, and interactions among the
parts. This constant interplay governs how the system manifests itself. A
system has life only now, when its component parts are present.

Sounds confusing? It isn't really. You put yeast, flour, water, and sugar   3
together to make bread. The bread isn't like any one of its ingredients, yet
it contains all of them.

Steam isn't like any of its parts, but it contains them all.   4

All human life is part of a system. We hear a lot about beating the sys-   5
tem, which would seem to say that all systems are bad. Not so. Some are
and some are not. The implications of systems thinking for personal, family, and societal behavior are evident everywhere today. . . .

An operating system consists of the   6
following:

A purpose or goal. Why does this sys-   7
tem exist in the first place? In families, the
purpose is to grow new people and to further the growth of those already here.

Essential parts. In families, this means   8
adults and children, males and females.

An order to the parts' working. In   9
families, this refers to the various family members' self-esteem, rules, and
communication.

Power to maintain energy in the sys-   10
tem so the parts can work. In families,
this power is derived from food, shelter,
air, water, activity, and beliefs about the

Virginia Satir (1916–1988) is known for her
pioneering work in exploring the way that family systems affect the mental health of family
members. She co-founded the Mental Health
Research Institute (Menlo Park, California),
which, in 1962, offered the first formal training in family therapy. Her key books include
Conjoint Family Therapy (1964), *Peoplemaking*
(1972), and *The New Peoplemaking* (1988). The
Avanta network, which she founded in 1977,
continues her work today.

"Systems: Open or Closed?" is excerpted from the
chapter of the same name in *The New Peoplemaking*
(Palo Alto, California: Science & Behavior Books,
1988).

emotional, intellectual, physical, social, and spiritual lives of the family members and how they work together.

Ways of interacting with the outside. In families, this means relating to changing contents, the new and different. 11

There are two types of systems: closed and open. The main difference between them is the nature of their reactions to change, both from the inside and from the outside. In a closed system, the parts are rigidly connected or disconnected altogether. In either case, information does not flow between parts or from outside in and inside out. When parts are disconnected, they often appear as if they are operating: information leaks in and out but without any direction. There are no boundaries. 12

An open system is one in which the parts interconnect, are responsive and sensitive to one another, and allow information to flow between the internal and external environments. 13

If one were to deliberately design a closed family system, the first step would be to separate it as completely as possible from outside interference, and to rigidly fix all roles for all time. The fact is, I don't believe anyone would deliberately design a closed system. Closed family systems evolve from certain sets of beliefs: 14

> People are basically evil and must be continually controlled to be good.
>
> Relationships have to be regulated by force or by fear of punishment.
>
> There is one right way, and the person with most power has it.
>
> There is always someone who knows what is best for you.

These beliefs are powerful because they reflect the family's perception of reality. And the family then sets rules according to their beliefs. In other words, in closed systems: 15

> Self-worth is secondary to power and performance.
>
> Actions are subject to the whims of the boss.
>
> Change is resisted.

In open systems: 16

> Self-worth is primary; power and performance, secondary.
>
> Actions represent one's beliefs.
>
> Change is welcomed and considered normal and desirable.
>
> Communication, the system, and the rules all relate to each other.

Most of our social systems are closed or very nearly so. A little change is   17
allowed, which in my opinion is the reason we have been able to limp along
as well as we have.

Now we come to an important philosophical question. Do you believe   18
that all human life deserves the highest priority? *I believe this with all my
being.* Therefore I unashamedly admit I will do everything I can to change
closed systems into open ones. An open system can choose to be open or
closed when it fits. The important word is choice.

I believe that human beings cannot flourish in a closed system; at best,   19
they can only exist. Human beings want more than that. The task of the
therapist is to see the light that shines in every person or family, and to
uncoil the wrappings that shroud that light.

Right now you and I could point to countless examples of closed sys-   20
tems, including dictatorships in current society, schools, prisons, churches,
and political groups. What about the system in your family? Is it open or
closed? If your communication now is mostly growth-impeding and if your
rules are inhuman, covert, and out of date, you probably have a closed family system. If your communication is growth-producing and your rules are
human, overt, and up to date, you have an open one. . . .

The following chart shows how the closed system applies to troubled   21
families, and the open system to nurturing families:

	CLOSED SYSTEM
SELF-ESTEEM	low
COMMUNICATION STYLES	indirect, unclear, unspecific, incongruent, growth-impeding blaming placating computing^2 distracting
RULES	covert, out-of-date, inhuman rules remain fixed; people change their needs to conform to established rules
	restrictions on commenting
OUTCOME	accidental, chaotic, destructive, inappropriate

Self-worth grows ever more doubtful and depends more and more   22
heavily on other people.

OPEN SYSTEM

SELF-ESTEEM	high
COMMUNICATION STYLE	direct, clear, specific, congruent, growth-producing
	leveling
RULES	overt, up-to-date, human rules; rules change when need arises
	full freedom to comment on anything
OUTCOME	related to reality; appropriate, constructive

Self-worth grows ever more reliable, confident, and draws increasingly 23
more from the self.

All right. When three or more people are related in any way and are 24
joined in one common purpose, they will develop into a system. This happens in families, with friends, and at work. Once established, the system remains very much in operation, even when not in evidence. If it's a closed system, it will probably operate on a *life-death, right-wrong* basis; fear permeates the atmosphere. If open, it probably operates on the basis of *growth, intimacy,* and *choice.*

Put very simply, your self-worth, your communication, together with your 25
rules and your beliefs, are the ingredients that make up your family system. Leveling communication and human rules characterize an open system and allow everyone in that system to flourish. Crippling communication and inhuman rules make a closed system, retarding and distorting growth.

Becoming aware of their system usually opens the way for family mem- 26
bers to become searchers and to stop berating themselves and others when things go wrong. People can ask "how" questions instead of "why" questions. Generally speaking, "how" questions lead to information and understanding, and "whys" imply blame and so produce defensiveness. Anything contributing to defensiveness contributes to low pot[3] and leads to potentially unsatisfying outcomes.

Another important part of any system is that it tends to perpetuate 27
itself. Once established, a system will stay the same until it dies or something changes it: a part breaks down from lack of care or because of a defect; or a catastrophic event affects the system. Sometimes even a minor incident can overwhelm the system, which indicates that the system's designers behaved as though change would never happen.

Each member in a system is a most significant factor in keeping the   28
system going as it is or changing it. Discovering your part in the system and
seeing others' parts is an exciting, although sometimes painful, experience.
And you can certainly see the importance of systems when you consider the
very life of the family depends on its system to a very large degree. . . .

NOTES

[1] For Satir, "peoplemaking" is the process by which families help or hinder the growth of their members.

[2] In Satir's framework of terms, "computing" denotes a personality style emphasizing super-rationality.

[3] In Satir's work, your "pot" is the place where you store good feelings. "Low pot" means that your good feelings are relatively absent.

QUESTIONS

1. Satir associates human flourishing with open family systems. What's her support for this association? Are you persuaded by her claim?

2. Satir does not offer details of specific open and closed family systems. Does the essay need this detail? Why or why not?

3. This essay analyzes family systems as either open or closed. Is the organization of systems analysis around a simple opposition a weakness or strength (or both) in this essay? Can you imagine a family system being partly open and partly closed?

SUGGESTION FOR WRITING

Satir claims there are many closed or nearly closed systems in "current society" and its institutions. Write an essay on a current social or cultural organization (such as a college department, a church, or a provincial government) or a current belief system (such as neo-conservatism), examining its degree of openness or closure.

In Search of a Modest Proposal

Fred Stenson

My gratitude to the education system for teaching my children to read lasted for many years. Whenever teachers were attacked in my earshot, I rose to defend them. Then my daughter hit Grade 9 and was taught to write the essay. 1

When she told me she had been assigned to write an essay, I felt a thrill. She was about to learn one of the great literary forms, used for hundreds of years to persuade and argue. In the hands of a great writer, the essay could shape society. Part of the thrill was also that she had finally reached a topic about which I knew something. I was eager to help, and she allowed that I could. 2

The essay, as I recall (it's been a few years), was about "why it is good to converse with seniors." I was surprised in that I didn't know my daughter held that opinion, and here she was making it the thesis of a personal essay. 3

When I asked her about the choice, she said, oh no, it was just one of a list that the teacher had given them to choose from. "But yet you chose it?" I countered. "Well, my small group did. We did all the preparation in group." 4

Teacher? Group? The whole point of a personal essay is to be personal. Her personal opinion. Something she wanted to convince others of. She waved this away as immaterial. Time was wasting. The essay was due on Friday. 5

The thesis statement, that it was good to visit with old people, had to be in paragraph one. That was mandatory. Also, the first paragraph had to contain the three arguments, one per sentence. After that, she must devote one paragraph to each argument. Restate the argument; give five points to support that argument. And so on. 6

Her arguments were on a very messy piece of paper, covered in many people's handwriting, the result of a brain-storming session in the small group. 7

"Seniors know a lot." 8

Albertan Fred Stenson is the author of several books of fiction and nonfiction focusing on the Canadian West. He has also written numerous film scripts. His novels *The Trade* (2000) and *Lightning* (2005) were nominated for the Giller Prize, and both novels won the Grant MacEwan author prize. Stenson was a founding member of the Writers Guild of Alberta. He lives in Calgary with his family and his partner, writer and teacher Pamela Banting.

"In Search of a Modest Proposal" was first published in *Alberta Views*, Jan./Feb. 2004: 14-15, and is reproduced with permission of the author.

"Seniors get lonely because their families neglect them." 9

"Seniors deserve respect." 10

"Seniors are nice." 11

"A lot of seniors are not neglected by their families," I said. "Some 12 seniors are not even slightly nice. I might turn out to be one of them."

Again, I was waved silent. My daughter and her friends were much 13 better qualified than I to determine how the subject should be approached, and what should be said about it.

My daughter had already started writing. I read what she had so far. 14

"It's fine," I said, "but you shouldn't use all those words like 'there- 15 fore' and 'consequently' at the start of every paragraph. I mean, really. 'Henceforth'?"

My daughter looked at me with pity. She pulled out a sheet, a class 16 handout, and she read: "Each paragraph is to be connected to the next paragraph by a transitional word or phrase at the beginning of the new paragraph. Use transitional words within each paragraph as well for greater unity and cohesion." There was a list. 'Henceforth' was on it.

"And you're repeating a lot," I said. "That's not good writing." 17

She pointed to a different place on the handout. 18

"Repeat important words and phrases." 19

"What's with all the adjectives and adverbs?" 20

"Says here: 'Use bright descriptive language.'" 21

"What else does it say?" 22

"Support each of your three arguments with five points, in three sepa- 23 rate paragraphs. Then repeat the three arguments in the concluding para- graph, ending with a strong conclusion statement."

"That's not an essay!" I cried. "That's, that's . . ." 24

"A formula," she said. "A formula I have to stick to, or I will flunk. 25 Now, let's get busy."

* * *

A couple of months later, it was parent/teacher day. I confronted my 26 daughter's Language Arts teacher with my concerns about how the essay was being taught. I suspect I buttered it on a bit thick about the tradition of Rousseau and Swift, and the great modern practitioners like Richler and Fussell.[1] The teacher was a pleasant, able-seeming woman, who instantly deflated me with agreement. No, theirs was not a creative approach to the essay. No, that approach probably would not endear the students to the essay form. Asked why it was so, she shrugged and said, "It's the curricu- lum, on which they will be tested. The results of the test will determine their future in high school. So we teach it that way."

I sought out the Grade 9 curriculum for Language Arts. Everything   27
was there. "Bright descriptive language." The mathematical equation: this
many arguments each supported by this many points. Special emphasis on
transitional words and phrases, the more the merrier. I said no more about
it. My daughter passed her provincial Language Arts exam and moved on
into high school.

Nonetheless, it is sad about the essay. I find myself thinking about   28
Jonathan Swift's "A Modest Proposal," the essay he published in 1729 to
address the problem of Irish poverty and starvation. He proposed that the
higher classes eat Irish children while they were still young and succulent,
thus reducing the number of poor to a more manageable level.

This "modest proposal" is the essay's thesis statement. When I exam-   29
ined the essay with the Alberta Language Arts curriculum in mind, I was
disturbed to find that Swift does not actually state his thesis until he has
expended over 1,000 words! His use of transitional devices is equally
shoddy. Out of 28 paragraphs, he uses transitional words and phrases
to begin only eight of them. Of the eight, six are an enumeration of his
six strongest points toward the essay's end. This enumeration is good
and would get him some important marks. *But,* "finally," "similarly" and
"in addition" are absent from the essay, leaving Swift's thoughts sadly
unconnected.

However, let us remember that this essay was written almost 300 years   30
ago. On that account, let us be kind to Mr. Swift and give him a "C." It
would be a shame to keep him out of Grade 10.

NOTE

[1] Jean Jacques Rousseau (1712–1778) was a Swiss-born French philosopher whose *Confessions* (1770, 1782) was influential in the evolution of the personal essay. Jonathan Swift is one of the authors featured in Readings. Mordecai Richler, who died in 2001, is primarily known as a Canadian novelist, but his journalism and essays are collected in four books, including *Shovelling Trouble* (1972). American Paul Fussell (b. 1924) has written books on war, class, and travel, among other topics.

QUESTIONS

1. Why does Stenson open his essay with comments on his appreciation of teachers and on his love for the essay as "one of the great literary forms"?

2. Stenson is writing a personal essay about the value of personal essays. How far does his own essay embody what he argues for? To help you answer this question, you might find it useful to refer to our discussion of informal and formal essays in Chapter 1.

3. Stenson clearly admires Jonathan Swift's "A Modest Proposal" (Readings), and, like Swift, he writes to criticize cultural and social attitudes and institutions. How does his use of satire and irony compare to Swift's?

SUGGESTIONS FOR WRITING

1. Stenson defends the role of "personal opinion" in the personal essay. Write an essay exploring the role of personal opinion in the essay form in general and referring to several essayists from the Readings.

2. What was your own experience of writing essays in junior high or high school? Was it like that of Stenson's daughter, or quite different? Do you now write essays in the way you were taught then? Write an essay on this topic.

Food Connections

David Suzuki

Food is what nourishes us, connects us with the Earth, and reminds us of the cycles of the seasons. But in the industrialized countries of the world, fresh fruit and vegetables are available throughout the year, and we often forget that food remains a gift of the soil, water, and air. A vivid reminder is a visit to a traditional market—especially those in Third World countries. Such markets assault our senses with an indelible collage of sounds—vendors hawking their products (and some of the live produce adding their own squawks); buyers haggling over price and old friends greeting and exchanging gossip; smells that range from the perfume of flowers and spices to nonrefrigerated meat and fish; and splashes of colours in clothing, fruits, and flowers.

Markets give us a sense of the people. That's not surprising, since food is what keeps us alive and every society has evolved elaborate rituals around the gathering of food. In poor countries, where only a few people own refrigerators, most have to shop for food daily. For them, the market is a focal point of their lives.

Markets at different times of the year reveal nature's rhythms in types of fruits, fish, and vegetables available. Variations in abundance, size, and variety of products may reflect the consequences of drought or a severe winter. In poor countries, the market products are invariably "indigenous" and grown locally. They give us an idea of the kind of agriculture practised in a locale and the variety of products grown or collected in the area. Blemishes and the odd shapes of fruit and vegetables tell us they are still grown by traditional methods. And the sharp aroma and flavour of these fresh fruits and vegetables are often a delightful shock for those of us from cities in rich countries.

I have seen the floating markets in Thailand, street markets in Shanghai, a covered market on the Amazon, and village

A third-generation Japanese Canadian born in Vancouver, David Takayoshi Suzuki was interned with his family in interior British Columbia during the Second World War. Suzuki went on to earn a PhD in zoology from the University of Chicago, carry out research on genetic adaptations in fruit flies, and enjoy a thirty-year career as a professor of zoology at the University of British Columbia. His later career has been devoted to the popularization of scientific and urgent environmental issues, notably as the host of *The Nature of Things*, a long-running CBC television show that has been shown worldwide. He is the author of over thirty-two books, including *Genethics* (1990), *Wisdom of the Elders* (1993), *The Sacred Balance* (2002), and *The Legacy* (2010).

"Food Connections" is an essay from Suzuki's book *Time to Change* (Toronto: Stoddart, 1994. 178–80). Reprinted with permission of The David Suzuki Foundation.

markets in Madagascar. On those visits, I feel not only the spirit of the local people, but a direct sense of connection to the land through the fruits and vegetables and the seasonal change. There is an immediate bond between people and the productive Earth.

It is the contrast with markets of Third World countries that gives us   5
a measure of our own society. Try looking at our markets as if you were a foreign visitor. In most urban centres in Canada, traditional markets have been superseded by "*super*markets." What a contrast to a village market. Our supermarkets are immense shopping opportunities under a single roof that offer everything from cosmetics to hardware and clothing. Oh, yes, and food, too. They are temperature-controlled and squeaky clean with little hint of the terrestrial origin of our nutrition. Not surprisingly, the word *dirt* in our society is a pejorative.

A television producer recounted a telling anecdote. While dating   6
a woman who had a university education, he took her to the country to buy some fresh vegetables. At a "U-pick" farm, they went to the field for cucumbers. The woman tugged at the producer's sleeve and asked, "What are those cucumbers doing on the ground?" When told they grow that way, she exclaimed in disgust, "But they're covered in *dirt!*" We have become so used to clean food presented in plastic packages that we no longer think about where it comes from. It's small wonder that a BBC April Fool's Day broadcast showing how farmers grow and harvest spaghetti as a crop was taken seriously by many viewers.

Seasonal variation in industrial societies is minimized by import-   7
ing many products that mature in specific seasons from different parts of the world—apples from New Zealand, asparagus from Peru, grapes from Argentina and, of course, everything from California. When I was a boy, the first fresh fruit or vegetables of the year that appeared on the table were a delight, a signal to celebrate the change of the seasons and a renewal of the productivity of the Earth. I regret the loss of that celebration today.

Food grown naturally *without* chemicals is marked "organic," as if it's   8
special, while food that has been treated with pesticides, herbicides, hormones, preservatives, and antibiotics requires no special label. So naturally grown food is no longer considered normal while food raised under total human control and management is.

The overriding concern in our supermarkets is with appearance. We   9
have become accustomed to near-perfect uniformity and the absence of blemishes. When I was a child, my mother would sit with a basket of apples and nick out the scabs and worms before cooking them or putting them in a bowl for us. We thought nothing of sharing those apples with other organisms. Today we aren't nearly as tolerant and demand bug-free products even

if it means poisoning air, water, and soil to get it. By fostering the illusion of escape from the vagaries of pests, abnormality, and seasons, we are no longer of the land—we have removed ourselves from nature.

This isn't just the nostalgic yearning of an aging man for the good old 10 days. We are paying a terrible price for our separation from the natural world. Traditional markets where those who consume can come into direct contact with produce and their producers are a strong reminder of our lost contract with Mother Earth.

VOCABULARY

indigenous—belonging to a particular region or country

QUESTIONS

1. Just as Virginia Satir (Readings) organizes her discussion of family systems into two types of system, so Suzuki organizes his systems analysis and argument into two categories: traditional markets and supermarkets. Are there any resemblances between these two kinds of markets and Satir's open and closed systems?

2. On what basis does Suzuki value traditional markets? What standard(s) of evaluation does he use?

3. In this essay, Suzuki speaks of his childhood. Why? Do you see any correlation between his childhood experience and his present opinions?

SUGGESTIONS FOR WRITING

1. "Food Connections" compares two market systems, but it is not organized as a formal comparison essay. Write an outline to show how you would reorganize Suzuki's essay to produce a point-by-point comparison (see Chapter 7). Would this reorganization alter Suzuki's thesis?

2. Explore the origins or distribution of an item of food that you consume regularly. You might choose to write a process essay exploring its path from growth and harvesting to your table, or an analysis of its distribution and sales (see Chapter 3).

It Always Costs

David Suzuki

I have long believed that we have to have greater scientific literacy at all levels of society if we are to have any hope of affecting the way science and technology are impacting on our lives. That's why I went into broadcasting.

But I have only recently realized that my underlying faith in the power of greater awareness is misplaced. First of all, we must understand that there is no such thing as a problem-free technology. However beneficent, technology always has a cost.

Think, for example, of DDT[1]—it killed malaria-carrying mosquitoes in huge numbers and without question saved millions of lives in tropical countries. But geneticists could have predicted that DDT would exert incredible selective pressure for mutations that would confer resistance to DDT in the mosquitoes and that within a few years large numbers would return. They did. But once committed to a chemical approach, we had to turn to other more toxic compounds.

The ecological damage from massive use of chemical sprays has been enormous because DDT is not specific and kills all insects. Furthermore, the compound is ingested by many organisms, so that initially minute quantities become concentrated up the food chain in a process called *biomagnification.* The final result was that DDT ended up in the shell glands of birds, affecting the thickness of egg shells and eventually causing heavy bird mortality.

There are numerous examples of how technological innovations have had detrimental side effects that eventually outweighed their benefits. It has been my assumption that what we needed was some kind of vehicle, like panels of citizens representing a broad range of interests, to do a cost/benefit analysis of all new technologies. The idea was that by carefully weighing the benefits and bad side effects, we could make a more informed decision on whether to allow a new technology to be used. My belief that this would help us avoid future problems was based on faith in our predictive capabilities. Indeed, much of the testing of environmental and health impacts is made on that faith. But we can't rely on such a system.

For biographic details, see the previous reading, Suzuki, David, "Food Connections."

"It Always Costs" is taken from *Inventing the Future* by David Suzuki. Reprinted with permission of Stoddart Publishing Co. Limited, North York, Ontario.

For one thing, our assessments are always limited. For example, suppose   6
we do an environmental impact assessment of drilling for oil in the high
Arctic. The studies, of necessity, are carried out in a limited time within a
restricted area. It is simply assumed that scaling up the observed effects of
the two drill holes by a factor of one hundred or more gives a reasonable
estimate of the impact of major exploration.

Well, there are effects called *synergistic;* several components interact to   7
give new or greater effects than the sum of their individual impact. Also,
during an assessment, you can bet industry will be on its best behaviour, so
the results will always be on the conservative side.

It is also true that even if a study is made over ten years (which it won't   8
be) we could never anticipate all the fluctuation of conditions in this sensitive area. I've known colleagues who have studied populations of animals
or plants over decades and find nice cycles and patterns that are predictable until suddenly completely unexpected fluctuations occur. They get out
more publications that way, but we ought, then, to be a lot more humble
about how *little* we know.

Finally, we know that major blowouts, spills or accidents are relatively   9
rare. Suppose one happens an average of once every twenty holes. By studying
two holes and finding no effect, we are not justified in concluding that drilling
one hundred holes will also be accident free. It would be just as invalid were an
accident to happen in one of the test holes to conclude that half of all drilling
sites will have a bad episode. The numbers are statistically meaningless.

Food additives, pesticides and drugs are extensively tested before they   10
are approved for use. But numerous cases inform us that we can't anticipate
all the effects. The DDT example is classic—at the time it was used, we
didn't even know about biomagnification, let alone its concentration in
bird shell glands.

Remember thalidomide[2] or DES?[3] Or consider the oral contraceptive. It   11
had been extensively tested (in Puerto Rico, of course) and shown to be effi-
cacious without detrimental side effects. It was only after millions of healthy,
normal women had taken the pill for years that epidemiologists could see
negative effects. No amount of pretesting could have anticipated them.

So we come to a terrible conclusion. Technology has enormous benefits.   12
They are undeniable—that's why we're hooked on it. Once technology is
in place, it becomes impossible to do without it and we can't go back to
doing things the old way. But the pretesting of any new technology is flawed
because it provides only a limited assessment of its impact. The tests are
restricted in size, scope and time and are based on what we decide a priori
might be a possible effect.

But how can we test for something that we don't know will happen? If   13
every technology has a cost, the more powerful the technology, the greater
its potential cost. We have to build into our judgements a large leeway for
our ignorance and err on the side of extreme caution. And perhaps it's time
to realize we don't have to do everything just because we can.

NOTES

[1] DDT—dichlorodiphenyltrichloroethane—has been used extensively as an insecticide, particularly
in combatting malarial mosquitoes. It is a persistent pesticide (it does not break down readily) and
is stored in human fat almost indefinitely. Tolerance to DDT is widely variable in humans and its
use has led to much controversy. It has been shown, in laboratory experiments, to be an "enzyme
inducer" that breaks down estrogen, which in birds mediates calcium metabolism. It is also readily passed through the placenta into the fetus. The use of DDT is now banned in Canada and the
United States, though DDT is still manufactured for export.

[2] Thalidomide, or alpha phthaloyl glutarimide, is a close relative of aminopteria, a drug known since
1950 to have teratogenic (causing monstrous genetic defect) properties. Thalidomide was introduced
for sale in Britain in April 1958. It was released for sale despite an almost complete lack of chemical and pharmacological testing, and of research into the scientific literature. It was touted as being
perfectly safe as a sedative for pregnant women despite testing that indicated that it could completely
shut down thyroid function. It caused birth defects such as shortened or absent limbs and flipper-like
appendages in more than 450 births as well as nerve damage in more than 400 adults and children.
Despite medical evidence of its effects, it continued to be sold until its withdrawal in November 1961.

[3] DES, or diethylstilbestrol, is a synthetic estrogen. It was widely prescribed to women in the United
States between 1938 and 1971 to prevent miscarriages and treat other complications of pregnancy.
Its use for pregnant women was halted in 1971 when the drug was found to affect the reproductive
system of children exposed to it in the womb. Women who took DES while pregnant have a slightly
elevated risk of breast cancer. "DES daughters"—daughters exposed to DES in the womb—have an
increased risk of a rare cancer of the vagina or cervix, as well as increased risk of reproductive tract
abnormalities, complications of pregnancy, and infertility. Sons exposed to DES also have some
increased health risks.

VOCABULARY

a priori—*a priori* here means being knowable by reasoning from something that is considered self-evident or presupposed from general experience

epidemiologists—those who study the incidence, distribution, and control of diseases in
large populations

QUESTIONS

1. Suzuki's title "It [technology] Always Costs" is also his thesis. How is his essay organized to support this thesis?

2. Why does Suzuki include his reassessments of the value of scientific research in his
essay? How do these inclusions affect his tone? Be specific about his attitudes to himself,
his readers, and his subject.

3. What does Suzuki's comment that the oral contraceptive was tested "in Puerto Rico, of course" reveal about his attitude to the scientific establishment? Do you think this comment affects Suzuki's credibility?

4. Is this essay written for scientists, for specialists in environmental issues, or for the general public? Does Suzuki's style define the audience he is aiming for? (For more on Suzuki's style, see Joyce MacDonald's essay comparing Suzuki with Merwin in the Sample Essays.)

SUGGESTION FOR WRITING

Do you agree that scientific advances *always* have costs? Write a letter to David Suzuki expressing your views on the costs and/or benefits of recent developments in science and technology, such as cloning, digital television, social networking, voice mail, the internet, and smartphones.

A Modest Proposal

For preventing the Children of Poor People
from being a Burthen to
their Parents, or the Country,
and for making them
Beneficial to the Publick.

Jonathan Swift

I t is a melancholly Object to those, who walk through this great Town,[1] or travel in the Country, when they see the *Streets,* the *Roads,* and *Cabbin-Doors,* crowded with *Beggars* of the female Sex, followed by three, four, or six Children, *all in Rags,* and importuning every Passenger for an Alms. These *Mothers* instead of being able to work for their honest Livelyhood, are forced to employ all their time in Stroling, to beg Sustenance for their *helpless Infants,* who, as they grow up, either turn *Thieves* for want of work, or leave their *dear native Country to fight for the Pretender in Spain,*[2] or sell themselves to the *Barbadoes.*[3]

I think it is agreed by all Parties, that this prodigious number of Children, in the Arms, or on the Backs, or at the *Heels* of their *Mothers,* and frequently of their *Fathers,* is *in the present deplorable state of the Kingdom,*[4] a very great additional grievance; and therefore whoever could find out a fair, cheap and easy method of making these Children sound and useful Members of the Commonwealth would deserve so well of the publick, as to have his Statue set up for a Preserver of the Nation.

But my Intention is very far from being confined to provide only for the Children of *professed Beggars:* It is of a much greater extent, and shall take in the whole number of Infants at a certain Age, who are born of Parents in effect as little able to support them, as those who demand our Charity in the Streets.

As to my own part, having turned my thoughts, for many Years, upon this important Subject, and maturely weighed the several *Schemes of other Projectors,* I have always found them grossly mistaken in their

Jonathan Swift (1667–1745) is often regarded as the foremost prose satirist to write in English. Born in Ireland of English parents, he was educated at Trinity College, Dublin, and then attempted a career in writing, politics, and the church in England. Most of his best-known works, including "A Modest Proposal" (1729) and the satiric fiction *Gulliver's Travels* (1726), were written during the thirty years between his appointment in 1714 as Dean of St. Patrick's (Anglican) Cathedral in Dublin and his death in 1745, a period in which he more and more took on the role of defender of Ireland against English absentee landlords and their upper-class Irish collaborators.

computation. It is true a Child, *just dropt from its Dam,* may be supported by her Milk, for a Solar year with little other Nourishment, at most not above the Value of two Shillings, which the Mother may certainly get, or the Value in *Scraps,* by her lawful Occupation of begging, and it is exactly at one Year old that I propose to provide for them, in such a manner, as, instead of being a Charge upon their *Parents,* or the *Parish,* or *wanting Food and Raiment* for the rest of their Lives, they shall, on the Contrary, contribute to the Feeding and partly to the Cloathing of many Thousands.

There is likewise another great Advantage in my Scheme, that it will prevent those *voluntary Abortions,* and that horrid practice of *Women murdering their Bastard Children;* alas! too frequent among us; sacrificing the *poor innocent Babes,* I doubt, more to avoid the Expence, than the Shame; which would move Tears and Pity in the most Savage and inhuman breast. 5

The Number of Souls in this Kingdom being usually reckoned one Million and a half; of these I calculate there may be about two hundred thousand Couple whose Wives are Breeders; from which number I Subtract thirty Thousand Couples, who are able to maintain their own Children, although I apprehend there cannot be so many under *the present distresses of the Kingdom;* but this being granted, there will remain an Hundred and Seventy Thousand Breeders. I again Subtract fifty Thousand for those Women who miscarry, or whose Children dye by accident, or disease within the Year. There only remain an hundred and twenty thousand Children of poor Parents annually born: The question therefore is, how this number shall be reared, and provided for, which, as I have already said, under the present Situation of Affairs, is utterly impossible by all the methods hitherto proposed, for we can *neither employ them in Handicraft,* or *Agriculture;* we neither build Houses, (I mean in the Country) nor cultivate Land: They can very seldom pick up a Livelyhood *by Stealing* till they arrive at six years Old, except where they are of towardly parts, although, I confess they learn the Rudiments much earlier, during which time, they can however be properly looked upon only as *Probationers,* as I have been informed by a principal Gentleman in the County of *Cavan,*[5] who protested to me, that he never knew above one or two Instances under the Age of six, even in a part of the Kingdom *so renowned for the quickest proficiency in that Art.* 6

I am assured by our Merchants, that a Boy or Girl, before twelve Years old, is no saleable Commodity, and even when they come to this Age, they will not yield above three Pounds, or three Pounds and half a Crown at most on the Exchange, which cannot turn to Account either to the Parents or the Kingdom, the Charge of Nutriment and Rags having been at least four times that Value. 7

I shall now therefore humbly propose my own thoughts, which I hope   8
will not be liable to the least Objection.

I have been assured by a very knowing *American* of my acquaintance in   9
London, that a young healthy Child well Nursed is at a Year old a most delicious, nourishing, and wholesome Food, whether *Stewed, Roasted, Baked,*
or *Boyled,* and I make no doubt that it will equally serve in a *Fricasie,* or a
Ragoust.

I do therefore humbly offer it to *publick consideration,* that of the hun-   10
dred and twenty thousand Children, already computed, twenty thousand
may be reserved for Breed, whereof only one fourth part to be Males, which
is more than we allow to *Sheep, black Cattle,* or *Swine,* and my reason is that
these Children are seldom the Fruits of Marriage, *a Circumstance not much
regarded by our Savages,* therefore *one Male* will be sufficient to serve *four
Females.* That the remaining hundred thousand may at a Year old be offered
in Sale to the *persons of Quality,* and *Fortune,* through the Kingdom, always
advising the Mother to let them Suck plentifully in the last Month, so as
to render them Plump, and Fat for a good Table. A Child will make two
Dishes at an Entertainment for Friends, and when the Family dines alone,
the fore or hind Quarter will make a reasonable Dish, and seasoned with a
little Pepper or Salt will be very good Boiled on the fourth Day,[6] especially
in Winter.

I have reckoned upon a Medium, that a Child just born will weigh   11
12 pounds, and in a solar Year if tollerably nursed encreaseth to 28 Pounds.

I grant this food will be somewhat dear, and therefore very *proper for*   12
Landlords, who, as they have already devoured most of the Parents, seem to
have the best Title to the Children.

Infant's flesh will be in Season throughout the Year, but more plentiful   13
in *March,* and a little before and after, for we are told by a grave Author[7]
an eminent *French* Physitian, that *Fish being a prolifick Dyet,* there are more
Children born in *Roman Catholick Countries* about nine Months after *Lent,*
than at any other Season: Therefore reckoning a Year after *Lent,* the Markets
will be more glutted than usual, because the number of *Popish Infants,* is at
least three to one in this Kingdom, and therefore it will have one other
Collateral advantage by lessening the Number of *Papists*[8] among us.

I have already computed the Charge of nursing a Beggars Child (in   14
which list I reckon all *Cottagers, Labourers,* and four fifths of the *Farmers)*
to be about two Shillings *per Annum,* Rags included, and I believe no
Gentleman would repine to give Ten Shillings for the *Carcass of a good fat
Child,* which, as I have said will make four Dishes of excellent Nutritive
Meat, when he hath only some particular friend, or his own Family to Dine
with him. Thus the Squire will learn to be a good Landlord, and grow

popular among his Tenants, the Mother will have Eight Shillings net profit, and be fit for Work till she produceth another Child.

Those who are more thrifty (*as I must confess the Times require*) may flay the Carcass; the Skin of which, artificially dressed, will make admirable *Gloves for Ladies,* and *Summer Boots for fine Gentlemen.* 15

As to our City of *Dublin,* Shambles may be appointed for this purpose, in the most convenient parts of it, and Butchers we may be assured will not be wanting, although I rather recommend buying the Children alive, and dressing them hot from the Knife, as we do *roasting Pigs.* 16

A very worthy Person, *a true Lover of his Country,*[9] and whose Virtues I highly esteem, was lately pleased, in discoursing on this matter, to offer a Refinement upon my Scheme. He said, that many Gentlemen of this Kingdom, having of late destroyed their Deer, he conceived that the want of Venison might be well supplied by the Bodies of young Lads and Maidens, not exceeding fourteen Years of Age, nor under twelve, so great a Number of both Sexes in every Country being now ready to Starve, for want of Work and Service: And these to be disposed of by their Parents if alive, or otherwise by their nearest Relations. But with due deference to so excellent a friend, and so deserving a Patriot, I cannot be altogether in his Sentiments, for as to the Males, my *American* acquaintance assured me from frequent Experience, that their flesh was generally Tough and Lean, like that of our Schoolboys, by continual exercise, and their Taste disagreeable, and to Fatten them would not answer the Charge. Then as to the Females, it would, I think with humble Submission, *be a loss to the Publick,* because they soon would become Breeders themselves: And besides it is not improbable that some scrupulous People might be apt to Censure such a Practice, (although indeed very unjustly) as a little bordering upon Cruelty, which, I confess, hath always been with me the strongest objection against any Project, however so well intended. 17

But in order to justify my friend, he confessed, that this expedient was put into his head by the famous *Sallmanaazor,* a Native of the Island *Formosa,*[10] who came from thence to *London,* above twenty Years ago, and in Conversation told my friend, that in his Country when any young Person happened to be put to Death, the Executioner sold the Carcass to *Persons of Quality,* as a prime Dainty, and that, in his Time, the Body of a plump Girl of fifteen, who was crucified for an attempt to Poison the Emperor, was sold to his Imperial *Majesty's prime Minister of State,* and other great *Mandarins* of the Court, *in Joints from the Gibbet,* at four hundred Crowns. Neither indeed can I deny, that if the same use were made of several plump young Girls in this Town, who, without one single Groat[11] to their Fortunes, cannot stir abroad without a Chair, and appear at the 18

Play-House, and *Assemblies* in Foreign fineries, which they never will Pay for; the Kingdom would not be the worse.

Some Persons of a desponding Spirit are in great Concern about that vast Number of poor People, who are aged, diseased, or maimed, and I have been desired to imploy my thoughts what Course may be taken, to ease the Nation of so grievous an Incumbrance. But I am not in the least pain about the matter, because it is very well known, that they are every Day *dying,* and *rotting,* by *cold,* and *famine,* and *filth,* and *vermin,* as fast as can be reasonably expected. And as to the younger Labourers they are now in almost as hopeful a Condition. They cannot get Work, and consequently pine away for want of Nourishment, to a degree, that if at any time they are accidentally hired to common Labour, they have not strength to perform it, and thus the Country and themselves are happily delivered from the Evils to come.   19

I have too long digressed, and therefore shall return to my subject. I think the advantages by the Proposal which I have made, are obvious, and many, as well as of the highest importance.   20

For, *First,* as I have already observed, it would greatly lessen *the Number of Papists,* with whom we are Yearly over-run, being the principal Breeders of the Nation, as well as our most dangerous Enemies, and who stay at home on purpose with a design *to deliver the Kingdom to the Pretender,* hoping to take their Advantage by the absence *of so many good Protestants,* who have chosen rather to leave their Country, than stay at home, and pay Tithes against their Conscience, to an *Episcopal Curate.*   21

Secondly, the poorer Tenants will have something valuable of their own, which by Law may be made liable to Distress,[12] and help to pay their Landlord's Rent, their Corn and Cattle being already seazed, and *Money a thing unknown.*   22

Thirdly, Whereas the Maintenance of an Hundred Thousand Children, from two Years old, and upwards, cannot be computed at less than Ten Shillings a piece *per Annum,* the Nation's Stock will be thereby encreased fifty thousand pounds *per Annum,* besides the profit of a new Dish, introduced to the Tables of all *Gentlemen of Fortune* in the Kingdom, who have any refinement in Taste, and the Money will circulate among ourselves, the Goods being entirely of our own Growth and Manufacture.   23

Fourthly, The constant Breeders, besides the gain of Eight Shillings *per Annum,* by the Sale of their Children, will be rid of the Charge of maintaining them after the first Year.   24

Fifthly, This food would likewise bring great *Custom to Taverns,* where the Vintners will certainly be so prudent as to procure the best receipts for dressing it to perfection, and consequently have their Houses frequented by   25 all the *fine Gentlemen,* who justly value themselves upon their Knowledge in good *Eating,* and a skillful Cook, who understands how to oblige his Guests, will contrive to make it as expensive as they please.

Sixthly, This would be a great Inducement to Marriage, which all wise 26 Nations have either encouraged by Rewards, or enforced by Laws and Penalties. It would encrease the care and tenderness of Mothers towards their Children, when they were sure of a Settlement for Life, to the poor Babes, provided in some sort by the Publick to their annual Profit instead of Expence. We should soon see an honest Emulation among the married Women, *which of them could bring the fattest Child to the Market.* Men would become as fond of their *Wives,* during the Time of their Pregnancy, as they are now of their *Mares* in Foal, their *Cows* in Calf, or *Sows* when they are ready to Farrow, nor offer to Beat or Kick them (as it is too frequent a practice) for fear of a Miscarriage.

Many other advantages might be enumerated. For Instance, the addi- 27 tion of some thousand Carcases in our exportation of Barreled Beef: The Propagation of *Swines Flesh,* and Improvement in the Art of making good *Bacon,* so much wanted among us by the great destruction of *Pigs,* too frequent at our Tables, which are no way comparable in Taste, or Magnificence to a well grown, fat Yearling Child, which Roasted whole will make a considerable Figure at a *Lord Mayor's Feast,* or any other Publick Entertainment. But this, and many others I omit, being studious of Brevity.

Supposing that one thousand Families in this City, would be constant 28 Customers for Infants Flesh, besides others who might have it at *Merry-meetings,* particularly *Weddings* and *Christenings,* I compute that *Dublin* would take off annually about Twenty Thousand Carcases, and the rest of the Kingdom (where probably they will be sold somewhat cheaper) the remaining Eighty Thousand.

I can think of no one Objection, that will possibly be raised against 29 this Proposal, unless it should be urged that the Number of People will be thereby much lessened in the Kingdom. This I freely own, and it was indeed one principal Design in offering it to the World. I desire the Reader will observe, that I Calculate my Remedy *for this one individual Kingdom* ✳ *of IRELAND, and for no other that ever was, is, or, I think, ever can be upon Earth.* Therefore let no Man talk to me of other Expedients: *Of taxing our Absentees at five Shillings a pound: Of using neither Cloaths, nor household Furniture, except what is of our own Growth and Manufacture: Of utterly rejecting the Materials and Instruments that promote Foreign Luxury: Of curing the Expensiveness of Pride, Vanity, Idleness, and Gaming in our Women: Of introducing a Vein of Parsimony, Prudence and Temperance: Of learning to Love our Country, wherein we differ even from LAPLANDERS, and the*

Inhabitants of TOPINAMBOO:[13] *Of quitting our Animosities, and Factions, nor Act any longer like the Jews, who were Murdering one another at the very moment their City was taken:*[14] *Of being a little Cautious not to Sell our Country and Consciences for nothing: Of teaching Landlords to have at least one degree of Mercy towards their Tenants. Lastly of putting a Spirit of Honesty, Industry and Skill into our Shopkeepers, who, if a Resolution could now be taken to Buy only our Native Goods, would immediately unite to Cheat and Exact upon us in the Price, the Measure, and the Goodness, nor could ever yet be brought to make one fair Proposal of just dealing, though often and earnestly invited to it.*

Therefore I repeat, let no Man talk to me of these and the like   30
Expedients, till he hath at least some Glimpse of Hope, that there will ever be some hearty and sincere Attempt to put them in Practice.

But as to my self, having been wearied out for many Years with offering   31
vain, idle, visionary thoughts, and at length utterly despairing of Success, I fortunately fell upon this Proposal, which as it is wholly new, so it hath something Solid and Real, of no Expence and little Trouble, full in our own Power, and whereby we can incur no Danger in *disobliging* England. For this kind of Commodity will not bear Exportation, the Flesh being of too tender a Consistance, to admit a long continuance in Salt, *although perhaps I could name a Country, which would be glad to Eat up our whole Nation without it.*

After all, I am not so violently bent upon my own Opinion, as to reject   32
any Offer, proposed by wise Men, which shall be found equally inno-cent, cheap, easy and effectual. But before something of that kind shall be advanced in Contradiction to my Scheme, and offering a better, I desire the Author, or Authors will be pleased maturely to consider two points. *First,* as things now stand, how they will be able to find Food and Raiment for an hundred thousand useless Mouths and Backs. And *Secondly,* there being a round Million of Creatures in human Figure, throughout this Kingdom, whose whole Subsistance put into a common Stock, would leave them in Debt of two Million of Pounds *Sterling,* adding those, who are Beggars by Profession, to the Bulk of Farmers, Cottagers and Labourers with their Wives and Children, who are Beggars in Effect; I desire those *Politicians,* who dislike my Overture, and may perhaps be so bold to attempt an Answer, that they will first ask the Parents of these Mortals, whether they would not at this Day think it a great Happiness to have been sold for Food at a year Old, in the manner I prescribe, and thereby have avoided such a perpetual Scene of Misfortunes, as they have since gone through, by the *oppression of Landlords,* the Impossibility of paying Rent without Money or Trade,

the want of common Sustenance, with neither House nor Cloaths to cover them from Inclemencies of Weather, and the most inevitable Prospect of intailing the like, or greater Miseries upon their Breed for ever.

I Profess in the sincerity of my Heart that I have not the least personal Interest, in endeavouring to promote this necessary Work; having no other Motive than the *publick Good of my Country,* by *advancing our Trade, providing for Infants, relieving the Poor, and giving some Pleasure to the Rich.* I have no Children, by which I can propose to get a single Penny; the youngest being nine Years old, and my Wife past Childbearing.

33

NOTES

1 Dublin, Ireland.

2 The Pretender is James Edward Stuart, who claimed (or "pretended" to) the throne lost by his father, James II, in 1688. (Because of his Catholic sympathies, James II had been overthrown by supporters of his Protestant daughter and son-in-law, Mary II and William II.) The French upheld James Stuart's claim because of his Roman Catholicism, and, by the Limerick Treaty of 1691, Irish Roman Catholics were granted the right to bear arms in the service of France, and thus, by affiliation, in the service of the Pretender.

3 Because of the poverty in Ireland, many Irish immigrated to British colonies in America and the West Indies, indenturing themselves to plantation owners for their passage.

4 Ireland had just suffered three successive bad harvests.

5 Soil conditions in county Cavan are particularly unsuited to tillage and require a great deal of capital to manage. Cavan also had a long history of high rents and exploitation.

6 Boiling was a way to render meat edible if it was beginning to turn bad.

7 François Rabelais (1494–1553) was a French humorist and satirist and anything but "grave."

8 "Papist" is a hostile name for a Roman Catholic. Swift, as an Anglican (Protestant) clergyman, might be expected to be hostile to Catholicism, but the hostility here is, of course, ironic.

9 It is not clear whether the "true Lover of his Country" refers to an actual person or not.

10 George Psalmanazar was a Frenchman who posed as a Formosan (modern Taiwanese). His fictitious accounts, *Historical and Geographical History of Formosa* (1704) and *A Dialogue between a Japanese and a Formosan about some points of the religion of the time* (1707), contained passages describing human sacrifice and cannibalism. The remainder of this paragraph is a paraphrase of one of the stories told by Psalmanazar.

11 A groat was a small British coin worth four pence.

12 Distress or distraint is the act of distraining or legally forcing a person to give up personal goods to be used as payment against debts.

13 The Tupinamba were a group of tribes, now extinct, that lived on the coast of Brazil from the mouth of the Amazon to the southern part of the state of São Paulo. Swift says that even those who live in places of extreme cold and heat love their countries better than the Anglo-Irish.

14 In AD 70, the Roman Emperor Titus laid siege to, captured, and destroyed Jerusalem. Throughout the period of siege and capture, the city was being torn apart internally by warring religious factions.

VOCABULARY

alms—anything given freely to relieve want

artificially—with skill or artifice

burthen—burden

crown—a coin worth five shillings, a shilling being worth 1/20 of a pound or five pence. Half a crown is, therefore, a coin worth 12½ pence.

dressing—preparing meat for the market, usually by bleeding and cleaning it

emulation—an attempt to equal or excel, here perhaps each other

gibbet—a gallows

importuning—pressing or urging with unreasonable requests

intailing (or usually, entailing)—settling something (for example, land, title, obligation) on a number of persons in succession so that it cannot be bequeathed to another person

joints—a large section of meat usually including a large bone or joint

probationers—those whose fitness is being tested

repine—to complain or fret

shambles—a slaughterhouse

squire—a country gentleman, particularly the principal landowner of a district

towardly—dutiful, tractable

vintner—not only the maker but also the seller of wines

QUESTIONS

1. In this essay, Swift speaks through a persona (a mask, or second self, created by the author). Give three or four examples that show that Swift is not speaking in his own voice.

2. List the main interests and characteristics of Swift's persona.

3. How does Swift use the gap between his own feelings and opinions and those of his persona to create and sustain the irony throughout the essay? What standard(s) of evaluation does the persona employ as he presents his solution to the terrible poverty in Ireland? What standards does Swift imply?

4. Can you identify any places where Swift steps out from behind his mask?

5. For what reasons, literary or otherwise, do you think Swift chose irony, rather than direct statement, as a strategy to persuade his audience to alleviate poverty in Ireland?

6. In a satiric essay, writers achieve their purpose by undermining the apparent thesis rather than by supporting it. What is the apparent thesis of "A Modest Proposal"? How does Swift undermine it?

7. Matters like spelling, punctuation, capitalization, and the use of italics were far less standardized in Swift's day than in ours. Do these or other features of Swift's style affect your reading of this essay? If so, how?

SUGGESTION FOR WRITING

Using Swift's essay as a model, write a "modest proposal" in which you present an outrageous solution to a current social problem. Follow the structure of "A Modest Proposal" and feel free to include verbal echoes from it. Remember that you will need to adopt a persona whose attitudes and values present to your readers an exaggerated version of their own. Like Swift, you want to shock your readers into a recognition of their moral inadequacies in not responding to a social need.

All for One, and One for All

Charles Taylor

Solidarity is essential to democratic societies; otherwise, they fall apart. 1
They cannot function beyond a certain level of mutual distrust or a
sense on the part of some members that other members have abandoned them. Many view the development of an individualistic outlook as
the greatest threat to solidarity. But this is closely linked to a diminishing
sense of common identity.

It's no accident, for example, that Europe's most successful welfare 2
states were created in ethnically homogeneous Scandinavia. People in those
countries had the sense that they could understand their neighbours and
fellow citizens, and that they shared a close link with them.

The challenge nowadays is to maintain that sense of intense solidarity 3
amid diversifying populations. There are two ways to do this. One is to hark
back to older modes of solidarity. French identity, for example, is based on
the country's unique brand of republican secularism, known as *laïcité*. But
France's efforts to shore up solidarity by insisting on *laïcité* and erecting a
dam against Muslim immigrants are both ineffective and counterproduc-
tive, because they exclude from a sense of
fully belonging to the nation many people
who are already in France.[1]

The other way to preserve solidar- 4
ity is to redefine identity. All democratic
societies are faced with the challenge of
redefining their identity in dialogue with
some elements that are external, and some
that are internal. Consider the influence of
feminist movements throughout the West.
These are not people who came from outside their countries. They are people who,
in some ways, lacked full citizenship, who
demanded it, and who redefined the political order by obtaining it.

The great task is to calm the fears 5
that our traditions are being undermined;
to reach out to people who are coming
to our lands from other countries; and to

Charles Taylor (b. 1931) is a Canadian philosopher who has held professorships at Oxford
University in England and McGill University in
Montreal. He has been active in politics and is
a defender of Canadian nationalism. In 1991,
he delivered the Massey Lecture that was
published as *The Malaise of Modernity*. He has
published *Reconciling the Solitudes: Essays
on Canadian Federalism and Nationalism*
(1993) and is most famous for his book
*Multiculturalism: Examining the Politics of
Recognition* (1994), which has been translated
into several languages. He follows in the philosophical tradition of Martin Heidegger, Hans-
Georg Gadamer, and Ludwig Wittgenstein.

"All for One, and One for All" was published in *The Globe
and Mail* on September 30, 2010. Reprinted with permission of the author.

find a way of recreating our political ethic around the kernel of human rights, equality, non-discrimination and democracy. If we succeed, we can create a sense that we belong together, even though our reasons for believing so may be different.

But increasing individualism—a focus on one's own ambitions and economic prosperity—in many countries poses a stubborn obstacle to realizing this vision. Indeed, the utter lack of a sense of solidarity among so many people—horrifyingly evident in the U.S. health-care debate—is undermining the very basis of what a modern democratic society is.   6

A society's sense of solidarity can be sustained only if all of its different   7 spiritual groups recreate their sense of dedication to it: if Christians see it as central to their Christianity, if Muslims see it as central to their Islam, and if the various kinds of lay philosophies see it as central to their philosophies.

Religion provides a profound and powerful base of solidarity, and to   8 marginalize it would be a big mistake, just as marginalizing atheistic philosophies would be a mistake. Democratic societies, in their tremendous diversity, are powered by many different engines of commitment to a common ethic. They cannot afford to switch off any of these engines and hope to maintain a political community.

Historically, the political ethic of confessional societies has been   9 grounded in a single, basic foundation. In Europe, various kinds of *laïque* societies have tried to invent themselves out of the ruins of the Christian foundation, but they have made the same mistake in another way, with a kind of Jacobin insistence on the civil religion of the Enlightenment.

Well, we can no longer have a civil religion—not one based on God,   10 or on *laïcité* and the rights of man, or, indeed, on any particular view. We live in uncharted territory. We face a challenge that is unprecedented in human history: creation of a powerful political ethic of solidarity self-consciously grounded on the presence and acceptance of very different views.

This can succeed only if we engage in vigorous exchange with each   11 other in order to create a kind of mutual respect for these different views. The advancing force of Islamophobia in Europe and the U.S., with its attempt to reduce Islam's complex and varied history to a few demagogic slogans, is the kind of utterly ignorant stupidity—there's no better description of it—on which democratic societies founder.

But that's true of any kind of dismissive view of the "other." Our soci-   12 eties will hold together only if we talk to each other with openness and frankness, and, in doing so, recreate a certain sense of solidarity from all our different roots.

NOTE

[1] In February 2011, French President Nikolas Sarkozy claimed that multiculturalism had failed in France. This statement followed German Chancellor Angela Merkel's claim in October 2010 that multiculturalism had failed in Germany and British Prime Minister Gordon Cameron's claim in February 2011 that multiculturalism had also failed in England.

VOCABULARY

laïcité—often transcribed as secularism, it is basically the separation of church and state

laïque—the adjectival form of *laïcité*

Enlightenment—a general term for Western intellectual history and development since the eighteenth century. Key thinkers include René Descartes and Immanuel Kant.

QUESTIONS

1. What are the two ways that Taylor suggests help to maintain solidarity among people?

2. Canada has a significant population of immigrants. How do you think Canada should address difficulties that arise when immigrants bring principles that conflict with Canadian laws and customs? For example, what should happen when an immigrant comes from a country that does not prohibit polygamy or multiple spouses? What are the political and ethical values at stake?

3. Part of Taylor's essay involves the separation of church and state. If religion is no longer the primary common ground for community solidarity, what principles are the grounds for political solidarity today?

SUGGESTION FOR WRITING

Charles Taylor ends with a caution against a "dismissive view of the 'other.'" Write an essay that explains an encounter you have had with an "other" and how you engaged with and gained an understanding of that "other."

Summer of Our Discontent Revisited[1]

Drew Hayden Taylor

I t seems that opinions about the treatment of the all-too-frequent Native   1
crisis are being voiced more openly. Or more accurately, there appears
to be a double standard in relation to blockades: a belief that perhaps
Natives are getting preferential treatment, and getting handled with kid
gloves.

Tell that to Dudley George,[2] the Ojibway man killed at Ipperwash.   2

Many critics outside and within the government have commented that   3
there seems to be two sets of laws in Canada: one for the Native people and
one for Whites. As I've often heard said, "You get White people blockading
a road or doing what the Indians are doing and the police would be in there
breaking things up faster than Mike Harris[3] can hit a golf ball. They should
treat them Indians like they would White people."

Equal rights—what a concept. That would be nice. Very nice in fact,   4
but in reality, unlikely. It does seem there is a double standard. Chief Tom
Bressette of the Stony-Kettle Reserve agrees with these irate voices, saying
that there are "two separate laws" for Indians and Whites, and that Indians
"get the lower end of the stick."

Drew Hayden Taylor (b. 1962) is an Ojibway
author who has written plays, stories, and
essays. He served as the Artistic Director
of the Native Earth Performing Arts theatre
from 1994 to 1997. Within the traditions of the
storyteller, Taylor's frequent use of humour
allows him to raise and address contemporary
issues that Aboriginal people face. "Summer
of Our Discontent Revisited" is included in
*Funny, You Don't Look Like One: Observations
of a Blue-Eyed Ojibway*, a collection of essays
and articles, many of which were published
in *Windspeaker, The Globe and Mail*, and *The
Toronto Star*, and aired on CBC Radio.

"Summer of Our Discontent Revisited" is reprinted from
*Funny, You Don't Look Like One: Observations of a
Blue-Eyed Ojibway*.

Anyone who is even slightly familiar   5
with the Native community is well aware
of the incredibly high levels of Aboriginal
people incarcerated in the provincial and
federal jails. While Native people make
up less than five percent of the general
population, they sometimes exceed forty
percent of those in jail.

You don't have to work for Revenue   6
Canada to know that something is wrong
with these numbers. Especially when you
take into consideration that Native culture, as a whole, never had jails nor a real
need for them. There was no institution-
alized punishment, no witness relocation,
no prison riots.

To go from a culture with no use for   7
jails, to an obscenely high incarceration

rate should tell these politicians and nay sayers something is dreadfully wrong. Either, in a scant few years, we as a people have become an anarchic gang of hoodlums with no appreciation of law or government, bent on overcrowding prisons for the hell of it, or there *is* a double standard. The justice system's famous inflexibility or inability to take into account different perceptions of what is right and what is wrong is legendary. For instance, White society reveres the nuclear family principle, while the Native community is structured around the extended family concept. Such misunderstanding led to incidents like "the scoop up"[4] when thousands of Native kids were forcibly removed from communities and put up for adoptions, and moved into residential schools.

Centuries of alienation, dispossession and insensitivity have also had their effect. When you take away from Native people their culture, their language and their land, it creates a vacuum. And as White scientists love to quote, nature hates a vacuum.   8

Logically, something has to fill this gaping black hole. Anger and frustration at what has been lost or taken rushes into that vacuum. Simple physics. And while I and the vast majority of Native people across this country do not condone violence, I challenge any people with this history not to be overcome by emotions such as these.   9

Hugh MacLennan was incredibly naive when he wrote his book *Two Solitudes*.[5] He couldn't even begin to understand how many solitudes there really are.   10

NOTES

[1] The title of this piece is a literary allusion to William Shakespeare's play *Richard III* that begins "Now is the winter of our discontent / Made glorious summer by this sun of York" (1.1.1-2).

[2] Dudley George was protesting the Canadian government's refusal to return land at Ipperwash to the people in 1995. George was shot on September 6, 1995, and later died in hospital.

[3] Mike Harris was the premier of Ontario from 1995 to 2002, including the time of the protest at Ipperwash.

[4] The "scoop up" includes the forced adoption policies for Aboriginal children in several Canadian provinces, as well as the residential school system where children were removed from their communities and placed in boarding schools for education.

[5] Hugh MacLennan's 1945 novel *Two Solitudes* is about the relations between the French and English in Canada. Taylor is obviously suggesting that there are many more historical conflicts between different groups in Canada.

QUESTIONS

1. Taylor suggests that there are "two sets of laws in Canada: one for the Native people and one for Whites." Do you agree with his assessment?

2. Taylor's reference to Dudley George is very brief. Have you ever heard of Dudley George before? Is Taylor's use of this reference effective in his argument?

3. Taylor claims that the justice system is unable "to take into account different perceptions of what is right and what is wrong." Given that different communities may have different ethical standards and practices, what do you make of this argument? Is this a valid form of reasoning? How would "different perceptions" be understood in terms of the law?

4. What is Taylor doing when he refers to white scientists, physics, and vacuums?

SUGGESTIONS FOR WRITING

1. Write an essay about the importance of cross-cultural understanding between those of Aboriginal ancestry and those of settler ancestry in Canada. How can we understand our history—the intertwinement of Aboriginal and settler histories—and respond to it politically and ethically?

2. Write a comparison essay in which you consider Drew Hayden Taylor's discussion of Aboriginal/settler-descendant relations in "Summer of Our Discontent Revisited" and Margaret Laurence's discussion of Aboriginal/settler-descendant relations in "The Loons" (Readings).

Inequality Is the Real Enemy

Polly Toynbee

The Impact of Inequality:
How to Make Sick Societies Healthier
by Richard G. Wilkinson
Routledge, 355 pages, £19.99 (£18.99)

D oes inequality really matter? The poor have what their grandparents 1
would think unimaginable luxuries—TVs, telephones and washing
machines. So why should it matter to them if in some unseen stratosphere the gated kleptocrats on company boards award themselves staggering sums of money? Does anyone really mind the gap?

That is a reasonable question and it niggles away at those on the left, 2
too. Equality has gone out of fashion. In Britain social justice under Labour
means heaving the poorest over the poverty threshold and lifting the life
chances of children from lower social classes. Tony Blair[1] said early on that
he was not bothered about wealth, only about abolishing poverty. Talk of
inequality sounds like the old politics of envy. Equality of opportunity, yes,
but equality for its own sake, why?

Here is the answer. Richard Wilkinson is a professor of social epide- 3
miology, an expert in public health. From that vantage point he sees the
world in terms of its physical and psychological wellbeing, surveying great
sweeps of health statistics through socio-
logical eyes. He has assembled a mountain of irrefutable evidence from all over
the world showing the damage done by
extreme inequality. However rich a country is, it will still be more dysfunctional,
violent, sick and sad if the gap between
social classes grows too wide. Poorer
countries with fairer wealth distribution
are healthier and happier than richer,
more unequal nations.

Life expectancy in rich nations corre- 4
lates precisely with levels of equality. So
Greece, with half the GDP per head, has
longer life expectancy than the US, the
richest and most unequal country with

Granddaughter of English historian Arnold
Toynbee, Polly Toynbee has written on social
issues for the *Guardian* newspaper in England
both before and after her tenure as social
affairs editor for the British Broadcasting
Corporation (1988-1995). Her books include
A Working Life (1971), *Lost Children: Story of
Adopted Children Searching for Their Mothers*
(1985), and *Hard Work: Life in Low-pay Britain*
(2003), which she researched by working as a
hospital porter, a nursery assistant, a call centre employee, and a labourer in a cake factory.

the lowest life expectancy in the developed world. The people of Harlem live shorter lives than the people of Bangladesh. When you take out the violence and drugs, two-thirds of the reason is heart disease. Is that bad diet? No, says Wilkinson, it is mainly stress, the stress of living at the bottom of the pecking order, on the lowest rung, the stress of disrespect and lack of esteem. Bad nutrition does less harm than depression.

The book blisters with research such as this: tests found that subordinate, low-status monkeys had high levels of the stress hormone, cortisol, which leads to arteriosclerosis. When the high-status monkeys were all put together and low-status monkeys put in another enclosure, all the pecking orders changed. When some previous high-rankers became subordinate they developed all the same physical symptoms, including a fivefold increase in arteriosclerosis within less than two years. Meanwhile some of the low-rankers who suddenly found themselves dominant had sharply dropped levels of stress hormone.

People, says Wilkinson, are the same. Social status and respect matter beyond anything, and the psychological damage done by being at the bottom is crippling. A survey of Whitehall civil servants[2] found junior ranks were three times more likely to die in a year than seniors, with a fine sliding gradation from top to bottom according to status.

Homicide rates (and other crimes) track a country's level of inequality, not its overall wealth. The fairest countries have the highest levels of trust and social capital. The US states that have the more equal income distribution also have most social trust: New Hampshire, the most equal, is least likely to agree that "most people would try to take advantage of you if they got the chance."

Wilkinson's message is that social environment can be more toxic than any pollutant. Low status and lack of control over one's life [are] a destroyer of human health and happiness. The wealth gap causes few to vote or participate in anything in a world of fear, conflict and hostility.

It is not primarily five a day fruit and veg or obesity that need targeting, but social injustice itself. An orphanage in hungry postwar Germany found that children on the same diet were found to have grown most under the kindest matron and least under the unkindest matron. Psyche matters more than vitamins, all through life.

Poverty in rich nations is not a number or the absence of a particular necessity. A poor vicar may bring up children well on lentils and respect. But for most people respect is measured in money. Low pay tells people that their labour and they themselves are worth little. Poverty is not, as Britain's Labour government imagines, a line to pull people over—it is a position on a line. If it tilts too sharply upwards, the pain of those at the bottom can be measured in hard statistics.

This book is evidence for what common sense already knows. Children   11
on free school meals, with no holidays to talk about, unable to afford the
school trips, who never invite anyone back to a shabby home, painfully
understand their place in the hierarchy from their first day at school. Adults
know the same, noses pressed up against the window of lifestyle shows on
television. This is a book that puts the numbers to a psychological truth:
inequality is the real enemy.

NOTES

[1] Tony Blair became leader of the British Labour Party in 1994 and prime minister of the United
Kingdom in 1997, a position he held until 2007. The Labour Party was originally a left-wing, social
democratic party with much of its support coming from trade unions; Blair became known for shift-
ing Labour away from a commitment to the redistribution of wealth, toward support for the market
economy.

[2] *Whitehall* is the name of a street in London, England where government buildings are concentrated;
the term is traditionally used to refer to the British civil service.

VOCABULARY

arteriosclerosis—disease involving hardening of the arteries

epidemiology—the branch of medicine dealing with epidemic diseases

psyche—the psychological or mental structure of a person

QUESTIONS

1. Early in her essay, Toynbee announces that "The poor have . . . TVs, telephones and
washing machines." What part of the world is the essay focused on? Can Toynbee's
thesis about inequality be applied to all parts of the world?

2. Toynbee thinks Richard Wilkinson's book provides an answer to her question: Why
should there be "equality for its own sake"? What is Wilkinson's answer to this
question?

3. A review is a kind of critique, and thus contains a mixture of summary/analysis and of
evaluative judgments. Does Toynbee's review lean more toward summary or evaluation? What standard of evaluation does she use to evaluate Wilkinson's book? How does
the thesis of the review differ from the thesis of the book?

SUGGESTION FOR WRITING

Toynbee and Wilkinson argue that large social or cultural issues have an important psychological dimension. Explore this claim by writing a review of an article, book, film, or TV
program on a social issue of importance to you.

Once More to the Lake

E. B. White   *August 1941*

One summer, along about 1904, my father rented a camp on a lake   1
in Maine and took us all there for the month of August. We all got
ringworm from some kittens and had to rub Pond's Extract on our
arms and legs night and morning, and my father rolled over in a canoe with
all his clothes on; but outside of that the vacation was a success and from
then on none of us ever thought there was any place in the world like that
lake in Maine. We returned summer after summer—always on August 1 for
one month. I have since become a salt-water man, but sometimes in summer there are days when the restlessness of the tides and the fearful cold of
the sea water and the incessant wind that blows across the afternoon and
into the evening make me wish for the placidity of a lake in the woods. A
few weeks ago this feeling got so strong I bought myself a couple of bass
hooks and a spinner and returned to the lake where we used to go, for a
week's fishing and to revisit old haunts.

I took along my son, who had never had any fresh water up his nose   2
and who had seen lily pads only from train windows. On the journey over
to the lake I began to wonder what it would be like. I wondered how time
would have marred this unique, this holy spot—the coves and streams, the
hills that the sun set behind, the camps and the paths behind the camps. I
was sure that the tarred road would have found it out, and I wondered in
what other ways it would be desolated. It
is strange how much you can remember
about places like that once you allow your
mind to return into the grooves that lead
back. You remember one thing, and that
suddenly reminds you of another thing.
I guess I remembered clearest of all the
early mornings, when the lake was cool
and motionless, remembered how the
bedroom smelled of the lumber it was
made of and of the wet woods whose scent
entered through the screen. The partitions
in the camp were thin and did not extend
clear to the top of the rooms, and as I was
always the first up I would dress softly so

E. B. (Elwyn Brooks) White (1899–1985) is a
highly regarded American author. Perhaps
most widely recognized for his popular children's books *Charlotte's Web* and *Stuart Little*,
White penned numerous essays and contributed to *The New Yorker* for many years. He
co-authored with William Strunk Jr. the commonly assigned writing textbook *The Elements
of Style*, which is still in use today. "Once More
to the Lake" was published in 1941.

as not to wake the others, and sneak out into the sweet outdoors and start out in the canoe, keeping close along the shore in the long shadows of the pines. I remembered being very careful never to rub my paddle against the gunwale for fear of disturbing the stillness of the cathedral.

The lake had never been what you would call a wild lake. There were 3 cottages sprinkled around the shores, and it was in farming country although the shores of the lake were quite heavily wooded. Some of the cottages were owned by nearby farmers, and you would live at the shore and eat your meals at the farmhouse. That's what our family did. But although it wasn't wild, it was a fairly large and undisturbed lake and there were places in it that, to a child at least, seemed infinitely remote and primeval.

I was right about the tar: it led to within half a mile of the shore. But 4 when I got back there, with my boy, and we settled into a camp near a farmhouse and into the kind of summertime I had known, I could tell that it was going to be pretty much the same as it had been before—I knew it, lying in bed the first morning, smelling the bedroom and hearing the boy sneak quietly out and go off along the shore in a boat. I began to sustain the illusion that he was I, and therefore, by simple transposition, that I was my father. This sensation persisted, kept cropping up all the time we were there. It was not an entirely new feeling, but in this setting it grew much stronger. I seemed to be living a dual existence. I would be in the middle of some simple act, I would be picking up a bait box or laying down a table fork, or I would be saying something, and suddenly it would be not I but my father who was saying the words or making the gesture. It gave me a creepy sensation.

We went fishing the first morning. I felt the same damp moss covering 5 the worms in the bait can, and saw the dragonfly alight on the tip of my rod as it hovered a few inches from the surface of the water. It was the arrival of this fly that convinced me beyond any doubt that everything was as it always had been, that the years were a mirage and that there had been no years. The small waves were the same, chucking the rowboat under the chin as we fished at anchor, and the boat was the same boat, the same color green and the ribs broken in the same places, and under the floorboards the same fresh-water leavings and débris—the dead helgramite, the wisps of moss, the rusty discarded fishhook, the dried blood from yesterday's catch. We stared silently at the tips of our rods, at the dragonflies that came and went. I lowered the tip of mine into the water, tentatively, pensively dislodging the fly, which darted two feet away, poised, darted two feet back, and came to rest again a little farther up the rod. There had been no years between the ducking of this dragonfly and the other one—the one that was part of memory. I looked at the boy, who was silently watching his fly, and it was my hands that held his rod, my eyes watching. I felt dizzy and didn't know which rod I was at the end of.

We caught two bass, hauling them in briskly as though they were   6
mackerel, pulling them over the side of the boat in a businesslike manner without any landing net, and stunning them with a blow on the back of the head. When we got back for a swim before lunch, the lake was exactly where we had left it, the same number of inches from the dock, and there was only the merest suggestion of a breeze. This seemed an utterly enchanted sea, this lake you could leave to its own devices for a few hours and come back to, and find that it had not stirred, this constant and trustworthy body of water. In the shallows, the dark, water-soaked sticks and twigs, smooth and old, were undulating in clusters on the bottom against the clean ribbed sand, and the track of the mussel was plain. A school of minnows swam by, each minnow with its small individual shadow, doubling the attendance, so clear and sharp in the sunlight. Some of the other campers were in swimming, along the shore, one of them with a cake of soap, and the water felt thin and clear and unsubstantial. Over the years there had been this person with the cake of soap, this cultist, and here he was. There had been no years.

Up to the farmhouse to dinner through the teeming, dusty field, the   7
road under our sneakers was only a two-track road. The middle track was missing, the one with the marks of the hooves and the splotches of dried, flaky manure. There had always been three tracks to choose from in choosing which track to walk in; now the choice was narrowed down to two. For a moment I missed terribly the middle alternative. But the way led past the tennis court, and something about the way it lay there in the sun reassured me; the tape had loosened along the backline, the alleys were green with plantains and other weeds, and the net (installed in June and removed in September) sagged in the dry noon, and the whole place steamed with midday heat and hunger and emptiness. There was a choice of pie for dessert, and one was blueberry and one was apple, and the waitresses were the same country girls, there having been no passage of time, only the illusion of it as in a dropped curtain—the waitresses were still fifteen; their hair had been washed, that was the only difference—they had been to the movies and seen the pretty girls with the clean hair.

Summertime, oh, summertime, pattern of life indelible, the fade-proof   8
lake, the woods unshatterable, the pasture with the sweetfern and the juniper forever and ever, summer without end; this was the background, and the life along the shore was the design, the cottagers with their innocent and tranquil design, their tiny docks with the flagpole and the American flag floating against the white clouds in the blue sky, the little paths over

the roots of the trees leading from camp to camp and the paths leading back to the outhouses and the can of lime for sprinkling, and at the souvenir counters at the store the miniature birch-bark canoes and the postcards that showed things looking a little better than they looked. This was the American family at play, escaping the city heat, wondering whether the newcomers in the camp at the head of the cove were "common" or "nice," wondering whether it was true that the people who drove up for Sunday dinner at the farmhouse were turned away because there wasn't enough chicken.

It seemed to me, as I kept remembering all this, that those times and those summers had been infinitely precious and worth saving. There had been jollity and peace and goodness. The arriving (at the beginning of August) had been so big a business in itself, at the railway station the farm wagon drawn up, the first smell of the pine-laden air, the first glimpse of the smiling farmer, and the great importance of the trunks and your father's enormous authority in such matters, and the feel of the wagon under you for the long ten-mile haul, and at the top of the last long hill catching the first view of the lake after eleven months of not seeing this cherished body of water. The shouts and cries of the other campers when they saw you, and the trunks to be unpacked, to give up their rich burden. (Arriving was less exciting nowadays, when you sneaked up in your car and parked it under a tree near the camp and took out the bags and in five minutes it was all over, no fuss, no loud wonderful fuss about trunks.) 9

Peace and goodness and jollity. The only thing that was wrong now, really, was the sound of the place, an unfamiliar nervous sound of the outboard motors. This was the note that jarred, the one thing that would sometimes break the illusion and set the years moving. In those other summertimes all motors were inboard; and when they were at a little distance, the noise they made was a sedative, an ingredient of summer sleep. They were one-cylinder and two-cylinder engines, and some were make-and-break and some were jump-spark, but they all made a sleepy sound across the lake. The one-lungers throbbed and fluttered, and the twin-cylinder ones purred and purred, and that was a quiet sound, too. But now the campers all had outboards. In the daytime, in the hot mornings, these motors made a petulant, irritable sound; at night, in the still evening when the afterglow lit the water, they whined about one's ears like mosquitoes. My boy loved our rented outboard, and his great desire was to achieve single-handed mastery over it, and authority, and he soon learned the trick of choking it a little (but not too much), and the adjustment of the needle valve. Watching him I would remember the things you could do with the old one-cylinder engine with 10 the heavy flywheel, how you could have it eating out of your hand if you got really close to it spiritually. Motorboats in those days didn't have clutches, and you would make a landing by shutting off the motor at the proper time and coasting in with a dead rudder. But there was a way of reversing them, if you learned the trick, by cutting the switch and putting it on again exactly on the final dying revolution of the flywheel, so that it would kick back against compression and begin reversing. Approaching a dock in a strong following breeze, it was difficult to slow up sufficiently by the ordinary coasting method, and if a boy felt he had complete mastery over his motor, he was tempted to keep it running beyond its time and then reverse it a few feet from the dock. It took a cool nerve, because if you threw the switch a twentieth of a second too soon you would catch the flywheel when it still had speed enough to go up past center, and the boat would leap ahead, charging bull-fashion at the dock.

We had a good week at the camp. The bass were biting well and the sun 11 shone endlessly, day after day. We would be tired at night and lie down in the accumulated heat of the little bedrooms after the long hot day and the breeze would stir almost imperceptibly outside and the smell of the swamp drift in through the rusty screens. Sleep would come easily and in the morning the red squirrel would be on the roof, tapping out his gay routine. I kept remembering everything, lying in bed in the mornings—the small steamboat that had a long rounded stern like the lip of a Ubangi, and how quietly she ran on the moonlight sails, when the older boys played their mandolins and the girls sang and we ate doughnuts dipped in sugar, and how sweet the music was on the water in the shining night, and what it had felt like to think about girls then. After breakfast we would go up to the store and the things were in the same place—the minnows in a bottle, the plugs and spinners disarranged and pawed over by the youngsters from the boys' camp, the Fig Newtons and the Beeman's gum. Outside, the road was tarred and cars stood in front of the store. Inside, all was just as it had always been, except there was more Coca-Cola and not so much Moxie and root beer and birch beer and sarsaparilla. We would walk out with a bottle of pop apiece and sometimes the pop would backfire up our noses and hurt. We explored the streams, quietly, where the turtles slid off the sunny logs and dug their way into the soft bottom; and we lay on the town wharf and fed worms to the tame bass. Everywhere we went I had trouble making out which was I, the one walking at my side, the one walking in my pants.

One afternoon while we were there at that lake a thunderstorm came 12 up. It was like the revival of an old melodrama that I had seen long ago with childish awe. The second-act climax of the drama of the electrical disturbance over a lake in America had not changed in any important respect. This was the big scene, still the big scene. The whole thing was so familiar, the first feeling of oppression and heat and a general air around camp of not wanting to go very far away. In midafternoon (it was all the same) a curious darkening of the sky, and a lull in everything that had made life tick; and then the way the boats suddenly swung the other way at their moorings with the coming of a breeze out of the new quarter, and the premonitory rumble. Then the kettle drum, then the snare, then the bass drum and cymbals, then crackling light against the dark, and the gods grinning and licking their chops in the hills. Afterward the calm, the rain steadily rustling in the calm lake, the return of light and hope and spirits, and the campers running out in joy and relief to go swimming in the rain, their bright cries perpetuating the deathless joke about how they were getting simply drenched, and the children screaming with delight at the new sensation of bathing in the rain, and the joke about getting drenched linking the generations in a strong indestructible chain. And the comedian who waded in carrying an umbrella.

When the others went swimming, my son said he was going in,   13
too. He pulled his dripping trunks from the line where they had hung all through the shower and wrung them out. Languidly, and with no thought of going in, I watched him, his hard little body, skinny and bare, saw him wince slightly as he pulled up around his vitals the small, soggy, icy garment. As he buckled the swollen belt, suddenly my groin felt the chill of death.

VOCABULARY

helgramite—a small water insect that resembles a centipede

Moxie—a carbonated beverage produced in the United States since 1884

Ubangi—a tribe of people named after the Ubangi river that separates the Democratic Republic of the Congo from the Republic of the Congo. The Ubangi people insert discs inside their upper or lower lips as a form of body modification.

QUESTIONS

1. White's essay has a descriptive, narrative style, and it does not have some of the conventional features of an essay such as an explicit thesis statement. Rather, the thesis is implied, and the essay reads very much like a story. What kind of structural and stylistic devices does White employ to achieve his effects?

2. Compare this essay to Margaret Laurence's short story "The Loons" (Readings). What are the similarities and differences between the two works? How does each narrator convey his or her reflections and remembrances of childhood experiences?

3. White ends his essay with a reference to "death," which is reminiscent of the "creepy sensation" he experiences earlier in the essay. How do these references contradict the dominant idyllic tone of the essay?

4. White insists on the continuity of the lake and its geography by repeating, "There had been no years." However, some things have changed. What are they, and what do these changes contribute to the essay?

SUGGESTION FOR WRITING

In a manner that is imitative of White's style, write an essay about a place that has meaningful memories to you. You will want to consider both your recollections and memories, and your current relationship to those past events.

[Shakespeare's Sister]

Virginia Woolf

What I find deplorable . . . is that nothing is known about women before the eighteenth century. I have no model in my mind to turn about this way and that. Here am I asking why women did not write poetry in the Elizabethan age,[1] and I am not sure how they were educated; whether they were taught to write; whether they had sitting-rooms to themselves; how many women had children before they were twenty-one; what, in short, they did from eight in the morning till eight at night. They had no money evidently; according to Professor Trevelyan[2] they were married whether they liked it or not before they were out of the nursery, at fifteen or sixteen very likely. It would have been extremely odd, even upon this showing, had one of them suddenly written the plays of Shakespeare, I concluded, and I thought of that old gentleman, who is dead now, but was a bishop, I think, who declared that it was impossible for any woman, past, present, or to come, to have the genius of Shakespeare. He wrote to the papers about it. He also told a lady who applied to him for information that cats do not as a matter of fact go to heaven, though they have, he added, souls of a sort. How much thinking those old gentlemen used to save one! How the borders of ignorance shrank back at their approach! Cats do not go to heaven. Women cannot write the plays of Shakespeare.

Be that as it may, I could not help thinking, as I looked at the works of Shakespeare on the shelf, that the bishop was right at least in this; it would have been impossible, completely and entirely, for any woman to have written the plays of Shakespeare in the age of Shakespeare. Let me imagine, since facts are so hard to come by, what would have happened had Shakespeare had a wonderfully gifted sister, called Judith, let us say. Shakespeare himself went, very probably—his mother was an heiress—to the grammar school, where he may have learnt Latin—Ovid, Virgil and Horace[3]— and the elements of grammar and logic. He was, it is well known, a wild boy who poached rabbits, perhaps shot a deer, and had, rather sooner than he should have done, to marry a woman in the neighbourhood, who bore him a child rather quicker than was right. That escapade sent him to seek his fortune in London. He had, it seemed, a taste for the theatre; he began by holding horses at the stage door. Very soon he got work in the theatre, became a successful actor, and lived at the hub of the universe, meeting everybody, knowing everybody, practising his art on the boards, exercising his wits in the streets, and even getting access to the palace of the queen. Meanwhile his extraordinarily gifted sister, let us suppose, remained at home. She was as adventurous, as imaginative, as agog to see the world as he was. But she was not sent to school. She had no chance of learning grammar and logic, let alone of reading Horace and Virgil. She picked up a book now and then, one of her brother's perhaps, and read a few pages. But then her parents came in and told her to mend the stockings or mind the stew and not moon about with books and papers. They would have spoken sharply but kindly, for they were substantial people who knew the conditions of life for a woman and loved their daughter—indeed, more likely than not she was the apple of her father's eye. Perhaps she scribbled some pages up in an apple loft on the sly, but was careful to hide them or set fire to them. Soon, however, before she was out of her teens, she was to be betrothed to the son of a neighbouring wool-stapler.[4] She cried out that marriage was hateful to her, and for that she was severely beaten by her father. Then he ceased to scold her. He begged her instead not to hurt him, not to shame him in this matter of her marriage. He would give her a chain of beads or a fine petticoat, he said; and there were tears in his eyes. How could she disobey him? How could she break his heart? The force of her own gift alone drove her to it. She made up a small parcel of her belongings, let herself down by a rope one summer's night and took the road to London. She was not seventeen. The birds that sang in the hedge were not more musical than she was. She had the quickest fancy, a gift like her brother's, for the tune of words. Like him, she had a taste for the theatre. She stood at the stage door; she wanted to act, she said. Men laughed in her face. The manager—a fat, loose-lipped man—guffawed. He bellowed something about poodles dancing and women acting—no woman, he said, could possibly be an actress. He hinted—you can imagine what. She could get no training in her craft. Could she even seek her dinner in a tavern or roam the streets at midnight? Yet her genius was for fiction and lusted to feed abundantly upon the lives of men and women and the study of their ways. At last—for she was very young, oddly like Shakespeare the poet in her face, with the same grey eyes and rounded brows—at last Nick Greene the actor-manager took pity on her; she found herself with child by that gentleman and so—who shall measure the heat and violence of the poet's heart when caught and tangled in a woman's body?—killed herself one winter's night and lies buried at some cross-roads where the omnibuses now stop outside the Elephant and Castle.[5]

That, more or less, is how the story would run, I think, if a woman in   3
Shakespeare's day had had Shakespeare's genius. But for my part, I agree
with the deceased bishop, if such he was—it is unthinkable that any woman
in Shakespeare's day should have had Shakespeare's genius. For genius like
Shakespeare's is not born among labouring, uneducated, servile people. It
was not born in England among the Saxons and the Britons. It is not born
today among the working classes. How, then, could it have been born among
women whose work began, according to Professor Trevelyan, almost before
they were out of the nursery, who were forced to it by their parents and
held to it by all the power of law and custom? Yet genius of a sort must have
existed among women as it must have existed among the working classes.
Now and again an Emily Brontë or a Robert Burns[6] blazes out and proves
its presence. But certainly it never got itself on to paper. When, however,
one reads of a witch being ducked, of a woman possessed by devils, of a wise
woman selling herbs, or even of a very remarkable man who had a mother,
then I think we are on the track of a lost novelist, a suppressed poet, of
some mute and inglorious Jane Austen,[7] some Emily Brontë who dashed
her brains out on the moor or mopped and mowed about the highways
crazed with the torture that her gift had put her to. Indeed, I would venture
to guess that Anon, who wrote so many poems without signing them, was
often a woman. It was a woman Edward Fitzgerald,[8] I think, suggested who
made the ballads and the folk-songs, crooning them to her children, beguiling her spinning with them, on the length of the winter's night.

This may be true or it may be false—who can say?—but what is true   4
in it, so it seemed to me, reviewing the story of Shakespeare's sister as I had
made it, is that any woman born with a great gift in the sixteenth century
would certainly have gone crazed, shot herself, or ended her days in some
lonely cottage outside the village, half witch, half wizard, feared and mocked
at. For it needs little skill in psychology to be sure that a highly gifted girl
who had tried to use her gift for poetry would have been so thwarted and
hindered by other people, so tortured and pulled asunder by her own contrary instincts, that she must have lost her health and sanity to a certainty.
No girl could have walked to London and stood at a stage door and forced
her way into the presence of actor-managers without doing herself a violence
and suffering an anguish which may have been irrational—for chastity may
be a fetish invented by certain societies for unknown reasons—but were none
the less inevitable. Chastity had then, it has even now, a religious importance

in a woman's life, and has so wrapped itself round with nerves and instincts that to cut it free and bring it to the light of day demands courage of the rarest. To have lived a free life in London in the sixteenth century would have meant for a woman who was poet and playwright a nervous stress and dilemma which might well have killed her. Had she survived, whatever she had written would have been twisted and deformed, issuing from a strained and morbid imagination. And undoubtedly, I thought, looking at the shelf where there are no plays by women, her work would have gone unsigned. That refuge she would have sought certainly. It was the relic of the sense of chastity that dictated anonymity to women even so late as the nineteenth century. Currer Bell, George Eliot, George Sand,[9] all the victims of inner strife as their writings prove, sought ineffectively to veil themselves by using the name of a man. Thus they did homage to the convention, which if not implanted by the other sex was liberally encouraged by them (the chief glory of a woman is not to be talked of, said Pericles,[10] himself a much-talked-of man), that publicity in women is detestable. Anonymity runs in their blood. The desire to be veiled still possesses them. . . .

That woman, then, who was born with a gift of poetry in the sixteenth century, was an unhappy woman, a woman at strife against herself. All the conditions of her life, all her own instincts, were hostile to the state of mind which is needed to set free whatever is in the brain. . . .   5

NOTES

[1] The Elizabethan age is roughly the period during which Elizabeth I was queen of England (1558–1603). This was the period during which Shakespeare and many other writers and artists produced a significant body of work.

[2] George Macaulay Trevelyan (1876–1962), born six years before Woolf, was an influential English historian.

[3] Ovid (43 BC–AD 17?), Virgil (70–19 BC), author of *The Aeneid,* and Horace (65–8 BC), inventor of the Horatian Ode, were Roman poets.

[4] The staple is the fibre of the wool. A wool-stapler would likely be a dealer in wool, not a common labourer.

[5] The Elephant and Castle pub in inner south London dates from 1765 and gives its name (unofficially) to the surrounding area.

[6] Emily Brontë (1818–1848) was notably the author of *Wuthering Heights,* a powerful novel of doomed romance set on the Yorkshire Moors. Robert Burns (1759–1796) was a poet of working-class origins who wrote extensively in the Scots dialect.

[7] Jane Austen (1775–1817) was the author of *Emma, Pride and Prejudice,* and other novels dealing with moral choice and social hierarchy.

[8] Edward Fitzgerald (1809–1883) was an English poet known particularly for his translations from the writings of Persian poet and mathematician Omar Khayyám.

[9] Currer Bell was the pen name of Charlotte Brontë (1816–1855), Emily Brontë's sister. George Eliot was the pen name of Mary Ann Evans (1819–1880), author of *Middlemarch* and other novels. George Sand was the pen name of the French novelist Lucile Aurore Dupin, later Baroness Dudevant (1804–1876), who dressed in men's clothes and smoked a pipe.

[10] Pericles (c. 495–429 BC) was an Athenian statesman. The Periclean age is the period when Athens dominated Greek political and cultural life.

QUESTIONS

1. Does Virginia Woolf use irony in this essay? If so, where and with what effect?

2. In *A Room of One's Own* (originally two lectures given to audiences interested in the arts and scholarship), Woolf invents a hypothetical example, a sister of Shakespeare's with the same creative drives as he had, but provides real examples of historical and contemporary views on women. It is generally assumed that it is the examples that make this section of *Room* nonfictional rather than fictional. Do you agree? Why or why not?

3. Why does Woolf agree with an unnamed bishop that "it is unthinkable that any woman in Shakespeare's day should have had Shakespeare's genius"? Is it for the same reasons that the bishop held this belief, or for some other reasons?

4. Woolf is making a case about women in the Elizabethan age. Does anything in the essay tell you whether she thinks her points apply to women in her own time as well?

SUGGESTIONS FOR WRITING

1. How much do the conditions that inhibited women's expression in the sixteenth century still apply today? Write an essay exploring this issue.

2. Can men and women write about issues of gender inequality in the same way? Write an essay comparing Virginia Woolf's approach to these issues with that taken by Scott Russell Sanders (also in Readings).

African National Identities Can't Be Built on Soccer Fever

Jonathan Zimmerman

C an sports make a nation? 1

   That's a strange question. Americans love high-profile athletic 2
events, as the current buildup to Super Bowl XLII illustrates. But
nobody hangs America's future upon sports.

   In Africa, though, it's quite common to do so. In a continent ravaged 3
by political and ethnic violence, people often invoke sports—especially
soccer—as [a] force for national unity. And nobody does so more than the
Ghanaians, who are hosts of the 16-country Africa Cup of Nations tournament at four sites around the country.

   "We all speak football," one headline announced this week. "Football— 4
A real source of unity," declared another. When Ghana celebrated a last-
minute defeat over Guinea in the tournament's opening match, one commentator wrote, "There were no distinctions as to who belonged to which political
party, religious sect, or ethnic division." Another editorialist compared Ghana's
stability to the ethnic violence plaguing Kenya. "Is it because Kenya does not
have an accomplished, unifying football team?" he asked.

   As a rabid supporter of Ghana's "Black Stars" soccer team, I can appreci- 5
ate the sentiment. But as a historian, I am also deeply worried by it. Over the
last century, sports have rarely spawned true national harmony and reconcili-
ation. Instead, they provide a convenient
tool for one part of a nation—or, even, for
one leader—to oppress the rest of it.

Jonathan Zimmerman is Professor of
Education and History, and Director of the
History of Education Program at New York
University's Steinhardt School of Culture,
Education, and Human Development. His
books include *Whose America? Culture Wars in
the Public Schools* (2002), *Innocents Abroad:
American Teachers in the American Century*
(2006), and *Small Wonder: The Little Red
Schoolhouse in History and Memory* (2009).

"African National Identities Can't Be Built on Soccer
Fever" is reprinted with permission of the author,
Jonathan Zimmerman, Professor of Education and
History, NYU Steinhardt.

   To take the most notorious example: 6
Adolf Hitler used the 1936 Olympic
Games in Berlin to "unify" Germany—
around the idea of Aryan superiority.

   With the next Olympics slated for 7
Beijing this summer, China has been jail-
ing dissidents and pushing poor people
from their homes to build stadiums.

   Here in Africa, tyrants have often 8
seized upon sports to bolster their power.
Zaire's Mobutu,[1] Nigeria's Sani Abacha,[2]
and especially Uganda's Idi Amin[3] all

poured vast resources into national sports programs. A former boxing and swimming champion, the 6-foot-4-inch Amin lavished cash upon the country's star athletes. He also competed with them personally, knocking out one of the country's leading boxers and offering 10,000 shillings to anyone who could defeat him in the breast stroke. (Amin lost to a brave challenger, in 1976, and promptly paid up.)

Did these antics help Amin "unify" Uganda? Perhaps. More than anything else, however, they helped him solidify his dictatorial regime. When a Voice of Uganda sports reporter criticized the national football team, Amin promptly fired him; and when two players were rumoured to have links to a Tanzania-based opposition group, he threw them both in prison. Only a last-minute appeal from their teammates on the eve of a big match saved them from likely torture and death.   9

Here in Ghana, the independence leader Kwame Nkrumah[4] promoted soccer to demonstrate the new nation's freedom from its former colonial masters. Nkrumah helped start the Africa Cup of Nations tournament, which would "earn for our dear continent a greater respectability and recognition at the universal level," he predicted.   10

But as a force for national unity and stability, soccer's record is pretty poor. Three years after Ghana's victory in the inaugural Africa Cup tourney, Nkrumah himself would be deposed.   11

Even worse, some governments use sports to divert attention from their own misdeeds. "It is good to see people talking about football in Sudan, and not about Darfur," said the coach of the Sudanese national team, which is competing in the Africa Cup for the first time in 32 years. Good for the butchers in Khartoum, perhaps; but not for the victims in Darfur, where an estimated 200,000 people have perished and 2.5 million have lost their homes.   12

Most of all, sports are unpredictable: Even the best team has to lose, now and then. And that's a slender reed for national identity, as was demonstrated by a recent editorial in the Accra Daily Graphic. The soccer team's first-round victory against Guinea had created a "national euphoria," the editorial noted, which "transcended ethnic, gender, age, political, and social barriers." But the Black Stars' lacklustre second match against a much weaker Namibian team squad gave the paper pause.   13

"The Daily Graphic believes that this nationalistic feeling will last for as long as the Black Stars continue to win their matches," the editorial explained. "The moment they are out, we will lose that feeling and our hearts will be broken."   14

My heart will break, too, if Ghana fails to win the Africa Cup. But my biggest hope is for the country, not for its soccer team.   15

NOTES

[1] Mobutu Sese Seko (1930–1997) was the president of Zaire (the Democratic Republic of the Congo) from 1965 to 1997.

[2] Sani Abacha (1943–1998) was the president of Nigeria from 1993 to 1998.

[3] Idi Amin (1925–2003) was the president of Uganda from 1971 to 1979.

[4] Kwame Nkrumah (1909–1972) was the president of Ghana from 1952 to 1966.

QUESTIONS

1. Zimmerman claims that "nobody hangs America's future upon sports." Do you agree or disagree with this claim?

2. Which dynamic do you think is stronger: sport as a unifier through common interest or sport as a divider through competition and team rivalry?

3. Zimmerman claims sport is a fragile basis for a nation. What other kinds of things contribute to nationhood or national unity?

SUGGESTION FOR WRITING

Write a comparison essay that analyzes the strengths and weaknesses of both Jonathan Zimmerman's and Kofi Annan's (Readings) arguments about sport and its relationship to politics.

Sample Essays

To Peacekeep or Not to Peacekeep

James Ash

n the 1990s peacekeeping became a booming business, and Canada established itself as a world leader in this endeavour. There are those, however, who criticize Canada's active support of and enthusiastic participation in UN peacekeeping operations. They believe that our armed forces should focus on territorial defence and that our defence dollar should be spent on the acquisition of new equipment; as for peacekeeping, they believe we should leave it to bigger powers. Such critics are mistaken. Peacekeeping is the best possible role for the Canadian Armed Forces, both from the pragmatic and the ethical point of view. 1

The most common objection to Canada's involvement in peacekeeping operations is that it ties up our limited military resources abroad and leaves nothing for the defence of Canada. It is hard to deny the truth of this allegation; we have so few actual soldiers in our army that it is hard to imagine that there are any of them left in Canada, considering our many peacekeeping commitments. But whom would these soldiers be guarding against? Any foreign power that attacks Canada will have to contend with the United States, and if the US were to attack us, it would be a very short war, whether our puny army was in Canada or Yugoslavia. Either we fight alongside the US or against them, and in either case the American military machine dwarfs our own so badly that the issue of territorial defence is hardly an issue at all. 2

This is not to say that we do not want an army that can engage in large-scale violence as efficiently as the next one, both as a point of national pride (it is nice to think that we could at least put up a fight before the Stars and Stripes flies over Parliament Hill) and as a sign that we are willing to do our part for collective security with our allies. However, peacekeeping is ideal training for war-making: it requires the same skills, and it provides the ideal environment for troops to practise them in, namely a real war. This same 3 rationale can be used to answer the objection that our defence dollar would be better spent on new equipment. Yes, our armed forces do need new equipment. But they are far more likely to get this equipment if they are abroad on peacekeeping missions than if they are at home involved in tame training exercises. A few body bags being flown home because small-arms fire can penetrate Canada's ancient armoured personnel carriers, or because our helicopters are too decrepit to evacuate Canadian wounded, is probably the only incentive that will actually get Canada's military the tools it needs to do the job.

We have yet to consider the merits of peacekeeping in and of itself. 4
The first is that it allows Canada to play a legitimate, independent foreign policy role. Canada will never be a superpower, but it has the misfortune (at times) to live next to one. Peacekeeping is an opportunity for Canada to play a real role in the world beyond its border, without being an American puppet. We are not following the US example with peacekeeping; we are setting one for them.

Setting an example is an idea that is central to this whole issue, because 5
peacekeeping is becoming a symbol of Canada at a time when the country desperately needs one. Peacekeeping allows Canada to be the best at something, to be famous, to earn awards. This argument may sound like an emotional one, but it is not entirely. Pragmatically, at a time when Canada is internally divided and economically exhausted, peacekeeping is a low-cost morale booster for a nation that seems to be wallowing in self-pity and cynicism.

Ultimately, though, all of these arguments for peacekeeping are 6
window-dressing. The bottom line is that Canada should commit its defence resources to peacekeeping because it is the right thing to do. War is bad; we take this to be a self-evident truth. Consequently, the only ethical role for a peacetime army is to try to prevent war. It may not always work, it may even never work, but it is something that, morally, we should try our best at anyhow. If it saves more lives than it costs, if it brings even temporary relief to parts of the world that have become living hells, if it serves as a small sign that the world will not stand by forever and let butchers and "ethnic cleansers" have their way, then peacekeeping should be supported by even the most hard-nosed pragmatist.

It seems, on balance, that there really is no good argument against 7
Canada's involvement in UN-sponsored peacekeeping, and several good arguments for it. Maybe it is time we gave our much-maligned government a little credit for something. It seems that we have found a government expenditure where taxpayers are getting more than their money's worth.

Perspectives on Addictions*

C. Jones

Like many Western nations, Canada has a long-standing problem   1
with addictions. Mothers Against Drunk Driving is a group formed
to fight the consequences of alcoholism; Vancouver's Downtown
Eastside is one of the drug capitals of the world. Since addiction is widespread and growing, it is important to understand its causes. Two recent
essays—both originating from the Vancouver area—address this issue
in interesting ways. In "Embraced by the Needle," Dr. Gabor Maté, an
Eastside physician, claims that addiction has its roots in emotional depri-
vation. In "Addiction in Free Markets," Bruce Alexander, a professor at
Simon Fraser University, and Stefa Shaler, a social worker assistant for the
government of British Columbia, argue that addiction rises from social dislocation. Seemingly very different in their detail, development, points, and
perspectives, these essays finally seem to offer complementary rather than
contradictory explanations of the causes of addiction.

The most obvious difference between "Embraced by the Needle" and   2
"Addiction in Free Markets" is in the kind of detail they use. "Embraced"
includes references to theories of brain chemistry and dysfunctional parenting. However, the details we remember from the essay are the stories about
individuals: Anna, who "wasn't wanted" (273); Carl, who "had dishwashing liquid poured down his throat . . . at age 5" (274); Wayne, who was
"hit a lot" and, at the end of the essay, "looks away and wipes tears from his
eyes" (275). In "Addiction," in contrast, the details are general rather than
specific. The authors describe the world "[a]t the beginning of the 21st century [as one where], for rich and poor alike, jobs disappear at short notice,
communities are weak and unstable, people routinely change lovers, families, occupations, co-workers, technical skills . . ." (203–4). The specific
examples that eventually turn up are still large-scale: "England mov[ing]
to a full-blown free market system between the late 16th and the early 19th
centuries" (204); "the history of Native Canadians" (205). Detail in the two
essays, then, reflects a dramatic contrast between focus on the individual
and focus on the general.

---

* Sample comparison essay

The same contrast is reflected in the way the essays are organized. Both 3
essays present a straightforward causal sequence. According to Maté, the
lack of "warm, non-stressed, calm interactions with the parenting figures"
(274) actually changes brain functioning, causing a greater need for external
calming and pleasure enhancing, a need which, in later life, can be temporarily satisfied by drugs. In Alexander and Shaler, the sequence can be summarized even more simply: free market societies create social dislocation,
and then social dislocation creates addiction. If both these sequences are
straightforward, the way the essays are organized differs significantly. We
remember the detail about addicts' lives in "Embraced" because it appears at
the beginning, middle, and end of the essay, wrapping the causal sequence
in a narrative framework. In "Addiction" the sequence is presented in a linear, analytic way. The essay discusses and defines addiction and dislocation;
it then gives extensive examples of the connections between the two before
finally arguing that understanding and reversing dislocation is necessary if
mass addiction is to be cured.

The roots of these differences between "Embraced by the Needle" and 4
"Addiction in Free Markets" lie in the different points Maté and Alexander
and Shaler are making, and the different perspectives that lie behind these
points. Maté's essay opens with his thesis: "Addictions always originate in
unhappiness, even if hidden. They are emotional anesthetics; they numb
pain" (273). "Unhappiness," "emotional," "numb": these terms indicate a
psychological perspective on the causes of addiction. Alexander and Shaler's
thesis, similarly announced in the first sentences, is that "[a]lthough any
person in any society can become addicted, free market societies universally
dislocate their members, leading to mass addiction" (203). Here terms like
"free market societies," "universally," and "mass addiction" point to the
more collective perspective of sociology.

Are these essays as different as they seem? Psychological and sociological 5
perspectives on the causes of addiction are different, but they are not mutu-
ally exclusive. One significant similarity between the essays is that Maté and
Alexander and Shaler have a similar sense of whom they are arguing against.
Maté insists that "[n]either physiological predispositions nor individual
moral failures explain drug addictions" (273). Alexander and Shaler see
their antagonists as the addiction professionals who "continue decades of
futile debate about whether addiction is a 'criminal' or a 'medical' problem
whereas, in fact, it is neither" (205). Furthermore, Maté acknowledges that
parental stress could come "from outside circumstances such as economic
pressure or political disruption" (274–75), whereas Alexander and Shaler
refer to the "painful void" that social dislocation creates (204).

The different ways that "Embraced by the Needle" and "Addiction in   6
Free Markets" handle detail and development, their different points and
perspectives, ensure that each essay charts a different area of causal explanation. However, the similarity in antagonists and the acknowledgment of the
other perspective reflect an important truth: while physiological and ethical
explanations of addiction are incompatible with psychological and sociological ones, these psychological and sociological explanations of cause are
not incompatible with each other. Judging from the material in these two
essays, it would be perfectly possible to show that free markets cause social
dislocations and that social dislocations, in turn, affect parental functioning and thus, via brain and emotions, increase the likelihood of addiction
in individuals. Neither essay presents this whole causal sequence, but when
compared, they provide strong evidence that both sociological and psychological factors are at work in causing addiction.

Reflecting on Population*

D. Jones

ed Byfield's essay "Health Canada Inadvertently Discloses Facts 1
Planned Parenthood Would Like to Suppress" appeared in *The Report,*
the Alberta-based newsmagazine that Byfield also edited, in March
2002. Byfield begins his essay by referring to a Health Canada study that suggests Canadians are working too hard, including too hard to have children. He then goes on to argue that the real threat to the world is not population growth but rather a "serious population decline, a 'birth dearth' that will wreak great havoc on the economies of much of the western world. . . . making the absence of kids the world's No. 1 economic problem" (222–23). Population is obviously an important issue to consider these days, but is this essay a credible contribution to that consideration? "Health Canada" seems to have logical strengths: a cause and effect argument supported by statistics and references to authorities on both sides of the case. These strengths are more apparent than real, however. Byfield's treatment of authorities is one-sided and his statistics, while thought-provoking, do not support his point. As a result, his causal argument fails to be logically convincing.

At first "Health Canada" seems to be a logical, well-supported essay 2
arguing for a startling position on world population. The essay has a clear causal argument: obsession with work leads to population decline; population decline will lead to economic chaos. This argument is supported by statistics taken from Health Canada and the American Enterprise Institute; in fact, Byfield's thesis statement appears to be a composite of opinions from these two institutions.

Byfield's position, if true, would demand a dramatic reassessment of 3
the way we see world population. Unfortunately, "Health Canada," despite the appearance of logic, fails to make this position logically credible.

It is true that Byfield refers to authorities from both sides of the argu- 4
ment about population, but these authorities are used very differently. Byfield does not give the arguments of experts who argue the dangers of population growth; instead he dismisses them in a series of satiric caricatures. Paul Ehrlich is one of the "prophets of doom" (222); Planned Parenthood is the "zealous preacher of the Save-the-World-with-Smaller-Families message" (223); the United Nations publishes "don't-have-kids

* Sample critique

propaganda" (223). On the other hand, Byfield quotes opinions from the American Enterprise Institute and Tom Bethell, a journalist writing in the *American Spectator,* and treats these opinions as fact. Such a one-sided handling of authorities diminishes the essay's credibility.

Equally lacking in credibility is Byfield's handling of evidence. At first 5 glance, the figures showing declines in the birth rate in certain Western and non-Western countries seem to support his claim for "serious population decline" (222). But further reflection, even on the examples given, suggests that even if Europe's birth rate is running at 1.4, this rate is more than balanced by the rates of India (3.5), Egypt (3.9), and Mexico (3). And what about the ones he does not quote? Oddly, given his starting place, he does not quote statistics for Canada and the United States; a chance remark about Thailand reveals that both countries have a birth rate above replacement level. Thus the statistics Byfield quotes and those he does not quote show that the world's population is increasing, not declining. Most damaging of all is the absence of any evidence that demonstrates current population trends are creating "the world's No. 1 economic problem" (223).

One-sided handling of authorities and selective evidence create a causal 6 argument that does not work. Its key fallacy is that of the single cause/single outcome. It is not very credible that an obsession with work demonstrated by one study in Canada should be reflected all over the world as a cause of birth-rate decline, especially when there is no mention of other causes commonly and convincingly cited, such as an increase in women's access to birth control and education and increases in standards of living. And can we believe that the main effect of a slowing in the increase of population—since that is what Byfield's statistics show—is going to be economic "havoc" (222)? It could be argued that "government welfare programs" (223) would be endangered in a few countries particularly affected by a falling birth rate—this is Byfield's one explanation (and a surprising one, given his other views) of what he means by "havoc." However, would this effect prove more important than the massive destruction of the environment and of rural societies that many experts argue to be the visible and present effect of population growth? To make his argument about economic "havoc" more credible, Byfield would need to outline alternative explanations and show why they should be dismissed or minimized.

Perhaps the real contribution of Ted Byfield's "Health Canada" is that, 7 by using statistics, reference to authorities, and causal argument, the essay sends the message that we need to bring logic to discussions of issues such as population. Unfortunately, because of its one-sided use of authorities, failure to link evidence to point, and flawed causal argument, the essay itself does not achieve logical credibility. Instead, the essay makes us recognize the need for our thinking on important subjects to contain the substance of logic, and not just its appearance.

Same-Sex Marriages: Tradition and Change*

E. Jones

When we think of the phenomenon of same-sex marriages in Canada, 1 we think of change, rapid change. Barely a distant dream before the twenty-first century, same-sex marriage suddenly underwent a period of acceptance as a series of court decisions between 2003 and 2005 legalized the practice in most provinces and territories. The culmination of this process was the Civil Marriage Act in 2005, which legalized such marriages across the country. However, this is far from the end of the story, even in the legal and political field, for Stephen Harper's 2005 campaign promise to organize a free vote on the question represents social currents that continue to be firmly opposed to this form of marriage. In the field of religion there is even more dramatic division, with, for example, the Roman Catholic Church lining up to oppose same-sex weddings and the United Church of Canada in support of them, but with substantial bodies of dissidents in both denominations. In this context it seems pertinent to ask: How should Canadian institutions respond to same-sex marriages? Should the state hold firm to its path of support, or remove support? Should the churches accept division in their ranks, or actively push towards acceptance? Though there are serious reasons behind the resistance to same-sex marriage, there are better practical and ethical reasons for both church and state to endorse not only legal marriage but also church ceremonies for same-sex couples.

Before we examine the main options available to the state and the 2 church, let's define the key terms *wedding* and *marriage*. A wedding is the act and ceremony of marrying. This wedding ceremony may be performed in a cathedral or a submarine. As long as it meets the church's criteria, the couple are married in the eyes of the church. They are not legally married, however, unless they meet the legal requirements for getting a marriage licence. These requirements used to specify that the couple must be a man and a woman; now they do not. It used to be possible for a same-sex couple to have a wedding in certain churches but not be legally married. Now it is possible for them to be legally married but not be able to have a wedding in the church of their upbringing or choice.

---

* Sample persuasive essay

The passing of the Civil Marriage Act is probably a testament to chang- 3
ing Canadian social values. It is true that there are still traditionalists who
argue that the main purpose of marriage is to create stable family structures
in which to raise children. If the status of the family is secure, they argue,
the society will be stable and prosperous. This argument has merit: children
invariably prefer, and seem to thrive on, the attention of two loving parents,
and two-parent families are usually more economically stable. However,
Canada is a pluralistic country. From Inuit trappers in Nunavut to community health workers in Newfoundland to Sikh business people living in
Vancouver, there are many ways to be Canadian. There are also many kinds
of Canadian families, including single-parent families, blended families,
and foster-home families. Good parenting goes on in these non-traditional
families, just as poor parenting goes on in some two-parent families. The
passing of the Civil Marriage Act suggests this social acceptance of plurality is extending to the committed relationships of this particular non-
traditional kind.

The development represented by the Civil Marriage Act should be sup- 4
ported for both practical and ethical reasons. The practical advantages for
same-sex couples are clear: couples who have entered into marriage have all
the rights of married couples, rights that include supplemental health care
benefits, pension benefits, and property rights. What may be less clear is
that when same-sex couples form committed relationships, we all benefit.
If Tom works so that Bill can finish his medical degree and then Bill helps
Tom through civil engineering training, the country has another doctor
and another civil engineer. On the ethical side, there are issues of social
and personal obligation. Because people in committed relationships make
sacrifices for each other and help each other to succeed, they deserve legal
protection if their relationships end.

However, supporting national legislation concerning same-sex mar- 5
riage is not the whole picture. There is another institution involved in for-
malizing committed relationships, namely the church. The lack of legal
status for church weddings does not mean that they are unimportant to
same-sex couples. Gays and lesbians with strong ties to a church want the
same blessing for their commitment to each other that other members of
the congregation feel entitled to. Same-sex couples also feel that churches
should provide moral leadership for the wider community. In evaluating
what churches can and should do, it is important to recognize the special
difficulties they face in struggling to cope with the practical and ethical
implications of marrying same-sex couples.

The ethical difficulty churches face in marrying same-sex couples is 6
that the historical precepts of most churches include injunctions against

same-sex relations. We should note, though, that these precepts also usually include injunctions concerning love, respect, faithfulness, and commitment. Churches insisting on a literal reading of historical scriptures generally stick to the injunction against same-sex relations and interpret precepts concerning love and commitment to apply to the restricted group of "the faithful"; less fundamentalist churches struggle over the degree to which following the "spirit" of love and respect allows divergences from the letter of scriptural "law." On this issue, the ethical value of leadership seems key: in an era when either tolerance or sectarianism could win out, churches that make same-sex couples fully participating members of their own congregations send a powerful message of inclusion to society as a whole.

If agreeing to marry same-sex couples is ethically desirable for churches,   7
the question remains: is it practically possible? As every church is well aware, marrying same-sex couples will outrage gender traditionalists, who may well be a congregation's most staunch supporters. What church wants to outrage its main source of volunteers and financial support, not to mention some of its most senior and respected clergy? Although churches that perform same-sex marriages may alienate gender traditionalists, churches that refuse to perform such marriages will almost certainly alienate their lesbian and gay members. Furthermore, performing same-sex marriages is likely to arouse the sympathy and commitment of a younger generation of potential churchgoers. Progressive churches will therefore attract more young people and ensure their own growth and vitality. The declining attendance of young people should make the marrying of same-sex couples a somewhat painful but still positive practical option in mainstream churches, if not in fundamentalist ones.

The issue of same-sex unions is particularly challenging to traditional-   8
ists, whether inside or outside the church, but they are perhaps missing one important aspect of the desire of many same-sex couples not only for legal marriage but also for church weddings. This desire for religious institutions to bless their commitment and sacrifice suggests that these traditional values are alive and well among same-sex couples. True leadership involves finding the best way to promote ongoing virtues in changing circumstances. By recognizing the ethical and practical value of both legal marriage and church weddings for same-sex couples, church and state would show true leadership.

The Problem of Environmental Costs: Suzuki vs. Merwin

Joyce MacDonald

We live in a time of great concern for the environment. We constantly need to evaluate almost everything we buy or consume in terms of what it may be doing to our atmosphere or water supply. We have a wide range of sometimes contradictory information at our fingertips telling us how we can, or should, help the environmental cause. While both David Suzuki, in his essay "It Always Costs," and W. S. Merwin, in "Unchopping a Tree," concern themselves with the problem of environmental costs, their messages are very different. Suzuki provides a very accessible essay using well-defined technical terms and a straight-forward, academic structure. His thesis, that we must just be a little more careful about the environment, is very practical. The entire tone of his essay, however, is somewhat emotionally detached. Merwin, on the other hand, provides an essay that uses complicated emotional imagery, a complex reverse-process structure, and a thesis that is totally impractical: all forest harvesting must be stopped. What Merwin's article has that Suzuki's lacks is a tone of emotional connection to the question of environmental costs. This sense of emotional connection is the truly necessary feature which causes the reader to take personal responsibility for the problems of the environment.

While Suzuki's use of well-defined technical jargon makes his essay accessible to his reader, it also creates a tone of emotional distance from the subject. He uses terms like "biomagnification" and "synergistic" accompanied by their definitions (310, 311). These terms may be accurate, but they are hardly descriptive. When Suzuki refers to a "bad episode" (311) on a drill site, he does not explain what the specific effects may be. Are they pollution, loss of wildlife, or loss of human life? When he writes about the "negative effects" (311) of the pill, he does not elaborate on how it affects a woman's mental health or how it may increase her risks of developing cancer. By eliminating description, Suzuki produces a tone of emotional distance from his subject. One brief description of the horror a mother would experience on the birth of a severely deformed thalidomide baby would be enough to arouse some sympathy in the reader. As it stands, the technical jargon only serves to distance the reader from the subject matter. While it explains everything clearly, it provokes no emotional response. Without emotional connection to the material, no sense of personal responsibility for the environment can be established.

Merwin, in contrast, uses elaborate imagery to evoke an emotional response in the reader, creating a tone of personal involvement. He uses the language of violation, saying that leaves, twigs, and nests have been "shaken, ripped, or broken off" and limbs "smashed or mutilated" (277). Attempts at restoration achieve "only the skeleton of the resurrection" (278). The death of the tree creates more of an emotional response than the fate of Suzuki's thalidomide babies. We are made to feel for the dead trees, whereas those deformed children are kept at a safe distance by nice technical language. The tone of personal emotional involvement created by Merwin is more conducive to creating a feeling of personal responsibility for those poor dead trees.

The tone created by Suzuki's academic essay structure also serves to distance the reader from the subject. The thesis, "technology always has a cost" (310), is given in the beginning. We are also handed our conclusion on a silver platter: We must "err on the side of extreme caution" (312). The reader never needs to search for any hidden meaning in this straightforward approach. The reader can remain emotionally detached from what he or she is reading. While use of the pronoun "we" throughout may seem like an effort to involve the reader, closer examination shows "we" to mean "the public in general" and not "you and I." Few of us will ever conduct "an environmental impact assessment" (311), so we can even further detach ourselves because the term seems to refer to the scientific community. The tone created is one of total emotional detachment in the reader. There are no conclusions to reason out. There is no personal stake in the state of the environment. No commitments need to be made by the reader.

Merwin's reverse process structure is more successful in creating a tone of personal involvement because the thesis is never stated and the conclusion is never drawn. Discovery of the point of the essay is an active process. The reader is included in the essay: "You will watch. . . . You will listen for the nuts to shift. . . . [Y]ou will hear whether they are indeed falling" (278).

The emotions the reader is supposed to feel are carefully explained: "It is as though its weight for a moment stood on your heart. . . . You are afraid the motion of the clouds will be enough to push it over" (279). The sheer complexity of the process increases the reader's sense of futility:

> It goes without saying that if the tree was hollow in whole or in part, and contained old nests of bird or mammal or insect, or hoards of nuts or such structures as wasps or bees build for their survival, the contents will have to be repaired where necessary, and reassembled, insofar as possible, in their original order, including the shells of nuts already opened. (277)

Recognition of the futility of the enterprise combined with the pre-   8
scribed feelings dictated by Merwin leaves us emotionally involved. We
are responsible for coming to our own conclusions. This sense of personal
responsibility is exactly what Merwin is after. Merwin wants us to take
personal responsibility for the environment. Without a sense of personal
responsibility, one does not make a commitment to a cause.

In criticism of Merwin, one might say that his proposal to stop defor-   9
estation is totally impractical, whereas Suzuki seems to have a very reasonable approach. The problem with Suzuki is that he generalizes wildly in his
assumption that we are "hooked" on modern technology and "can't go back
to doing things the old way" (311). What about the conservation movement
that advocates returning to simpler methods around our own homes? Suzuki
ignores the ideas of composting and recycling to reduce household wastes
and using compost as an alternative to chemical fertilizers. These are certainly
old ways to deal with our modern problems. In speaking about technology
on a large scale, Suzuki misses these small individual efforts. Perhaps there
are ways in which large-scale technologies can return to simpler, less destructive techniques. Just to say that it can't be done shows a lack of faith. On the
other hand, Merwin's proposal seems totally impractical, until it is analyzed
more closely. His demand for a halt to tree chopping is an overstatement. It
is almost like bartering; he asks for much more than he ever hopes to receive.
If he is lucky he will get more than he has at present. Instead of asking for
a halt to deforestation, he really is asking for a slowdown of the devastation. Where Merwin seems to ask for too much, Suzuki seems to show no
faith and asks for too little. Suzuki seems to buy the technological quick fix,
whereas Merwin rejects it as not good enough.

While Suzuki seems to be all practicality and accessibility in his essay,   10
he lacks the tone of personal emotional involvement achieved by Merwin.
The future of the environment may depend much less on what the scientific community dictates than on the contributions made by individuals
who take a personal stand on the issue and do everything in their power to
make things better. Merwin asks his reader to become involved, to accept
the challenge, to change the world. If we do not aim at something better
than what we have, we will never have anything better and we may end up
with something even worse.

Laurence's "The Loons": Insight or Stereotype?*

F. Smith

Following the main character Vanessa MacLeod's development from the age of eleven to eighteen, Margaret Laurence's short story "The Loons" focuses on the white girl's relationship with a Métis girl named Piquette Tonnerre. Vanessa's attitudes change during the story—from naive romanticism to "embarrassment and pity" (Laurence, "Time" 271) to accepting her share of collective responsibility for Piquette's death. This final change allows the reader to think that Vanessa gains insight into her would-be friend's life, what Laurence herself called "the pain and bewilderment of one's knowledge of other people" (270). But does Laurence actually portray Vanessa as achieving a mature understanding of Piquette and of their relationship by the end of the story? Laurence critics provide a range of answers to this question. Critics Jon Kertzer and Peter Easingwood agree that Vanessa MacLeod grows in understanding, whereas critics Janice Acoose and Tracy Ware lay more emphasis on the persistence of destructive racial stereotypes in Vanessa's views and in the story as a whole. An analysis of characterization, narrative structure, figurative language, and point of view in "The Loons" suggests that, while Laurence shows Vanessa struggling with her conceptions of Piquette and maturing in certain ways, she also demonstrates Vanessa's inability to escape the historical and social limits of her understanding.

Narrative structure and characterization combine to show Vanessa's changing attitudes toward Piquette. Laurence presents the story of the girls' relationship in three key summer incidents separated by four-year intervals. At the beginning of the story, Vanessa is eleven, the white, healthy, well-educated, imaginative daughter of a doctor; Piquette is older, having "failed several grades" ("The Loons" 259), partly because, Vanessa tells us, she spent months in hospital under Dr. MacLeod's care for treatment of tuberculosis of the bone. Piquette is Métis, daughter and granddaughter of "French half-breeds" (258) who live in a ramshackle dwelling and periodically end up in jail for being drunk and disorderly. Although the girls are classmates, they are not friends: to Vanessa, Piquette is little more than "a vaguely embarrassing presence" (259).

1

2

---

* Sample research essay

When Dr. MacLeod arranges for Piquette to accompany the family to   3
their summer cottage at Diamond Lake for health reasons, Vanessa tries
to assimilate Piquette into the worlds she knows, the world of the summer cottage and the world of books. She is too immature to understand
why Piquette refuses to play house (in her mother's absence, Piquette cooks
for the family) or to enter into the romantic fantasies that Vanessa con-
cocts when she discovers that the Tonnerres are actually "Indians, or as
near as made no difference" (261). Laurence underscores Vanessa's inability
to understand Piquette's reality by having Vanessa accept at face value the
excuse Piquette offers: "I thought it was probably her slow and difficult
walking that held her back" (263). When Piquette refuses to be assimilated,
Vanessa retreats first into the cottage world she knows, and then into the
pain of her father's death.

In the next stage of the narrative, Laurence shows Vanessa achieving a   4
more mature understanding of Piquette. When Piquette, now seventeen,
with beautiful eyes and a "soft and slender body" (264), approaches her in
the Regal Café, Vanessa, who knows "a little more than I had that summer
at Diamond Lake" (264), feels at first a mixture of shame, guilt, embarrassment, and contempt. Her observation that Piquette is teetering, but
not because of her tubercular leg, suggests that Piquette has been drinking,
though this may be a product of Vanessa's naive and stereotypical thinking
rather than a fact. Then Piquette reveals that she is about to marry a tall,
handsome, blond guy with a classy name who works in the stockyards in
the city. For a moment Piquette's "defiant face" becomes "unguarded and
unmasked," and in her eyes Vanessa sees a "terrifying hope" (265). For
a moment, Vanessa claims, "I really did see her" (265), without the pre-
conceptions and stereotypes that had clouded their earlier encounter. This
moment of empathy and recognition brings with it this insight: "I could
only guess how great her need must have been, that she had been forced to
seek the very things she so bitterly rejected" (265).

This moment of empathy does not bring the two girls into closer rela-   5
tion, however. Piquette again drops out of Vanessa's consciousness until,
returning from her first year of college, she hears among her mother's bits
of dredged-up gossip that Piquette and her two young children were killed
when the Tonnerre shack caught fire in the winter. Vanessa, receiving this
news with "a kind of silence around the image in my mind of the fire and
the snow," wishes "I could put from my memory the look that I had once
seen in Piquette's eyes" (266). Having seen that look, however, Vanessa cannot blank out Piquette's death as she had blanked out so much of the young
Métis woman's life. While revisiting the lake (now renamed Lake Wapakata

for greater tourist appeal) one evening, Vanessa becomes aware that the loons have vanished under the pressure of human development, as her father had long ago predicted. In Vanessa's mind, as Laurence's language makes clear, the disappearance of the birds is linked with Piquette's death:

> I did not know what had happened to the birds. Perhaps they had gone away to some far place of belonging. Perhaps they had been unable to find such a place, and had simply died out, having ceased to care any longer whether they lived or not. 6
>
> I remembered how Piquette had scorned to come along, when my father and I sat there and listened to the lake birds. It seemed to me now that in some unconscious and totally unrecognised way, Piquette might have been the only one, after all, who had heard the crying of the loons. (266) 7

This is the progression, then, that leads Jon Kertzer to claim in his book 8 *That House in Manawaka* that Vanessa arrives at "understanding and feeling compassion for Piquette's plight" (68). In his article on "The Realism of Laurence's Semi-Autobiographical Fiction," Peter Easingwood makes a similar claim, arguing that Vanessa's maturing understanding is evident in the growth of her "psychological compulsion to question reality" (126). In other words, Easingwood identifies Vanessa's need to question her prejudices, although she has yet to find ways of answering the questions. Read in this way, the story addresses Vanessa's struggle to overcome what she realizes to be unfounded and destructive preconceived ideas about Piquette. Where Kertzer suggests Vanessa has developed compassion, Easingwood claims that she recognizes the need for compassion but has not yet found a way to achieve it. Janice Acoose is not convinced; she maintains that Vanessa's "understanding of reality is filtered through a racist, classist, and male-privileged ideological value system" (79).

Critical debate about Vanessa's perspective centres around the meta- 9 phor of the loons. Vanessa's fascination with the loons is introduced in the first stage of the story, when, unable to interest Piquette in joining her, she sits on the pier with her father to watch the birds rise from their nests and to hear their cry: "Plaintive, and yet with a quality of chilling mockery, those voices belonged to a world separated by aeons from our neat world of summer cottages and the lighted lamps of home" ("The Loons" 262-63). Dr. MacLeod immediately echoes the narrative comment: "'They must have sounded just like that . . . before any person ever set foot here'" (263). When Vanessa tries to make Piquette feel sorry that she hadn't come along, Piquette again refuses the role of "junior prophetess of the wilds" (261), referring to the loons as "a bunch of squawkin' birds" (263). It is this incident Vanessa remembers at the end of the story when she reflects "that in some uncon-scious and totally unrecognised way, Piquette might have been the only one, after all, who had heard the crying of the loons" (266).

This image identifying Piquette with the loons, it can be argued, encap-sulates Vanessa's awareness that Piquette's fate, like that of the loons, is a consequence of the destruction both of nature and of Aboriginal peoples brought about by white settlement, of which she is a part. A number of crit-ics claim that this is a mature vision, a valid moment of powerful empathy. Michelle Gadpaille, for instance, sees this image as "a lament for the passing of an entire way of life among the Indians, epitomized by the haunting call of the loons" (qtd. in Ware 79). However, Tracy Ware, who summarizes the comments of a number of critics on the loons, argues that this symbol-ism "is a misrecognition because it ignores the historical struggles of both Natives and Metis while assigning both to 'a world separated by aeons from our neat world of summer cottages'" (79), along with the loons. Ware's position is shared by Acoose, who claims that indigenous women "have been variously portrayed as creatures of nature . . . or suffering, helpless victims" (74) by non-indigenous writers.

These seem to be valid critiques of the maturity of Vanessa's under-standing. While Vanessa's vision at the end of the story certainly shows more genuine empathy for Piquette than she demonstrated earlier, it does seem to identify the loons as helpless victims of white expansion and mod-ernization and Aboriginal people as "suffering, helpless victims." The impli-cations of this view for actions against Aboriginal people are outlined in Acoose's accounts of the beating, rape and murder of young Aboriginal women (69-70, 85-88); they are also evident in *Stolen from Our Embrace*, Suzanne Fournier and Ernie Crey's chilling account of the abduction of children from Aboriginal communities. Thus Vanessa's final image is not mature in the sense of offering us a vision of Métis and Indian people that moves beyond destructive stereotypes.

Whether Laurence shares this limitation, or "misrecognition" (79), as Ware claims, remains the question. Acoose argues that despite her sym-pathies for the Métis, Laurence does indeed perpetuate destructive stereo-types. Piquette, according to Acoose, is "represented as a victim who is consistently victimized" (79). Laurence, that is, characterizes Piquette as the victim of every possible disadvantage: she is not only racially mixed, socially underprivileged, marginalized from town, and subjected to the kind of racial stereotyping so freely voiced by Vanessa's mother and grandmother but has also suffered from tuberculosis and has been abandoned by her mother to the care of a father and grandfather with drinking problems. This negative stereotyping, Acoose argues, ignores the many positive role models among indigenous people (88).

Assessing the validity of this argument requires an examination of   13
Laurence's use of point of view in the story and a closer look at the images and language of the ending.

In "The Loons," as in the other stories in *A Bird in the House,* the point   14
of view is first person. It is tempting to assume that the story is narrated by eighteen-year-old Vanessa, since she is the focus of its third and final narrative stage. There is also an older narrative voice, however, the voice that in the first paragraph situates both Jules Tonnerre and Vanessa in historical time as it describes the shack built by Jules "some fifty years before, when he came back from Batoche with a bullet in his thigh, the year that Riel was hung and the voices of the Metis entered their long silence" and the shack as it appeared in the thirties, "when I was a child" (258). The presence of this narrative voice contradicts Ware's claim that Laurence shares Vanessa's "misrecognition": Laurence does not "ignore the historical struggles of both Natives and Metis" (Ware 79) but locates the story in relation to them.

This narrative voice recurs at various points in the story, most notice-   15
ably in the final episode. This narrator introduces the crucial moment in this episode by saying, "I went up to Diamond Lake for a few days that summer" (266): "that summer," like the phrase "when I was a child" in the first paragraph, tells us that this narrator is older than the Vanessa who acts in the scene. The language of the final sentence reinforces this distance between older and younger self through its emphasis on the provisional, time-bound quality of this insight: "It *seemed* to me *now* that . . . Piquette *might have been* the only one, after all, who had heard the crying of the loons" (266; italics mine).

This claim that there is critical distance between Laurence and the   16
Vanessa who identifies Piquette with the loons is further supported by a second look at figurative language at the end of the story. On her visit to the lake, Vanessa has avoided the family cottage, sold after her father's death, "not wanting to witness my long-ago kingdom possessed now by strangers" (266). Her "kingdom" has suffered other changes: a "large and solid pier built by the government" (266) has replaced the pier built by her father; stores have proliferated; and the settlement, with its "hotels, a dance hall, cafés with neon signs, the penetrating odours of potato chips and hot dogs" (266), now seems like "a flourishing resort" (266).

It is not only the loons that have disappeared but also the world of   17
Vanessa's childhood and the father who shared that world with her. But just as Vanessa's "distance from her youthful excesses is the source of most

of the [story's] irony" (Ware 76), so Laurence's irony marks the distance between the older narrative voice and the younger Vanessa. The loons' call is twice described as both mocking and plaintive ("The Loons" 262-63, 266). The elegiac tone of the ending suggests that Vanessa at eighteen hears only the plaintive tones. She does not hear the other half, the half that mocks any idea of permanence, whether of people, of places, or of the creatures that predated them both. Given who Vanessa is and the social world she inhabits, Laurence seems to be saying, this is as much understanding as she is capable of at this moment. Laurence's framing of the loon metaphor thus makes it into a social and historical critique of Vanessa's understanding, not an endorsement of it.

This reading of "The Loons" is reinforced by the comments about time   18 that Laurence makes in her essay "Time and the Narrative Voice." What she means by time in fiction, Laurence says, is not "absolute time—which I don't believe to exist," but "historical time, variable and fluctuating" (268). This conception of time is at odds with Easingwood's claim that the story is "an evocation of atmospheric stillness, a momentary glimpse of a way of life belonging to the past which has almost completely disappeared" (124). Although Easingwood demonstrates that Vanessa's romantic vision of Piquette "is spoiled by [her] confrontation with known reality" (124), he nonetheless desires to retain a romantic vision of the past where the "momentary glimpse" fixes the Métis in a misrepresented history. The way of life may belong to the past, but "the pain and bewilderment of one's knowledge of other people" (Laurence, "Time" 270) are like time itself, "variable and fluctuating" (268).

In Laurence's "The Loons," then, point of view and figurative language   19 convey a more critical perspective on the question of the maturity of narrator Vanessa's understanding than initial responses to characterization and narrative structure might suggest. There is good reason to raise issues of destructive stereotyping in relation to the story, as critics Janice Acoose and Tracy Ware do. However, it finally becomes clear that through the story Laurence herself critiques the successive stereotypes that Vanessa employs in trying to understand Piquette. Acoose suggests that instead of presenting negative stereotypes of indigenous people, non-indigenous writers and the media should present strong indigenous role models and the full range of indigenous personalities. It is also possible to do what Laurence does in "The Loons" and critique stereotyping by showing how it operates in a basically sympathetic character who achieves some maturity and awareness, but not enough to overcome the blinkers of family, social status, and relative privilege.

Works Cited

Acoose, Janice. "Fenced In and Forced to Give Up: Images of Indigenous Women in Selected Non-Indigenous Writers' Fiction." *Iskwewak—Kah' Ki Yaw Ni Wahkomakanak: Neither Indian Princesses nor Easy Squaws.* Toronto: Women's Press, 1995. 69-88. Print.

Easingwood, Peter. "The Realism of Laurence's Semi-Autobiographical Fiction." *Critical Approaches to the Fiction of Margaret Laurence.* Ed. Colin Nicholson. Vancouver: U of British Columbia P, 1990. 119-32. Print.

Fournier, Suzanne, and Ernie Crey. *Stolen from Our Embrace: The Abduction of First Nations Children and the Restoration of Aboriginal Communities.* Vancouver: Douglas & McIntyre, 1997. Print.

Kertzer, Jon. *"That House in Manawaka": Margaret Laurence's* A Bird in the House. Toronto: ECW P, 1992. Print.

Laurence, Margaret. "The Loons." *A Bird in the House: Stories.* Toronto: McClelland & Stewart, 1970. 114-27. Print. [Reprinted in Readings 258-66. Page references are to this text.]

——. "Time and the Narrative Voice." *The Narrative Voice.* Ed. John Metcalf. Toronto: McGraw-Hill Ryerson, 1972. 156-60. Print. [Reprinted in Readings 268-72. Page references are to this text.]

Ware, Tracy. "Race and Conflict in Garner's 'One-Two-Three Little Indians' and Laurence's 'The Loons.'" *Studies in Canadian Literature* 23.2 (1998): 71-84. Print.

Nostalgia in Tim Bowling's "Na Na Na Na, Hey Hey Hey, Goodbye"*

C. Stonehouse

Tim Bowling's entertaining essay about NHL hockey, "Na Na Na Na, Hey Hey Hey, Goodbye," is an exploration of the author's own ambivalent attitude toward that sport in Canada. On the one hand, Bowling demonstrates his love and appreciation for the game. On the other hand, however, Bowling recognizes the many real problems that have become inseparable from the culture of hockey in Canada, including corporate ownership and violence. Bowling never really resolves his dilemma about hockey, remaining in a "love/hate" relationship with the game throughout the essay. Interestingly, though, while cataloguing his reasons for and against supporting the game, Bowling generates a feeling of nostalgia. *The Oxford English Dictionary* explains that nostalgia derives from the Greek roots "nostos," meaning "home," and "algia," meaning "pain." M. H. Abrams's *A Glossary of Literary Terms* explains that "nostalgia" is a longing for a past that is pristine and idyllic—like the garden of Eden before the Fall of Adam and Eve. Thus, nostalgia is a painful separation from and longing for one's home, a home that is also construed as one's personal or ancestral past. Bowling's nostalgia for hockey as it was in the past is evident in his references to his own childhood, his linking of hockey to distinctly Canadian icons, and his understanding of hockey as narrative.

Bowling's childhood memories of hockey are tinged with a fondness and a longing that are characteristic of nostalgia. For instance, speaking of his childhood in the early 1960s, Bowling says, "I'd play with hockey cards on the linoleum floor of the kitchen, passing a marble back and forth and re-enacting great goals and saves as my mother clattered dishes in the sink nearby" (211). Bowling's first hockey memory is in his kitchen, the domestic space of home, and Bowling is alongside his mother, a symbol, perhaps, of love, comfort, and belonging. Furthermore, Bowling states, "When I was a boy, the boards, ice and score clock were free of advertising; goals and assists meant more than salaries; and players and teams had distinct characters" (215). Here, hockey in Bowling's childhood is understood as pristine, untouched, and not yet corrupted by corporate culture.

1

2

---

* Sample analysis essay

This vision of hockey in Bowling's past is contrasted with a present day hockey game at which "you're . . . bombarded with supersonic noise and flashing lights and company logos" (215). Bowling's recollection of playing hockey with marbles on his kitchen floor is nostalgic in that it exemplifies a longing for home, domesticity, and love; his recollection of the blank "boards, ice and score clock" (215) is nostalgic in its description as pure and idyllic: hockey has not yet fallen into the corruption of corporate takeover and violence.

Bowling's nostalgia for the old-fashioned game of hockey is not only evident in the description of his childhood but also in his linking of hockey to Canadian icons. For example, Bowling mentions the instance in which Canadian icemakers placed a loonie under the ice at the 2002 Winter Olympic Games in Salt Lake City, and he notes that Team Canada won the gold medal that year (214). Here, the loonie—the Canadian one-dollar coin—stands for Canada, the home to which the players will bring back the gold medal. Team Canada is away from and yet linked to the nation to which it belongs. Moreover, Bowling states that his absence from watching NHL hockey is "like fasting after binging on double-doubles and maple creams down at the local Tim Hortons" (215). Bowling compares watching hockey to eating Tim Hortons' doughnuts, and so links one Canadian reference (hockey) with another (Tim Hortons' doughnuts). In this case, Bowling longs to watch hockey just as he longs to binge on maple creams. His separation from both hockey and doughnuts is pained.

Bowling's nostalgia can be noted in the way he associates hockey with narrative or story. Bowling states that he is compelled to watch NHL hockey because of "the primal pull of narrative" (212). Like the constructed and idyllic story of one's nostalgic past, this narrative is "primal"—the first or original story—and "pull[s]" one into it, seemingly against one's own will. Bowling says that the NHL is "the Great Canadian Novel, a tale replete with villains and heroes, prima donnas and blue collar types, triumph and failure, hope and revenge" (212). He gives examples of moments in that narrative: "six out of seven Sutter brothers from Viking, Alberta, made the big time and Bobby Clarke overcame diabetes to realize his professional dreams" (213). Thus, Canadian hockey is a soap opera, a page-turner that Bowling cannot put down. Like nostalgia, the author has a fondness for it and feels pain at his separation from it. When Bowling goes to a theatre to watch the film *Howards End* instead of watching game seven of the Stanley Cup, what he really wants to do is come home and watch the narrative of his own home-grown Canadian hockey. Bowling finally notices the extremity of his obsession with the Canadian hockey story. Upon leaving the theatre, he pulls a group of teenagers aside, only to find that they do not know the results of the game (212). Bowling must wrench himself away from his nostalgia to "begin the process of cultural de-programming that would find [him], a decade later, completely indifferent to the labour dispute between the NHL team owners and players" (212).

At the end of his essay, Bowling asks, "Can I resist the lure of *nostalgia*   5 and the pull of narrative?" (215, my emphasis). This statement is the only one in which Bowling mentions the word "nostalgia," but the notion of nostalgia is prevalent throughout his essay. From his recollection of child-hood memories of hockey, which include domestic and motherly images, to his linking of hockey to Canadian national icons, to his connection of hockey to narrative, Bowling wishes to come back to a past in which hockey was free from corruption, a past which was also supposedly idyllic, innocent, and comforting. Perhaps Bowling's desire is typical of twenty-first century Canadians who remember or have heard about their ancestor pioneers. Bowling's "Na Na Na Na, Hey Hey Hey, Goodbye" is not just an exploration of the author's reasons for liking or disliking the game of hockey: it is an engagement with the fond memories of his past, an engage-ment that might apply, in one way or another, to many Canadians.

Works Cited

Abrams, M. H. *A Glossary of Literary Terms*. 8th ed. Boston: Thomson, 2005. Print.

Bowling, Tim. "Na Na Na Na, Hey Hey Hey, Goodbye." *Alberta Views* Dec. 2005-Jan. 2006: 46-49. Print. [Reprinted in Readings 211-16. Page references are to this text.]

Paperback Oxford English Dictionary. 6th ed. Oxford: Oxford UP, 2006. Print.

Tone in William Carlos Williams's "This Is Just to Say"*

L. Strong

William Carlos Williams presents his poem "This Is Just to Say" (Rhetoric 86) as a casual note of apology most likely written from one lover to another. Although the poem is deceptively simple, Williams leaves it open to different signifying possibilities that complicate the tone. If we read the poem on a simplistic level, we can perceive the speaker's tone as casual yet honest—in an informal manner, the speaker shows his honesty by admitting his wrong. If we read the poem with scrutiny, we can perceive the speaker's tone as vengeful and haughty—the speaker teases his lover by acknowledging not only that he can freely eat the plums but also that he can skilfully use rhetoric to justify the act and earn forgiveness. 1

The word "this," in the title of the poem, is open to more than one possible meaning. It can refer either to the note of apology or to the act of eating the plums. If we read "this" as a reference to the note, then the speaker's tone is either honest or haughty: he either leaves the note because he wants to admit his wrong or because he wants to declare his action and thus tease his lover. If we read "this" as a reference to the act of eating the plums, then the speaker's tone is vengeful: he eats the plums as a statement of vengeance toward his lover. Similarly, the word "just," also in the title, is open to more than one possibility. It can mean *merely*, or it can mean *legally valid* or *fair*. If we read "just" as a synonym for *merely*, then the speaker takes a casual tone: he implies that his act and the note are not very important. If we read "just" as *legally valid*, then the speaker is saying "this is fair to say"—the tone is then one of retribution. Hence, the tone of the title alters between honest, haughty, casual, and vengeful according to the way in which we read the words "this" and "just." 2

The phrase "forgive me," in the final stanza of the poem, is also open to a number of signifying possibilities: we can read the phrase in a simplistic way as an honest plea; we can read it ironically, as though the speaker taunts his lover by temporarily taking a formal tone rather than a casual one; or we can read it as an appeal for forgiveness that is cuttingly undermined because it is juxtaposed with the lines "they were delicious / so sweet / and 3

---

* Sample essay on literature

so cold" (10–12). The latter reading is perhaps the most interesting. The phrase "forgive me" momentarily privileges obligation over temptation; by following it with a description of the taste and feel of the plums, however, the speaker ultimately takes a snide tone—he cleverly nullifies his wrong by justifying the sensual. Thus, like the words "this" and "just" in the title of the poem, the tone of the phrase "forgive me" varies. We can read it as honest, ironic, or snide.

Although Williams presents his poem as a note of apology, he also presents it as a poem that appears in his collection of poems. What is Williams's purpose in presenting this poem as a piece of literature? In order to answer this question, we may view the poet in the same way that we view the speaker. Like the speaker, the poet creates a seemingly simple work that relays a casual and honest tone, as if the poem can precisely depict and justify the meaning of a particular incident. Essentially, however, he creates a complex piece of literature in which the tone is dependent upon the way we read the words. Williams thus comments on the power of language. We accept words as justifications for action, even though "just saying" is only saying. Perhaps "this" poem then, is "just to say" that there is no single truth or ideal justice that language can express.   4

Handbook for Final Editing

(Part 3)

A Final Editing: The Process

A1 Strategies for Final Editing

Final editing is the last stage of the writing process, your last chance to eliminate the kinds of errors that can distract and annoy your reader. Here are some tips.

1. Wait at least a day after you have finished writing your essay. If you try to edit immediately, you will miss errors.

2. Use a spell-checker and other editing software to pick up errors. Then print out a hard copy and edit it. You will notice errors that you missed onscreen.

3. Read your essay aloud. You or your listener will notice awkward sentences, lack of transitions, and other problems that you might overlook on the page.

4. Make a list of the kinds of errors you frequently make (such as problems with pronoun agreement, apostrophes, and commas) and watch particularly for them.

5. Begin editing with the last sentence in your conclusion. Read each sentence separately and work your way back to the first sentence in your introduction. This procedure will help you to see what you have actually written, not what you have memorized.

The chart on the following pages lists in alphabetical order the most common errors in sentence structure, grammar, mechanics, and format. This chart also includes common marking symbols, an example of each error, and page references to explanations and exercises in the handbook. When you get an essay back, note your errors on the chart and keep the chart handy when you edit your next essay.

A2 Identifying Common Problems

Term	Marking Symbol	Example of Common Error (bold indicates error to be corrected)	Page Reference
abbreviation	*Abbrev*	The **pres.** of the company will visit **AB & SK** this **yr.**	464
adjective form	*Adj*	Skirmish was the **most ugliest** dog.	397
adverb form	*Adv*	Skirmish barked **real** loud.	397
apostrophe	⟨'⟩ *Apos*	We offer exciting **childrens'** programs.	444
capitalization	*Caps*	My **Mother** and I lived in the **north.**	463
colon	⊙ /ː\	The camp offered activities such **as:** canoeing, swimming, and tennis.	453
comma	⟨'⟩ /\	Bill enjoys **tennis,** and football.	447
comma splice, comma fault	*CS, CF*	Loons are an endangered **species, pollution** is destroying their habitat.	415
dangling modifier	*DM*	**After running a marathon,** exhaustion is inevitable.	399
dash	⊖ \∕	The storm ripped and scattered all the shingles—**on the new roof.**	454
diction	*Dic*	Alison decided **to partake** in the game.	436
documentation	*Doc*	Macbeth echoes the witches' opening words when he says, "So foul and fair a day I have not seen." **(No in-text citation)**	478
essay format	*EF*	**Gender stereotypes in *Macbeth*.**	466
faulty coordination	*F Coord*	Adam was terrified **and** he burst into laughter.	405
faulty subordination	*F Subord*	**Although** Irene wanted to stop smoking, **however,** she lacked the willpower.	406
fragment	*SF, Frag*	**Which is the main reason for Allan's success.**	414
fused sentence	*FS*	The baby is **hot she** must have a fever.	417
hyphen	⊖ \∕	The **well^prepared** athlete must be mentally and physically fit.	461
italics	*Ital.*	This summer I read Tolstoy's **War and Peace.**	458
misplaced modifier	*MM*	I **hardly** have any money.	399
mixed construction	*Mix*	One reason he is often late **is because** his car has chronic battery problems.	418
numbers	*Num*	**15** employees were fired; **three hundred and forty seven** went on strike.	463

Term	Marking Symbol	Example of Common Error (bold indicates error to be corrected)	Page Reference
parallelism	*//ism*	Our servers must be hard-working, intelligent, **and they can't insult the customers.**	402
parentheses	*(/) (/)*	During the second period, **(the** fans were holding their **breath,)** our team scored.	455
passive voice	*Passive*	After **the ghost was seen by Hamlet,** he hated his uncle more intensely.	395
possessive pronouns	*P Poss*	The jury made **it's** decision.	384
pronoun agreement	*P Agr*	**Every student** must check **their** bag at the door.	385
pronouns of address	*P Add P Shift*	By the end of the movie, **you** could see that the hero had matured.	433
pronoun case	*P Case*	**Her** and I have been married almost twelve years.	382
pronoun reference	*P Ref*	Fred doesn't know whether to get married or join the navy **which** makes him uneasy.	387
quotation format	*Quot F*	Hamlet's despair is clear when he says, **"O that this . . . into a dew."**	474
quotation introduction	*Quot*	^ "The woods are lovely, dark and deep." The speaker wants to rest.	471
quotation marks	*(") \"/*	Mio liked Munro's story **Boys and Girls.**	456
semicolon	*(;) /;*	When the movie **ended;** the audience burst into applause.	451
sentence length and structure	*S Var*	**Hamlet misses his father. He is angry at his mother. He hates his uncle.**	423
spelling	*Sp ( )*	Elizabeth was **to** angry to speak.	460
split infinitive	*Split*	The rebels struggled **to strongly resist** the government forces.	399
subject–verb agreement	*S/V Agr*	The director's **use** of gimmicky special effects **were attacked** by the critics.	393
transitions	*Trans*	Peter wants to lose **weight.** ^ **He** refuses to diet.	426
usage/wrong word	*WW*	Houdini was a master of **allusion.**	438
verb forms	*VF*	After Sophy **had drank** the last beer, she **laid** on the couch and fell asleep.	389
verb tenses	*T, Tense*	Hamlet **grieves** for his father, but he **concealed** his feelings.	392
wordiness	*Wordy*	**Due to the fact that** the tickets sold out in the first half hour, many fans were disappointed.	423

B Grammar: Parts of Speech

A language is a system of communication in which the parts work together to produce messages understood by both sender(s) and receiver(s). In traditional approaches to grammar, English words are divided into eight categories according to their function in sentences. These categories are referred to as **parts of speech**. In this chapter we discuss the eight parts of speech in five sections: Nouns; Pronouns; Verbs; Adjectives and Adverbs; and Conjunctions, Prepositions, and Interjections.

Just as you can drive a car without being able to describe all its parts and how they operate, so you can speak and write English without knowing all about parts of speech. When your car breaks down or starts running rough, however, you need at least a little knowledge to get it fixed. That's also the case with language. Some basic understanding of the parts of speech will help you to avoid or correct problems with grammar, sentence structure, and punctuation. Without these distractions, you and your reader can focus on the act of communication.

B1 Nouns

A **noun** is a word that names a person, place, or thing.

1a Common Nouns and Proper Nouns

Common nouns, which are not capitalized except in special circumstances, refer to objects as members of a class. **Proper nouns**, which are always capitalized, refer to a specific person, place, or thing.

COMMON NOUNS	PROPER NOUNS
baby	Suzie
park	Elk Island Park
toy	Lego

For more on capitalization, see G3b Capitalization.

1b Concrete Nouns and Abstract Nouns

Concrete nouns, such as those in the lists on the previous page, refer to objects with an external physical existence. **Abstract nouns** refer to ideas, feelings, and concepts, such as justice, frustration, and Einstein's theory of relativity. The terms *abstract* and *concrete* are not pigeonholes into which every word must fit; they are end points on a continuum, as the example below illustrates.

MOST CONCRETE	MOST ABSTRACT
Barkley, beagle, dog, pet	animal, living thing

Both concrete and abstract nouns have their place in good writing. Concrete nouns will anchor your writing in the everyday world your readers share. Much of the power of W. S. Merwin's essay "Unchopping a Tree" (Readings), for example, comes from his use of concrete nouns: *leaves, twigs, nests.* He doesn't make vague statements about the destruction of the environment; he makes us *see* the impact of our actions. If your writing tends to be vague, check whether you can make your language more concrete.

Abstract nouns, on the other hand, allow us to put concrete experience within a broader framework. In "Shooting an Elephant" (Readings), for instance, George Orwell places his encounter with a rogue elephant within the context of imperialism. Without the context provided by this abstract idea, the essay would lack the depth that has kept it relevant for more than seventy years. In the sections on gathering material in this text, you will find suggestions for how to arrive at the categories—the abstract level of thinking—that will give your writing a broader meaning.

Exercise 1

Circle the abstract nouns in the following paragraph. Then rewrite the paragraph to create a better balance between abstract nouns and concrete nouns. Add specific examples to illustrate your points.

> Pets contribute a great deal to people's sense of well-being. Pets make people feel safe in their environment. Pets also provide entertainment. They create a sense of attachment to the world because people have to provide for their needs.

1c Singular Nouns, Plural Nouns, and Collective Nouns

Singular nouns refer to one person, place, or thing. **Plural nouns** refer to more than one person, place, or thing.

SINGULAR	PLURAL
deer	deer
girl	girls
box	boxes
baby	babies
man	men

These examples illustrate the most common ways of making singular nouns into plural nouns. If you are unsure of the plural form of a noun, check a dictionary.

Note: It is important to understand the difference between the singular and plural form of nouns and the possessive form, which indicates *belonging to.*

Singular	Singular Possessive	Plural	Plural Possessive
society	society's	societies	societies'

For guidelines on forming possessives, see F1b Using Apostrophes to Show Possession.

   Collective nouns are words that refer to a group, such as *band, committee, company, herd, team.* If the collective noun refers to the group acting as a unit, it is considered singular (*The band plays every night*). If the collective noun refers to the group members acting as individuals, it is considered plural (*The band disagree about getting a new manager*). Collective nouns also have plural forms that refer to more than one group: *bands, committees, companies, herds, teams.*

   Being able to recognize singular, plural, and possessive forms of nouns will help you with spelling, subject–verb agreement (see B3c), and pronoun agreement (see B2b).

Exercise 2

Put C beside the collective nouns in the following list. Then give the plural form of each collective noun you labelled.

1. woman	4. goose	7. flock	10. match
2. party	5. cactus	8. foot	11. company
3. family	6. potato	9. sock	12. squid

NOUNS

1d Uses of Nouns

Understanding the two basic uses of nouns will help you to identify and correct errors in sentence structure and grammar.

Nouns as subjects A sentence must have two basic components: a **verb**, which names the action or state of being (see B3), and a **subject**, which tells who or what performs the action or manifests the state of being. The subject will be a noun or pronoun (for pronouns as subjects, see B2a). In the most common sentence pattern in English, the subject comes before the verb.

> Rain [subject noun] fell [verb].
>
> The committee [subject noun] is meeting [verb].

In some cases the subject will appear after the verb.

> Here (there) are [verb] three books [subject noun].
>
> Through the open window came [verb] the wail [subject noun] of a siren.

Two or more nouns joined by a conjunction (see B5a) may function as the subject of a verb.

> Sunil and Misha [subject nouns] are [verb] angry.
>
> Neither reward nor punishment [subject nouns] improved [verb] the dog's behaviour.

To find the subject of a sentence, first locate the verb or verbs. Then ask yourself who or what performed the action or manifested the state of being.

Note: When the verb is in the passive voice, the subject is the thing acted upon rather than the agent of the action or state of being.

> Active voice: The dog [subject] bit the letter carrier.
>
> Passive voice: The letter carrier [subject] was bitten by the dog.

For more on active and passive voice, see B3d Active and Passive Voice.

Nouns as objects Nouns also function as **objects** in various grammatical constructions. While you are unlikely to make mistakes in using nouns as objects, understanding the difference between subjects and objects will help you with subject–verb agreement (see B3c) and with pronouns (see B2b).

Direct object A direct object is defined as one or more nouns or pronouns that follow the verb and receive its action.

> Subject-verb-direct object
>
> [who or what] did [who or what]
>
> Jamal [subject] hit [verb] the puck [direct object].
>
> His line [subject] scored [verb] three goals [direct object] and killed off [verb] two penalties [direct object].

Indirect object An indirect object answers the question "to whom or what?" about the direct object, without the use of *to*. The indirect object comes before the direct object.

> The father [subject] gave [verb] the baby [indirect object] a cookie [direct object].
>
> The librarian [subject] sent [verb] the interlibrary loan service [indirect object] a request [direct object] for four books.

Object of a preposition The noun or pronoun that ends a prepositional phrase and completes its meaning is called the object of the preposition. (For more on prepositions, see B5b.)

> The woman with the <u>sunglasses</u> [object of the preposition *with*] is my aunt.
>
> The soldiers fought for their <u>country</u> and their <u>lives</u> [objects of the preposition *for*].

Note: Do not confuse the object of a preposition with the subject of a sentence. The subject of a sentence never appears in a prepositional phrase. Make sure the verb agrees with the subject.

> The team [subject] with the best scores [object of the preposition] wins [not *win*] the tournament.

Exercise 3

The verbs in the following sentences have been underlined for you. Circle nouns used as subjects. Put square brackets [ ] around nouns used as objects.

1. Down the street <u>march</u> the bands in the Rose Bowl parade.

2. There <u>are</u> seventy-six trombones in the big parade.

3. Flutes and drums also <u>twitter</u> and <u>bang</u>.

4. The twins <u>play</u> trumpet.

5. In front of each band, baton twirlers <u>strut</u> their stuff.

B2 Pronouns

A **pronoun** is a word that takes the place of a noun, usually when the noun has already been mentioned and repeating it would be awkward.

> Scientists created a megavirus.
>
> *They* [pronoun] accidentally let *it* [pronoun] escape from the lab.

2a Uses of Pronouns: Pronoun Case

Personal pronouns Since pronouns take the place of nouns, they serve the same primary functions in sentences: as subjects and as objects. As you can see from the following chart, however, most subject pronouns have different forms from the equivalent object pronouns.

	SUBJECT PRONOUNS		OBJECT PRONOUNS		POSSESSIVE FORM
	Singular	*Plural*	*Singular*	*Plural*	
First person	I	we	me	us	my, mine/ our, ours
Second person	you	you	you	you	your, yours
Third person	he, she, it	they	him, her, it	them	his, her, hers, its/their, theirs

If you use a subject pronoun where you should use an object pronoun, or vice versa, you have made an error in **pronoun case**.

Uses of subject pronouns

1. To replace nouns in the subject position of the sentence.

   NOT   Her and me went to a movie.

   BUT   She and I went to a movie.

Note: Errors in pronoun case often occur when only one subject noun is replaced by a pronoun.

   NOT   My brother and me bought a car together.

   BUT   My brother and I bought a car together.

2. When the subject pronoun is followed by an explanatory noun.

   NOT   Us students were enraged by the exam.

   BUT   We students were enraged by the exam.

3. After comparisons using *than* and *as*.

> NOT   The other team is weaker than us.
>
> BUT   The other team is weaker than we [are].

4. As the subject of a subordinate clause beginning with *that*.

> NOT   Mr. Ramsay said that him and his sister had rented the house on the corner.
>
> BUT   Mr. Ramsay said that he and his sister had rented the house on the corner.

Uses of object pronouns

1. As the object of a verb.

> NOT   The coach told Rajiv and he to come early.
>
> BUT   The coach told Rajiv and him to come early.

2. After a preposition.

> NOT   The manager left a message for my roommate and I.
>
> BUT   The manager left a message for my roommate and me.

Notes: (1) *Me* is not an informal form of *I*. *Me* is a perfectly acceptable object pronoun. (2) Don't substitute *myself* for *me* when you need an object pronoun.

> NOT   Please contact either the supervisor or myself if you have problems.
>
> BUT   Please contact either the supervisor or me if you have problems.

Relative pronouns   In addition to the personal pronouns, there are six **relative pronouns**: *that, which, who, whoever, whom, whomever*. These pronouns can link a subordinate clause (see C1d) to the preceding noun or pronoun.

That and *which* can be used as either subject or object pronouns.

> The hand that rocks the cradle rules the world.
>
> Toshimi bought a pound of tea, which she gave to a friend.

Who and *whoever* are subject pronouns. Use them to replace or refer to a subject noun.

> Dr. Wong is the distinguished biologist. She will give the opening address.
>
> Dr. Wong is the distinguished biologist who will give the opening address.
>
> Someone has the best cards. That person will win the poker game.
>
> Whoever has the best cards will win the poker game.

Whom and *whomever* are object pronouns. Use them to refer to an object noun.

> Claudius is a smooth politician. Hamlet distrusts him.
>
> Claudius is a smooth politician whom Hamlet distrusts.

You may invite the people you wish to invite.

You may invite whomever you wish to invite.

As these examples suggest, you can check your usage of *who/whoever* and *whom/whomever* by substituting an appropriate personal pronoun.

You may invite [they/them] if you wish to invite [they/them].

If you would use *them* rather than *they*, then you should choose the object pronoun *whomever* rather than the subject pronoun *whoever*.

You will find guidelines for punctuating clauses beginning with a relative pronoun in F2e Non-restrictive and Restrictive Modifiers.

Exercise 4

Revise the following sentences to correct all errors in pronoun case. Put C beside a correct sentence.

1. For now, let's keep this plan a secret between you and I.

2. Caterina said that her and Bill might get married this summer.

3. Give the money to whoever you like.

4. Us residents strongly oppose the increase in property taxes.

5. Luis has consistently put more effort into this project than she.

6. Direct all complaints to the caretaker or myself.

7. My youngest sister, whom lives in Ontario, is a painter.

8. Her and her mom fight all the time.

9. Nobody works harder than us.

10. The person who finishes first gets to leave early.

Possessive pronouns When you want to show ownership, use these possessive pronouns: *my/mine, our/ours, your/yours, his, her/hers, its, their/theirs, whose*. Remember that possessive pronouns do not take apostrophes.

1. Don't confuse the possessive pronoun *its* with the contraction *it's* (it is).

    POSSESSIVE The board has made its ruling.

    CONTRACTION It's obvious that no one was listening.

2. Don't confuse the possessive pronoun *whose* with the contraction *who's* (who is).

    POSSESSIVE We must decide whose responsibility this is.

    CONTRACTION Who's responsible for this?

3. Don't confuse the possessive pronoun *their* with the dummy subject *there* or the contraction *they're*.

> POSSESSIVE The Inuit in the region are close to settling their land claim.
>
> DUMMY SUBJECT There are still a few issues to be resolved.
>
> CONTRACTION They're close to signing a treaty.

4. Don't confuse the possessive pronoun *your* with the contraction *you're*.

> POSSESSIVE Don't forget to put your signature on the expense claim.
>
> CONTRACTION If you don't hurry, you're going to be late.

Exercise 5

Revise the following sentences to eliminate all errors in the use of possessive pronouns.

1. The company management has stated it's final position on the union's proposal.

2. If your satisfied with this offer, then we will accept it.

3. We still don't know whose going to teach this class.

4. Luigi and Caterina devoted all of there attention to running the pet store.

5. That beautiful cottage on the shore of the lake is their's.

2b Pronoun Agreement

Pronouns must agree in number with the nouns to which they refer. Singular pronouns must replace or refer back to a singular noun; plural pronouns must replace or refer back to plural nouns. This rule applies to possessive pronouns as well as to subject and object pronouns. If nouns and pronouns do not agree in number, there is an error in **pronoun agreement.**

Most pronoun agreement errors occur in these contexts:

1. When the noun refers to a type of person: *the patient, the student, the player.* You can correct this error by making the subject plural.

> NOT   The first-year student may have problems adjusting to their new freedom.
>
> BUT   First-year students may have problems adjusting to their new freedom.

2. When a singular noun is followed by a prepositional phrase ending with a plural noun (*of the workers, of the children*).

> NOT   One of the children left their lunch on the kitchen table.
>
> BUT   One of the children left his lunch on the kitchen table.
>
> OR   One of the children left her lunch on the kitchen table.

3. When the writer is trying to avoid gender bias. If you don't want to imply that a singular subject (*the single parent, the nurse, the engineer*) is always male or female, you may make errors in pronoun agreement.

> *Every doctor* these days complains that paperwork encroaches on the time *they* can spend with their patients.

Although this error in pronoun agreement is gradually becoming more acceptable, you may want to avoid it with these strategies.

a. Make the subject plural (*single parents, nurses, engineers*).

b. Use *him or her, he or she* (never *he/she* or *s/he*) to refer to a singular subject.

> Typically, a two-year-old will insist that he or she be the focus of all attention.

This strategy works well in a single sentence but becomes cumbersome in a longer piece of writing.

c. Rewrite the sentence to avoid pronouns.

> Typically, a two-year-old insists on being the focus of all attention.

d. Refer to the subject with masculine pronouns in one paragraph and feminine pronouns in the next.

4. When the subject is an indefinite pronoun. In formal writing, use singular pronouns to refer to *each* and to words that end with *–body, –one*, and *–thing: anybody, everybody, nobody; anyone, everyone, no one; anything, everything, nothing.*

> INFORMAL SPOKEN Everyone wanted to have their picture taken.
>
> FORMAL WRITTEN Everyone at the convention wanted his or her vote on this issue recorded.

5. When the subject is a collective noun (see B1c). If the sentence indicates unanimous action, the collective noun takes a singular verb and singular pronouns. If the sentence indicates members of the group acting individually, the collective noun takes a plural verb and plural pronouns.

> The committee is circulating the minutes of its [not *their*] last meeting.
>
> The committee were fighting over the size of their [not *its*] bonuses.

Exercise 6

Correct all the errors in pronoun agreement in the following sentences.

1. When a firm meets government pollution emission standards, their expenses increase.

2. The steelworker wants to have some control over their working conditions.

3. A cancer patient may be misled by quack cures that seem to promise them miraculous results.

4. The House of Commons said that they will enforce new security measures. Everyone entering the building will be searched to determine whether they are carrying firearms.

5. Because it loses less energy than copper wire, fibres are used to transmit thousands of signals simultaneously in enormous bandwidths.

2c Pronoun Reference

Errors in pronoun reference occur whenever a pronoun does not clearly refer to a specific noun. Here are some ways to correct ambiguous pronouns.

1. Keep the pronoun close to the noun to which it refers.

> NOT Luigi told George that he was a terrible baseball player. He was furious.
>
> BUT George was furious because Luigi called him a terrible baseball player.
>
> OR Because Luigi was furious, he called George a terrible baseball player.

2. Use pronouns to refer only to nouns or pronouns, not to possessive adjectives such as *his, her, Shakespeare's.*

> James snapped the guitar's neck that belonged to his mother.

In this sentence, *that* refers to the guitar's neck, an error suggesting that only the guitar's neck belonged to James's mother. The next sentence shows how you could make clear that the whole guitar belonged to James's mother.

> James snapped the neck of his mother's guitar.

3. Make sure *that, this,* and *which* refer to a specific noun or pronoun, not to the idea in the preceding sentence or clause. Clarify vague pronoun references by rewriting the sentence or supplying the missing noun or pronoun.

> NOT He did not know whether she would leave or wait for him. This made him anxious.
>
> BUT He did not know whether she would leave or wait for him. This uncertainty made him anxious.
>
> OR He was anxious because he did not know whether she would leave or wait for him.

4. Do not use *they* to refer to people in general or to the author of a text.

> NOT They said hurricanes are affected by the rain cycles in Africa.
>
> BUT Meteorologists say hurricanes are affected by the rain cycles in Africa.

NOT	They say in Shaw's play *Major Barbara* that the only crime is poverty.
BUT	In Shaw's play *Major Barbara*, Undershaft says that the only crime is poverty.

5. Do not use *it* or *they* to refer to an implied subject. Supply the missing noun or rewrite the sentence.

NOT	I spent two weeks studying for the exam, but it didn't improve my grade.
BUT	I spent two weeks studying for the exam, but this effort did not improve my grade.
OR	Two weeks of studying for the exam did not improve my grade.
NOT	I wrote to the Canada Revenue Agency about my income tax assessment, but they have not yet replied.
BUT	I wrote to the Canada Revenue Agency about my income tax assessment, but the taxation officials have not yet replied.
OR	I have not yet received a reply to my letter to the Canada Revenue Agency about my income tax assessment.

Exercise 7

Revise the following sentences to eliminate ambiguous pronoun references.

1. An important part of being a successful goalie is building up a determination to defend the net. It must occupy his or her complete attention.

2. Many people who renovate to make their houses more energy efficient are unaware that it will increase their property value and are surprised when they assess their property for increased taxes.

3. Gradually the public began to accept the theory of evolution, which forced the clergy into less vocal opposition.

4. She left flowers in the teacher's office who had been such a help to her.

5. The two children hid their margarine sandwiches from their classmates because they were ashamed to let them see how poor they were.

Review Exercise 1

Revise this paragraph to eliminate errors in pronoun agreement and ambiguous pronoun references.

There are serious problems with the way the province administers health care to their citizens. Both consumers and providers are frustrated with the way it is run. They agree that waiting lists are too long and that life-saving treatment is being rationed based on a person's medical history and their future usefulness to society. Doctors and other health care professionals have fled to the United States, which is more lucrative and less stressful. A patient with enough money may also seek treatment for their medical problems in the United States. The provincial government has imposed stringent cost-cutting measures for several years, and now they promise it will improve again. Given these problems, it is easy to see why they are proposing throwing out the old system and implementing a new one, which is what some people in the medical, political, and general communities want.

B3 Verbs

A **verb** is a word that expresses action, existence, possession, or sensation.

> He *plays* hockey. (Action)
>
> I *am* here. (Existence)
>
> You *have* the measles. (Possession)
>
> The bread *smells* mouldy. (Sensation)

A **verb phrase** is made up of the main verb plus one or more **auxiliary (helping) verbs** that indicate time or condition.

> He *is playing/has been playing* hockey.
>
> I *may be/might have been* here.
>
> Do you have the measles? Soon we will have the measles.
>
> The bread *should* not *smell* mouldy.

Here is a list of the most common auxiliary verbs:

1. forms of *to be: am, is, are, was, were, be, been, being*
2. forms of *to have: have, has, had, having*
3. forms of *to do: do, does, did, done*
4. others: *can, could, may, might, must, shall, will, should, would, ought to, have to, supposed to, used to*

To name a verb, give its infinitive form, as in the list of auxiliary verbs above: *to run, to listen*.

3a Principal Parts of Verbs

Principal parts of regular verbs Regular verbs, as their name suggests, form their principal parts in a regular, predictable way. The four main parts of a verb are the present tense, the past tense (formed by adding *–ed* to the present tense), the present participle (formed by adding *–ing* to the present tense), and the past participle (formed by adding the appropriate form of the auxiliary verb *to have* to the past tense).

The present tense usually expresses habitual action (Every day I *walk* to school), whereas the present participle is used with an auxiliary to express ongoing action (I *am walking* to school now). The simple past expresses action that began and ended in the past (I *lived* in Toronto for five years). The past participle expresses action that began in the past and continues to the present (I *have lived* in Canada for twenty years) or action that ended before a subsequent event (I *had lived* in Germany before I came to Canada).

PRESENT	PAST	PRESENT PARTICIPLE	PAST PARTICIPLE
walk	walked	walking	walked
fill	filled	filling	filled

Principal parts of irregular verbs Irregular verbs form their principal parts in various unpredictable ways. Here are three different patterns of irregular verbs.

PRESENT	PAST	PRESENT PARTICIPLE	PAST PARTICIPLE
drink	drank	drinking	drunk
burst	burst	bursting	burst
steal	stole	stealing	stolen

The present participle of irregular verbs is always formed by adding *–ing* to the present tense. It's the past tense and the past participle that may cause problems. You need either to memorize these forms or to check your dictionary. Here are some of the most troublesome irregular verbs to watch for in your writing.

Principal parts of troublesome verbs

INFINITIVE	PAST TENSE	PAST PARTICIPLE
to be	was	been
to break	broke	broken
to choose	chose	chosen
to come	came	come
to cost	cost	cost
to go	went	gone
to lay (place)	laid	laid
to lie (recline)	lay	lain
to hang (a person)	hanged	hanged

INFINITIVE	PAST TENSE	PAST PARTICIPLE
to hang (a picture)	hung	hung
to lead	led	led
to rise	rose	risen

Note 1: Don't confuse *lose* and *loose*.

> NOT   She is afraid that she will loose her mind.
>
> BUT   She is afraid that she will lose her mind.

Note 2: Be sure to add the past tense ending to *use* and *suppose* when they are followed by an infinitive.

> NOT   Rosa use to play soccer.
>
> BUT   Rosa used to play soccer.
>
> NOT   Alix is suppose to make dinner.
>
> BUT   Alix is supposed to make dinner.

Note 3: In speech, the contractions for "would have" (*would've*) and "should have" (*should've*) sound like "would of" and "should of." These forms are never correct.

> NOT   You should of seen *The Lord of the Rings*.
>
> BUT   You should have seen *The Lord of the Rings*.

Exercise 8

Correct any errors in verb usage in the following sentences. Put C beside a correct sentence.

1. Because he had laid in the sun all afternoon, he was horribly sunburnt.

2. I'll put my money in a safe place so I won't loose it.

3. After three months in her new job, she still wasn't sure what she was suppose to do.

4. When the soldiers surrendered, they laid down their weapons in the sand.

5. The car loan costed more than he had anticipated.

6. I need to borrow your vacuum cleaner because mine is broke.

7. The clues have lead the detective straight to the murder suspect.

8. I have a headache, so I think I'll lay down for an hour.

9. Their bubble of happiness finally burst.

10. After she had drank all of the magic potion, she suddenly felt very tall.

VERBS

VERBS

3b Verb Tenses

Verb tenses indicate the *time* of existence, action, possession, or sensation. The basic tenses in English are the present, past, and future. The tenses used in a sentence or series of sentences must accurately indicate the time relationships involved.

> She walks to the door. She opens her umbrella. She leaves. (All verbs in the present tense)
>
> She walked to the door. She opened her umbrella. She left. (All verbs in the past tense)
>
> When she finishes her meal [present tense], she will walk to the door, open her umbrella, and leave [future tense]. (Change in tense necessary to indicate time relationships)

Unnecessary shifts in tense Unnecessary shifts in tense occur when the verb forms do not correspond to the time relationships. In the following sentence, the tense shifts are confusing.

> When she finished her meal, she walks to the door, opens her umbrella, and will leave.

If you are caught up in the ideas you are trying to convey, you may switch from present to past or vice versa without noticing. These suggestions will help you keep your tenses consistent.

1. When you are writing about literary works, keep your analysis and your account of events in the present tense:

   NOT   The small-town setting of William Faulkner's "A Rose for Emily" *explains* the attitude of the townspeople toward Emily because people in small communities traditionally *rejected* and *excluded* those who *were* different from them. Faulkner's description of the setting *emphasizes* Emily's isolation. Most of the action *took place* in and around the house where Emily *lived* all her life.

   BUT   The small-town setting of William Faulkner's "A Rose for Emily" *explains* the attitude of the townspeople toward Emily because people in small communities traditionally *reject* and *exclude* those who *are* different. Faulkner's description of the setting *emphasizes* Emily's isolation. Most of the action *takes place* in and around the house where Emily *has lived* all her life.

2. Use the simple present or past tense in preference to *–ing* verbs.

   NOT   Freud *is discussing* the relationships among the id, ego, and superego.

   BUT   Freud *discusses* the relationships among the id, ego, and superego.

3. If you sometimes omit verb endings, writing "he learn" instead of "he learns" or "he learned," check each verb.

4. If you know you have a problem with verb tenses, proofread your final draft a paragraph at a time, checking all verbs to make sure that (a) they are in the same tense or (b) changes in tense are justified by the time relationships.

Exercise 9

Underline all the verbs and verb phrases in the following paragraph. Then correct unnecessary tense shifts. Do not make any other changes.

> I was walking around the pet store, trying to decide what kind of pet I could keep in my new apartment, when I remember Hammy, the curious brown hamster. I saw him in Zellers when I first moved to Canada. For very little money my parents buy Hammy for me, a black hamster for my brother Paul, a whole complex of compartments and tubes of hamster housing, a running wheel, a ten-kilogram bag of food, and sawdust to cover the bottom of the cages. When we were setting it all up in my bedroom, my uncle comes in and forbids us to keep our pets upstairs—they would have to live in the basement with the dogs. We live in his house; therefore, we have to live by his rules. But later that week I go away to summer camp and forget about poor Hammy. While I learned about canoeing, painting, and weaving, and while I went hiking, exploring, and swimming, Hammy's food bowl was getting emptier and emptier. I come back to find him lying on his side, thin, quiet, and cold.

3c Subject–Verb Agreement

Verbs must agree with their subjects in number: if the subject of the sentence is singular, the verb must be singular; if the subject is plural, the verb must be plural.

> The engine is hot. (Singular subject, singular verb)
>
> The engines are hot. (Plural subject, plural verb)

By the time you reach college or university, you probably won't make subject–verb errors very often. When you do, you may have lost track of the subject, as in the following cases.

1. Prepositional phrase between the subject and the verb. Remember that the noun in the prepositional phrase (of the *children,* between the *hedges,* beneath the *sheets*) is never the subject of the sentence.

> NOT The reaction to these incidents were quick and angry.
>
> BUT The <u>reaction</u> to these incidents <u>was</u> quick and angry.

VERBS

2. Phrases that imply a plural subject when the actual subject is singular: *as well as*, *in addition to*, *along with*, *including*.

    NOT   The cost, including parts and labour, were far more than the estimate.

    BUT   The <u>cost</u>, including parts and labour, <u>was</u> far more than the estimate.

3. Indefinite pronouns that may seem plural but take a singular verb:

anybody	anyone	anything	each (of)
everybody	everyone	everything	either (of)
nobody	no one	nothing	neither (of)
somebody	someone	something	

    NOT   Each of the passengers have a headphone.

    BUT   <u>Each</u> of the passengers <u>has</u> a headphone.

    NOT   Neither of the soldiers were wounded.

    BUT   <u>Neither</u> [one] of the soldiers <u>was</u> wounded.

4. *There is/are* constructions. In these constructions, the subject comes after the verb. *There* is never the subject of the sentence.

    NOT   There is three important issues to consider.

    BUT   There <u>are</u> three important <u>issues</u> [subject] to consider.

5. Singular subjects joined with *or*.

    NOT   John or Carol are meeting you at the airport.

    BUT   <u>John</u> or <u>Carol</u> <u>is meeting</u> you at the airport.

6. A combination of singular and plural subjects joined with *either . . . or, neither . . . nor, not only . . . but also*. With these constructions, the verb agrees with the subject closer to it.

    NOT   Neither the students nor the teacher were satisfied with the test results.

    BUT   Neither the students nor the <u>teacher</u> <u>was</u> satisfied with the test results.

    Note: In these constructions, it is best to put the plural subject second.

    Neither the teacher nor <u>the students</u> <u>were</u> satisfied with the test results.

Exercise 10

Underline the subject of the sentence. Then circle the correct verb form.

1. There (doesn't/don't) seem to be any books or articles on this subject.

2. Banff National Park, with its breathtaking scenery, its nature programs, and its plentiful campsites, (attracts/attract) millions of visitors every year.

3. Neither of the women (was/were) willing to vote for the candidate.

4. Not only the athletes but also the coach (is/are) tired at the end of the game.

5. The demand for luxury products (is/are) decreasing.

3d Active and Passive Voice

Verbs have two voices: active and passive. In the **active voice**, the subject of the sentence performs the action. In the **passive voice**, the subject is acted upon.

ACTIVE   Jasmine drove the car.

PASSIVE   The car was driven by Jasmine.

Uses of the passive voice Usually the active voice is preferable because it is more direct and concise. Sometimes, however, the passive voice is necessary, as in the following instances.

1. When the agent of the action is understood, unimportant, or unknown:

> I was born in Saskatoon.
>
> The roads were sanded regularly.

2. When you want to focus attention on the procedure and the results rather than on the agent.

> Ten milligrams of sodium chloride were placed in a beaker.

Passive constructions are often used in scientific writing to suggest that the steps and outcome will be the same no matter who performs the experiment. Researchers who place more emphasis on their own role in the experiments use the active voice more often.

Misuses of the passive voice

1. Avoid the passive voice when the active voice would be more concise, more direct, or more emphatic.

> NOT   It was reported to the president by the vice-president that an agreement was reached between the workers and the management.
>
> BUT   The vice-president reported to the president that the workers and the management had reached an agreement.

2. Avoid mixing the active and passive voices in the same sentence.

> NOT   Psychologists have found that more realistic estimates of control over future events are made by mildly depressed people.
>
> BUT   Psychologists have found that mildly depressed people make more realistic estimates of their control over future events.

VERBS

Exercise 11

Identify the verbs in the following sentences as active or passive. Revise sentences in which the passive voice is inappropriate or ineffective.

1. The desire by Swift in "A Modest Proposal" for better food, clothing, and housing for the Irish is expressed.

2. Their house was bombed during the war.

3. Skilled helicopter pilots lifted terrified flood victims from their rooftops.

4. The autopsy on the famous racehorse was performed this morning.

5. The demand for better employment opportunities was forcefully expressed by the Métis in Alberta and Saskatchewan.

Exercise 12

Write a paragraph in which all the verbs are in the active voice. Then rewrite the paragraph so that all the verbs are in the passive voice. Bring both paragraphs to class for discussion. What are the strengths and weaknesses of each? Does a mixture work best?

Review Exercise 2

Correct all problems with subject–verb agreement, tense shifts, troublesome verbs, and inappropriate use of the passive voice in the following paragraph.

Unlike Steven Spielberg's *Saving Private Ryan,* which was released just prior to this film, *The Thin Red Line* is not portraying any single battle or story from the Second World War. Instead it examined the mental and emotional chaos that goes hand in hand with combat. Whereas *Saving Private Ryan* was a tribute to the men of D-Day, *The Thin Red Line* is a much less celebratory salute to the human spirit. The film's slow-paced imagery of scenery and marching men present no easy answers and the line between good and evil as well as sanity and madness is frequently blurred. The film has been made in a style quite outside the norm in the Hollywood war movie genre, and it is very effective. It should of won an Academy Award, but its unconventional style made it loose out to *Saving Private Ryan.* Nevertheless, *The Thin Red Line* was among the finest of contemporary war films.

B4 Adjectives and Adverbs

4a Adjectives

An **adjective** is a word that describes (or *modifies*) a noun or pronoun. Single-word adjectives may appear before a noun, after a noun, or after a state-of-being verb (*appears, is, feels, looks, sounds, tastes,* and so forth).

> The *old, bent* man hobbled down the street.
>
> The man, *old* and *bent,* hobbled down the street.
>
> He was *old* and *bent.*

Phrases and clauses can also be used as adjectives.

> An hour *of exercise* will give you more energy.
>
> The woman *dancing the lead role* is Karen Kain.
>
> People *who live in glass houses* shouldn't throw stones.

For more information on phrases and clauses, see C Writing Better Sentences.

Comparative forms of adjectives Most adjectives have comparative forms. The comparative and superlative forms of short adjectives are most often made by adding *–er* or *–est: full, fuller, fullest.* Longer adjectives add *more* or *most: beautiful, more beautiful, most beautiful.* In a few cases, the word changes completely: *good, better, best.*

The **comparative form** is used for comparing two things:

> A peacock is more beautiful than a turkey.

The **superlative form** is used for comparing something with all the other members of its class.

> The peacock is the most beautiful bird in the world.
>
> [The peacock is the most beautiful of all the birds in the world.]

A few adjectives, such as *unique* and *perfect,* are considered absolutes. They have no comparative or superlative form.

4b Adverbs

An **adverb** is a word that describes (modifies) a verb, adjective, or another adverb. Many adverbs end in *–ly.*

> Keisha ran *quickly.*
>
> She ran *very* fast.
>
> Keisha ran *more* quickly.

Phrases and clauses can also be used as adverbs modifying a verb.

> Keisha ran *into the street.*
>
> Keisha ran *until she came to the river.*

For more information on phrases and clauses, see C Writing Better Sentences.

Comparative forms of adverbs Adverbs that end in *–ly* form the comparative and superlative by adding *more* or *most: fashionably, more fashionably, most fashionably.*

Most adverbs that do not end in *–ly* change form in the comparative and superlative: *well, better, best.*

4c Troublesome Adjectives and Adverbs

Careful writers make sure they use the following adjectives and adverbs appropriately.

Farther and Further Although these words are often used interchangeably, the current trend is to use *farther* to indicate distance (*farther into the cave*) and *further* to indicate "to a greater degree" (*his argument went further*).

Good and Well *Good* is an adjective: a good book, a good cookie.

Well is usually an adverb: to draw well, to swim well. (Exception: in regard to health, *well* is an adjective. *She is not well.*)

Hopefully *Hopefully* is often used as a sentence modifier meaning "I hope" or "perhaps," as in "Hopefully, the construction work will be finished by May." But *hopefully* is really an adverb meaning "full of hope," as in this example:

> Dressed in Halloween costumes, the children shouted hopefully at the door.

Real and Really *Real* is an adjective: a real job, a real diamond. *Really* is an adverb: a really good job, a really expensive diamond.

Than and Then *Then* is an adverb meaning "at that time": Then he went home.

Than is a preposition or conjunction that introduces the second term of a comparison: faster than a speeding bullet.

Do not use *then* when you are making a comparison.

> NOT   faster *then* a speeding bullet

Exercise 13

Correct all errors in the use of adjectives and adverbs in the following sentences.

1. Fatima did good on her math test.

2. Matthew is the tallest of the two brothers.

3. Oscar has the most unique website.

4. The novel was better then the movie.

5. Ping's mother is real fit now that she is lifting weights.

4d Misplaced and Dangling Modifiers

Adjectives and adverbs, as we suggested above, are modifiers. A modifier is a word, phrase, or clause that supplies further information about another word in the sentence. For clarity, a modifier must be as close as possible to the word it modifies, and there must be a word in the sentence for it to describe. If these conditions are not met, the modifier is either **misplaced** or **dangling**.

Misplaced modifiers Misplaced modifiers are single words (such as the adverbs *especially, almost, even, hardly, just, merely, nearly, only, scarcely*) or phrases that are too far away from the word they describe to be clear.

> This film *only* runs fifty-eight minutes. (Is this the only film that runs fifty-eight minutes, or does it run only fifty-eight minutes?)
>
> She told him *on Friday* she was quitting. (Did she tell him on Friday, or is she quitting on Friday?)

You can easily correct a misplaced modifier by moving it as close as possible to the word it describes.

> Only this film runs fifty-eight minutes. **OR** This film runs only fifty-eight minutes.
>
> On Friday she told him she was quitting. **OR** She told him she was quitting on Friday.

A special type of misplaced modifier is a **split infinitive.** An infinitive is *to* + a verb: *to walk, to think, to breathe*. An infinitive is split when an adverb is placed between *to* and the verb: *to seriously think*. Try to avoid splitting an infinitive when the resulting construction is awkward.

> SPLIT INFINITIVE Alex tried to carefully prepare for the exam.
>
> REVISED Alex tried to prepare carefully for the exam.

Exercise 14

Revise the following sentences to eliminate misplaced modifiers.

1. The Wongs were amazed to see a bear on the main street while vacationing in Jasper.

2. Selina needed time to mentally prepare for the lawyer's questions.

3. Antonio stared at the attractive young women across the aisle over his glasses.

4. Marissa had nearly driven all the way home when she stopped to pick up a hitchhiker.

5. Beena was just trying to rapidly read through the whole chapter before class.

Dangling modifiers The implied subject of an introductory adverbial phrase must be the same as the subject of the main clause. If the two subjects are not the same, the phrase is called a **dangling modifier**. The phrase dangles because there is no word for it to modify.

> Bitterly regretting his misspent youth, his days in jail seemed endless.
>
> [implied subject of *regretting: he;* subject of *seemed: his days*]
>
> When empty, return them to the store.
>
> [implied subject and verb: *they are;* understood subject of *return: you*]

You can correct a misplaced modifier by moving it closer to the word it modifies. To correct a dangling modifier, you have to revise the sentence. You can do this in two ways:

1. Expand the dangling modifier into a subordinate clause.

   > Because he bitterly regretted his misspent youth, his days in jail seemed endless.
   >
   > When the bottles are empty, return them to the store.

2. Revise the main clause to give it the same subject as the implied subject of the phrase.

   > Bitterly regretting his misspent youth, the prisoner endured seemingly endless days in jail.
   >
   > When empty, the bottles should be returned to the store.

Exercise 15

Revise the following sentences to eliminate all dangling modifiers.

1. Determined to finish her essay, all interruptions were ignored.

2. After hearing the manager's plans to reorganize the office, it was difficult for the workers to remain calm.

3. A lover of movies since childhood, his plan was to become an actor.

4. When recovering from major surgery, strenuous exercise should be avoided.

5. Just before starting school, Domingo's parents moved to Halifax.

Review Exercise 3

Revise the following sentences to correct all errors in the use of adjectives and adverbs, including misplaced and dangling modifiers.

1. He scarcely knew anyone at the party, but he had a gooder time then he expected.

2. Even after studying all night, many of the exam questions seemed unfamiliar.

3. To successfully jump farther, you'll need a more perfect pair of track shoes.

4. After a hot, strenuous day of sightseeing, the hotel pool looked real inviting.

5. Rayna is the oldest of the two sisters; hopefully she will graduate this year.

6. On the most terriblest night of my life, the engine exploded while showing off my car to my friends.

7. By enforcing regulations to properly dispose of hazardous wastes, the environment will be preserved.

8. In writing stories for popular magazines, readers want a happy ending more then a gloomier one.

9. When underage, Louis XIV's ministers had charge of the government.

10. By blaming the poor for their problems, responsibility to create a juster society quicker can be avoided by politicians.

B5 Conjunctions, Prepositions, and Interjections

5a Conjunctions

A **conjunction** is a word that joins words, phrases, clauses, or sentences. Conjunctions are of two main types: **coordinating conjunctions** and **subordinating conjunctions.**

Coordinating conjunctions The coordinating conjunctions are *and, but, or, nor,* and sometimes *for, so, yet. (For* can also be used as a preposition; *so* and *yet* can also be used as adverbs. These words are conjunctions only when they introduce clauses.) Remember the acronym BOYSFAN: But, Or, Yet, So, For, And, Nor. Coordinating conjunctions join words, phrases, clauses, or sentences that are equal in importance, as in these examples.

> richer *or* poorer
>
> in through the window *and* out through the door

They hadn't seen the movie, *nor* had they read the book.

The strikers offered to reopen negotiations. *But* the company refused.*

Correlative conjunctions (*either–or, neither–nor, not only–but also*) are two-part conjunctions that connect closely related words, phrases, or clauses of equal importance.

Neither Toshimi *nor* Tariq has missed a day of work.

The military *not only* closed the airports *but also* barricaded the roads.

Parallelism When sentence elements are joined by a coordinating conjunction or correlative conjunction and have the same grammatical construction, they are referred to as parallel. Use parallel structure to give equal weight to words, phrases, and clauses of equal importance; to help your reader follow the steps in a process; or to make comparisons more vivid.

She was lucky, intelligent, and brave. (Adjectives of equal importance)

Before you leave, close the windows, turn off the lights, and lock the doors. (Steps in a process)

The cowardly fail because of their fear, but the courageous succeed in spite of their fear. (Comparison in parallel clauses)

Faulty parallelism As its name suggests, faulty parallelism occurs whenever sentence elements are not parallel. You can correct faulty parallelism by balancing words with words, phrases with phrases, and clauses with clauses.

NOT PARALLEL To write an effective conclusion, restate your thesis, summarize your main points, and the broader context of your subject should be suggested.

PARALLEL To write an effective conclusion, restate your thesis, summarize your main points, and suggest the broader context of your subject.

NOT PARALLEL As a winner you will achieve success, and respect will also come your way.

PARALLEL As a winner, you will achieve both success and respect.

---

* While it is grammatically permissible to use coordinating conjunctions at the beginning of sentences, some readers object, especially in formal academic writing. Check with your instructor.

Exercise 16

A. Circle coordinating conjunctions and correlative conjunctions in the following sentences. Draw a line to connect the parts of correlative conjunctions.

1. Neither Ritchie nor Lawanda is going to the concert, so Janelle has two extra tickets.

2. Finding a job can be a lengthy and discouraging process, for success depends not only upon the job seeker's qualifications but also upon economic factors over which he or she has no control.

3. It was almost May. Yet snow lingered in patches of shade and ice clung to the riverbank on frosty mornings.

B. Revise the following sentences to correct faulty parallelism.

1. Many children do poorly in school because of inadequate diet, poor instruction, and they are not very interested.

2. To prevent shock, cover the victim with a blanket, speaking reassuringly.

3. To clean this oven, I need either atomic weapons or perhaps a miracle will happen.

4. You could end your speech with a quotation, by asking a question, or suggest the broader implications of your subject.

5. The successful candidate for this position must be self-motivated, have an ability to learn quickly, and reliability is very important.

C. Write five sentences of your own containing parallel elements. Include parallel words, parallel phrases, and parallel clauses. Use correlative conjunctions in at least one sentence. Underline the parallel elements.

Subordinating conjunctions Subordinating conjunctions join clauses of less importance to main clauses. Here is a list of the words most commonly used as subordinating conjunctions.

Note: These words can also be used as other parts of speech, such as prepositions and adverbs. They are called subordinating conjunctions *only* when followed by a clause.

after	because	in order that	until
although	before	provided that	when
as	even though	since	where
as long as	if	unless	while

Relative pronouns (*that, which, who, whoever, whom, whomever*) also function as subordinating conjunctions (see B2a).

CONJUNCTIONS

Conjunctive adverbs Subordinating conjunctions are sometimes confused with conjunctive adverbs. Conjunctive adverbs are words that express logical relationships between clauses; they include words such as *accordingly, besides, consequently, furthermore, hence, however, likewise, moreover, nevertheless, otherwise, still, therefore, thus.* Here is an easy way to remember the difference: subordinating conjunctions must come at the beginning of a clause, whereas conjunctive adverbs can be moved to different positions.

> The Prime Minister called an election even though [subordinating conjunction] his party clearly could not win.

> The Prime Minister called an election; however [conjunctive adverb], his party clearly could not win.

> The Prime Minister called an election; his party clearly could not win, however [conjunctive adverb].

Clauses beginning with subordinating conjunctions are punctuated differently from clauses with conjunctive adverbs, so it is important to know the difference. For more on punctuating clauses, see C Writing Better Sentences; F2 Comma; and F3 Semicolon.

Exercise 17

Circle subordinating conjunctions in the following sentences. Underline conjunctive adverbs.

1. We won't go hiking unless it stops raining.

2. It is raining; therefore, the hike has been cancelled.

3. When the power went out, office workers were trapped in elevators.

4. Fossil fuels contribute to global warming; many people are thus switching to hybrid cars.

5. Many species that are now on the endangered list will be extinct in twenty years.

Coordination and subordination Coordination and subordination help you to use the structure of the sentence to emphasize your main point. Use **coordination** to join points of equal importance. To create coordination, join words, phrases, and clauses with coordinating or correlative conjunctions.

Use **subordination** to join points of unequal importance. To create subordination, put your main point in the main clause and your less important point in a subordinate clause or phrase.

> Although everyone was aware of the problem, no one knew what to do about it.

> Marta had her car serviced before she set out on her journey.

The clause or phrase at the end of the sentence always gets more emphasis. Thus, for maximum emphasis, put your main idea in a main clause and put that clause at the end of the sentence. Notice the difference in the emphasis given to the main clause in these two sentences.

> Although the meeting was well publicized, it attracted little interest.
> (Putting the main clause last gives it maximum emphasis)

> The meeting attracted little interest even though it was well publicized.
> (Putting the subordinate clause last evens the emphasis given to both clauses)

Faulty coordination Faulty coordination occurs if you join ideas that are unrelated or not of equal importance.

> UNRELATED IDEAS The movie was boring and pretentious and hundreds of people lined up for hours to see it.

> REVISED Although the movie was boring and pretentious, hundreds of people lined up for hours to see it.

> UNEQUAL IDEAS Hamlet is Prince of Denmark and he is disillusioned by his mother's hasty remarriage.

> REVISED Hamlet, Prince of Denmark, is disillusioned by his mother's hasty remarriage.

Don't use *and* as an all-purpose conjunction. Although *and* can sometimes be a weak signal of causal connection (I was late and I missed the bus), it's best to use *and* only when you want to signal that what follows is a coordinate fact or idea.

> NOT   Dan was chronically tired and he had anemia.

> BUT   Dan was chronically tired because he had anemia.

Exercise 18

Revise the following sentences to correct errors in coordination.

1. Angus is an ardent outdoorsman and conservationist and he lives in rural New Brunswick.

2. In the summer, Andrea enjoys working in the garden, taking long walks, and she likes to read romances.

3. Marco forgot to pay a speeding ticket and he received a summons to appear in court.

4. To function effectively as a social worker, you need to be both knowledgeable and compassion is important.

5. As far as I can tell, Ingrid has no interest either in getting a job and school doesn't interest her.

CONJUNCTIONS

Faulty subordination Faulty subordination occurs when subordinating conjunctions are used inappropriately. Here are the most common causes of this error.

1. Attaching the subordinating conjunction to the wrong clause.

   FAULTY Although they missed the plane, they left in plenty of time to reach the airport.

   REVISED They missed the plane although they left in plenty of time to reach the airport.

2. Using an imprecise subordinating conjunction, especially *since* and *as*. *Since* can mean "because," but *since* can also mean "from the time that." If these two meanings might be confused, use *because* to indicate a causal connection.

   CONFUSING Since she broke her ankle, she has been housebound.

   CLEAR Because she broke her ankle, she has been housebound.

   CLEAR From the time she broke her ankle, she has been housebound.

   As can be used to mean *because*, but it's best to use *as* to mean "while."

   CLEAR As Felicity struggled to listen to the lecture, her mind began to wander.

   CONFUSING As Raul is the manager, he thinks he should make all the decisions.

   CLEAR Raul thinks he should make all the decisions because he is the manager.

3. Using two conjunctions that mean the same thing.

   MIXED Because he did not want to pay a late penalty for his income tax, so he rushed to the post office just before midnight.

   REVISED Because he did not want to pay a late penalty for his income tax, he rushed to the post office just before midnight.

   OR He did not want to pay a late penalty for his income tax, so he rushed to the post office just before midnight.

4. Using too many subordinate clauses in a sentence. Avoid beginning and ending a sentence with similar subordinate clauses. Also avoid piling up clauses beginning with relative pronouns, such as *that, which,* and *who.*

   EXCESSIVE SUBORDINATION Because she was afraid of a hailstorm, she covered all the windows because the force of the hail might break them.

   REVISED Fearing a hailstorm, she covered all the windows to protect them.

EXCESSIVE SUBORDINATION The novelist who wins this contest which is sponsored by a major publisher will be taken on a cross-country tour that begins July 1.

REVISED The novelist who wins this contest, sponsored by a major publisher, will be taken on a cross-country tour beginning July 1.

Exercise 19

Revise the following sentences to correct faulty subordination. Write C beside a correct sentence.

1. When Jing-Mei learned about the fashion opportunities in Montreal when she was living in Lethbridge, she packed her bags and bought an airline ticket.

2. Since Karl had a seizure caused by an allergic reaction, he has been cautious about all medications.

3. Because the assistant manager is autocratic and arrogant, therefore no one wants to work with her.

4. As the main character ties his sense of masculinity to clan traditions, he feels threatened when these structures begin to crumble.

5. Although Amin desperately needed a job, he was determined never again to work for his father.

Review Exercise 4

Revise the following sentences to eliminate faulty parallelism, faulty coordination, and faulty subordination.

1. To complete this degree, you could take three more courses or a thesis could be written.

2. Although he loved her, he didn't want to marry her although she was rich.

3. The house that burned down, which used to belong to the Santos family, who moved here from Guatemala, was designed by an architect who is well known.

4. Maria had three goals in life: to complete her degree, travelling to Asia, and she wanted to start her own business.

5. Julia has travelled extensively in the Far East and she teaches dance.

6. Because the roads through the mountains were hazardous, he decided to fly home because he didn't want to drive.

7. They vowed to remain married for better and worse, for richer and poorer, and whether or not they were both healthy.

8. As Timothy was the last to be hired, he was also the first to be fired.

9. He had forgotten about the test until the class started, although he did well on it.

10. Charles Dickens is an important nineteenth-century novelist who experienced poverty as a child and who is very sympathetic to poor children in his novels.

5b Prepositions

Prepositions are those little words you probably learned from *Sesame Street* that indicate relationships in time, space, manner, and so forth. Here is a partial list of prepositions.

against	by	into	through	upon
around	down	of	to	with
at	for	on	toward	within
before	from	onto	under	without

The noun or pronoun that follows the preposition is called the **object of the preposition.** If you speak English as a first language, you are not likely to make mistakes with prepositions. You may, however, make errors in subject–verb agreement because you confuse the object of the preposition with the subject of the sentence (see B3c).

5c Interjections

An **interjection** is a word "thrown into" a sentence to express emotion, such as *hurray, oh, well,* and less polite words. An interjection at the beginning of a sentence is set off with a comma. An interjection in the middle of a sentence is set off with a pair of commas.

Oops, I dropped my wallet in a puddle.

It must have been, oh, ten years since I saw you last.

Interjections are seldom used in formal academic writing.

C Writing Better Sentences

In academic writing, as in most business and professional writing, the basic unit of *thought* is the paragraph, which generally states a point and then develops that point through details and examples. Within each paragraph, the basic unit of *expression* is the sentence. The boundaries of the sentence are clearly marked by a capital at the beginning and a period at the end, and the words, as you no doubt learned in grade school, express a complete idea. Your readers will expect sentences that are well structured and correctly punctuated. The aim is not correctness for its own sake, but correctness as an aid to meaning. Poorly constructed, badly punctuated sentences are hard to understand.

Consider an extreme example. In the following paragraph, we have removed all internal punctuation and introduced problems in sentence structure.

> John A. Macdonald was a colourful prime minister before Confederation he had proved his skill as a politician by clinging to power for over thirty years it showed he was bold shrewd and stubborn although he drank heavily still he maintained a firm grip on his party and the country because he helped to bring about the birth of a nation and was serving his country in its infancy he is known as the Father of Confederation a man with great historical importance and also who had many weaknesses Macdonald continues to fascinate historians and biographers.

Notice that without periods or other punctuation to mark sentence boundaries, it is hard to tell how ideas fit together. Was Macdonald a colourful prime minister before Confederation? Of course not—there was no prime minister before Confederation. Was he bold, shrewd, and stubborn although he drank heavily? No, he possessed those character traits regardless of his alcohol consumption.

This paragraph illustrates the difficulties caused by the absence of sentence boundaries. Sentences that run together like this are called *fused sentences.* The wrong punctuation, resulting in *sentence fragments* and *comma splices,* may create similar problems for your reader. We discuss these problems in detail below, along with other errors in sentence structure. First, however, we will discuss clauses and phrases, the building blocks from which sentences are constructed. Understanding these building blocks will help you to write better sentences.

C1 Recognizing Complete Sentences: Clauses and Phrases

1a Main Clauses

In formal academic writing, any words punctuated as a sentence must contain a **main clause**. A main clause (also known as an *independent clause*) consists of one or more subjects and one or more verbs that together express a complete idea. A main clause may take the form of a statement, a question, or a command.

> The boy [subject] hit [verb] the ball. (Statement: declarative sentence)
>
> Did [verb] the boy [subject] hit [verb] the ball? (Question: interrogative sentence)
>
> Hit [verb] the ball [*you* is the understood subject]. (Command: imperative sentence)

A main clause may contain more than one subject and/or more than one verb.

> Jack and Jill ran.
>
> Jack and Jill ran and played.

It may also contain adjectives that *modify* (describe or give additional information about) the subject or adverbs that modify the verb (see B4).

> The ramshackle [adjective] cabin [subject] burned [verb] quickly [adverb].

Remember this definition: a main clause is a group of words with a subject–verb core that can stand alone as a complete sentence.

1b Phrases

A main clause may also contain one or more **phrases.** A phrase is a group of words that does not contain a subject–verb core. The three most common types of phrases are prepositional, participial, and infinitive phrases.

Prepositional phrases **Prepositional phrases** begin with a preposition (see B5b) and end with a noun (see B1) or pronoun (see B2).

> The referee on the sideline is waving a flag. (*On the sideline:* prepositional phrase modifying *referee*)

Participial phrases **Participial phrases** all begin with a participle (the *-ing* or past tense form of a verb) and end with a noun or pronoun (see B3a and F2e).

The player lying on the ground has broken her ankle. (*Lying on the ground:* participial phrase modifying *player*)

She will be carried to the ambulance parked just off the field. (*Parked just off the field:* participial phrase modifying *ambulance*)

Infinitive phrases **Infinitive phrases** begin with an infinitive (*to* + a verb) and end with a noun or pronoun.

Jill wanted to help Jack. (*To help Jack:* infinitive phrase modifying *wanted*)

1c Simple and Compound Sentences

A sentence that consists of one main clause and its modifiers is called a **simple sentence.** A sentence that contains two or more main clauses is called a **compound sentence.** The main clauses may be joined with a semicolon, a comma and a coordinating conjunction (*and, but, or, nor, for, so, yet*), or a semicolon and a conjunctive adverb (such as *therefore, thus, however, consequently*).

SIMPLE SENTENCES	Civil unrest has increased. Many people have fled the country.
COMPOUND SENTENCES	Civil unrest has increased; many people have fled the country.
	Civil unrest has increased, so many people have fled the country.
	Civil unrest has increased; consequently, many people have fled the country.

Exercise 1

First label each of the following constructions MC (main clause) or P (phrase). Then for each main clause, underline the subject(s) once and the verb(s) twice.

1. After leaving the theatre and catching a cab

2. We walked and talked together for hours; finally, we headed home

3. On Sunday Vijay phones his mother

4. A bandage over the exposed wound but no painkillers

5. Her dream was to see Paris and die happy

1d Subordinate Clauses

Like main clauses, **subordinate clauses** contain a subject and verb. Unlike main clauses, however, subordinate clauses (also known as dependent clauses) cannot stand alone as complete sentences. As its name suggests, a subordinate clause is *subordinate to* or *dependent upon* the main clause. Subordinate clauses may, for example, add extra information or qualify the statement made in the main clause. The precise relationship is signalled by the subordinating conjunction or relative pronoun that introduces the subordinate clause (for lists of the most common subordinating conjunctions and relative pronouns, see B5a Conjunctions).

> *When we finished dinner,* we went to a movie.
>
> The movie, *which starred Colin Firth and Keira Knightley,* was entertaining.

If the ideas are not logically related (as in *Although I like chicken, I went to the store*), the error is called **faulty subordination** (see B5a).

Subordinate clauses that begin with a relative pronoun (see B2a) describe the preceding noun or pronoun.

> The next car *that I buy* will be an energy-efficient hybrid.

The relative pronoun may also function as the subject of the subordinate clause.

> The car *that hit the lamppost* was a total writeoff.

Note: Often *that* is omitted when it is not the subject. Don't overlook subordinate clauses of this type.

> The horse he picks [*that he picks*] never wins.

1e Complex and Compound-Complex Sentences

A sentence that contains one main clause and one or more subordinate clauses is called a **complex sentence.** A sentence that contains two or more main clauses and one or more subordinate clauses is called a **compound-complex sentence**.

The subordinate clause may come before or after the main clause, or it may come between the subject and verb of the main clause. If the subordinate clause comes before the main clause, put a comma after it. This use of the comma is covered in F2b.

**COMPLEX
SENTENCES**

If you are cold, then put on a sweater.

Everyone left *as soon as the meeting ended.*

The candidate *who gets* the most votes will become the next mayor.

**COMPOUND-COMPLEX
SENTENCE**

Although the oil industry reported record profits, one company laid off five thousand workers, and another company closed two plants.

You should now have a better grasp of what makes a complete sentence. A grammatically complete sentence must contain at least one main clause. It may contain more than one main clause; it may also contain one or more subordinate clauses and any number of phrases. But without a main clause, it is not a complete sentence.

Exercise 2

Put square brackets around the main clause(s) in the following sentences. Put parentheses around subordinate clauses. Underline the subject of a main or subordinate clause once; underline the complete verb (the main verb + any auxiliaries) twice.

1. While the fighting persists, the airport will remain closed.
2. The supplies that would prevent deaths from injuries and starvation have been delayed.
3. I am worried about my parents, who are helpless victims of the civil war.
4. Although many attempts have been made to enforce a cease-fire, the fighting has increased.
5. Hopes for an early solution are fading because neither side will compromise.

Exercise 3

A.   Label the following sentences simple, compound, complex, or compound-complex. Put square brackets around main clauses and put parentheses around subordinate clauses. Underline the subject of a main or a subordinate clause once; underline the complete verb (the main verb + any auxiliaries) twice.

1. Smoking in the hospital was prohibited, so patients huddled outside the doors in freezing temperatures.
2. *Othello* is the tragedy of a man who "loved not wisely, but too well."

3. Some people believe that tuition should be affordable enough for anyone to attend post-secondary institutions; others believe that tuition should be increased and loans made available to those who need them.

4. As the runners surged toward the finish line, the crowd cheered wildly.

5. The distraught parents searched the campground, the lakeshore, and the surrounding woods for their missing child.

6. The weather, which had remained warm for several days, suddenly turned bitterly cold.

7. In the grey dawn of a cold November morning, the hunter stood motionless at the edge of the clearing, waiting patiently, cold fingers ready to press the button on the sleek silver camera.

8. Before you take an exam, get a good night's sleep and eat a healthy meal.

B.   Create two sentences of your own of each type discussed above (simple, compound, complex, compound-complex). Put square brackets around main clauses and parentheses around subordinate clauses. Underline the subject(s) of each main and subordinate clause once; underline the complete verb (the main verb + any auxiliaries) of each clause twice.

C2 Correcting Errors in Sentence Structure

Understanding the difference between main clauses, subordinate clauses, and phrases will help you to identify and correct common errors in sentence structure. Here we will discuss four common problems: sentence fragments, comma splices, fused sentences, and mixed constructions. The first three problems result from failing to punctuate sentences correctly. Mixed constructions occur when grammatically incompatible elements are linked together.

2a Sentence Fragments

As its name implies, a **sentence fragment** is a grammatically incomplete sentence. The sentence may be incomplete because the subject or verb has accidentally been omitted. More often, a subordinate clause or phrase has been punctuated as a sentence.

In advertising, personal essays, and fiction, sentence fragments may be used intentionally for emphasis.

> No more war.

In academic writing, sentence fragments are less acceptable because they seem too informal. They may also be confusing, especially if they are accidental.

To correct sentence fragments, supply the missing word(s) or attach the fragment to the appropriate sentence.

FRAGMENT The president given the choice of resigning or being impeached.

COMPLETE SENTENCE The president was given the choice of resigning or being impeached. (Auxilliary verb added)

FRAGMENT Even though students had been warned that they would be expected to write an in-class essay. Many of them arrived late.

COMPLETE SENTENCE Even though students had been warned that they would be expected to write an in-class essay, many of them arrived late. (Subordinate clause attached to the main clause)

FRAGMENT Shakespeare's play *Richard III* deals with fundamental human problems. Such as the conflict between good and evil.

COMPLETE SENTENCE Shakespeare's play *Richard III* deals with fundamental human problems, such as the conflict between good and evil. (Phrase attached to main clause)

Exercise 4

Revise the following sentences to correct sentence fragments.

1. Many students decide not to hold part-time jobs. Because they need time to study.
2. Although the benefits of pollution regulations outweigh the costs. Every regulation has an impact on the Canadian economy.
3. Genetically modified foods, sometimes known as "Frankenfoods."
4. In the last act of the play, when the hero and the villain confront each other.
5. Genetic manipulation could be useful in the treatment of some diseases. Such as diabetes.

2b Comma Splices

The **comma splice** (sometimes called the *comma fault*) occurs when two main clauses are joined only by a comma, with no conjunction to show how the clauses are related. Each of the following sentences contains a comma splice.

1. Women become addicted to working out at the gym, they look a little too healthy in their skin-tight pants and bra-tops.
2. She wanted to win the prize, she practised hours every day.

3. If you expect too much you are sure to be disappointed, if you expect too little you may be pleasantly surprised.

4. Many transit users make the mistake of boarding the bus empty-handed, they have nothing with which to mark off their territory.

5. The causeway brings more tourists to Prince Edward Island, they don't stay as long.

Whenever you join two separate ideas, you need more than a comma to show how they are related. There are five ways to correct comma splices. Choose the method that best expresses the relationship between the clauses.

CORRECTING COMMA SPLICES

1. If the clauses are long or the ideas are not closely related, separate the clauses with a period.

   Women become addicted to working out at the gym. They look a little too healthy in their skin-tight pants and bra-tops.

2. If the ideas are of equal importance, join the clauses with a comma and the appropriate coordinating conjunction (*and, but, or, nor, for, so, yet*).

   She wanted to win the prize, so she practised hours every day.

3. If the ideas are closely related and parallel in structure, join the clauses with a semicolon.

   If you expect too much, you are sure to be disappointed; if you expect too little, you may be pleasantly surprised.

4. If the ideas are closely related and the second clause expresses a contrast, qualification, or addition to the first, join the clauses with a semicolon and the appropriate conjunctive adverb (for a list of conjunctive adverbs, see B5a). If the conjunctive adverb is a word of more than one syllable, set it off with a comma.

   Many transit users make the mistake of boarding the bus empty-handed; consequently, they have nothing with which to mark off their territory.

5. If the clauses are not of equal importance, put the less important idea into a subordinate clause. Notice that when the subordinate clause comes first, it is separated from the main clause by a comma.

   Although the causeway brings more tourists to Prince Edward Island, they don't stay as long.

Note: If you join two independent clauses with only a comma and a conjunctive adverb, you will have created a comma splice. Make sure that you use a semicolon to join the clauses.

SENTENCES

Exercise 5

Choose the most appropriate method to correct comma splices in the following sentences.

1. Holden wants to be like the ducks, no one seems to notice them.

2. The southern half of the province has received very little rain for the third consecutive year, poor crops are expected.

3. The competition in high school is intense, some students use alcohol to escape from the pressure to succeed.

4. Olena has very limited vision, voice-sensitive computer software is enormously helpful to her.

5. Ultra-light aircraft are easy to fly, however they can be very difficult to land.

Exercise 6

Circle all comma splices in the following paragraph. Then correct the comma splices, using the most appropriate method.

> The lack of physical activity involved when a child interacts with the computer is another pitfall of this technology, children learn a great deal through physical activity. Alphabet puzzles, active games, playdough, and colouring are a few examples of popular learning activities, these games require children to be physically active. They not only introduce children to new concepts, they also enable children to express themselves creatively. It is difficult to hold children's attention without these games, consequently trying to teach small children on computers, without these games, is somewhat risky. Extensive computer use may increase learning disorders, it may also create a generation of couch potatoes. Computers prevent children from interacting with the natural environment, this is an important part of a child's mental and physical growth.

2c Fused Sentences

Fused sentences (sometimes called *run-on sentences*) contain two or more main clauses, but there is no punctuation to show how the clauses are related.

> Television networks make money by selling advertising time therefore programs must appeal to people who can afford the products advertised.

> Cellphones are not a status symbol anymore most people have them.

Fused sentences can be corrected in the same way as comma splices. Be sure not to create a comma splice by merely putting a comma between main clauses.

Exercise 7

Revise the following fused sentences by adding conjunctions and adjusting punctuation as necessary.

1. It is easy to make this delicious dessert just follow these instructions.

2. Some adolescents are sullen, rebellious, and lazy others work to support themselves and to help their families.

3. Einstein abhorred the practical use of his theories by the military in the future we may find more humanitarian uses for his concepts.

4. Some leaders brutally impose their policies they get sullen compliance at best.

5. The window display stopped passersby in their tracks it featured a mannequin wrapped in a bloody sheet with a boot on its neck.

2d Mixed Constructions

A **mixed construction** will occur if you begin a sentence with one grammatical construction and complete it with one that is different and incompatible. Any of the errors listed below will produce a mixed construction.

Putting a subordinate clause before or after a linking verb Readers expect linking verbs, such as *is* and *was,* to be followed by a noun or noun clause, not by a subordinate clause that modifies the verb. Formulations like *an example of this is when* and *the reason for this is because* are typical of this sort of mixed construction.

> MIXED *An example* of his hostility *is when* he turns his homicidal bull loose on the mushroom pickers.

> MIXED *One reason* she dropped out of school *is because* she was in constant conflict with authority.

You can revise these sentences by supplying the missing noun or noun clause.

> REVISED An example of his hostility is his decision to turn his homicidal bull loose on the mushroom pickers.

> REVISED One reason she dropped out of school is her constant conflict with authority.

Another way to revise these sentences is to replace the linking verb.

> REVISED He shows his hostility when he turns his homicidal bull loose on the mushroom pickers.

> REVISED She dropped out of school because she was in constant conflict with authority.

Omitting the subject Leaving out the subject typically produces sentences like this:

> MIXED In this documentary makes the point that gorillas are a seriously endangered species.

This sentence is confusing because the prepositional phrase *In this documentary,* which normally introduces a grammatically complete sentence, seems to be the subject of the sentence. You could revise by omitting the preposition.

> REVISED This documentary makes the point that gorillas are a seriously endangered species.

Or you could keep the prepositional phrase and add a subject to the main clause.

> REVISED In this documentary, the filmmaker shows that gorillas are a seriously endangered species.

Leaving out part of a comparison Sentences that begin with phrases such as *the more, the less, the worse, the further* suggest a comparison. You will confuse your reader if you fail to complete the comparison.

> MIXED The less time I have, I have a lot to do.

You could revise this sentence by pairing *less* with *more.*

> REVISED The less time I have, the more I have to do.

Mixing a question and a statement Be clear about whether or not you are posing a question or making a statement. You will confuse your readers if you mix a question with a statement.

> MIXED The little boy plaintively asked his mother when will she finish writing her essay?

You could revise this sentence by rephrasing the question as direct speech.

> REVISED The little boy plaintively asked his mother, "When will you finish writing your essay?"

SENTENCES

You could also make the question a statement.

REVISED The little boy plaintively asked his mother when she would finish writing her essay.

Exercise 8

Revise the following sentences to eliminate mixed constructions.

1. *A Man for All Seasons* shows that the reason Sir Thomas More becomes a martyr is because he is willing to die for his beliefs.
2. An example of her cunning is when she persuades her client not to consult another lawyer.
3. By denying that the government intended to raise taxes increased the credibility gap between the Minister of Finance and the public.
4. The more Yvette loathed her family, she did not want to live with them.
5. The frustrated mother asked her daughter when will she ever grow up?

Review Exercise 1

Correct all the fragments, comma splices, and fused sentences in the paragraph below.

For most of my life I have used and appreciated good knives, this comes from growing up on a farm. Where I often needed a good knife. I quickly learned to distinguish a good quality knife from one of poor quality. Finding a good knife was often difficult. Because most knives are made by companies that care more about profit than about quality. Consequently I always kept an eye out for knives made in the early part of the century knives constructed then are usually made from better quality materials. I faithfully attended auctions and garage sales. In the hope of finding these early knives. I had to be content with whatever style I found, there were not many styles available.

Review Exercise 2

Rewrite the following paragraph to eliminate sentence fragments, comma splices, fused sentences, and mixed constructions. Do not omit any of the ideas in the paragraph.

From January to mid-June is when the bay is covered with ice. Then twice-weekly air transportation replaces the three-hour ferry trip to the mainland. On a clear, windless day the twenty minutes in the air can be heavenly. A sightseer's bliss. Below you can spot moose and caribou, you can follow snowmobile trails as they wend their way over and around ponds, brooks, hills and dales. The snow gleaming and glistening like a fairy-tale scene. But this is no Boeing 747 this only is a four-seater Cessna commonly referred to as a matchbox with wings. You squeeze and squirm into a bearable position, draping yourself over bags of mail, boxes of freight, and the luggage you brought. Your knees bump against your chin, you clench your teeth in preparation for take-off. Hoping and praying that the weather remains good. If it doesn't you are in for the most unpleasant twenty minutes of your life.

D Writing Better Paragraphs

In Part 1 (Rhetoric) we stress the importance of writing paragraphs with a main point developed through reasons, examples, and other relevant details. In Part 3 (Handbook), C Writing Better Sentences, we show how to correct errors in sentence structure. This chapter will give you tips on polishing your writing: using sentence structure to create emphasis and to signal movement from point to detail; using transitions to indicate relationships in space, time, and logic; and making every word count. This kind of polishing will help your reader move surely and easily from point to detail and back again.

Without this kind of polishing, your ideas may be hard to follow. Consider this paragraph analyzing symbolism in Margaret Atwood's novel *Cat's Eye:*

> The most important symbol in Margaret Atwood's novel is the cat's eye. *Cat's Eye* is the title. *The Dictionary of Symbols and Imagery* by Ad de Vries gives several meanings of both cats and eyes. Cats have several symbolic interpretations, both good and evil. The eye also has both good and evil interpretations. Cats are beautiful and cuddly on the outside. They are highly independent. They are thought to be the most cunning and untrustworthy of all animals. The duality of their nature is most apparent in their "inverted playfulness" (de Vries 86). Cats turn the act of killing a mouse into a game. The eye can be either evil or protecting. De Vries says that "the divinity can be malevolent: the evil eye, one that scorches" (171). The eye can also be a charm against evil. The Eye of Horus in folklore protects against the Evil Eye of envy, malice, and the like (de Vries 172). The main character of the novel is Elaine. As a child Elaine carries her cat's eye marble everywhere. It is a charm that she hopes will protect her from the cruelty of the girls at school. She finally realizes that she has become like the glass marble. Glass eyes are unmoving and unfeeling.

This paragraph is hard to understand for three main reasons:

1. **Lack of sentence variety** All the sentences have the same basic structure and are about the same length. As a result, it's hard to distinguish the ideas from the examples that support them.
2. **Lack of transitions** There are no words, phrases, or clauses that establish relationships between sentences. As a result, it is hard to tell

whether the writer intended a particular statement to reinforce, qualify, or contradict another statement or to suggest a cause-and-effect relationship.

3. **Wordiness** Because sentence structure and transitions are not used effectively, the writing is wordy. Readers get bogged down in unnecessary repetition.

If you compare the paragraph opposite with the revised version below, you can see just how big a difference these simple changes make.

> The most important symbol in Margaret Atwood's novel is the image of the cat's eye that gives the book its title. According to Ad de Vries in the *Dictionary of Symbols and Imagery,* both the cat and the eye have several symbolic meanings, good and evil. Cats have a dual nature: beautiful and cuddly on the outside, they are nevertheless highly independent and thought to be the most cunning and untrustworthy of all animals. The duality of their nature is most apparent in their "inverted playfulness" (de Vries 86): they turn the act of killing a mouse into a game. Similarly, the eye can be either an Evil Eye, "one that scorches" (de Vries 171) or a protecting presence, like the Eye of Horus that serves as a charm against the Evil Eye of envy and malice (de Vries 172). As a child Elaine, the main character of the novel, uses her cat's eye marble as a charm to protect herself against the cruelty of the girls at her school. By the end of the novel Elaine realizes that she has become like the glass marble, unmoving and unfeeling.

D1 Creating Sentence Variety

1a Sentence Length

Your main points will be clearer and more emphatic if you express them in short sentences. Use longer sentences to gather details, reasons, and examples that support and develop your main points.

> In constructing the Imperial Hotel in Tokyo, Frank Lloyd Wright had to solve several architectural problems [main point: 16 words]. He had to deal with difficulties created by earthquake tremors, correct the weak soil base of the hotel site, and keep the building from cracking [series of explanations: 25 words].

1b Sentence Patterns

The basic sentence pattern in English is subject + verb + object (*Jennifer hit the ball*). If all of your sentences follow this pattern, however, your writing

PARAGRAPHS

will soon become as monotonous as a Grade 1 reader. You will also make it more difficult for your reader to distinguish major and minor points.

1c Common Sentence Patterns

Here are the most common sentence patterns:

The loose sentence: subject + verb + modifier

> The team lost money, despite better players and an improved stadium.

This is the most common sentence pattern and is thus the easiest for most readers to understand. The modifier gains emphasis because it is placed at the end of the sentence. Readers would expect the sentence that follows it to focus on the improvement in players and the stadium.

The periodic sentence: modifier + subject + verb

> Despite better players and an improved stadium, the team lost money.

Because we have to wait for the subject and the verb, this sentence pattern creates suspense and interest. It puts maximum emphasis on the fact that the team lost money, so readers would expect the next sentence to deal with this issue.

The embedded sentence: subject + modifier + verb

> The team, despite better players and an improved stadium, lost money.

This sentence pattern slows the reader down because the subject and the verb are separated by a lengthy modifier. It is useful if you want to imitate the process of thinking through a problem. It also leads readers to expect that the next sentence will begin to explore the real reasons for the team's inability to make a profit.

The balanced construction: parallel main clauses

> The team gained good players and a better stadium; it still lost money.

The balanced construction creates a compound sentence in which two closely related main clauses with the same structure are joined with a semicolon; a comma and a coordinate conjunction; or a semicolon and a conjunctive adverb. It is especially useful when you want to create a contrast or to suggest a choice between two equal possibilities.

In the following example, notice how emphatic the balanced construction seems after the longer sentences that precede it.

> It would seem from watching CNN that crime has reached epidemic proportions. The truth is that crime statistics are declining. Crime has not grown; fear has.

Sentences with other parallel elements For maximum effect, arrange parallel words, phrases, or clauses in an order of ascending interest, with the most important detail last.

> Although the team is still losing money, it has better players, an improved stadium, and fiercely loyal fans.

For more on parallelism, see B5a Conjunctions.

Rhetorical questions Asking a question actively engages your reader in the process of reading and thinking about your subject. You may give your essay an inductive pattern of organization by asking a question that the essay will explicitly answer.

> The team has better players and an improved stadium. So why is it still losing money?

Or you may pose a question ironically, creating a bond with your reader by assuming that you would both agree on the answer:

> *Ever After* glitters with the predictable Hollywood sparkle. Would Prince Henry really have looked twice if this beautiful brain belonged to a homely peasant girl rather than Drew Barrymore?

Questions of this type backfire if your reader disagrees with you. Consequently, some instructors ban questions altogether. If you do use questions, use them sparingly and make sure your answer is clear. Peppering your work with questions will create a tone that seems hectoring or indecisive (for more on tone, see E Creating an Appropriate Tone).

Varying the structure of your sentences will help you to avoid monotony and to clarify the relationships among ideas, explanations, and details. On the other hand, if every sentence follows a different pattern, your reader will find your paragraph confusing. Here are some guidelines for varying sentence structure effectively.

1. Keep the structure of topic sentences fairly simple. When you are making major points, you don't want to lose your reader in elaborate sentence patterns.

2. Change your sentence structure when you introduce an explanation. If your explanation takes more than one sentence, keep the sentences in similar patterns.

3. When you shift from explanation to details, change your sentence pattern.

4. Keep similar sentence patterns for all your details.

PARAGRAPHS

Exercise 1

A. Write a brief paragraph analyzing sentence variety in the paragraph below. How many words are there in the shortest sentence? The longest? What is the average sentence length? Are there sentences that could be shortened to emphasize main points? Are there sentences that could be combined to present details more concisely? Which sentence patterns does the writer use from among those described in this section? Which sentences could be given a different pattern to signal a shift in thought?

> The equal value of boys and girls does not mean that fair treatment will be identical treatment. We need to set aside the idea that because girls and boys have equal value they will have identical needs. We need to adopt a more gender sensitive approach to education. We need to realize that boys are in trouble. They need more freedom than we permit them in the earlier grades. They need more movement. They need educators who understand their developmental maturation so that they will remain persistent and encouraging in their language skills development beyond the primary grades. We need to realize that although girls have come a long way in math and science, they still have dangers to face. We need to recognize their developmental sensitivities as well. We should be prepared for the likelihood that they may need more attention in junior high than they did in elementary school. We also need to be sensitive enough to pay attention before they start asking for it.

B. Rewrite the paragraph to make the changes you identified.

D2 Making Transitions

Transitional words and phrases are important for two reasons. They increase your reader's understanding of how your ideas are related. They also create a sense of continuity, both within and between paragraphs, because one idea leads smoothly to the next.

2a Sentence and Paragraph Hooks

Sentence hooks are words and phrases used to create continuity. You can hook sentences together with pronouns, demonstrative pronouns, synonyms, and repeated words and phrases.

Pronouns After the first reference by name, use pronouns and possessive pronouns to indicate a continuity of subject. Make sure that the reference is clear (see B2c).

> Margaret Atwood has written several novels. *Her* most recent is . . .
> *She* has also written . . .

Demonstrative pronouns To avoid repeating your last point, refer to it with a demonstrative pronoun (*this, that, these, those*) and a noun that identifies the subject to which you are referring.

> During the Depression, prairie farmers suffered because of the severe drought. *This problem* . . .

> Macbeth murders Duncan and is responsible for the murder of Banquo and several others. *These acts* of violence . . .

Synonyms and repeated words and phrases Keep your reader's attention on your subject by repeating key words and phrases or by using synonyms. Notice the continuity created by the repetition of "race" and "racism" in the following paragraph.

> So what is racism? Racism is the idea, whether in the back of your mind or deep in your heart, that there are large groupings within humanity that can be distinguished as separate races, and that the race you belong to is superior to other races in mind, body, and character. The problem with this concept, outside of the monstrous behaviour that such a belief justifies, is that the very notion of race has no scientific value. It is true that there are differences as to how people from different parts of the planet look. That much is obvious. But most of us are unaware that we differ in only 5% of our bodily features. This hardly seems like enough to classify us as separate "races." And even though some of these differences are dramatic, we also note that there is as much variation *within* a so-called race as *between* the so-called races. And how do we deal with people of mixed-"race" parentage? How do we describe them? And what about those sub-"race" nationalities that look significantly like peoples of other "races," such as the African Kalahari Desert dwellers who appear to be Asians, or the Australian and Dravidian Aborigines who appear to be straight-haired Africans?

Paragraph hooks are words and phrases that recall key ideas to create continuity between paragraphs.

1. Repeat single words or phrases or use synonyms to link the last sentence of one paragraph to the first sentence of the next.

> LAST SENTENCE OF PARAGRAPH 1   His pride thus leads him to reject his friends' offers of help.

> FIRST SENTENCE OF PARAGRAPH 2   His pride also prevents him from helping himself.

PARAGRAPHS

2. Use phrases, clauses, or occasionally whole sentences that briefly recall the ideas of one paragraph at the beginning of the next.

> FIRST TOPIC SENTENCE Mackenzie King, Diefenbaker, and Pearson . . .

> SECOND TOPIC SENTENCE These three prime ministers were not the only ones to favour such a policy. . . .

2b Transitional Words and Phrases

Transitional words and phrases are means of indicating relationships in time, space, and logic.

RELATIONSHIP		SAMPLE TRANSITIONAL WORDS AND PHRASES
time		before, after, meanwhile, as soon as, during, until, then
space		on the right, near, farther away
logic	1. addition	and, another, a second, also, too, furthermore, moreover, not only . . . but also, first, second, etc.
	2. contrast	but, in contrast, yet, however, on the other hand, nevertheless, otherwise
	3. similarity	just as, like, likewise, similarly, in the same way
	4. examples	for example, for instance, to be specific, in particular, to illustrate
	5. cause and effect	therefore, thus, so, for, hence, because, consequently, as a result, accordingly
	6. concession and qualification	although, despite, while it is true that . . .
	7. emphasis	most important, a crucial point, significantly, of overwhelming importance

You can use these transitional words and phrases to provide continuity both within paragraphs and between paragraphs.

Exercise 2

Make a list of all the transitional devices in the following paragraph. Then identify each device by type as specifically as possible (such as pronoun, synonym, contrast).

> For a long time, meat consumption in Western countries has been on the rise. This reliance on meat is a facet of "advanced" societies. Many tribal societies, for example, do hunt animals; however, they largely subsist on nuts and vegetables. A lot of animals other than humans also have a herbivorous diet. In the last ten or fifteen years, the media have begun to report more on the consequences of a high-meat, low-vegetable diet. As a result, more people have adopted a diet that is either vegetarian (no meat products) or vegan (no meat products and nothing that comes from animals, such as dairy and eggs). Nevertheless, those who don't eat meat are still very much in the minority, especially in a place such as Alberta where people proudly display "I love Alberta beef" stickers on their car bumpers. The question therefore remains: What is better, a vegetarian diet or a diet that includes meat?

Exercise 3

Identify transitions in two paragraphs from one of the following essays (Part 2, Readings). Then write a paragraph discussing the kinds of transitions the author uses and their effectiveness.

1. Linda Hogan's "The Voyagers"
2. George Orwell's "Shooting an Elephant"
3. Virginia Satir's "Systems: Open or Closed?"

D3 Being Concise

When you write a draft, you may find yourself making false starts on sentences and using inexact, wordy language because you are still working out your ideas. Or you may repeat ideas instead of giving evidence to support them.

You can see both problems in the following draft paragraph from an essay comparing homeless people and nomads.

> There is a difference between being a homeless person and being a nomad. Being homeless is a state of mind; being a nomad is a way of life. Although homeless people have no place to live, many of them do not want a home. When they are placed in shelters or housing, they leave because they do not want ties with family or society.

Homeless people have very few possessions, and because they really have no permanent place to stay, they somewhat tend to carry their rather few possessions around with them. Nomads, on the other hand, move from place to place, usually seasonally. Although they have no fixed residence, they tend to stay in different spots within a certain territory. It is a feature of traditional nomads that they live in family groups or small communities. When they move, the whole group moves together. Modern nomads don't have a permanent residence. At different times they may travel to different family members. When they arrive, they may stay with different family members for a few months at a time. When they travel, they take most of the things they own and put them in a storage facility. They take only the most essential things with them when they move. They leave things that are not essential behind. In these ways nomads are different from homeless people.

When you revise, try to be more concise. Here are some suggestions:

1. Choose exact nouns, verbs, and modifiers.

   NOT   When they travel, they take most of the things they own and put them in a storage facility. (18 words)

   BUT   When they travel, they store most of their belongings. (9 words)

2. Replace vague words, such as *very, somewhat, really,* and *rather* with more exact words.

   NOT   Homeless people have very few possessions, and because they really have no permanent place to stay, they somewhat tend to carry their rather few possessions around with them. (28 words)

   BUT   Because homeless people have no permanent place to stay, they tend to carry their few possessions around with them. (19 words)

3. Avoid carelessly repeating words and ideas.

   NOT   They take only the most essential things with them when they move. They leave things that are not essential behind.

   BUT   They take only the most essential things with them.

4. Don't overuse *there is/are* and *it is . . . that* to introduce sentences.

   NOT   There is a difference between being a homeless person and being a nomad.

   BUT   Being a homeless person is different from being a nomad.

   NOT   It is a feature of traditional nomads that they live in family groups or small communities.

   BUT   Traditional nomads live in family groups or small communities.

5. Reduce sentences to clauses, clauses to phrases, and phrases to single words.

> NOT   At different times they may travel to different family members. When they arrive, they may stay with different family members for a few months at a time. (27 words)

> BUT   They may travel to different family members, staying for a few months with each one. (15 words)

Exercise 4

Revise the following groups of sentences to make them more concise.

1. A study has been done on smokers. This study revealed that much smoking is an automatic response to certain activities. These activities might be driving, typing, reading, or drinking alcohol and coffee.

2. Being a video game player, I find it my duty to give a good name to video games because I find them challenging. I would like to change people's attitudes toward video games by giving some information in the hope that many people will discard their belief that these are mindless games and learn that these games require many years of practice.

3. Despite the costumes and castles, the heroine of *Ever After* seems remarkably like an independent modern woman. She is bright, feisty, innovative, brave, and craftily clever. Surely she has watched *Oprah*. She has her priorities straight. She is someone any contemporary woman would want to be. She values work. She fights to keep the family farm and instead of pining away when the going gets tough she gets busy. This Cinderella is a woman of action.

4. Convenience food is a product of technology and contains many negative things. A large majority of our food is loaded with preservatives and other harmful chemicals. You only need to read the back of any packaged food to identify numerous unknown ingredients.

5. He drove his car down the highway. He drove his car very fast. He was travelling about 150 km an hour. Suddenly he hit a very icy section of the road. The car went out of control and slid quite quickly in the direction of the ditch.

Exercise 5

Rewrite the following paragraph to make it more concise.

> There is a book called *Roots of Empathy* that is about a very effective program Mary Gordon developed that cuts down on the amount of bullying and aggression in the classroom. The program involves classroom visits by a parent and baby. Each month the parent and baby visit the classroom. There is also an instructor with special training. Each month the instructor visits the classroom a week before the baby comes. The

instructor talks a lot with the children about the really important changes they may see in the baby since the last visit. The next week the parent and baby visit the classroom. The children always sing a rather special welcoming song. They carefully observe the way the baby acts and they play very happily with the baby. The next week, the special instructor returns. The instructor talks to the children about what they observed. The instructor helps the children make connections between the baby's feelings and actions and things they have experienced in their own lives. It is the purpose of this interaction to help the children deal with their feelings and emotions. The children may share stories about being afraid, or the things that frighten them. Another time they may write poems about things that make them angry or sad. These visits help the children to develop emotional literacy. Emotional literacy is a term that describes a person's ability to understand another person's feelings and respond with empathy. Research studies have been carried out to test the effectiveness of this program. These research studies show that participation in this program reduces bullying and other kinds of aggressive behaviour in the classroom.

Review Exercise

A.   Write a brief paragraph analyzing the strengths and weaknesses of the paragraph below in terms of the points covered in this chapter. Does it make good use of a variety of sentence lengths and sentence patterns? Are transitional devices used effectively? Is it sufficiently concise?

Computer-typed assignments definitely depersonalize a child's work. Teachers can no longer identify a student through the handwritten craft, but must ultimately depend on the little name typed in the corner. Moreover, children gain personal satisfaction when they see their personal finished product. I work with young children who are learning English as a second language, and these children definitely feel a sense of achievement when they create the perfect B or S. It may take a great deal of time to acquire these skills, and an individual's penmanship is less important than it was years ago. Personally, I believe creativity is an essential part of our education. As a young girl I continually practised my handwriting, in order to achieve the aesthetic appeal of my mother's handwriting. Unfortunately, I no longer strive for this quality and the majority of my writing is done on the computer. Thus, although computers make the writing process easier for children, it is wiser to implement them at a later stage after they have mastered the art of handwriting.

B.   Rewrite the paragraph to remedy any problems you have identified.

E Creating an Appropriate Tone

Formal academic writing does not have to be stuffy or difficult to read. Indeed, you want to create a sense of yourself as a friendly, reasonable person writing for equally friendly, reasonable readers who may be less well informed or hold a different opinion. You create this tone by choosing appropriate pronouns of address, by using an appropriate level of diction, and by using words that accurately convey your meaning.

E1 You and Your Reader: Pronouns of Address

The **pronouns of address** you choose for a piece of writing set up a particular relationship among writer, reader, and subject. First-person pronouns suggest a conversation between friends. If you were writing about a personal experience, you would naturally use first-person pronouns (*I, me, my/ mine, we, us, our/ours*), as George Orwell does in "Shooting an Elephant" (Readings). Second-person pronouns, on the other hand, suggest a conversation between teacher and learner. Thus if you were giving directions on how to carry out a process, you would use second-person pronouns, as W. S. Merwin does in "Unchopping a Tree" (Readings). You might also use second-person pronouns to draw your reader into a hypothetical situation: "What would you do if you encountered a bear?"

Third-person pronouns suggest a more detached, objective point of view. Most often in college and university essays, you will want to keep your reader's attention focused on your subject, so you will use third-person pronouns (*he, she, it, they*). Most of the essays in the Readings, you will notice, are in the third person.

Some instructors forbid the use of first-person pronouns in academic writing. Others permit limited use of first-person pronouns when you clearly need to indicate your agreement or disagreement with a position or to express consensus with your readers. Follow these guidelines to ensure that you use the first person only when necessary and that you do so as unobtrusively as possible.

USING FIRST-PERSON REFERENCES

1. Avoid using "I" when you can rewrite the sentence to give a more general application.

    NOT   I had a hard time figuring out what these two lines mean.
    (Implies it's your fault)

    BUT   The meaning of these two lines is hard to grasp.
    (Implies that others would have the same difficulty)

2. Avoid apologetic expressions such as "this is only my opinion" and "I hope I will be able to show."

3. Avoid stilted expressions such as "one" and "this writer."

4. Use "I" as necessary when giving a personal example to support a point.

5. Use "I would argue" or similar wording when necessary to make a clear distinction between your position and the position you are arguing against.

6. Use "we" sparingly to refer to people in general. Be careful not to overgeneralize.

    NOT   We all remember our high school teachers with affection.

    BUT   Many of us remember our high school teachers with affection.

7. Keep expressions such as "I think" or "we have seen" inconspicuous by putting them inside the sentence.

    NOT   We have seen that oil is a major factor in the politics of the Middle East.

    BUT   Oil, as we have seen, is a major factor in the politics of the Middle East.

8. Avoid using "you" to refer to people in general (see E1b).

    NOT   By the end of the play, you can see that Macbeth is desperate.

    BUT   By the end of the play, Macbeth is obviously desperate.

1a Using Third-Person Pronouns: *He, She, They*

Although *he* and other masculine singular pronouns have traditionally been used to refer to both men and women, as in the example "The driver is responsible for the safety of all passengers in *his* vehicle," many people feel that this usage contributes to gender stereotyping. To avoid alienating your reader, try to use more inclusive language, but be careful not to introduce errors in pronoun agreement, as in "The driver is responsible for the safety of all passengers in *their* vehicle." Here are some suggestions for avoiding both sexist language and pronoun agreement errors. For more on the latter, see B2b Pronoun Agreement.

Using Inclusive Language

1. Reword the sentence to eliminate unnecessary gender pronouns.

    NOT The average commuter drives his car fifty kilometres a day.

    BUT The average commuter drives fifty kilometres a day.

2. Make the noun and pronouns plural.

    NOT   The enterprising executive sends his managers to study foreign business practices.

    BUT   Enterprising executives send their managers to study foreign business practices.

3. Alternate references to boys and girls, men and women in examples.

    NOT   Teachers sometimes complain about their students: "He never does his homework," "He constantly disrupts the class," "He never listens."

    BUT   Teachers sometimes complain about their students: "She never does her homework," "He constantly disrupts the class," "She never listens."

Exercise 1

Revise each of the following sentences to eliminate errors in the use of pronouns of address. Put C beside a correct sentence.

1. In this essay I hope to show that poison imagery pervades *Hamlet*.
2. We all remember junior high school dances with warm nostalgia.
3. To train a dog effectively, you should avoid games that involve pitting the dog's strength and agility against yours.
4. By the end of the novel, you can see that the protagonist is doomed.
5. The average student finds that working ten hours a week is about all he can handle in addition to his school work.

1b Avoiding Shifts in Pronouns of Address

Once you have decided on first-, second-, or third-person pronouns as your basic mode, be consistent in using them. If you shift pronouns without good reason, you will confuse or jar your reader.

The most common problem is the inappropriate use of first- or second-person pronouns in a piece of writing that is primarily in the third person, as in the following example:

> The student board governing the residence hall recently approved the installation of a security system designed to curb theft and vandalism by outsiders. With this system, you have locked doors, identification cards, security guards, and an obligatory sign-in procedure for visitors. Unfortunately, the system is ineffective because most of the damage is done by students who live in the residence.

You could eliminate the inappropriate shift to "you" in this paragraph by beginning the second sentence with "This system includes."

Exercise 2

Decide whether this paragraph would be most effective written in the first, second, or third person. Then revise the paragraph so that the pronouns of address are consistent.

> When you are on the borderline between adolescence and adulthood but still on the side of childhood, it is possible to have a bit of both worlds. One can choose to act responsibly or irresponsibly, and still usually have someone to cover up for you. After crossing the line, however, it is not as easy to forget responsibility and allow someone else to pick up the pieces of the bad choices. Different people cross the line at different times in their lives, and some people never cross it. However, it is an irreparable change. One cannot really remove the marks and responsibilities of adulthood without invoking the scorn of society.

E2 Choosing Appropriate Diction

One important element in creating an appropriate tone, as we have seen, is choosing the right pronouns of address. Equally important is your choice of **diction**: the individual words that make up your sentences. If you rely too heavily on formal, abstract language, your writing will seem stuffy and hard to understand. If, however, your writing is too informal, your reader may not take your opinions seriously.

Here are some guidelines for achieving a balance.

1. Eliminate very informal language and slang; they suggest you do not take your subject seriously.

   NOT   Bolivia has a lot of social and economic problems.

   BUT   Bolivia has many [a great many] social and economic problems.

> NOT   Hamlet was cheesed off by his mom's hasty marriage to his uncle.
>
> BUT   Hamlet was infuriated by his mother's hasty marriage to his uncle.

2. While the presence of some contractions (*don't, can't*) will give your writing a friendlier tone, too many contractions will make your writing seem too casual for a formal essay.

> NOT   Hamlet decides he'll feign madness while he's gathering proof that the ghost's telling the truth.
>
> BUT   Hamlet decides he will feign madness while he is gathering proof that the ghost is telling the truth.

3. Eliminate or define specialized vocabulary that may be unfamiliar to your reader.

> NOT   Self-worth is affirmed when one's self-image is validated by one's significant others.
>
> BUT   People like themselves better when their ideas and feelings about themselves are confirmed by those they care about.

4. Rewrite sentences that are too abstract or too grandiose.

> NOT   The interpersonal interaction between volunteer counsellors and clients can provide the opportunity for both parties to gain a sense of self-worth and significance in the midst of our institutionalized society. (Too abstract)
>
> BUT   Meetings between volunteer counsellors and clients can help both to feel more worthwhile.
>
> NOT   Throughout history man has struggled to understand his place in the ever-changing world in which he was only one infinitesimal link in the infinite chain of being. (Too grandiose and sexist)
>
> BUT   Men and women often struggle to understand their place in the world.

5. Eliminate expressions that are too apologetic or argumentative.

> NOT   I hope I will be able to show that some doctors over-prescribe medications because they want to meet their patients' expectations. (Too apologetic)
>
> BUT   Some doctors over-prescribe medications because they want to meet their patients' expectations.
>
> NOT   Any fool can see that the emission of greenhouse gases is a worldwide problem.
>
> BUT   The emission of greenhouse gases is a worldwide problem.

USAGE

Exercise 3

Rewrite the following paragraph so that its tone is appropriate for a university essay. You may need to check your dictionary to find replacements for some words.

> Perhaps there's no greater influence on the teeming masses of humanity than the society around them. People are coerced into buying bling-bling they don't need, cutting their locks in a manner that doesn't compliment their faces, and voting for rubber-ducky candidates they don't believe in. Then why should it be shocking that society is eliciting impressionable youth into anorexia or anabolic steroids? After all, the female concern with becoming ectomorphs is nothing more than a response to the male's expectation for a certain body type. Equally obviously, the male concern with abs and pecs is nothing more than a response to the contemporary glorification of exercise. By conforming to society's formal standards of what's appealing, anorexics and anabolic steroid users are simply buying into something that others around them deem attractive. As I hope I have shown, this isn't their fault—it's everybody's fault. It is because of everybody that youth are becoming sucked into the unhealthy lifestyles that march in tandem with being physically perfect.

E3 Choosing the Right Word: Usage

Some diction problems are not a matter of being too formal or too informal, but of confusing the meanings of similar words. Mistakes in **usage** may confuse your reader; they also undermine your credibility. To ensure that such mistakes don't mar your writing, check definitions in a dictionary whenever you are uncertain about the meanings of words. The following list will give you an idea of the kinds of words that are commonly misused.

1. *Affect* and *Effect*

   a. *Affect* is usually a verb.

      The early frost affected the tomatoes.

   b. *Effect* is usually a noun.

      The effect of the early frost on the tomatoes was obvious.

2. *Allude* and *Elude*

   a. Use *allude* when you mean "to refer to," as in an allusion to the Bible or the Quran.

      Forster frequently alludes to the Bible in his essay "My Wood."

   b. Use *elude* when you mean "to avoid" or "escape."

      The clever thief eluded the police for seven years.

3. *Allusion* and *Illusion*

   a. An *allusion* is a reference to a piece of literature, a historical event or figure, or a popular movie or television show.

     The speaker's frequent allusions to characters in popular television shows entertained the audience.

   b. An *illusion* is something that deceives by creating a false impression. An *illusion* can also refer to the state of mind in the person who is deceived.

     The use of perspective in the painting created the illusion of depth.

     Alison clung to the illusion that Juan would never forget her.

4. *Ambiguous* and *Ambivalent*

   a. Use *ambiguous* when you mean "having different possible interpretations."

     Jean-Paul left an ambiguous message on my answering machine.

   b. Use *ambivalent* when you refer to a person's having opposing emotional attitudes toward a single object.

     Taylor is ambivalent about attending law school: one moment she's keen, the next she can't stand the idea.

5. *Among* and *Between*

   a. Use *among* when you refer to more than two things.

     Divide the candy canes evenly among all the Christmas hampers.

   b. Use *between* when you refer to two things.

     Divide the prize money between the two winners.

6. *Amount* and *Number* (See also 16. *Less* and *Fewer*)

   a. Use *amount* to refer to things considered as a mass.

     Melt a small amount of butter in a pan.

   b. Use *number* to refer to things that can be counted as individual units.

     A small number of delegates attended the convention.

7. *Compare with* and *Compare to*

   a. Use *compare with* when you examine the similarities and differences in things.

     A comparison of the American Senate with the Canadian Senate strengthens the argument for electing senators.

   b. Use *compare to* when you want to point out the similarities in two things.

     I would compare her eating habits to those of a pig.

8. *Complement* and *Compliment*

   a. Use *complement* when you want to indicate something that completes or rounds out (noun) or the act of completing or rounding out (verb).

      He was born without a full complement of toes.

      This purse will complement your outfit.

   b. Use *compliment* to indicate an expression of praise or flattery (noun) or the act of praising or flattering (verb).

      Serena was embarrassed by her boss's compliments.

      I must compliment our server; he kept all the orders straight despite the changes.

9. *Continually* and *Continuously*

   a. Use *continually* when you mean "persistently."

      Our conversation was continually interrupted by the ringing of the telephone.

   b. Use *continuously* when you mean "without ceasing."

      The kitchen tap dripped continuously for two weeks.

10. *Differ from* and *Differ with*

    a. Use *differ from* to indicate that two things are unalike.

       The stage version of the play differs enormously from the film version.

    b. Use *differ with* to express disagreement with a person.

       I wish to differ with your assessment of the mayor's voting record.

11. *Different from* (not *different than*)

    The effects of an expectorant cough syrup are different from the effects of a cough suppressant.

12. *Elusive* and *Illusory*

    a. Use *elusive* when you want to describe something that is good at escaping or difficult to define or express.

       The elusive mouse disappeared through a crack in the wall.

       The specific implications of the new immigration policy remained elusive.

    b. Use *illusory* when you want to describe something that is false or unreal.

       The benefits of the proposed tax reduction are illusory.

13. *Eminent* and *Imminent*

    a. Use *eminent* when you mean "prominent" or "notable."

       He married into an eminent Quebec family.

    b. Use *imminent* to refer to a danger or threat near at hand.

       Flooding was imminent after the heavy rains.

14. *Flaunt* and *Flout*

   a. Use *flaunt* to refer to a conspicuous display of a person's attributes or possessions.

   Only the newly rich flaunt their wealth.

   b. Use *flout* to mean "to treat with scorn or contempt."

   Rebellious teens often flout authority.

15. *Imply* and *Infer*

   a. Use *imply* to mean "hint at."

   His lack of response to her entreaties implied his refusal to grant her wish.

   b. Use *infer* to mean "make an educated guess" or "draw a conclusion."

   The detective inferred from the blood on the sheets that the victim had been murdered in his sleep.

16. *Less* and *Fewer*

   a. Use *less* to refer to things considered as a mass.

   Although I am earning more, I seem to have less spending money.

   b. Use *fewer* to refer to things that can be counted.

   Fewer students than expected signed up for this course.

17. *Like* and *As*

   a. Use *like* when you are not introducing a clause.

   He looks like his father.

   b. Use *as* to introduce a clause.

   That night she dressed as she did when she was a girl.

18. *Partake of* and *Take part in*

   a. Use *partake of* when you mean "to have a share of something" (usually a meal).

   The guests were invited to partake of the enormous turkey.

   b. Use *take part in* when you mean "to join or participate."

   Will you take part in our volleyball game?

19. *Principle* and *Principal*

   a. *Principle* means "a fundamental belief."

   Most Canadians accept the principle of universal medical coverage.

   b. *Principal* means "most important," "first in rank."

   My principal objection is that cuts in services will inflict the most damage on the most vulnerable members of the community.

   He is the principal dancer with the Royal Winnipeg Ballet company.

USAGE

20. *Realize*

    a. Realize can mean "to make real," as in "to realize a profit."

    b. *Realize* can also mean "to understand fully," as in "to realize that he was wrong." You can avoid confusing these two meanings of realize if you use "realize that" when you mean "understand fully."

        NOT   He realized his mother's unhappiness.

        BUT   He realized that his mother was unhappy.

21. *Simple* and *Simplistic*

    a. Use *simple* when you mean "plain, easy to understand."

        Follow these simple directions.

    b. Use *simplistic* when you want to indicate something has been over-simplified. *Simplistic* always conveys a negative judgment.

        The premier offered only simplistic solutions to complex problems.

22. *Uninterested* and *Disinterested*

    a. Use *uninterested* to mean "not interested in."

        I am uninterested in politics.

    b. Use *disinterested* to mean "impartial."

        We need a disinterested third person to settle our dispute.

Exercise 4

Revise the following sentences to correct errors in usage. Sentences may contain more than one error.

1. From the noise in the lecture theatre, it is reasonable to imply that a large amount of people were quite disinterested in the topic.

2. Engineers must realize their responsibility to protect the environment.

3. Even on formal occasions, Ted dresses like he is going to a hockey game.

4. The principle difference in my two jobs is that I now work less hours and make more money.

5. The results of the medical tests were different than what the doctor had predicted.

Review Exercise

Identify problems with pronouns of address, level of diction, and usage in the paragraph below. Then rewrite the paragraph so that the tone is appropriate for an academic essay.

    I will begin by discussing television news and how it radically effects our lives. The news informs us about local and world events; however, we are bombarded with scads of information that is at times impossible to digest and understand. This information overload gives us the allusion that we are learning about and connecting with other countries, when in reality we are merely sitting in the living room, watching a square apparatus. We find the television news convenient because we can gain a summary of what's happening in the world in only half an hour. This is great when you are busy with your own life, but is such a summary possible or does television just create the allusion that it is possible? Every evening, as I watch CNN, I learn about the day's horrible travesties. Although for a brief period I'm disgusted by corporations flaunting government regulations or touched by the latest eminent disaster, I quickly become disinterested. The television news doesn't motivate me to do something or to help someone. Personally, I believe that if I were speaking in person to someone, I would be more likely to join a hand and help him. The news somewhat depersonalizes the personal because the main goal is to spew out as much information as possible in the shortest amount of time. The principle reason is that people only have enough time to partake in a simplistic version of the truth.

USAGE

F Punctuation

F1 Apostrophe

The **apostrophe** is used to indicate missing letters in *contractions* and to show *possession*.

1a Recognizing Plurals, Contractions, and Possessives

Plurals, contractions, and possessives are often confused because they sound the same.

> PLURAL Three bikes have been stolen in the last week.
>
> CONTRACTION This bike's for sale. (*Bike's* = bike is)
>
> POSSESSIVE The bike's front wheel is warped. (Front wheel belonging to the bike)

In order to use apostrophes correctly, you need to be able to distinguish among these three forms. The following points will help you.

1. Only nouns and indefinite pronouns (such as *everybody, someone, anything*) take an apostrophe to show possession.

2. Be careful, especially with proper nouns, not to add an apostrophe when you want to indicate a plural.

    > PLURAL All the Lees [plural of *Lee*] want to invite you to their reunion.
    >
    > POSSESSIVE The Lees' garage burned down last year. (The apostrophe shows that the garage belonged to the Lees.)

3. Do not use an apostrophe with possessive pronouns (*yours, hers, its, ours, theirs*).

    > NOT This problem is your's to solve.
    >
    > BUT This problem is yours to solve.
    >
    > NOT The dog pressed it's nose against the window.
    >
    > BUT The dog pressed its nose against the window.

1b Using Apostrophes to Show Possession

Making indefinite pronouns and singular nouns possessive

1. To make an indefinite pronoun possessive, add 's.

    Everybody's salary will be affected by the budget cutbacks.

2. To make a singular noun possessive, add 's.

    This little boy's epilepsy is getting worse.

3. To make a singular noun that ends with *s* possessive, add 's. Do not add only an apostrophe.

    Charles's car is in the shop again.

    The albatross's death haunted the Ancient Mariner.

Making plural nouns possessive

1. If the plural noun ends in *s*, add only an apostrophe.

    Both boys' bathing suits were lost.

    All the students' marks were excellent.

2. If the plural noun does not end in *s*, add 's.

    All children's toys, men's coats, and women's shoes are on sale.

Showing joint possession and separate possession

1. Joint possession: To indicate that two or more people possess something together, add 's to the last name.

    Tom and Brenda's house is for sale.

2. Separate possession: To indicate that two or more people possess things separately, add 's to each name.

    Tom's and Brenda's cars are for sale.

Exercise 1

Add an apostrophe or 's where necessary in the following sentences.

1. Sonya and Edwards bicycles were found as a result of their parents determined efforts.
2. Our boss main interest is in creating stronger international business connections.
3. The childrens destructive behaviour alarmed the staff.
4. This problem is nobodys fault but yours.
5. The Huis trailer was broken into.

APOSTROPHE

1c Other Uses of the Apostrophe

1. Expressions of time can be used as possessives. Be sure that the placement of the apostrophe indicates whether the noun naming the time period is singular or plural.

> I'll contact you in a month's time. (One month)
>
> We wasted two weeks' work.

2. To make letters plural, italicize the letter and add *'s*.

> Have you dotted your *i*'s and crossed your *t*'s?

3. To put a word referred to as a word in the plural, italicize the word and add *'s*.

> There are too many *however*'s in this sentence.

4. To make an abbreviation plural, you can add either *s* or *'s*.

> All the SPCAs in this province are running out of money.
>
> All the YMCA's in the city offer day camps.

5. To make a date plural, add *s* or *'s*.

> Throughout most of the 1980s Canada faced a constitutional crisis.

Note: Forming plurals without the apostrophe is becoming the preferred usage for both abbreviations and dates.

Exercise 2

Correct missing or misused apostrophes as necessary in the following sentences.

1. Hockey violence among fans as well as players has increased since the 1980's.
2. Nadeem spent a months holiday doing volunteer work at a mens shelter.
3. Its distracting when a speaker uses too many *you knows*.
4. Are these books yours or theirs?
5. The RCMPs response times to serious crimes have improved since the 1990s.

Exercise 3

Make a list of words with missing or misused apostrophes in signs, advertisements, and similar material. Bring your list to class for discussion.

F2 Comma

2a Main Clauses

Use a **comma** to separate main clauses joined by a coordinating conjunction (*and, but, or, nor, for, so, yet*).

> Inflation is under control, but unemployment is still a problem.
>
> No one has succeeded in proving the existence of UFOs, yet many have tried.

2b Subordinate Clauses

Use a comma to set off a subordinate clause at the beginning of a sentence.

> When economic conditions are poor, the incidence of family violence increases.
>
> Because the highways were icy, we postponed our trip.

2c Introductory Phrases

Use a comma to set off long (more than five words) or potentially confusing phrases at the beginning of a sentence.

> In his search for the meaning of life, he examined many religions. (Long phrase)
>
> In winter, darkness comes early. (Could be misread)

2d Items in a Series

Use a comma to separate more than two items joined by *and* or *or*. Include a comma before the conjunction so that the last two items are not read as a unit.

> We watched the children slide, swing, and climb.
>
> The horses galloped over the field, across the stream, and down the road.
>
> He ordered toast, eggs, coffee, and milk for breakfast. (Comma indicates that four items were ordered)

2e Non-restrictive and Restrictive Modifiers

Non-restrictive modifiers are clauses, phrases, and single words that add information about the preceding noun or pronoun but are not necessary to specify its meaning. Non-restrictive modifiers can be omitted without changing the basic meaning of the sentence.

> My dog[, who barks a lot,] sometimes disturbs the neighbours.

COMMA

In this sentence, "my dog" identifies what disturbs the neighbours. The non-restrictive modifier "who barks a lot" adds the why or how.

Restrictive modifiers, in contrast, cannot be omitted because they help to define the preceding noun or pronoun.

> Dogs [that bark a lot] disturb the neighbours.

Without the modifier, this sentence would suggest that all dogs are a neighbourhood nuisance; the modifier restricts the meaning to "dogs that bark a lot."

Use a pair of commas to set off non-restrictive modifiers. Do *not* set off restrictive modifiers.

Punctuating non-restrictive and restrictive modifiers

Clauses beginning with relative pronouns

a. *Which* clauses are almost always **non-restrictive,** and so should be set off with commas.

> The latest James Bond film, which opens Friday, is sure to be a hit.

b. *That* clauses are almost always **restrictive** and therefore do not take commas.

> The hand that rocks the cradle rules the world.

c. Clauses beginning with *who, whom,* or *whose* may be either non-restrictive or restrictive.

> NON-RESTRICTIVE Sutton, who injured his knees in a skiing accident, is slowly recovering.
>
> RESTRICTIVE Athletes who injure their knees often recover slowly.

Participial phrases These are phrases beginning with the past participle or *–ing* form of a verb. Participial phrases are condensed clauses. When they come after nouns, they follow the same rules as they would if expanded into clauses.

> NON-RESTRICTIVE Jennifer Aniston, starring in this summer's blockbuster, made her name in television.
>
> RESTRICTIVE The window broken by vandals will have to be replaced.

Appositives These are nouns or noun phrases that rename the preceding noun or pronoun. They may be either non-restrictive or restrictive. Set off non-restrictive appositives with commas.

> NON-RESTRICTIVE The Beatles, the most important rock group of the sixties, sold millions of records.
>
> RESTRICTIVE The film *The Compleat Beatles* is a history of the group's rise and fall.

Adjectives following nouns These are always **non-restrictive** and are therefore set off with commas.

> NON-RESTRICTIVE The dialogue, [which was] witty and fast-paced, made the play memorable.
>
> NON-RESTRICTIVE Lear, angry at his fate, railed against the heavens.

2f Parenthetical Expressions

Use commas to set off transitional words and phrases and other expressions that break the flow of the sentence.

> Developing countries, in contrast, may be resource-rich but capital-poor.
>
> This situation, I believe, leads to economic instability.
>
> Well, I'd better be going.
>
> There were, amazingly enough, thirty thousand people at the demonstration.

2g Dates and Place Names

Use a comma with dates and place names when more than one item of information is given.

> The centre of the Canadian automobile industry is Windsor, Ontario.
>
> Canada officially entered the Second World War on September 10, 1939.

2h Quotations

Use a comma to set brief quotations off from introductory material.

> One minister said, "This policy should never have been adopted."
>
> "This policy," said one minister, "should never have been adopted."

Exercise 4

Use a pair of commas to set off non-restrictive modifiers in the following sentences. Do not enclose restrictive modifiers with commas.

1. Children who are taught how to express their feelings are less likely to become bullies.
2. My parents traded in their SUV, which was a gas guzzler, for a more fuel-efficient hybrid.

COMMA

3. Miriam Toews, an award-winning Manitoba writer, will read from her novel *A Complicated Kindness*.

4. The triumphant Leafs, passing the Stanley Cup between them, skated around the rink.

5. The DVD that you borrowed from the library is two days overdue.

6. The driver, who has three prior convictions for drunk driving, has been charged in the hit-and-run accident.

7. *Akeelah and the Bee*, a documentary about spelling contests, provides fascinating glimpses into the lives of the contestants.

8. The employee who has the highest sales this month will receive a bonus.

9. The Canadian forces exhausted by their tour of duty in Afghanistan were sent home.

10. Many voters unhappy with the government's record switched their allegiance in the next election.

Exercise 5

Add commas, where appropriate, to the following sentences.

1. Because he could find no way to avoid the task he got to work.

2. In the morning light shone through the cracks in the roof.

3. Marvin on the other hand is steady hard-working and rather unimaginative.

4. Indeed some of these arguments deserve closer attention.

5. The negotiators were tired and hungry so they made little progress.

6. According to William Blake "Imagination has nothing to do with Memory."

7. In 1842 the Webster–Ashburton Treaty between Canada and Britain defined the Canadian frontier.

8. The United States and Britain declared war on Japan on December 8 1941 the day after the bombing of Pearl Harbor Hawaii.

9. Returning home after a strenuous workout Julia showered reached for a cold drink and collapsed on the sofa.

10. First Night festivities offer participants musical performances street theatre plays readings and a spectacular finale complete with fireworks.

Exercise 6

If you have problems with commas, decide which three uses of the comma you most need to focus on to increase the clarity and effectiveness of your writing. Make a list with examples of each of the three types of comma problems and bring your list to class for discussion.

F3 Semicolon

The **semicolon** is used in two ways: to join main clauses and to join a series of phrases or clauses that is too complicated for commas alone to clarify.

3a When to Use a Semicolon

1. Use a semicolon to join main clauses.

   a. When the ideas are closely related and there is no coordinating conjunction (*and, but, or, nor, for, so, yet*) to join the clauses.

      Mary was an idealist; Martha was a pragmatist.

   b. With a coordinating conjunction when the clauses are long or contain commas.

      The hard-boiled detective, as we have seen in the works of Dashiell Hammett, Raymond Chandler, and Ross MacDonald, is a distinctively American creation; but the amateur sleuth, popularized by British writers such as Dorothy Sayers, Agatha Christie, and Michael Innes, also appears in American fiction.

   c. When the second clause begins with a conjunctive adverb (*accordingly, besides, consequently, furthermore, hence, however, likewise, moreover, nevertheless, otherwise, still, therefore, thus*). Put a comma after a conjunctive adverb of more than one syllable. (See Note in F3b.)

      Byron's poetry soon eclipsed Scott's; therefore, Scott turned to writing novels.

      Few members of the legislature thought an election was necessary; nevertheless, the premier called one.

2. Use a semicolon to separate items within a series that contains commas.

   The defence attorney called three witnesses: her client's brother, who testified that his sister was with him the night of the crime; the brother's caretaker, who testified that he saw the defendant arrive at 10:15 p.m.; and the brother's neighbour, who glimpsed the sister as she left at 11:30 p.m.

3b When Not to Use a Semicolon

1. Do not use a semicolon to join a main clause and a subordinate clause.

   NOT   The restaurant switched to Fair Trade coffee; because the manager knew that customers would support the change.

   BUT   The restaurant switched to Fair Trade coffee because the manager knew that customers would support the change.

   OR   The restaurant switched to Fair Trade coffee; the manager knew that customers would support the change.

SEMICOLON

Note: Some writers misuse semicolons because they confuse subordinating conjunctions and conjunctive adverbs. Here is an easy way to remember the difference: conjunctive adverbs can be moved to different positions in a clause, whereas subordinating conjunctions cannot.

> The premier called an election; however [conjunctive adverb], few members of the party thought an election was necessary.

> The premier called an election; few members of the party thought an election was necessary, however.

> The premier called an election even though [subordinating conjunction] few members of the party thought an election was necessary.

2. Do not overuse semicolons. Too many semicolons will make your writing seem stuffy, as in the following passage.

> NOT   A good opera for beginners is *Carmen.* It is always a hit; it is packed full of recognizable tunes. The lead mezzo-soprano has to ooze with sex and burn with a fiery bitchiness; she has to be the consummate gypsy. In this story love is not the conqueror or sustainer; it is a colourful bird, rebellious and inconsistent. No one knows where it will perch; worse, no one knows when it will fly away. The key to *Carmen* is not heart-breaking emotion; it is passionate drama. If done well *Carmen* becomes absolutely thrilling; if done poorly the music is still great.

Notice how the passage is improved when some ideas are joined through subordination rather than coordination.

> BUT   A good opera for beginners is *Carmen.* Packed full of recognizable tunes, it is always a hit. The lead mezzo-soprano has to be the consummate gypsy, oozing with sex and burning with a fiery bitchiness. In this story love is not the conqueror or sustainer but a colourful bird, rebellious and inconsistent. No one knows where it will perch; worse, no one knows when it will fly away. Passionate drama, not heartbreaking emotion, is the key to *Carmen.* Done well, the opera is absolutely thrilling; done poorly, the music is still great.

Exercise 7

Add semicolons where appropriate to the following sentences.

1. Early in the play, Macbeth seems to recognize the futility of his ambition to remain king nevertheless he pursues his bloody ambitions.

2. Lady Macbeth has been described as fiendish however some critics argue that she is the ideal wife.

3. Macbeth believes the witches' prophecy that he will be killed by no man born of a woman he therefore feels invincible.

4. After the murder, Lady Macbeth, partly because she lacks Macbeth's vivid imagination, focuses on the immediate need to hide incriminating evidence but this strategy, which ignores Macbeth's susceptibility to supernatural fears, sets in motion the chain of events that dooms them both.

5. When Macbeth is terrified by his imagination, he arouses sympathy when he acts, he arouses contempt and hatred.

F4 Colon

Usually the **colon** indicates that what follows is an expansion of what has already been said. Use a colon for the following purposes:

1. To introduce a list that follows a complete clause. The items following the colon should be grammatically parallel.

> Car manufacturers have introduced several improvements: better restraint systems, better pollution control devices, and better rust-proofing.

Note: Do not use a colon when the list begins with *such as* or *for example*.

> Car manufacturers have introduced several improvements, such as better restraint systems, better pollution control devices, and better rust-proofing.

2. To introduce a phrase or clause that explains the preceding statement.

> He wanted only one thing out of life: to make money. (Explanatory phrase)

> My new car is a real lemon: it has broken down for the third time this month. (Explanatory clause)

3. To introduce a quotation. Both the quotation and the sentence that introduces it must be grammatically complete.

> Goldberg dismissed the arguments against changes in the Fisheries Act: "Contrary to the opinions expressed by packers and the fisheries unions, the proposed changes are not designed to increase federal control over the fishing industry."

Note: Do not use a colon when the sentence introducing the quotation ends with *that*.

> In his essay "African National Identities Can't Be Built on Soccer Fever," Jonathan Zimmerman states that "Americans love high-profile athletic events" (345 Readings).

COLON

Exercise 8

Add colons, where appropriate, in the following sentences. Put C beside any sentence that is correctly punctuated.

1. The setting was perfect for a horror movie a foggy night, an isolated house, shrieks and groans coming from unseen sources.

2. Monique is saving her money with one goal in mind to travel for a year.

3. When you are preparing for a long winter drive, be sure to bring some emergency equipment such as a sleeping bag, a candle, and several chocolate bars.

4. Macbeth clings to the witches' prophecies, saying that "I will not be afraid of death and bane, / Till Birnam forest come to Dunsinane."

5. Alexander and Shaler argue that there is a direct relationship between addiction and dislocation "Most people who cannot achieve a reasonable degree of psychosocial integration find that they must develop 'substitute' lifestyles in order to endure" (204 Readings).

Exercise 9

Write a paragraph in which you use colons in each of the three ways described above. Then replace the colons with dashes or other types of punctuation. Discuss with your classmates how these changes affect the tone of the paragraph.

F5 Dash

A **dash** (or pair of dashes) indicates an interruption in a train of thought or in the structure of the sentence. It creates an air of informality and so should be used sparingly in formal writing. Use the dash for the following purposes:

1. To set off abrupt shifts in thought.

    My Aunt Sadie—you remember her, don't you?—lived to be a hundred.

2. To set off a list when it comes in the middle of a sentence.

    She had established her goals in life—to travel, to have an interesting career, to develop close relationships—before she was sixteen.

Note: When the list comes at the end of the sentence, use a colon unless you want to indicate special emphasis, for which you use a dash.

    COLON Before she was sixteen, she had established her goals in life: to travel, to have an interesting career, to develop close relationships.

Exercise 10

Write a paragraph using dashes for the purposes described. Then replace the dashes with colons or other punctuation. Discuss with your classmates how the punctuation affects the tone.

DASH

F6 Parentheses

Use **parentheses** in these ways:

1. To enclose bibliographical information in the body of your essay.

> Tim Bowling's "Na Na Na Na, Hey Hey Hey, Goodbye" (2006) is a discussion of the author's ambivalent attitude toward NHL hockey.

2. To enclose explanatory material, such as brief definitions and historical information.

> British drivers open the bonnet (hood), put luggage in the boot (trunk), and fill their tank with petrol (gas).

> Mozart (1756–1791) was an accomplished musician by the time he was six.

3. To indicate that explanatory material is relatively unimportant.

> The mayor (who was re-elected by a slim majority) promised to improve transportation in the city.

If you want to emphasize explanatory material, set it off with dashes. If you don't want either to emphasize or to minimize its importance, set it off with commas.

Note: Don't use parentheses to enclose essential information.

> NOT   At a council meeting this morning, the mayor (who holds stock in several land development companies) disqualified herself from voting on the proposal to annex areas north and west of the city.

> BUT   At a council meeting this morning, the mayor—who holds stock in several land development companies—disqualified herself from voting on the proposal to annex areas north and west of the city.

6a Punctuating Material in Parentheses

1. If a complete sentence in parentheses is contained within another sentence, do not begin the parenthetical sentence with a capital letter or end it with a period.

> When spring finally arrived (winter had seemed endless), children suddenly appeared on the street.

2. If the phrase, clause, or sentence within parentheses requires a question mark or an exclamation mark, put the appropriate punctuation mark inside the closing parenthesis.

> Although credit cards sometimes lead people disastrously into debt (and who hasn't been appalled by a monthly statement?), they are essential for many business transactions.

Review Exercise 1

Insert commas, semicolons, colons, dashes, and parentheses where appropriate in the following sentences.

1. Let's divide our supplies into two categories inexpensive items in constant use and expensive items used only occasionally.

2. *Spider-Man* which attracted large audiences in 2002 spawned plenty of spinoff accessories.

3. There are two types of crimes in which the perpetrator deliberately chooses to break the law crimes of desperation and crimes of defiance.

4. A woman with a limited income perhaps a single parent might steal food for example to feed her family.

5. In *Hard Times* Dickens vividly portrays the monotonous mechanical lives of factory workers in his description of Coketown "It contained several large streets all very like one another . . ." (p. 213)

6. The goal of modern correctional institutions should not be punishment or revenge it should be the rehabilitation of the whole person.

7. *The Stone Angel* (1964) established Margaret Laurence as an important Canadian novelist.

8. The Pope needed only to show Galileo the instruments of torture Galileo's medical knowledge of what those instruments would do accomplished the rest.

9. When I returned home most unexpectedly I might add I was astounded at the changes that had occurred during my absence.

10. Ancient Chinese and Hindu societies had much in common both were unified through stable religious and cultural patterns both had little curiosity about foreign lands both were exploited by the West.

F7 Quotation Marks

This section covers the appropriate use of quotation marks as punctuation. For information on the format of quotations, the use of ellipses, and the integration of quotations into your writing, see H2 Quotations.

Use **quotation marks** to indicate direct speech, quotations from other writers, and titles of short works.

1. Put quotation marks around direct speech.

   DIRECT SPEECH Marie said, "I should get more exercise."

   INDIRECT SPEECH Marie said that she should get more exercise.

2. Put quotation marks around three or more consecutive words from any printed material.

   Virginia Woolf imagines what life would have been like for an equally talented sister of Shakespeare's, a sister who had "a taste for the theatre" and "a gift like her brother's, for the tune of words" (341 Readings).

3. Use single quotation marks for quotations within quotations.

> In her essay "Time and the Narrative Voice," Margaret Laurence states that "[i]n 'The Loons,' the narrative voice is also that of the older Vanessa" (271 Readings).

4. Use quotation marks to enclose titles of brief works (essays, magazine and newspaper articles, poems, short stories, songs, single episodes of a television series) that are part of larger works.

> Margaret Laurence's short story "The Loons" is a story in her collection of interconnected short stories, *A Bird in the House.*

5. You can put quotation marks around words referred to as words, but it's often clearer to italicize them (see F8 Italics).

> You use "because" three times in this sentence.

Do not put quotation marks around slightly informal expressions.

> NOT   Michaela needs to learn to "stand up" for herself.

7a Using Other Punctuation with Quotation Marks

1. Place commas and periods inside quotation marks.

> "Many plant species," he said, "are in danger of extinction."

2. Place colons and semicolons outside quoted material.

> Dan Gardner argues that "violence in black markets tends to be cyclical": when a powerful figure controls established networks, violence is minimized; but when something disrupts the status quo, "all hell breaks loose" (234 Readings).

3. a. Place other punctuation marks (question marks, exclamation marks, dashes) inside the quotation marks if they punctuate only the quoted words.

> The first lines of Keats's poem "La Belle Dame sans Merci" are "O, what can ail thee, knight-at-arms, / Alone and palely loitering?"

b. Place these punctuation marks outside the quotation marks if they punctuate the sentence containing the quotation.

> Do you agree with Keats's statement that "Beauty is truth, truth beauty"?

Exercise 11

Add or remove quotation marks as necessary in the following sentences.

1. Azim wished his brother would "buzz off" so that he could study.

2. Whenever you use a welding torch, said the shop teacher, make sure you wear goggles to protect your eyes.

QUOTATION MARKS

3. Jaylon said that "he could rap like Eminem."

4. Marika asked her teacher, What does Swift mean by the phrase deliver the Kingdom to the Pretender?

5. In his essay Na Na Na Na, Hey Hey Hey, Goodbye, Tim Bowling admits that he still smiles "with goofy fondness at the common graffiti of my childhood— Jesus Saves, Esposito Scores on the Rebound" (213).

F8 Italics

Slanted writing indicates italics in typeset and word-processed material. In typed and handwritten work, indicate by underlining. Use **italics** in the following ways.

1. For the titles of works published separately (books, plays, magazines, newspapers, CDs, films, television series). Titles of works that have been published separately are italicized even when these works are included in anthologies.

   > The students referred to *Hamlet* in their copies of the *Norton Introduction to Literature.*

2. For the names of ships and airplanes, works of art, and long musical compositions.

   > The choir practised three months for the performance of Handel's *Messiah.*

3. For words and letters referred to as words or letters.

   > The word *truly* does not contain an *e.*

4. For foreign words and phrases that have not been incorporated into English.

   > The setting epitomized what the Germans would call *Gemütlichkeit.*

5. For emphasis.

   > Library materials *must* be returned by the end of term.

   Be careful not to overuse italics for emphasis, especially in formal academic writing.

Exercise 12

Add or remove quotation marks and italics as necessary in the following sentences.

1. Annie Proulx's short story Brokeback Mountain, which appeared in the New Yorker in 1997 and in the short story collection Close Range: Wyoming Stories in 1999, was recently made into a film.

2. There was a great "to-do" over the sinking of the Titanic.

3. Margaret Wente's column on The Decline of Public Language was published in the Globe and Mail on August 13, 2005.

4. George asked, How many m's are there in the word accommodate?

5. The French word tristesse suggests not merely sorrow but melancholy.

6. In his essay Food Connections, David Suzuki points out that the word dirt in our society is a pejorative.

7. Allison Crowe's song By Your Side is available on the CD "Live at Wood Hall."

8. The Sound of Music, a perennial favourite on stage and screen, was based on the book The von Trapp Family Singers by Maria von Trapp.

9. Many children still learn the classic nursery rhyme Baa, Baa, Black Sheep, which begins with the question Baa, baa, black sheep, have you any wool?

10. How many times does the phrase Quoth the raven, Nevermore appear in Poe's poem The Raven?

Review Exercise 2

Insert punctuation as necessary in the paragraph below. Do not make any other changes. The paragraph is from an essay on *Dubliners*, a collection of short stories by James Joyce.

The final story of Dubliners returns to the subject of the first story mortality. Joyce divides The Dead into two separate scenes the Christmas gathering of family and friends and the hotel room where the main character Gabriel and his wife Gretta spend the night. Gabriel who is named for the archangel of good news Luke 1:26 believes he is the master of his surroundings. During the Christmas gathering he certainly seems to be in control. He is responsible for drunk Freddy he carves the turkey and he gives the speech. In the second scene Gabriel comes to the realization that he is not in control. When he and Gretta arrive at their hotel room Gabriel is consumed by passion and wants to dominate his wife. As he says he wants to be master of her strange mood p. 235. Gretta however is overwhelmed by long-buried grief for the young man who died for love of her. When Gretta tells her husband about Michael Furey Gabriel is forced to realize that it is death that controls people's lives. Many characters in Dubliners long to escape from their city and their lives most obviously Eveline in the story of that name and Chandler in A Little Cloud. Only Gabriel realizes there is no escape except through death.

Review Exercise 3

Bring to class an advertisement that uses a variety of punctuation. What is the effect of the punctuation? What tone does it create?

G Spelling and Mechanics

G1 Spelling

Here are some tips that will help you to proofread for spelling errors more efficiently.

1. Check the spelling of the subjects you are writing about, including titles, authors' names, place names, technical terms, and so on. If you put your instructor's name on your title page, check the spelling of that too.

2. Use the spell-checker on your word processor. If you are a weak speller, pay attention to the spell-checker in your word processing program, and your word processor lacks this feature, consider buying one. You might also consider buying a current dictionary. Spell-checkers will pick up most typos and commonly misspelled words. They will not, however, consistently pick up homonyms: *to/too, there/their/they're, your/you're, it's/its, compliment/complement.* Nor will they pick up typos that would be legitimate words in a different context, such as insurance "clams" (for "claims").

3. Spell-checkers may show Canadian spellings (*labour/defence/centre*) as errors. If you find this irritating, you can add Canadian spellings to the spell-checker or select Canadian English from the language options of your word-processing software.

4. Be consistent in your use of either Canadian or American spellings. Don't write *theatre* in one sentence and *theater* in the next.

5. Some instructors regard errors in the use of apostrophes as spelling mistakes, whereas others see them as punctuation errors. Either way, apostrophe errors can significantly undermine the quality and the credibility of your writing. If you are not sure how to use apostrophes, check F1, Apostrophes, and try to memorize the rules.

6. If you are not sure how to spell a word, don't guess. Consult a dictionary.

7. Don't rely on spell-checkers to find all your spelling errors. Print out a hard copy and read it carefully, sentence by sentence. Make a list of the words you often misspell and check your work for them.

Headliners on the list of commonly misspelled words include the following. It's worthwhile to memorize them:

COMMON SPELLING ERRORS

a lot, acquire, among, argument, conscience, conscious, definitely, depdendant (n.)/dependent (adj.), develop, embarrass, environment, even though, existence, interest, occurred, occurrence, prejudiced, privilege, rhyme, rhythm, separate, similar, subtly, tragedy, unnecessary, weird

Exercise 1

Correct all the spelling errors in the following sentences. Most sentences contain more than one error. Correct any errors in the use of apostrophes.

1. Tanis intrest in school has increased noticably since she seperated from her husband.

2. At the begining of the term, Tanis draged herself to all her class, but her heart was definately not in her studys.

3. Like most people, Tanis was embarassed by her marriage problems and rather lonly as well, but now she is enjoying her independance.

4. She is also acheiving better grades, especially in her childrens' literature and micro computer managment courses.

5. Eventhough Tanis worrys that people might be prejudice against a women who has decided to abandon the priviledges of the affluent middle class, she has decided to devote her summer to an enviromental protection project on Bafln Island.

G2 Hyphens

Use a **hyphen** in these ways:

1. With some compound words: *brother-in-law, major-general, buy-in.*

   Note: Other compound words are written as a single word (*textbook, stepmother, railway*) or as two words (*income tax, down payment, gallows humour*). There is no set pattern for forming compound words, so check your dictionary.

2. With two-word numbers (from twenty-one to ninety-nine) and with fractions used as adjectives. Do *not* hyphenate when the fraction functions as a noun.

   > The gas tank was one-third full. (*One-third* as adjective)
   >
   > One third of the students withdrew from the course. (*One third* as noun)

3. To join two words that function as a single adjective and convey a single idea. If this construction comes after the noun, do *not* hyphenate unless the construction is conventionally spelled with a hyphen. Do *not* hyphenate if the construction contains an *–ly* adjective.

> a well-organized essay
>
> The essay is well organized.
>
> a poorly organized essay

4. With the prefixes *self* (*self-sufficient*), *ex* (*ex-wife*); with prefixes that come before proper nouns (*anti-Catholic*); with the suffix *elect* (*president-elect*).

5. To prevent confusion: *re-mark* (mark again), *ten-year-old* children/ten *year-old* children.

6. To show that two or more prefixes share a common root.

> The results of both the pre- and the post-test were excellent.

2a How to Hyphenate Words at the End of a Line

Avoid dividing a word at the end of a line whenever possible.

Do not hyphenate

1. One-syllable words. (*Dragged,* for example, should not be hyphenated.)
2. Words of six or fewer letters even if they contain two or more syllables. (Do not hyphenate *diet, beauty, elegy.*)
3. Words in more than two consecutive lines in a paragraph, the last word in a paragraph, or the last word on a page.

To hyphenate a word If you occasionally need to hyphenate a word, follow these rules:

1. Try to divide it into two approximately equal parts that convey the sense of the whole word.
2. Divide the word between syllables, making sure that the first part of the word contains at least three letters: *com-fort, impor-tance.*
3. If a double consonant appears at the end of a word because you have added a suffix (*running, committed*), divide the word between the double consonants (*run-ning, commit-ted*). If the double consonant is part of the root word, divide between the root word and the suffix (*drill-ing*).
4. Include a one-letter syllable with the first part of the word (*tabu-late* not *tab-ulate*).

HYPHENS

Exercise 2

Hyphenate each of the following words as if it appeared at the end of a line. Put C beside a word that should not be hyphenated.

1. conferred
2. usable
3. heroes
4. recommend
5. stipulate
6. butterfly
7. begged
8. spilling
9. definitely
10. language

G3 Numbers, Capitalization, and Abbreviations

3a Numbers

Use numerals (1, 2, 3, . . .):

1. To express numbers in scientific and technical writing.
2. For a series of numbers.
3. For numbers that cannot be expressed in two words.
4. For dates.
5. For page, verse, act, scene, and line numbers.

Use words:

1. For numbers that can be expressed in one or two words.
2. When you begin a sentence with a number.

3b Capitalization

All proper nouns are capitalized. A proper noun names a specific person, place, or thing.

> We'll meet this afternoon for a picnic in the *park*. (Common noun)

> We'll meet this afternoon for a picnic in *Central Park*. (Proper noun)

Use capitalization in the following ways.

1. Capitalize titles of family members when the title substitutes for a name.

   > I asked Mother for a ride downtown.

   Do *not* capitalize titles of family members if they are preceded by a possessive pronoun: my father, your aunt, their brother.

2. Capitalize the names of languages, nationalities, and religions: English, Canadian, Buddhism.

NUMBERS

3. Do *not* capitalize the name of an academic discipline unless it's the name of a language: chemistry, psychology, French.

4. Capitalize the names of specific courses: Chemistry 101, Psychology 260.

5. Capitalize the names of faculties: the Arts Faculty, the Faculty of Education.

6. Capitalize the words *college* and *university* when used with the name of an institution (Camrose Lutheran College). Do *not* capitalize these words when used alone: "The drama department at the university has an excellent reputation."

7. Capitalize the days of the week and the months, but not the seasons: Tuesday, January, spring.

8. Capitalize *Native* and *First Nations* when referring to Aboriginal peoples. Do *not* capitalize colour words used to refer to ethnic groups: black, white.

9. Do *not* capitalize the names of directions unless they are used as place names.

> Turn north after you cross the bridge.
>
> The old priest had lived in the North for twenty years.

10. Do *not* capitalize to create emphasis.

3c Abbreviations

1. Use abbreviations sparingly in most essays. If it's desirable to abbreviate a term you repeat frequently, give the term in full the first time; then give the abbreviation.

> Sudden infant death syndrome (SIDS) is not fully understood. It seems, however, that SIDS occurs more frequently in the winter months.

2. Do *not* abbreviate days of the week or months of the year.

3. Put *BC* (before Christ) after the year to refer to dates before the birth of Christ.

> Socrates committed suicide in 399 BC.

Use *AD* (in the year of our Lord) before the year to refer to dates after the birth of Christ up to AD 500.

> Venice was founded by refugees from Attila's Huns in AD 452.

Some writers prefer to use *BCE* (before the common era) and *CE* (common era). Both these abbreviations appear after the year.

4. Do not abbreviate *and* with an ampersand (&) unless you are copying the name of an organization (McClelland & Stewart) or following a particular style of documentation, such as APA.

5. Avoid abbreviations for Latin terms, such as e.g. (*exempli gratia*) or i.e. (*id est*). Instead, write out their English equivalents.

> NOT   From then on he was considered a coward; e.g., no one forgot that he had saved himself first when the hotel caught fire.
>
> BUT   From then on he was considered a coward; for example, no one forgot that he had saved himself first when the hotel caught fire.
>
> NOT   Susan gradually came to understand the erosion of self-esteem caused by racism: i.e., the assumption that a person's worth could be reliably assessed by the colour of his or her skin.
>
> BUT   Susan gradually came to understand the erosion of self-esteem caused by racism: that is, the assumption that a person's worth could be reliably assessed by the colour of his or her skin.

6. Avoid using *etc.* Use a phrase such as "and so on" or "and similar items" at the end of the list, or use "such as" or "for example" at the beginning of the list.

> NOT   Unemployment in this region has increased because of plant closures, the decline in tourism, the decreased demand for agricultural produce, etc.
>
> BUT   Unemployment in this region has increased because of factors such as plant closures, the decline in tourism, and the decreased demand for agricultural produce.

Exercise 3

Correct all errors in the use of numbers, capitalization, and abbreviations in the sentences below.

1. On October thirtieth, the V.P. announced that the Northern end of the railway line had finally been completed.

2. My Brother & I like to go camping for 2 weeks every Summer.

3. The native friendship centre in our area hosts an annual barbecue to which everyone in the neighbourhood is invited. 151 people attended last year.

4. On our trip to the middle east last december, we noticed considerable tension between fundamentalist christians and muslims.

5. When Susan and her husband were robbed in an outdoor café in Rome, they lost most of their valuables: their passports, wallets, traveller's cheques, cameras, etc.

H Format

H1 Essay Format

Here are the most common conventions for the **format** of the essay and the title page. Be sure to confirm your choice of format with your instructor. For information on documenting the sources you use, see H3 Documentation.

1a Manuscript Conventions

Most students use a word processor to write their papers. Familiarize yourself with the formatting functions of your word-processing program for optimum efficiency. Either your instructor or the technical support staff at your college or university can help you with special items such as page or section breaks, hanging indents for bibliographical lists, and so forth.

If you are handing in a hard copy of your paper, staple or clip the pages in the top left corner. Do not use any other method to secure the pages. If you are submitting your paper electronically, follow all manuscript conventions and give your document a concise file name that clearly identifies you and the assignment. Always keep a copy of your essay.

Manuscript conventions for word-processed essays

1. Choose a standard font and size such as Times New Roman and 12 point for all parts of your essay and title page. Make sure you have a spare black ink cartridge for your printer.

2. Use white, 8½ × 11 inch paper in your printer. For drafts, you can save paper by printing on both sides, but your final copy should be printed only on one side of the page.

3. Double space all parts of your essay. Indent each paragraph with one tab and do not leave extra lines between indented paragraphs.

4. The default margins are sufficient; they are usually set at 2.5 cm or 1 inch all around a page of text.

5. Insert automatic page numbers according to the system of documentation you are using. All pages, including the first or title page and the

Works Cited or References list, can be numbered. Using an automatic header saves space and effort.

Conventions for handwritten essays

1. Use blue or black ink and make sure your writing is legible.

2. Use white, 8½ × 11 inch ruled paper but not loose-leaf, notepaper, or other kinds of punched paper. Write only on one side of the page.

3. To double space, skip every other line. Indent each paragraph 1 inch and do not leave extra lines between indented paragraphs.

4. Leave generous margins of at least 2.5 cm or 1 inch all around a page.

5. Number your pages consecutively, including the first or title page and the Works Cited or References list.

1b Title Page

A title page or cover sheet creates a first impression and provides necessary information. Take the time to present your work effectively. Do not scribble a title page at the last minute before handing in your essay.

Title The title is important. At a minimum, it should make clear which topic you are addressing. Never simply label your paper "Essay 1." If you pay attention to the titles in essays and articles that you read, you will see that good titles are usually a short form of the thesis.

In all styles of title page format, present the title in regular font and size. Capitalize the first word and all other words except articles (*a, an, the*), coordinating conjunctions (*and, but, or, . . .*), short prepositions (*on, at, in, of, for*), and the *to* in infinitives. Do not underline the title of your essay or put quotation marks around it. Do not put a period after it.

If your title includes the name of a work you are analyzing, put the title in quotation marks or use italics, following the rules outlined in the sections on Quotation Marks and Italics (F7 and F8).

For the format of your title page, follow the system of documentation you are using in your essay. Two of the most widely accepted styles of documentation are those of the Modern Language Association (MLA), used primarily in the humanities, and the American Psychological Association (APA), used in the sciences and social sciences. Some

FORMAT

instructors, however, will want you to prepare a generic title page with the title in the middle and your name, the date, and class information in the bottom right corner.

Title page format—MLA According to the *MLA Handbook*, you do not need a separate title page. Instead, your information and title appear double-spaced on the first page of your essay. With the automatic page numbering in place (as discussed earlier), put the following information in separate lines at the top left-hand corner in regular font and size: your name, your instructor's name, the course number, and the date. Next comes your title, centred, immediately above the beginning of your text. Here is a scaled-down sample in the MLA style:

Strong 1

L. Strong

Professor Loverso

English 101 (20)

28 June 2011

Tone in William Carlos Williams's "This Is Just to Say"

In "This Is Just to Say," one of William Carlos Williams's subjects is the complexity of language.

Title page format—APA The *APA Publication Manual* prescribes a separate title page with three distinct parts. First is the running head (not to exceed 50 characters) with essay title (or abbreviated title) in uppercase and the page number. The page number should be about 2.5 cm or 1 inch from the right-hand margin. Next is the title, in uppercase and lowercase, centred and positioned in the upper part of the page. Below the title, APA format requires your name and institutional affiliation; however, for most academic papers, you should also include the instructor's name, the date, and your course number. Third is an author note, which sets out the author's departmental affiliation, acknowledgments, disclaimers, and contact information. An author's note is usually required only for publishable material, not student assignments, theses, or dissertations. Here is a scaled-down sample in the APA style:

The Problem of Environmental Costs:

Suzuki vs. Merwin

Joyce MacDonald

3 March 2011

Sociology 101

Professor Smith

Grant MacEwan University

H2 Quotations

Quotations can be very effective tools to improve your writing. Quotations should not be thought of as a mere requirement for an assignment, however; rather, they should serve a specific purpose. For example, in essays on literature, it is usually essential that you quote the text you are analyzing. In research writing, you often will support your position by drawing upon secondary sources such as experts or authorities in relevant fields. When used for these purposes, quotations can strengthen or clarify your writing.

There is no set standard for how many quotations you should use in an essay. You will need to use your own judgment to decide if a quotation is necessary. Remember, however, that an essay should be about *your* ideas. If the essay includes too many quotations, your own voice and ideas may get lost. If the quotations begin to dominate an essay, the reader may wonder what you, and not the quotations, are saying.

These guidelines will help you decide when quotations are most effective.

2a When to Quote

1. When the precise wording of a short passage of prose, such as the definition of a key term, is the starting point for your analysis or evaluation of a concept, theory, proposal, or text. For example, you may find that a particular writer makes good distinctions between the different meanings for the terms *female, feminine,* and *feminist.*

2. When you are integrating research from an authority in a subject. For example, if you were writing about technology and its social effects, you would want to include statements from authorities who hold both positive and negative opinions of technology.

3. When you offer your own interpretation. Essays on literature often require that you present your opinion of a text. You need to explain why you reach your conclusions, and you can do this by quoting specific passages from the text. For example, you might make the following argument:

Tim Bowling overstates his argument about hockey when he suggests that boys are "sexually abused by their coaches" (213) because not all boys are subjected to such abuse, such abuse is not limited to hockey culture, and not all coaches abuse boys.

2b When Not to Quote

1. When you can paraphrase or summarize information without loss of meaning or impact. Both paraphrasing and summarizing demonstrate that you understand what you have read because you are able to put the material into your own words. You may paraphrase a writer's ideas to make the language more accessible to your reader. For example, scholarly writing can often employ very complicated terminology, and you may want to state an idea using plain language. You should summarize material when you wish to emphasize major ideas or concepts from a text. For example, academic studies will often include extensive data, examples, or analyses. You may find that you wish to focus on the conclusions a researcher draws rather than on specific examples in his or her study (for more on summarizing, see Chapter 2). Whenever you paraphrase or summarize materials, you

must include appropriate bibliographic information (see Chapter 11 and H3 Documentation).

2. When you state statistics or well-known facts. For example, you need not quote the fact that the Second World War lasted from 1939 to 1945. Usually you should refrain from quoting passages that consist mostly of statistics, numbers, examples, technical jargon, and similar material.

3. When writing a thesis statement. Do not rely on other people's ideas or cliché phrases to make your thesis.

4. When the quotation merely repeats your point. You can generally integrate the two (see H2c, number 3).

5. When you have already used a particular passage. Do not repeat quotations of significant length.

2c How to Use Quotations

1. Introduce the source. If the quotation comes from a previously unmentioned person, identify the person by first and last names; otherwise, use only the last name. For sources other than people (such as reference books, institutions, or governments), state the official title of the source.

> NOT   It seems clear that "social environment can be more toxic than any pollutant."

> BUT   Toynbee summarizes Wilkinson's argument this way: "social environment can be more toxic than any pollutant" (331).

2. Make sure you give readers enough context to understand the quotation. There are two important contexts to consider: the context of the original material and the context of your own writing. It is commonly understood that you should not take something out of context. For example, consider the following sentence:

> Jonathan Swift argues that children are "a most delicious, nourishing, and wholesome Food" (316).

This statement seems to indicate that Swift supports cannibalism. The sentence fails to communicate Swift's irony. When quoting, you must represent the original materials in their appropriate context.

Similarly, you should indicate why or how a quotation is relevant to your purpose. Do not include a quotation for no purpose or to appear important. Instead, when you quote something, you must explain the point it illustrates or supports. Notice that the following statement not only acknowledges the irony in the quotation from Swift but also gives the writer's interpretation of the purpose of Swift's irony:

> When he claims that children are "a most delicious, nourishing, and wholesome Food" (316), Jonathan Swift is using irony to critique the English and the Anglo-Irish for the political and economic policies that are consuming the Irish people.

3. Ensure that your point about the quotation is clear. Do not use rhetorical questions to make your point. Do not assume that the meaning of the quotation or how you are using the quotation is self-evident.

NOT   In her review of Richard G. Wilkinson's book on social inequality, Polly Toynbee claims that "for most people respect is measured in money" (331). Money is very important to people, and who wouldn't want to make a lot of money?

BUT   While Polly Toynbee states that "for most people respect is measured in money" (331), her review of Richard G. Wilkinson's book on social inequality demonstrates that the distribution of wealth, not wealth itself, determines the levels of respect and health in any society.

4. Instead of introducing quotations (or paraphrases and summaries) with "he/she says/writes," use verbs that reveal the degree of certainty with which the author makes statements. You can convey how the author uses ideas and information (or how you perceive the author to be using ideas and information) by using verbs such as these: *acknowledges, argues, articulates, avoids, claims, concludes, confirms, demonstrates, denies, disproves, engages, estimates, evades, expands, hopes, hypothesizes, ignores, illustrates, proves, recognizes, reveals, speculates, states, theorizes.* Consider the following examples:

John Smith *says* that "95% of people disagree with smoking bylaws."

John Smith *confirms* that "95% of people disagree with smoking bylaws."

John Smith *speculates* that "95% of people disagree with smoking bylaws."

John Smith *estimates* that "95% of people disagree with smoking bylaws."

In each example, the meaning of the quotation changes substantially, even though the quotation is the same.

5. Ensure that your point is related to the quoted material. Students will sometimes make a statement about a text which is either unsupported by the quotation or inaccurate to the text.

NOT   Dan Gardner thinks that "it is a mistake to think law enforcement can eliminate the drug trade and the violence swirling around it" (235). Being a police officer is a dangerous job, and the police take great risks to protect the average citizen.

BUT   When Dan Gardner claims that "it is a mistake to think law enforcement can eliminate the drug trade and the violence swirling around it" (235), he suggests that the problems with drugs and violence cannot be solved by the police force alone; rather, the main problem lies with market forces such as supply and demand.

6. Integrate quotations into your own writing. Do not merely insert a sentence-length quotation between two of your own sentences. Do not string quotations together.

NOT   Silence is important in the novel *Obasan*. Naomi's silence "is a discourse that cures precisely because it simultaneously mimics and resists" (Kamboureli 209).

BUT   Smaro Kamboureli asserts that in *Obasan*, Naomi paradoxically "practices the talking cure but does so in silence." Often, Naomi's silence "is a discourse that cures precisely because it simultaneously mimics and resists" (209).

NOT   The anthropologist Louis Leakey situated Jane Goodall in Gombe to study chimpanzees. "Gradually I was able to move nearer the chimpanzees, until at last I sat among them, enjoying a degree of acceptance that I had hardly dreamed possible." "I was to discover as much as possible about the way of life of the chimpanzee before it is too late—before encroachments of civilization crowd out, forever, all nonhuman competitors (Goodall 275–76)."

BUT   Jane Goodall was situated in Gombe to study chimpanzees, where she "sat among them, enjoying a degree of acceptance that [she] had hardly dreamed possible." Goodall states that she "was to discover as much as possible about the way of life of the chimpanzee before it is too late—before encroachments of civilization crowd out, forever, all nonhuman competitors" (275–76).

7. Use the correct terminology. Usually, it is not advisable to refer to a quotation as a quotation in your writing. Quotation marks ("") or indented lines (for long quotations) indicate that something is a quotation. Therefore, you need not write, "The following quote shows that . . . " or "As the previous quotation demonstrates . . . " If you find you must draw attention to a quotation as such, use the correct terminology. *Quote* is a verb; *quotation* is a noun. I may *quote* an authority in my writing, but I am using a *quotation* to support my point.

2d How to Format Quotations

Quotations are most often used for support, clarification, or analysis. They should be as short as possible. Avoid quoting materials that are irrelevant to your writing and its purpose. Try to isolate key words, phrases, or clauses that best articulate the point you want to make.

Quotations almost always require **in-text citations**: parenthetical references indicating their source. The format for in-text citations varies according to the style guide used in specific disciplines. You will find guidelines for MLA style (commonly used in literary studies) and APA style (commonly used in the social sciences) in H3 Documentation.

Integrating quotations Since quotations should be as short as possible, you will most often integrate quotations directly into your own sentence by using quotation marks.

The format for short prose quotations (from an article, a book, a short story, or a play written in prose, for example) differs slightly from the format for short poetry quotations.

- **Prose:** A quotation of four lines of text or less (MLA style) or of fewer than 40 words (APA style) should be integrated into your own sentence. Put the in-text citation in parentheses after the closing quotation mark, followed by the end punctuation for the sentence.

    In his article on globalization, James Howard Kunstler argues that American suburbs filled with box stores are "the greatest misallocation of resources in the history of the world" (255).

- **Poetry:** When quoting a poetry passage of fewer than four lines, use a slash (/) to indicate line breaks in the verse. The parenthetical reference follows the closing quotation mark and includes line numbers (act.scene.line numbers for verse plays divided into acts and scenes, such as the plays of Shakespeare: *Macbeth* 1.1.5–7).

    In the poem "This Is Just to Say," we can read the phrase "forgive me" as an appeal for forgiveness that is cuttingly undermined because it is juxtaposed with the lines "they were delicious / so sweet / so cold" (10–12).

There are three principal ways to introduce integrated quotations: with a colon; with an active verb and a comma; with no punctuation.

- **Colon:** Ensure that the writing before the colon is a complete sentence.

    David Suzuki offers an important insight into the impact of technology: "If every technology has a cost, the more powerful the technology, the greater its potential cost" ("It Always Costs" 312).

- **Active verb with a comma:** Use the author's name with an active verb (such as *writes, states, claims, argues*). The quotation must be a complete sentence.

  Speaking about Africa in his article on sport and nation, Jonathan Zimmerman writes, "In a continent ravaged by political and ethnic violence, people often invoke sports—especially soccer—as [a] force for national unity" (345).

  Note that the comma can be replaced with *that:*

  Speaking about Africa in his article on sport and nation, Jonathan Zimmerman writes that "[i]n a continent ravaged by political and ethnic violence, people often invoke sports—especially soccer—as [a] force for national unity" (345).

- **No punctuation:** If possible, try to quote key phrases or clauses within the grammatical structure of your own writing.

  Reflecting upon the allure of hockey to Canadians, Tim Bowling concludes that "the primal pull of narrative" (212) is what most strongly links almost every Canadian to the national sport.

Indenting quotations Occasionally you may need to quote a longer passage. In essays on literature, you may want to offer a detailed analysis of numerous literary qualities of the text. In research writing, you may want to quote a particularly convincing argument or an intricate line of reasoning. Quotations too long to integrate smoothly into your own writing should be indented.

Because of their length, indented quotations must be able to stand alone as independent and complete thoughts. Therefore, indented quotations will usually have a more definite grammatical separation from preceding materials. The most common way to introduce an indented quotation is to use a colon, as in the following examples. Do not put quotation marks around the quotation unless you are quoting dialogue that contains quotation marks.

- **Prose:** In MLA style, if a quotation exceeds four text lines, then you need to indent the quotation. If you are using APA style, the cut-off point for indented quotations is 40 or more words of text. An indented quotation is signalled by a break in the paragraph. The quoted text is indented from the left-hand margin of the page: 2.5 cm or 1 inch in MLA style and 1.25 cm or ½ inch in APA style. Font size and spacing remain consistent with the rest of the text in the essay. The parenthetical reference follows the final punctuation of the quotation.

In "Addiction in Free Markets," Bruce K. Alexander and Stefa Shaler criticize dominant media institutions for perpetuating false information about the benefits of free market systems:

> They [the media] endlessly publicize new medical explanations for the puzzling epidemic of "drug" addiction and hopeful new solutions. They continue decades of futile debate about whether addiction is a "criminal" or a "medical" problem whereas, in fact, it is neither. In free market society, the spread of addiction is primarily a political and spiritual problem. (205)

- **Poetry:** When you are quoting poetry that exceeds three lines of verse, the quotation must start on a new line and be indented 2.5 cm or 1 inch from the left-hand margin. Any formal or stylistic features, such as capitalization and length and placement of lines, must be retained in the formatting.

In the final stanza of "This Is Just to Say" (Rhetoric 86), Williams's speaker describes the plums in sensuous language:

> Forgive me
>
> they were delicious
>
> so sweet
>
> and so cold (9–12)

2e How to Indicate Deletions, Insertions, and Errors

Quotations are subject to the basic grammatical rules of clarity and coherence. As a general rule, they should be consistent with the rest of the writing in terms of tense, number, and agreement. Sometimes it is necessary to change a quotation for clarity, correctness, or brevity. Three special cases occur.

Deletions Use an ellipsis (. . .) to indicate an omission within a quotation. In this example, the specific items have been deleted since they were not relevant to the writer's purpose.

> ORIGINAL Five items—a purse, a watch, a wallet, a ring, a necklace— were stolen.
>
> QUOTATION WITH DELETION "Five items . . . were stolen."

When you quote only part of a sentence within the grammatical structure of your own writing, as in the example from Tim Bowling on page 475, it is generally not necessary to use an ellipsis to indicate that you have omitted material that came before or after the quotation.

Insertions Put square brackets around words added to clarify something in the quotation or to make the quotation fit into the grammatical structure of your sentence.

> ADDITION "Unlike the warriors of older tribes, however," Sanders points out, "they [the soldiers of his youth] would have no say about when the battle would start or how it would be waged" (294).

> CHANGE Sanders points out that modern soldiers "have no say about when the battle [will] start or how it [will] be waged" (294).

Error in the text Put [*sic*] (Latin for "so," "thus") after the error to indicate typographical errors, deviant spellings, grammatical mistakes, or confused wording in the original.

> According to one study, "Each of the provinces are [*sic*] contributing to the problem of acid rain."

Exercise 1

This exercise is designed to give you practice in integrating quotations. Introduce the quotation appropriately, quote only the most relevant material, and punctuate correctly.

1. "This may be true or it may be false—who can say?—but what is true in it, so it seemed to me, reviewing the story of Shakespeare's sister as I had made it, is that any woman born with a great gift in the sixteenth century would certainly have gone crazed, shot herself, or ended her days in some lonely cottage outside the village, half witch, half wizard, feared and mocked at." (342) In this quotation, Virginia Woolf explains her reason for writing about Shakespeare's imaginary sister.

2. In "Inequality Is the Real Enemy," Polly Toynbee makes the following point:

    > "Does inequality really matter? The poor have what their grandparents would think unimaginable luxuries—TVs, telephones and washing machines. So why should it matter to them if in some unseen stratosphere the gated kleptocrats on company boards award themselves staggering sums of money? Does anyone really mind the gap?" (330)

3. The idea that blindness is a mental rather than a physical condition is clear when Gloucester perceives in Act 4, Scene 1, lines 21-26 of *King Lear* he:

    > Stumbled when I saw. Full oft 'tis seen,
    > Our means secure us, and our mere defects
    > Prove our commodities. O dear son Edgar
    > The food of thy abused father's wrath!
    > Might I but live to see thee in my touch
    > I'd say I had eyes again!

4. An added benefit, Swift's narrator notes, is that this proposal will decrease the number of Roman Catholics in Ireland.

> For, *First*, as I have already observed, it would greatly lessen *the Number of Papists*, with whom we are Yearly over-run, being the principal Breeders of the Nation, as well as our most dangerous Enemies, and who stay at home on purpose with a design *to deliver the Kingdom to the Pretender*, hoping to take their Advantage by the absence *of so many good Protestants*, who have chosen rather to leave their Country, than stay at home, and pay Tithes against their Conscience, to an *Episcopal Curate*. (318)

H3 Documentation

Research writing, scholarly writing, and academic writing usually require you to cite—that is, to indicate the origin of—any materials or ideas you have taken from books, scholarly articles, internet sources, online databases, or other sources. The main purposes of documentation are to acknowledge your use of secondary sources and to differentiate within your writing between your own ideas and the ideas of other people. Additionally, good documentation practices allow your readers to find interesting or relevant materials quickly and easily, which helps the research process for everyone involved. When using secondary sources, you need to document both direct quotations and paraphrased ideas. Failure to acknowledge secondary sources constitutes plagiarism. For more detailed information on plagiarism, see Chapter 11.

With the increasing ease of access to online information and the consequent debates about intellectual property rights, file sharing and copyright issues, open source materials, and many other questions related to information and technology, it is arguable that information is becoming free for the taking. Similarly, information on many websites appears to have no author, implying that it does not belong to anyone and therefore does not need to be documented. This is not the case in formal writing. For academic writing such as research papers, it is essential that you document any secondary materials in your essay, even if it is a simple web page.

This section focuses on two documentation styles introduced earlier in the chapter: Modern Language Association (MLA) and American Psychological Association (APA). The two main requirements for documentation are in-text citations and a list of secondary sources at the end of the essay. An in-text citation is usually a parenthetical reference in the body of the essay. The list of sources, entitled Works Cited (MLA) or References (APA),

DOCUMENTATION

consists of a complete itemization of sources alphabetized by the author's last name. Each in-text citation must correspond to an entry in the Works Cited or References list. Similarly, each entry in the Works Cited or References list should correspond to an in-text citation. One always requires the other.

3a Direct Quotations, Paraphrase, and Ideas

Most students understand that any direct quotation of three or more words needs to be documented. However, a direct quotation is not the only situation where documentation is necessary. When you paraphrase someone else's work—often phrased as "putting the idea into your own words"—the idea still originates from someone else and needs to be documented. Therefore, when you are conducting research, it is important to keep track of what you read so that you have a clear understanding of where ideas or quotations originate. A good strategy is to take detailed notes as you read research materials. You also need to document any ideas from secondary sources that you have put into your own words or incorporated into your argument. In each case, you must have an in-text citation and an entry in the Works Cited or References list. For more information on summarizing other people's ideas, see Chapter 2.

Primary and secondary sources A primary source is usually the main text under discussion. For example, if you were studying William Shakespeare's *The Tempest,* the play itself would be the primary source. Any research materials you gathered—such as scholarly criticism on Shakespeare—would be secondary sources. Secondary sources, as the name implies, often address the primary source or an idea, concept, or theme relevant to the primary source. A Works Cited or References list includes both primary and secondary sources.

3b Systems of Documentation: MLA and APA

This section outlines the basic documentation guidelines for the two systems we have been discussing: Modern Language Association (MLA) and American Psychological Association (APA). While other systems exist (such as *The Chicago Manual of Style*), MLA and APA are commonly used for literary studies and social sciences, respectively. If you are unsure about which system to use, ask your instructor.

Documentation is not difficult; it merely requires careful attention to details of style and punctuation that may seem arbitrary. However, these styles have evolved to give order to a diverse realm of information. As grammar gives shape and coherence to language, documentation gives shape and coherence to research. Failure to adhere to rules of documentation results in a scattered, confusing research essay that can be difficult and frustrating to follow.

Below you will find examples of the most common types of documentation for books, articles, and online sources. Because of the diverse range of materials available to researchers, this section cannot cover every type of secondary source. If you need more information, consult a style manual: the *MLA Handbook for Writers of Research Papers* (MLA) or the *Publication Manual of the American Psychological Association* (APA). These manuals are very detailed and thorough. They are available in most school libraries.

When writing a Works Cited or References entry for a print source, you should always take the bibliographic information from the title page of the work. Do not take information from the cover of the book. The title page is most often identified by the small-print information (such as copyright and publisher details) on the reverse side of the page.

3c MLA Style

Literature courses usually ask that you document sources in MLA style. MLA style requires in-text citations and a Works Cited list.

In-text citations An in-text citation is necessary when you include a direct quotation, paraphrase, or idea from a primary or secondary source. Include enough information to identify the source of the material. Most frequently, you will need to include the author's name and the page number (line number for poetry; act.scene.line number for plays so divided). If you use more than one work by an author, you will need to include a short form of the title. Because online sources often do not have page numbers, you should cite the paragraph number, if given. The in-text citation should point the reader to the relevant entry in the Works Cited list. An in-text citation usually follows the closing quotation mark of a quotation.

- Author identified in sentence

  In Margaret Laurence's "The Loons," narrator Vanessa MacLeod reveals that she did not want "to witness [her] long-ago kingdom possessed now by strangers" (266).

- Author not identified in sentence

  One critic argues that in Africa "tyrants have often seized upon sports to bolster their power" (Zimmerman 345).

- Paraphrased idea, more than one work by the same author

Margaret Laurence claims that the distinction between first- and
third-person narration does not meaningfully apply to her work
because her focus is on the main character, not the narrative
perspective ("Time" 268-69).

- An online source with paragraph numbers

John Smith claims that Margaret Laurence's short story "The Loons"
creates a "problematic parallel between Piquette and the loons" (par. 22).

- An online source with no page number, paragraph numbers, or
other identifying markers

Near the end of his article, John Smith claims that Margaret Laurence's
short story "The Loons" creates a "problematic parallel between Piquette
and the loons."

- Quotations within quotations

Secondary materials often contain references to or direct
quotations from both primary and secondary sources. Try
to avoid significant use of such quotations: references, not
to mention readers, can easily become confused. If you
find it necessary to use a quotation within a quotation,
follow these examples. Note that the quotation within the
quotation is indicated by single quotation marks.

1. A quotation from a primary source within a quotation from a
    secondary source. The parenthetical reference is to the secondary
    source, which will appear in the Works Cited list.

    In "Fenced In and Forced to Give Up," Janice Acoose points out
    that, unlike the many "Metis who characteristically use and are loyal
    defenders of their Mitchif language, the Metis in Laurence's fiction
    are people whose language is 'neither Cree nor French'" (80).

2. A quotation from a secondary source within a secondary source.
    Within the parenthetical reference, begin with *qtd. in* (quoted
    in) followed by the author of the secondary source in which you
    found the quotation and the page number of the quotation. You
    need to include only the secondary source in which you found the
    quotation in your Works Cited list.

    Thomas King observes that non-indigenous writers who use
    Aboriginal materials are "limited in their variety of characters,
    themes, structures, and images" (qtd. in Acoose 74).

Works Cited A Works Cited list is a bibliography of all primary and
secondary sources used in an essay. It starts on a separate page at the end

of the essay. Every entry in a Works Cited list should refer to one or more in-text citations of that work in the body of the essay.

The following examples give representative entries for a Works Cited list in MLA style. The most common sources in a Works Cited list include books, articles, and online sources.

Books   A standard Works Cited entry for a book includes the author's name (last, first), the title of the book (including subtitle, if any), the city of publication, the publisher, the year of publication, and the medium of publication consulted (for example, *Print* or *Web*). Follow the punctuation and formatting as outlined in the examples. You should also cite any other relevant information about the text, including translations, editions, series, and so on. If you are unsure of what information to include, ask your instructor for clarification.

- **A work by a single author:** Many books have a single author. This is perhaps the most basic entry. Note that the title of the book is italicized and the main words capitalized.

  Solie, Karen. *Short Haul Engine.* London: Brick, 2001. Print.

- **A work by two or more authors:** When citing a book with two or three authors, alphabetize the entry by the name that appears first in the list of authors on the title page. Do not alphabetize the remaining names. Invert only the name of the first author in the list; leave the other authors' names in normal order. This book with two authors is also a translation:

  Horkheimer, Max, and Theodor W. Adorno. *Dialectic of Enlightenment.*
      Trans. John Cumming. New York: Continuum, 1972. Print.

  When citing a book with four or more authors, either present all names in the order in which they appear in the book (with the first author's name inverted) or present the first author's name (inverted) and add *et al.*

- **An anthology or a compilation:** An anthology or a compilation is a collection of works by different people, selected and arranged by an editor or editors. To cite an entire collection, alphabetize the entry by the last name of the editor, followed by a comma and "ed." If there is more than one editor, follow the format for books by two or more authors and add "eds." (For individual entries in an anthology or compilation, see below.)

  Mitchell, Allyson, Lisa Bryn Rundle, and Lara Karaian, eds. *Turbo
      Chicks: Talking Young Feminisms.* Toronto: Sumach, 2001. Print.

- **An individual work in an anthology or a compilation:** To cite a selection from an anthology or a compilation, alphabetize the entry by the last name of the author, not the editor. Put quotation marks around the titles of short works, such as essays, poems, and short stories. However, italicize the titles of works previously published in independent form, such as novels and plays, as well as the title of the anthology or compilation. Give the edition, if any, after the title of the anthology or compilation. Then add *Ed.* (for "Edited by") and list the name(s) of the editor(s), in normal order. Follow with the city of publication, the publisher, and the year of publication. Include the page numbers for the complete selection, not just the pages you have cited. Conclude with the medium of publication.

  Vanderhaeghe, Guy. "Cages." *The Harbrace Anthology of Literature.*
  4th ed. Ed. Jon C. Stott, Raymond E. Jones, and Rick Bowers.
  Toronto: Thomson Nelson, 2006. 1204-17. Print.

- **Two or more works by the same author(s):** When you cite more than one text by the same author, abbreviate the author's name in second and any subsequent references with three hyphens in a row, followed by a period. Alphabetize the author's name as usual in the Works Cited list, and order the author's works alphabetically, ignoring any initial *A*, *An*, or *The.*

  Zwicky, Jan. *Robinson's Crossing.* London: Brick, 2004. Print.
  ---. *Wisdom & Metaphor.* Kentville: Gaspereau, 2003. Print.

Articles Scholarly journals or periodicals are extremely common research sources. You may also draw upon magazine articles, newspaper articles, or encyclopedia entries. Most journal entries for a Works Cited list will be for a specific essay in a particular journal. The entry will include the author's name, the title of the article, the journal's title, the volume (and issue) of the journal, the year of publication, the page numbers, and the medium of publication (for example, *Print* or *Web*).

- **A scholarly article in a scholarly journal:** Note that no period follows the title of the journal. The volume and issue numbers of the journal are separated with a period; when no issue number exists, the volume number stands alone without a period.

  Brooks, Peter. "Aesthetics and Ideology: What Happened to Poetics?"
  Critical Inquiry 20.3 (1994): 509-23. Print.

- **A scholarly article in a collection:** These sources are cited in the same way as individual works in an anthology (see above) if they have not been previously published.

  Kilgour, Maggie. "The Function of Cannibalism at the Present Time."
  Cannibalism and the Colonial World. Ed. Francis Barker, Peter
  Hulme, and Margaret Iversen. New York: Cambridge UP, 1998.
  238-59. Print.

- If the article appeared first in a journal and has been reprinted in a collection, give the complete information for the journal publication. Then add *Rpt. in* and the information for the collection.

  Windle, Phyllis. "The Ecology of Grief." *Bioscience* 42 (May 1992):
  363-66. Rpt. in *Ecopsychology: Restoring the Earth, Healing the Mind.*
  Ed. Theodore Roszak, Mary E. Gomes, and Allen D. Kanner. San
  Francisco: Sierra Club, 1995. 136-45. Print.

- **A magazine article:** For magazines that are published weekly or biweekly, the date reference should include the day, month, and year of publication. For magazines that are published monthly or bimonthly, the date reference should include the month and year of publication. Do not include the volume and issue numbers of magazines.

  Stenson, Fred. "In Search of a Modest Proposal." *Alberta Views*
  Jan.-Feb. 2004: 14-15. Print.

- **A newspaper article:** When citing a newspaper article, include the author and title of the article as well as the title of the newspaper (omit any leading *A, An,* or *The*), the date, edition, section, and page number(s). If the article spans more than one page or appears on non-consecutive pages, this should be noted with the first page followed by a plus sign (for example, C4+).

  Curry, Bill. "Ottawa Wants Kyoto Softened." *Globe and Mail* 12 May
  2006, Alberta ed.: A1+. Print.

- **An encyclopedia entry:** Encyclopedia entries may or may not include author information. If the author is named, alphabetize the entry by the author's last name. If the author is unnamed, alphabetize the entry by the first significant word of the title. You do not need to cite page numbers for encyclopedia entries. Do not list the entry by the encyclopedia editor's name.

  "David Suzuki." *The Canadian Encyclopedia: Year 2000 Edition.* 2000 ed.
  Ed. James H. Marsh. Toronto: McClelland & Stewart, 1999. Print.

Electronic and online sources Electronic and online sources are much more recent developments than book technologies, and they are still developing and changing more rapidly than print culture. Therefore, the standards for documenting online sources are not as well established, though the principles are the same. The main objective is to identify the source of the information as completely as possible. Essentially, citations of electronic materials contain the same information as print sources as well as relevant electronic details. Include the author's name (if given), title of the work, information about print publication (if any), information about electronic publication (title of the work, name of overall website in italics, and publisher or sponsor of the site), date of publication (day, month, year, as available), the medium of publication (*Web*), and the date of access (day, month, year). Because electronic and online information can change so rapidly, it is very important to include the date of access for any citation. It is not necessary to include the URL of the website in the citation. Much online information is unpaginated; sometimes paragraph numbers are given, other times not. Cite what information is available to you.

- **A web page:** Authors of web pages are often not listed. If no author is listed, alphabetize the entry by the first significant word in the title of the work.

  "No Agreement on Role of Abortion Pill in Fatal Infections." *CNN.com.* Cable News Network, 11 May 2006. Web. 12 May 2011.

- **An article in an online database:** Full-text articles are increasingly becoming available through online databases. When citing an article from an online database, you cannot simply cut and paste the entry from the search results into your Works Cited list. Rather, follow the same rules for citing a print article and add the title of the database (in italics), the medium of publication consulted (*Web*), and the date of access (day, month, year). Refer to the section on citing journal articles for help on citing online journal articles.

  Scanlan, Margaret. "*Anil's Ghost* and Terrorism's Time." *Studies in the Novel* 36.3 (2004): 302-17. *Academic Search Premier.* Web. 12 May 2011.

3d APA Style

Social science disciplines such as psychology and sociology most frequently use APA style for research papers in college courses. APA style requires in-text citations and a References list at the end of research papers.

In-text citations An in-text citation is necessary when you include a direct quotation, paraphrase, or idea from a primary or secondary source. Include enough information to identify the source of the material. Most frequently, you will need to include only the author's name and the year of publication; for direct quotations, you will need to include the page number as well. For online sources that have no pagination, you should include the paragraph number by using *para.* followed by the number. The in-text citation should point the reader to the relevant entry in the References list.

- Author identified in sentence

  Smith (2005) analyzes the effects of behavioural drugs on children.

- Author not identified in sentence

  Recent research (Smith, 2005) analyzes the effects of behavioural drugs on children.

- In-text citation for a single work with two authors

  Smith and Liu (2004) found that behavioural drugs had few side effects.

- In-text citation for a single work with three to five authors

  First in-text citation: Smith, Liu, and Johnson (2004) found that behavioural drugs had few side effects.

  Subsequent in-text citations: Smith et al. (2004) also found that the number of people taking such drugs had risen significantly over the past five years.

- In-text citation for a single work with six or more authors

  Cox et al. (2008) found that the prevalence of chronic medication use in children increased from 2002 to 2005.

- Direct quotation using the author's name

  Taylor (2006) concludes that behavioural drugs have "significant side effects" (p. 288).

- Direct quotation not using the author's name

  One researcher concludes that behavioural drugs have "significant side effects" (Taylor, 2006, p. 288).

- Citation of another work within a secondary source

  Johnson's study (as cited in Smith & Jones, 2004) confirms that behavioural drugs can have negative side effects.

- Direct quotation from an online source with paragraph numbers

  Taylor's study (2003) finds "negligible side effects" (para. 3) in all but
  one type of drug.

- Direct quotation from an online source that does not include page
  numbers or paragraph numbers, but has headings

  Taylor's study (2003) finds "negligible side effects" (Results section, para.
  1) in all but one type of drug. [In this case, *para. 1* indicates the first paragraph following the section heading.]

References list A References list is a bibliography of all primary and
secondary sources used in an essay. It starts on a separate page entitled
References at the end of the essay. Every entry in the References list
should refer to one or more in-text citations of that work in the body of
the essay.

The following examples give representative entries for a References list
in APA style. The most common entries include books, articles, and online
sources.

Books A standard References list entry for a book includes the author's
name (last name and initials), the year of publication (in parentheses), the
title of the work in italics, the city (and state or province, or if outside the
United States and Canada, city and country) of publication, and the publisher. Follow the punctuation and format as outlined in the examples. You
should also cite any other relevant information about the text, including
translations, editions, and series. If you are unsure of what information to
include, ask your instructor for clarification.

- **A work by a single author:** Many books have a single author. This
  is perhaps the most basic entry. Note that the title of the book is
  italicized and only the first word is capitalized (the first word in a
  subtitle and any proper nouns are also capitalized).

  Solie, K. (2001). *Short haul engine.* London, ON: Brick Books.

- **A work by two or more authors:** When citing a book with up
  to seven authors, alphabetize the entry by the name that appears
  first in the list of authors on the title page; do not alphabetize the
  remaining names. Invert all the names in the list. Use an ampersand (&) between the last two names in the list. This book with
  two authors is also a translation. Note that no period follows the
  closing parenthesis of the original date of publication.

Horkheimer, M., & Adorno, T. W. (1972). *Dialectic of enlightenment* (Cumming, J., Trans.). New York, NY: Continuum. (Original work published 1944)

When citing a book with eight or more authors, list the first six names in the order in which they appear in the book, insert an ellipsis (. . .), and add the last author's name.

- **An anthology or a compilation:** An anthology or a compilation is a collection of works by different people, selected and arranged by an editor or editors. To cite an entire collection, alphabetize the entry by the last name of the editor, followed by a comma and *(Ed.)*. If there is more than one editor, follow the format for books by two or more authors and add *(Eds.)*. (For individual entries in an anthology or compilation, see below.)

Mitchell, A., Rundle, L. B., & Karaian, L. (Eds.). (2001). *Turbo chicks: Talking young feminisms.* Toronto, ON: Sumach Press.

- **An individual work in an anthology or a compilation:** To cite a selection from an anthology or a compilation, alphabetize the entry by the last name of the author, not the editor. Do not put quotation marks around the titles of short works, such as essays, poems, and short stories. Capitalize only the first word of the title and the subtitle (if any), and any proper nouns. Add *In* and then list the names of the editors, in normal order. Then, add *(Ed.)* or *(Eds.)* (depending on the number of editors) after the last editor's name. After the title of the anthology or compilation, give the edition of the anthology or compilation (if any) in parentheses, along with the page numbers for the complete selection (not just the pages you have cited). Conclude with the place of publication followed by the publisher.

Vanderhaeghe, G. (2006). Cages. In J. C. Stott, R. E. Jones, & R. Bowers (Eds.), *The Harbrace anthology of literature* (4th ed., pp. 1204–1217). Toronto, ON: Thomson Nelson.

- **Two or more works by the same author(s):** When you cite more than one text by the same author, include the name of the author in each entry. Entries are ordered chronologically by date, citing the earliest work first.

Zwicky, J. (2003). *Wisdom & metaphor.* Kentville, NS: Gaspereau Press.

Zwicky, J. (2004). *Robinson's crossing.* London, ON: Brick Books.

Articles Scholarly journals or periodicals are extremely common research sources. You may also draw upon magazine articles, newspaper articles, or encyclopedia entries. Most journal entries for a References list will be for a specific essay in a particular journal. The entry will include the author's name, the year of publication, the title of the article, the title of the journal, the volume (and issue) of the journal, and the page numbers of the article.

- **A scholarly article in a scholarly journal:** Note that a comma separates the journal title and the volume number. The volume number is italicized, but the issue number is not italicized. Note that the journal title retains its capitalization.

  Brooks, P. (1994). Aesthetics and ideology: What happened to poetics? *Critical Inquiry, 20*(3), 509–523.

- **A scholarly article in a collection:** These sources are cited in the same way as individual works in an anthology (see above) if they have not been previously published.

  Kilgour, M. (1998). The function of cannibalism at the present time. In F. Barker, P. Hulme, & M. Iversen (Eds.), *Cannibalism and the colonial world* (pp. 238–259). New York, NY: Cambridge University Press.

- If the article appeared first in a journal and has been reprinted in a collection, give the information for the journal publication at the end of the entry in parentheses, preceded by *Reprinted from.*

  Windle, P. (1995). The ecology of grief. In T. Roszak, M. Gomes, & A. Kanner (Eds.), *Ecopsychology: Restoring the earth, healing the mind* (pp. 136–145). San Francisco, CA: Sierra Club Books. (Reprinted from *Bioscience, 42* (1992, May), 363–366)

- **A magazine article:** When citing magazine articles, give the date as it is published on the magazine (month for monthly publications, day and month for weekly publications). Also, include any volume numbers.

  Wells, P. (2006, April 10). Spring break summit. *Maclean's, 119* (15), 16–18.

- **A newspaper article:** When citing newspaper articles, include the author, the date of the article, the title of the article, the name of the newspaper, and page number(s). Sometimes newspaper articles are discontinuous: cite all pages on which the article appears (as follows).

If no author is given, alphabetize the article by the first significant word in the title and put the date in parentheses after the title.

Freeman, A. (2006, May 15). Bush ready to deploy guardsmen to Mexican border. *The Globe and Mail*, pp. A1, A11.

- **An encyclopedia entry:** Encyclopedia entries may or may not include author information. If the author is named, alphabetize the entry by the author's last name. If the author is unnamed, alphabetize the entry by the first significant word of the title. After the title, list the edition, volume and page numbers, if available, in parentheses. List publisher information. Do not list the entry by the encyclopedia editor's name.

David Suzuki. (1999). In J. H. Marsh (Ed.), *The Canadian encyclopedia: Year 2000 edition* (2000 ed., p. 2277). Toronto, ON: McClelland & Stewart.

Electronic and online sources References for online sources should accomplish two objectives: to tell readers where to access a document and to provide an internet address or reference that works. A reference to an online resource should include a document title, a date, an address, and, if possible, an author. Many scholarly articles include a digital object identifier (DOI), which provides an ongoing link to the article on the web. If an article includes a DOI (which appears as doi:xxxxxx), add it to the end of an entry instead of a URL. It is not necessary to include a date of access in an entry unless the online resource might change (for example, a Wiki).

- **A web page:** Authors of web pages are often not listed, or the author may be an institution or corporation. If no author is listed, alphabetize the entry by the first significant word of the title of the document. If the author is an institution, alphabetize the entry using the institution's name.

Cable News Network. (2006, May 11). No agreement on role of abortion pill in fatal infections. Retrieved from http://www.cnn.com/ 2006/HEALTH/05/11/abortion.pill.hearing.ap/index.html

- **An article in an online database:** Full-text articles are increasingly becoming available through online databases. When citing an article from an online database, it is not necessary to include the database information. Rather, follow the same rules for citing a print article and add the electronic source of the article.

Pitt, L., Kilbride, M., Nothard, S., Welford, M., & Morrison, A. P. (2006). Researching recovery from psychosis: A user-led project. *The Psychiatrist, 31*, 55–60. doi:10.1192/pb.bp.105.008532

3e Format of Works Cited or References List

Several basic formatting conventions are common to both MLA and APA styles:

1. The title Works Cited (MLA) or References (APA) is centred at the top of the page without any special formatting (that is, no bold, no italics, no quotation marks, no change in font size).

2. Entries are alphabetized by the author's last name, as explained earlier.

3. Entries authored by institutions are alphabetized in the same manner as authored texts.

4. Entries with no identifiable author are alphabetized by the first significant word in the title (that is, not *The, A,* or *An*). This can be particularly relevant for internet sources.

5. Entries are double-spaced with no extra spaces between entries.

6. Entries longer than one line are formatted with a hanging indent; that is, subsequent text lines are indented 1.25 cm or ½ inch (one tab). Most word processors have an automatic function for formatting text to hanging indent.

Glossary of Rhetorical Terms

Analyze To divide something into parts in order to understand both the parts and the whole. This can be done by *systems analysis* (where the object is divided into its interconnected parts), *process analysis* (where the object is divided into stages of development), and *cause/effect analysis* (where the object is divided into the reasons that brought it into being, or into its consequences). The main purpose of analysis is to explain something, such as a concept, a text, an event, or a set of data, by examining its parts in detail.

Cause/effect analysis *See* Analyze.

Compare To show the similarities and differences between two things, or among more than two things, in order to reveal the qualities of each more clearly.

Comparison, basis of The common element in terms of which two or more things are compared. Topics that can be put in the form "Compare X and Y in terms of Z" specify the basis of comparison, Z. The basis of comparison tells you which features of the things you are comparing are relevant and thus gives you a focus for gathering information and writing your essay.

Comparison, methods of organizing The *block method* consists of organizing your *middle paragraphs* so that you finish everything you have to say about one of the things you are comparing before taking up another. The *point-by-point method* consists of organizing your middle paragraphs so that in each paragraph or series of paragraphs you discuss only one aspect of each of the things you are comparing.

Conclusion The concluding paragraph in your essay provides the chance for both you and your reader to step back from the essay and survey the development of your *thesis*. The conclusion should restate the thesis, tie together the points developed in the *middle paragraphs*, and mention the wider implications of the discussion, if any. A good conclusion will not have substantial repetition of words or phrases from the *introduction*.

Context The social, historical, and/or cultural situation in which a text is written or produced.

Deductive and inductive structure These terms provide the most common way of making a distinction between essays that begin with the *thesis* (deductive structure) and essays that lead up to a thesis at or toward the end of the essay (inductive structure).

Development, methods of The uses of *evidence* and detail to give substance to a point.

Diction A writer's level of word usage (formal, informal, colloquial) and particular word choices. An aspect of *style* that also contributes to *tone*.

Discuss An ambiguous term frequently used in essay topics. It does not mean "summarize the relevant information." Check the essay topic carefully to determine whether you are expected to *analyze*, *compare*, or *evaluate* a body of information. "Discuss the significance of X in Y" means to analyze the relationship between X and Y; "discuss X and Y" means to compare X and Y; "discuss the validity of X" means to evaluate X.

Evaluate To determine the strengths or weaknesses of something—a plan, a performance, a work of art, or a theory, for example. Evaluation usually examines an idea, position, argument, or viewpoint and often determines the effectiveness or validity of its presentation.

Evaluation, standard of A set of criteria based on accumulated judgments of things of the same kind that you can use as a standard against which to measure the material you are evaluating. The most common standards of evaluation are aesthetic (how effective is the relationship between form and content in the work?), logical (how convincing is the reasoning?), practical (will it work and is it useful?), and ethical (is it morally right or wrong?).

Evidence The factual information, examples, and references to and quotations from authorities that you use to support your thesis.

Genre and subgenre We use the term *genre* to refer to the broad kinds of text (for example, novel, play, film). We use *subgenre* to refer to more specific types within the form (for example, Gothic novel, Greek tragedy, film noir).

Inductive structure *See* Deductive and inductive structure.

Introduction The introductory paragraph prepares your reader both intellectually and emotionally for the essay to follow. It establishes the context by defining necessary terms, giving historical background, and so forth, and indicates the structure of the essay by mentioning, in order, the main points you plan to cover. The introduction usually ends with your *thesis*.

Literary analysis The analysis of a literary text or performance that focuses not only on the *theme* or *thesis* of the work but also on the presentation and *style*. For example, a film may be about dogs, but the film may present the theme of dogs as a comedy, a tragedy, or a documentary. Therefore, literary analysis will consider the *genre and subgenre* of the work through *subject*, *structure*, *development*, *tone*, and *theme* or *thesis*.

Middle paragraphs Paragraphs between the *introduction* and *conclusion* that explain and illustrate subpoints of the *thesis*. The purpose of each paragraph is defined by a ***topic sentence*** that links the paragraph to the thesis. Middle paragraphs usually contain both explanations of the point made in the topic sentence and specific details illustrating that point. Transitional words and phrases show how points, explanations, and details are related.

Middle paragraphs, order of There are four common ways of organizing a sequence of middle paragraphs.

1. *Chronological order:* The arrangement of material according to units of time. The simplest chronological order starts with events furthest away in time and ends with events closest in time.

2. *Spatial order:* The arrangement of material according to locations in space. Spatial order may move from near to far, top to bottom, right to left, and so forth.

3. *Logical order:* The arrangement of material according to a chain of reasoning. The order in which material is presented is determined by the need to establish one point so that it will serve as the basis for the next.

4. *Order of ascending interest:* The arrangement of material to lead up to the most important or most interesting point. An order of ascending interest may also accommodate a chronological, spatial, or logical order. *See also* Comparison, methods of organizing.

Peer-reviewed Often called "refereed," peer-reviewed materials are publications that have been examined and approved by experts in a particular field of study. The information and analysis in these publications are usually considered reliable, current, and consistent with the scholarship in the field. Such publications are used as ***secondary sources*** in a ***research paper***.

Persona The mask or second self created by the author, especially in poetry and in ironic essays where the stated thesis and the implied thesis are completely different. In "A Modest Proposal" (Readings), for example, Swift creates a persona who argues that eating the poor is the best way to solve the problems created by them. Swift's real thesis is that his readers need to see the Irish poor as human beings and find a humane solution to their problems.

Primary source Any first-hand source of information, such as the literary work you are analyzing, a performance you have seen, your own observations and experience, the raw data from a scientific experiment, or the historical documents on which historians base their interpretations of events.

Process analysis *See* Analyze.

Research paper An extended analysis, comparison, or evaluation essay that includes information from ***secondary sources*** as well as from ***primary sources***. A research paper is not merely a summary of other writers' ideas; it is an essay in which you develop your own opinion on your subject and use your research material as part of your evidence to support that opinion.

Secondary source Material that provides information about, or criticism and analysis of, a ***primary source***. A historian, for example, may write a book (secondary source) interpreting the meaning of historical documents (primary sources). An anthropologist may collect data (primary sources) about various cultures and write an article comparing those cultures (secondary source). A literary critic may write a review (secondary source) of a new novel (primary source). In secondary sources, material is selected and presented to support a particular point of view.

Structure The selection and ordering of parts in a written work or performance. *See also* Middle paragraphs, order of.

Style The distinctive way of writing that belongs to a particular writer. For analytic purposes, it is helpful to see style as consisting of a writer's use of *diction*, image and symbol, figurative language and allusions, and sentence structure.

Subgenre *See* Genre and subgenre.

Subject The text, issue, theory, or proposal that a writer writes about. If your essay topic is "Assess the role of the peasants in the French Revolution," the subject of your essay is the role of the peasants in the French Revolution.

Systems analysis *See* Analyze.

Theme The main statement made about a subject in fiction, drama, poetry, film, and imaginative literature generally. A theme is usually implied, whereas a *thesis* is usually stated directly.

Thesis The main statement made about a subject in nonfiction. The purpose of the essay is to develop and confirm the thesis. In your essay, the thesis statement will consist of an opinion with one or more reasons to support it. Like the hypothesis in a scientific experiment, the thesis is the statement or assertion you are proving.

Tone The attitude a writer takes to a subject and to a reader, the equivalent of "tone of voice" in conversation. The tone of a work can be described as serious or light, witty or ponderous, condescending or apologetic, and in many other similar ways. In your own essays, think of tone as a product of *diction* and pronouns of address.

Topic sentence The sentence in a *middle paragraph*, usually at the beginning, that states the main idea of the paragraph and shows how the material in the paragraph supports the *thesis* of the whole essay. Topic sentences are thus the bridge between the generalization you make in your thesis statement and the specific details you give in your middle paragraphs. An "umbrella" topic sentence covers points made in more than one paragraph.

Answer Key to Part 3: Handbook for Final Editing

A Final Editing: The Process

Students should be made aware of the five strategies for final editing as well as the chart Identifying Common Problems.

B Grammar: Parts of Speech

Exercise 1 (p. 378) deal, sense, well-being, environment, entertainment, sense, attachment, world, needs

Answers to the paragraph rewrite will vary.

Exercise 2 (p. 379) The collective nouns are found in 2, 3, 7, and 11. The plural forms of each of these nouns are *parties, families, flocks, and companies.*

Exercise 3 (p. 381)

1. bands (circled); [street] [parade]
2. trombones (circled); [parade]
3. flutes and drums (circled)
4. twins (circled); [trumpet]
5. twirlers (circled); [band] [stuff]

Exercise 4 (p. 384)

1. between you and me
2. she and Bill
3. to whomever
4. We residents
5. C
6. or me.
7. who lives
8. She and her mom
9. Nobody . . . than we
10. C

Exercise 5 (p. 385)

1. its
2. you're
3. who's
4. their
5. theirs

Exercise 6 (p. 386)

1. its expenses increase
2. steelworkers want . . . their; or steelworker . . . his or her working conditions

3. Cancer patients . . . them
4. it will enforce. Everyone . . . he or she is carrying; or People . . . they
5. they lose

Exercise 7 (p. 388)

1. This determination must occupy
2. these changes will increase . . . when the city assesses
3. of evolution, an acceptance that forced
4. in the office of the teacher who
5. to let the other children

Review Exercise 1 (p. 388) There are serious problems with the way the province administers health care to *its* citizens. Both consumers and providers are frustrated with the way *the health care system* is run. They agree that the waiting lists are too long and that life-saving treatment is being rationed based on *patients'* medical *histories* and their future usefulness to society. Doctors and other health professionals have fled to the United States, where *their jobs are* more lucrative and less stressful. *Patients* with enough money may also seek treatment for their medical problems in the United States. The provincial government, *which* imposed stringent cost-cutting measures for several years, now *promises* that *health care* will improve again. Given these problems, it's easy to see why *the government* proposes throwing out the old system and implementing a new one, *a plan* some people in the medical, political, and general communities want.

Exercise 8 (p. 391)

1. had lain
2. lose
3. supposed
4. C
5. cost
6. broken
7. have led
8. lie
9. C
10. had drunk

Exercise 9 (p. 393) I <u>was walking</u> around the pet store, trying to decide what kind of pet I <u>could keep</u> in my new apartment, when I <u>remembered</u> Hammy, the curious brown hamster. I <u>saw</u> him in Zellers when I first <u>moved</u> to Canada. For very little money my parents <u>bought</u> Hammy for me, a black hamster for my brother Paul, a whole complex of compartments and tubes of hamster housing, a running wheel, a ten-kilogram bag of food, and sawdust to cover the bottom of the cages. When we <u>were setting</u> it all up in my bedroom, my uncle <u>came</u> in and <u>forbade</u> us <u>to keep</u> our pets upstairs—they <u>would have to live</u> in the basement with the dogs. We <u>lived</u> in his house; therefore, we <u>had to live</u> by his rules. But later that week I <u>went</u> away to summer camp and <u>forgot</u> about poor Hammy. While I <u>learned</u> about canoeing, painting, and weaving, and while I <u>went</u> hiking, exploring, and swimming, Hammy's food bowl <u>was getting</u> emptier and emptier. I <u>came</u> back to find him <u>lying</u> on his side, thin, quiet, and cold.

Exercise 10 (p. 394)

1. There don't seem to be any <u>books or articles</u> on this subject.
2. <u>Banff National Park</u> . . . attracts
3. <u>Neither</u> . . . was willing
4. <u>coach</u> is tired
5. <u>demand</u> . . . is decreasing

Exercise 11 (p. 396)

1. Passive. In "A Modest Proposal" Swift expresses the desire of the Irish for better food, clothing, and housing.
2. Passive. OK
3. Active.
4. Passive. OK
5. Passive. The Métis in Alberta and Saskatchewan forcefully expressed their demand for better employment opportunities.

Exercise 12 (p. 396) Answers will vary.

Review Exercise 2 (p. 396) Unlike Steven Spielberg's *Saving Private Ryan*, which was released just prior to this film, *The Thin Red Line* <u>does not portray</u> any single battle or story from the Second World War. Instead it <u>examines</u> the mental and emotional chaos that goes hand in hand with combat. Whereas *Saving Private Ryan* <u>is</u> a tribute to the men of D-Day, *The Thin Red Line* is a much less celebratory salute to the human spirit. The

film's slow-paced imagery of scenery and marching men <u>presents</u> no easy answers and the <u>lines</u> between good and evil as well as sanity and madness <u>are</u> frequently blurred. The <u>style of the film steps</u> outside the norm <u>of</u> the Hollywood war movie genre <u>and is</u> very effective. It should <u>have</u> won an Academy Award, but its unconventional style made it <u>lose</u> out to *Saving Private Ryan*. Nevertheless, *The Thin Red Line* <u>is</u> among the finest of contemporary war films.

Exercise 13 (p. 399)

1. Fatima did well on her math test.
2. Matthew is the taller of the two brothers.
3. Oscar has a unique website.
4. The novel was better than the movie.
5. Ping's mother is very fit now that she is lifting weights.

Exercise 14 (p. 400)

1. While vacationing in Jasper, the Wongs were amazed to see a bear on the main street.
2. Selina needed time to prepare mentally for the lawyer's questions.
3. Antonio stared over his glasses at the attractive young women across the aisle.
4. Marissa had driven nearly all the way home when she stopped to pick up a hitchhiker.
5. Beena was trying to read rapidly through the whole chapter just before class.

Exercise 15 (p. 400)

1. She was determined to finish her essay, so she ignored all interruptions.
2. After hearing the manager's plans to reorganize the office, the workers had difficulty remaining calm.
3. Because he had loved movies since childhood, he planned to become an actor.
4. When recovering from major surgery, you should avoid strenuous exercise.
5. Just before Domingo started school, his parents moved to Halifax.

Review Exercise 3 (p. 401)

1. He knew scarcely anyone at the party, but he had a better time than he expected.
2. Although he had studied all night, many of the exam questions seemed unfamiliar.

3. To jump even farther, you'll need a better pair of track shoes.
4. After a hot, strenuous day of sightseeing, the tourists thought the hotel pool looked very inviting.
5. Rayna is the older of the two sisters; she hopes to graduate this year.
6. One terrible night, while I was showing off my car to my friends, the engine exploded.
7. If we regulate the disposal of hazardous wastes, we can preserve the environment.
8. In writing stories for popular magazines, you should remember that readers always want a happy ending.
9. When Louis XIV was underage, his ministers had charge of the government.
10. By blaming the poor for their problems, politicians avoid responsibility to create a more just society.

Exercise 16 (p. 403)

A

1. Neither__nor ("neither," "nor," and "so" should be circled)
2. not only__but also ("for," "not only," and "but also" should be circled)
3. "yet" and "and" should be circled

B

1. Many children do poorly in school because of inadequate diet, poor instruction, and lack of interest.
2. To prevent shock, cover the victim with a blanket and speak reassuringly.
3. To clean this oven, I need either atomic weapons or a miracle.
4. You could end your speech with a quotation, a question, or a suggestion.
5. The successful candidate for this position must be self-motivated, a quick learner, and reliable.

C Answers will vary.

Exercise 17 (p. 404)

1. unless (circled)
2. therefore (underlined)
3. when (circled)
4. thus (underlined)
5. that (circled)

Exercise 18 (p. 405)

1. Angus, who is an ardent outdoorsman and conservationist, lives in rural New Brunswick.
2. In the summer, Andrea enjoys working in the garden, taking long walks, and reading romances.
3. Marco forgot to pay a speeding ticket, so he received a summons to appear in court.
4. To function effectively as a social worker, you need to be both knowledgeable and compassionate.
5. As far as I can tell, Ingrid has no interest in either getting a job or going to school.

Exercise 19 (p. 407)

1. When Jing-Mei was living in Lethbridge, she heard about the fashion opportunities in Montreal, so she packed her bags and bought an airline ticket.
2. Ever since [or Because] Karl had a seizure caused by an allergic reaction, he has been cautious about all medications.
3. Because the assistant manager is autocratic and arrogant, no one wants to work with her.
4. Because the main character ties his sense of masculinity to clan traditions, he feels threatened when these structures begin to crumble.
5. Amin desperately needed a job, but he was determined never again to work for his father.

Review Exercise 4 (p. 407)

1. To complete this degree, you could take three more courses or write a thesis.
2. Although he loved her and she was rich, he didn't want to marry her.
3. The house that burned down was designed by a well-known architect; it had been owned by the Santos family, who had come from Guatemala.
4. Marla had three goals in life: to complete her degree, to travel to Asia, and to start her own business.
5. Julia, a dance teacher, has travelled extensively in the Far East.
6. He decided to fly home because he didn't want to drive on the hazardous mountain roads.
7. They vowed to remain married for better and worse, for richer and poorer, and in sickness and health.
8. Because Timothy was the last to be hired, he was also the first to be fired.
9. Although he had forgotten about the test until the class started, he did well on it.

10. Charles Dickens, an important nineteenth-century novelist, experienced poverty as a child, so in his novels he is very sympathetic to poor children.

C Writing Better Sentences

Exercise 1 (p. 411)

1. After leaving the theatre and catching a cab (P)
2. We walked and talked together for hours (MC); finally, we headed home (MC)
3. On Sunday (P); Vijay phones his mother (MC)
4. A bandage over the exposed wound but no painkillers (P)
5. Her dream was to see Paris and die happy (MC); to see Paris and die happy (P)

Exercise 2 (p. 413)

1. (While the fighting persists,) [the airport will remain closed.]
2. [The supplies (that would prevent deaths from injuries and starvation) have been delayed.]
3. [I am worried about my parents,] (who are helpless victims of the civil war.)
4. (Although many attempts have been made to enforce a cease-fire,) [the fighting has increased.]
5. [Hopes for an early solution are fading] (because neither side will compromise.)

Exercise 3 (p. 413)

A

1. [Smoking in the hospital was prohibited,] [so patients huddled outside the doors in freezing temperatures.] (Compound)
2. [Othello is the tragedy of a man] (who "loved not wisely, but too well.") (Complex)
3. [Some people believe (that tuition should be affordable enough for anyone to attend post-secondary institutions)]; [others believe (that tuition should be increased and loans made available to those who need them).] (Compound-Complex)
4. (As the runners surged toward the finish line,) [the crowd cheered wildly.] (Complex)
5. [The distraught parents searched the campground, the lakeshore, and the surrounding woods for their missing child.] (Simple)
6. [The weather, (which had remained warm for several days,) suddenly turned bitterly cold.] (Complex)

7. In the grey dawn of a cold November morning, [the hunter stood motionless at the edge of the clearing, waiting patiently,] cold fingers ready to press the button on the sleek silver camera. (Simple)
8. (Before you take an exam,) [(you) get a good night's sleep and eat a healthy meal.] (Complex)

B Answers will vary.

Exercise 4 (p. 415)

1. Many students decide not to hold part-time jobs because they need time to study.
2. Although the benefits of pollution regulations outweigh the costs, every regulation has an impact on the Canadian economy.
3. Genetically modified foods are sometimes known as "Frankenfoods."
4. In the last act of the play, the hero and villain confront each other.
5. Genetic manipulation could be useful in the treatment of some diseases, such as diabetes.

Exercise 5 (p. 417)

1. Holden wants to be like the ducks because no one seems to notice them.
2. The southern half of the province has received very little rain for the third consecutive year; therefore, poor crops are expected.
3. The competition in high school is intense; in fact, some students use alcohol to escape from the pressure to succeed.
4. Olena has very limited vision, so voice-sensitive computer software is enormously helpful to her.
5. Ultra-light aircraft are easy to fly; however, they can be very difficult to land.

Exercise 6 (p. 417) Answers will vary.

Exercise 7 (p. 418)

1. It is easy to make this delicious dessert; just follow these instructions.
2. Some adolescents are sullen, rebellious, and lazy; however, others work to support themselves and to help their families.
3. Einstein abhorred the practical use of his theories by the military, and in the future we may find more humanitarian uses for his concepts.

4. Some leaders brutally impose their policies, but they get sullen compliance at best.

5. The window display stopped passersby in their tracks because it featured a mannequin wrapped in a bloody sheet with a boot on its neck.

Exercise 8 (p. 420)

1. *A Man for All Seasons* shows that Sir Thomas More becomes a martyr because he is willing to die for his beliefs.

2. Her cunning is revealed when, for example, she persuades her client not to consult another lawyer.

3. The Minister of Finance increased the credibility gap between himself and the public by denying that the government intended to raise taxes.

4. The more Yvette loathed her family, the less she wanted to live with them.

5. The frustrated mother asked her daughter, "When will you ever grow up?"

Review Exercise 1 (p. 420) Growing up on a farm where I often needed a good knife, I quickly learned to distinguish a good quality knife from one of poor quality. Finding a good knife was often difficult because most companies now making knives care more about profit than about quality. Consequently I always kept an eye out for knives constructed in the early part of the century. Knives constructed then are usually made from better quality materials. I faithfully attended auctions and garage sales in the hope of finding those early knives. There were not many styles available, so I had to be content with whatever style I found.

Review Exercise 2 (p. 420) The bay is covered with ice from January to mid-June, so twice-weekly air transportation replaces the three-hour ferry trip to the mainland. On a clear, windless day the twenty minutes in the air can be heavenly, a sightseer's bliss. You can spot moose and caribou and follow snowmobile trails as they wend their way over and around ponds, brooks, hills, and dales. The snow gleams and glistens like a fairy-tale scene. This is no Boeing 747, however; it is only a four-seater Cessna, commonly referred to as a matchbox with wings. You squeeze and squirm into a bearable position, positioning yourself over bags of mail, boxes of freight, and your luggage. Your knees bump against your chin as you clench your teeth in preparation for take-off. You hope and pray that the weather remains good because if it doesn't, you are in for the most unpleasant twenty minutes of your life.

D Writing Better Paragraphs

Exercise 1 (p. 426) Answers will vary.

Exercise 2 (p. 429) This (demonstrative pronoun); for example (example); however (contrast); In the last ten or fifteen years (time); As a result (cause and effect); Nevertheless (contrast); therefore (cause and effect).

Exercise 3 (p. 429) Answers will vary.

Exercise 4 (p. 431)

1. One study of smokers revealed that much smoking is an automatic response to certain activities such as driving, typing, reading, or drinking alcohol and coffee.

2. Because I play video games and find them challenging, I would like to give them a good name. I hope that people will stop thinking of video games as mindless when they learn that these games require many years of practice.

3. Despite the costumes and castles, the heroine of *Ever After* seems independent and modern. She is bright, feisty, innovative, and brave with clear priorities. She values work and proves herself a woman of action when she fights to keep the family farm.

4. Packaged convenience food, a product of technology, contains preservatives and many other harmful chemicals.

5. While he was travelling down the highway at 150 km an hour, he hit a very icy section, lost control, and slammed into the ditch.

Exercise 5 (p. 431) *Roots of Empathy* focuses on an effective program Mary Gordon developed that reduces classroom bullying and aggression. The program involves monthly classroom visits by a parent and baby. A specially trained instructor visits the classroom a week before the baby's arrival to speak with the children about the important changes they might see in the baby since the last visit. When the parent and baby visit, the children sing a welcoming song and then observe the way the baby acts and play happily with the baby. Following the visit, the instructor helps the children make connections between the baby's feelings and actions and their own experiences. Ideally, this helps the children to embrace their own feelings and emotions, such as fear. The children are also encouraged to write poems about their feelings, which helps develop emotional literacy. Studies suggest that participation in this program reduces bullying and other kinds of aggression in the classroom.

Review Exercise (p. 432) Answers will vary.

E Creating an Appropriate Tone

Exercise 1 (p. 435)

1. Poison imagery pervades *Hamlet*.
2. Many of us remember junior high school dances with warm nostalgia.
3. C.
4. By the end of the novel, the protagonist is doomed.
5. Average students find that working ten hours a week is about all they can handle in addition to their school work.

Exercise 2 (p. 436) Answers will vary.

Exercise 3 (p. 438) Answers will vary.

Exercise 4 (p. 442)

1. From the noise in the lecture theatre, it's reasonable to infer that a large number of people were quite uninterested in the topic.
2. Engineers must recognize their responsibility to protect the environment.
3. Even on formal occasions, Ted dresses as if he were going to a hockey game.
4. The principal difference between my two jobs is that I now work fewer hours and make more money.
5. The results of the medical tests were different from what the doctor had predicted.

Review Exercise (p. 442) Answers will vary.

F Punctuation

Exercise 1 (p. 445)

1. Sonya's and Edward's, parents'
2. boss's
3. children's
4. nobody's
5. Huis'

Exercise 2 (p. 446)

1. fans, 1980s
2. month's, men's
3. It's, *you know*'s

4. yours, theirs
5. RCMP's, times

Exercise 3 (p. 446) Answers will vary.

Exercise 4 (p. 449)

1. no commas
2. , which was a gas guzzler,
3. , an award-winning Manitoba writer,
4. , passing the Stanley Cup between them,
5. no commas
6. no commas
7. , a documentary about spelling contests,
8. no commas
9. , exhausted by their tour of duty in Afghanistan,
10. no commas

Exercise 5 (p. 450)

1. Because he could find no way to avoid the task,
2. In the morning,
3. Marvin, on the other hand, is steady, hard-working, and rather unimaginative.
4. Indeed,
5. The negotiators were tired and hungry, so
6. According to William Blake,
7. no commas
8. The United States and Britain declared war on Japan on December 8, 1941, the day after the bombing of Pearl Harbor, Hawaii.
9. Returning home after a strenuous workout, Julia showered, reached for a cold drink, and collapsed on the sofa.
10. First Night festivities offer participants musical performances, street theatre, plays, readings, and a spectacular finale complete with fireworks.

Exercise 6 (p. 450) Answers will vary.

Exercise 7 (p. 452)

1. ; nevertheless,
2. ; however,
3. woman; he
4. ; but
5. sympathy; when

Exercise 8 (p. 454)

1. The setting was perfect for a horror movie: a foggy night, an isolated house, shrieks and groans coming from unseen sources.

2. Monique is saving her money with one goal in mind: to travel for a year.
3. C
4. C
5. Alexander and Shaler argue that there is a direct relationship between addiction and dislocation:

Exercise 9 (p. 454) Answers will vary.

Exercise 10 (p. 454) Answers will vary.

Review Exercise 1 (p. 456)

1. Let's divide our supplies into two categories: inexpensive items in constant use and expensive items used only occasionally.
2. *Spider-Man,* which attracted large audiences in 2002, spawned plenty of spinoff accessories.
3. There are two types of crimes in which the perpetrator deliberately chooses to break the law: crimes of desperation and crimes of defiance.
4. A woman with a limited income, perhaps a single parent, might steal food, for example, to feed her family.
5. In *Hard Times*, Dickens vividly portrays the monotonous, mechanical lives of factory workers in his description of Coketown: "It contained several very large streets all very like one another . . ." (213).
6. The goal of modern correctional institutions should not be punishment or revenge; it should be the rehabilitation of the whole person.
7. *The Stone Angel* (1964) established Margaret Laurence as an important Canadian novelist.
8. The Pope needed only to show Galileo the instruments of torture; Galileo's medical knowledge of what those instruments would do accomplished the rest.
9. When I returned home—most unexpectedly, I might add—I was astounded by the changes that had occurred during my absence.
10. Ancient Chinese and Hindu societies had much in common: both were unified through stable religious and cultural patterns; both had little curiosity about foreign lands; both were exploited by the West.

Exercise 11 (p. 457)

1. Azim wished his brother would buzz off so that he could study.
2. "Whenever you use a welding torch," said the shop teacher, "make sure you wear goggles to protect your eyes."
3. Jaylon said that he could rap like Eminem.

4. Marika asked her teacher, "What does Swift mean by the phrase 'deliver the Kingdom to the Pretender'?"
5. In his essay "Na Na Na Na, Hey Hey Hey, Goodbye," Tim Bowling admits that he still smiles "with goofy fondness at the common graffiti of my childhood—'Jesus Saves, Esposito Scores on the Rebound'" (213).

Exercise 12 (p. 458)

1. Annie Proulx's short story "Brokeback Mountain," which appeared in the *New Yorker* in 1997 and in the short story collection *Close Range: Wyoming Stories* in 1999, was recently made into a film.
2. There was a great to-do over the sinking of the *Titanic.*
3. Margaret Wente's column on "The Decline of Public Language" was published in the *Globe and Mail* on August 13, 2005.
4. George asked, "How many *m*'s are there in the word *accommodate?*"
5. The French word *tristesse* suggests not merely sorrow but melancholy.
6. In his essay "Food Connections," David Suzuki points out that the word *dirt* in our society is a pejorative.
7. Allison Crowe's song "By Your Side" is available on the CD *Live at Wood Hall.*
8. *The Sound of Music,* a perennial favourite on stage and screen, was based on the book *The von Trapp Family Singers* by Maria von Trapp.
9. Many children still learn the classic nursery rhyme "Baa, Baa, Black Sheep," which begins with the question "Baa, baa, black sheep, have you any wool?"
10. How many times does the phrase "Quoth the raven, Nevermore" appear in Poe's poem "The Raven"?

Review Exercise 2 (p. 459) The final story of *Dubliners* returns to the subject of the first story—mortality. Joyce divides "The Dead" into two separate scenes: the Christmas gathering of family and friends and the hotel room where the main character, Gabriel, and his wife, Gretta, spend the night. Gabriel, who is named for the archangel of good news (Luke 1:26), believes he is the master of his surroundings. During the Christmas gathering, he certainly seems to be in control. He is responsible for drunk Freddy, he carves the turkey, and he gives the speech. In the second scene, Gabriel comes to the realization that he is not in control. When he and Gretta arrive at their hotel room, Gabriel is consumed by passion and wants to dominate his wife. As he says, he wants to be master of her strange mood (235). Gretta, however, is overwhelmed by long-buried grief for the young man who died for love of her. When Gretta tells her husband about Michael Furey, Gabriel is forced to realize that it is death that controls people's lives. Many characters in *Dubliners* long to escape from their city and their lives, most obviously Eveline in the story of that name and Chandler in "A Little Cloud." Only Gabriel realizes there is no escape except through death.

Review Exercise 3 (p. 459) Answers will vary.

G Spelling and Mechanics

Exercise 1 (p. 461)

1. *Tanis's interest* in school has increased *noticeably* since she *separated* from her husband.
2. At the *beginning* of the term, Tanis *dragged* herself to all her *classes*, but her heart was *definitely* not in her *studies*.
3. Like most people, Tanis was *embarrassed* by her marriage problems and rather *lonely* as well, but now she is enjoying her *independence*.
4. She is also *achieving* better grades, especially in her *children's* literature and *micro-computer management* courses.
5. *Even though* Tanis *worries* that people might be *prejudiced* against a *woman* who has decided to abandon the *privileges* of the affluent middle class, she has decided to devote her summer to an *environmental* protection project on *Baffin* Island.

Exercise 2 (p. 463)

1. con-ferred
2. C
3. C
4. recom-mend
5. stipu-late
6. butter-fly
7. C
8. spill-ing
9. defin-itely
10. lan-guage

Exercise 3 (p. 465)

1. On October 30, the Vice-President announced that the northern end of the railway line had finally been completed.

2. My brother and I like to go camping for two weeks every summer.
3. The Native Friendship Centre in our area hosts an annual barbecue to which everyone in the neighbourhood is invited. Last year, 151 people attended.
4. On our trip to the Middle East last December, we noticed considerable tension between fundamentalist Christians and Muslims.
5. When Susan and her husband were robbed in an outdoor café in Rome, they lost most of their valuables: their passports, wallets, traveller's cheques, cameras, and so on.

H Format

Exercise 1 (p. 477)

1. Virginia Woolf's thoughts on "Shakespeare's Sister" are "that any woman born with a great gift in the sixteenth century would certainly have gone crazed, shot herself, or ended her days in some lonely cottage outside the village, half witch, half wizard, feared and mocked at" (342).
2. In "Inequality is the Real Enemy," Polly Toynbee questions whether or not people are concerned about inequality: "The poor have what their grandparents would think unimaginable luxuries—TVs, telephones and washing machines. So why should it matter to them if in some unseen stratosphere the gated kleptocrats on company boards award themselves staggering sums of money?" (330).
3. The idea that blindness is a mental state rather than a physical condition is clear when Gloucester in *King Lear* perceives that

    > I stumbled when I saw. Full oft 'tis seen,
    > Our means secure us, and our mere defects
    > Prove our commodities. O dear son Edgar
    > The food of thy abused father's wrath!
    > Might I but live to see thee in my touch
    > I'd say I had eyes again! (4.1.21-26)

4. An added benefit, Swift's narrator notes, is that this proposal will decrease the number of Roman Catholics in Ireland "with whom we are Yearly overrun, being the principal Breeders of the Nation, as well as our most dangerous Enemies, and who stay at home on purpose with a design *to deliver the Kingdom to the Pretender* . . . " ("A Modest Proposal" 318).

Index